T0272618

The Universal Sport

Books by Thomas Hauser

General Non-Fiction

Missing
The Trial of Patrolman Thomas Shea
For Our Children (with Frank Macchiarola)
The Family Legal Companion
Final Warning: The Legacy of Chernobyl
(with Dr. Robert Gale)
Arnold Palmer: A Personal Journey
Confronting America's Moral Crisis
(with Frank Macchiarola)
Healing: A Journal of Tolerance and
Understanding
With This Ring (with Frank Macchiarola)
Thomas Hauser on Sports
Reflections

Boxing Non-Fiction

The Black Lights: Inside the World of
Professional Boxing
Muhammad Ali: His Life and Times
Muhammad Ali: Memories
Muhammad Ali: In Perspective
Muhammad Ali & Company
A Beautiful Sickness
A Year at the Fights
Brutal Artistry
The View from Ringside
Chaos, Corruption, Courage, and Glory
I Don't Believe It, but It's True
Knockout (with Vikki LaMotta)
The Greatest Sport of All
The Boxing Scene
An Unforgiving Sport
Boxing Is . . .

Box: The Face of Boxing
The Legend of Muhammad Ali
(with Bart Barry)
Winks and Daggers
And the New . . .
Straight Writes and Jabs
Thomas Hauser on Boxing
A Hurting Sport
A Hard World
Muhammad Ali: A Tribute to the Greatest
There Will Always Be Boxing
Protect Yourself at All Times
A Dangerous Journey
Staredown
Broken Dreams
In the Inner Sanctum
The Universal Sport

Fiction

Ashworth & Palmer
Agatha's Friends
The Beethoven Conspiracy
Hanneman's War
The Fantasy
Dear Hannah
The Hawthorne Group
Mark Twain Remembers
Finding the Princess
Waiting for Carver Boyd
The Final Recollections of Charles Dickens
The Baker's Tale

For Children

Martin Bear & Friends

The Universal Sport

Two Years inside Boxing

Thomas Hauser

The University of Arkansas Press
Fayetteville
2023

Copyright © 2023 by Thomas Hauser. All rights reserved. No part of this book should be used or reproduced in any manner without prior permission in writing from the University of Arkansas Press or as expressly permitted by law.

978-1-68226-239-9 (paper)
978-1-61075-804-8 (electronic)

27 26 25 24 23 5 4 3 2 1

Manufactured in the United States of America

⊗ The paper used in this publication meets the minimum requirements of the American National Standard for Permanence of Paper for Printed Library Materials Z39.48–1984.

Library of Congress Cataloging-in-Publication Data

Names: Hauser, Thomas, author.
Title: The universal sport: two years inside boxing / Thomas Hauser.
Description: Fayetteville: The University of Arkansas Press, [2023] | Summary:
 "A compilation of previously published material, The Universal Sport gathers
  Thomas Hauser's best pieces from 2021 and 2022, where he offers accounts of
  this period's most important fights and compelling issues, covering the return
  of Madison Square Garden, the endgame for Manny Pacquiao, an ascendant
  moment for English boxing, and the most anticipated fight in the history of
  women's boxing between Katie Taylor and Amanda Serrano. Also included are
  Hauser's take on a historic account of boxing's very first Black world champion,
  a review of Ken Burns's Ali biopic, an appreciation of Oscar De La Hoya, and a
  commentary on the exploitation of anti-Russian sentiment at the heart of the
  Canelo-Bivol fight"—Provided by publisher.
Identifiers: LCCN 2023013529 (print) | LCCN 2023013530 (ebook)
 | ISBN 9781682262399 (paperback) | ISBN 9781610758048 (ebook)
Subjects: LCSH: Boxing.
Classification: LCC GV1133 .H34485 2023 (print) | LCC GV1133 (ebook)
 | DDC 796.83—dc23/eng/20230425
LC record available at https://lccn.loc.gov/2023013529
LC ebook record available at https://lccn.loc.gov/2023013530

For Chris Davis, Randy Roberts, Michael Buffer, David Diamante,
Roy Langbord, David Berlin, Arne Lang, and Gerry Cooney

Boxing fans and friends

Contents

Author's Note

The Universal Sport contains the articles about professional boxing that I wrote in 2021 and 2022.

The articles I wrote about the sweet science prior to 2021 have been published in *Muhammad Ali & Company*; *A Beautiful Sickness*; *A Year at the Fights*; *The View from Ringside*; *Chaos, Corruption, Courage, and Glory*; *I Don't Believe It, but It's True*; *The Greatest Sport of All*; *The Boxing Scene*; *An Unforgiving Sport*; *Boxing Is . . .*; *Winks and Daggers*; *And the New . . .*; *Straight Writes and Jabs*; *Thomas Hauser on Boxing*; *A Hurting Sport*; *A Hard World*; *Muhammad Ali: A Tribute to The Greatest*; *There Will Always Be Boxing*; *Protect Yourself at All Times*; *A Dangerous Journey*; *Staredown*; *Broken Dreams*; and *In the Inner Sanctum*.

Fighters and Fights

The fight reports in collections of my articles published by the University of Arkansas Press are usually presented in rough chronological order. But it makes sense to begin this volume with a fight of particular historical note.

The Importance of Taylor–Serrano

On April 30, 2022, women's boxing took a giant step forward when Katie Taylor and Amanda Serrano met in the ring at Madison Square Garden in a sensational fight with Taylor winning a split decision. It was the first time ever that two women headlined a card in the fabled arena, a fight to determine who would be recognized as the best pound-for-pound female fighter in the world, and the most anticipated fight in the history of women's boxing. Not only was it the biggest women's fight ever; it might have been the best.

Let's put Taylor–Serrano in context.

The New York City Golden Gloves created a women's amateur boxing tournament in 1995. Seventeen years later, women's boxing became an Olympic sport. But women's boxing had never penetrated the mainstream sports market in the United States. There were a few blips on the radar screen—Laila Ali vs. Jacqui Frazier because of their famous fathers; Christy Martin because of her presence on Mike Tyson undercards. But in truth, not even boxing insiders followed women's boxing in a serious way.

Last year, John Sheppard (who oversees BoxRec.com) reported that, internationally, one out of every seven women's fights was for a sanctioning body "championship" belt. Sheppard further noted that the world sanctioning organizations have created more women's "championship" belts than there are active women boxers.

It's hard to take a sport like that seriously.

That brings us to Taylor–Serrano.

Taylor, who entered the ring with a 20–0 (6 KOs) record, has taken women's boxing to a new level. A native of Ireland who lives in the United States, she won a gold medal at the 2012 London Olympics and has held the four major sanctioning-body 135-pound belts for three years.

Katie is articulate and self-effacing with a vulnerable quality about her. She projects a comforting image for women's boxing in an age when many people still aren't used to seeing women impose themselves so violently on each other. I asked her once, "When you reached an age when the punches hurt and boxing became serious for you, was the motivation you were most aware of when you got in the ring to defend yourself or attack?"

"That's an interesting question," Taylor answered.

But she declined to answer it.

And one thing more. Katie is willing to go in tough. After winning a questionable decision over Delfine Persoon at Madison Square Garden in 2019, she gave Persoon a rematch and outpointed her convincingly. Not many fighters—male or female—would have taken that rematch.

Serrano (previously 42–1–1, 30 KOs) has been fighting professionally since 2009 and is billed as a "seven-weight world champion," having won belts in divisions ranging from 115 to 140 pounds. That emphasizes the manner in which women's belts are handed out today, like candy from a gumball machine. But Amanda can fight and, in the ring, evokes images of another Nuyorican star—Héctor Camacho, a slick southpaw with sharp claws.

"I shine under pressure," Amanda says.

Serrano has been trained from her first days in the gym by Jordan Maldonado. On the downside, Maldonado was charged in 2007 with the criminal sale of controlled substances, pled guilty, and spent a year in prison. The indictment, Chris Mannix of *Sports Illustrated* reported, stemmed from a federal investigation of two gyms that were alleged to be "drug supermarkets that peddled steroids, cocaine, ecstasy, and OxyContin." Amanda and her sister figured in the investigation, with Mannix reporting, "Cindy faced nine years but avoided prison. Amanda's case never went to court."

Taylor–Serrano was packaged as "the biggest fight in women's boxing history." It was certainly the most heavily promoted.

At the February 2 kickoff press conference in New York, Madison Square Garden executive vice president Joel Fisher hailed the event as a watershed moment in women's boxing and declared, "This is history."

Jake Paul (who replaced Lou DiBella as Serrano's promoter) brought a massive social media platform to the promotion, which was aimed in large measure at New York's Irish American and Nuyorican communities and marketed as a statement of women's empowerment.

Each woman, the media was told, would receive a seven-figure purse.

Serrano seemed excited by the magnitude of the event. She had more to win and Taylor had more to lose in the impending confrontation. "I respect Katie Taylor," Amanda said. "There's going to be no bad words between us. But in the ring, it's something different."

Taylor was less enamored of the spotlight. If Katie had her way, she wouldn't be going to press conferences and answering the same questions in interview after interview. But that's the way professional boxing works.

"This fight is more important than we realize," Katie declared. "Not only are we breaking the ceiling for female purses, but we have actually changed perceptions of the sport. If our careers have only achieved that, then all the hard days in the gym have been absolutely worth it."

There were the usual fight-week activities, including open media workouts and a visit by Taylor and Serrano to the Empire State Building. The promotion had an agreement with World Wrestling Entertainment for the latter to push the event on its social media platforms (which claim a combined audience of 167 million followers). WWE Raw women's champion Bianca Belair and former WWE Raw women's champion Becky Lynch served as "honorary captains" for Team Serrano and Team Taylor, respectively.

Taylor had opened as an 11-to-10 betting favorite. By fight week, the odds had flipped to favor Serrano by a similar margin. The two women had one opponent in common. Katie pitched a shutout over Miriam Gutiérrez in 2020. One year later, Amanda fell one round shy of doing the same. As a footnote, Taylor defeated Cindy Serrano in 2018, winning all ten rounds on each judge's scorecard.

At a February 7 press conference in London, Taylor acknowledged, "I'm expecting the toughest fight of my career." But then she proclaimed, "I know that I won't be found short on grit and heart. I know my mind can take me to places I have no right to go because I've been there before. That question has been answered. I'm not sure that Amanda has answered that question yet."

Serrano matched Taylor verbally from the start. That's the easy part of boxing.

"I have everything," Amanda said in London. "There's no questioning my heart, my skills, my power, and my chin. I have all the tools to beat Katie Taylor. I just have to go out there and be smart."

Amanda was more subdued during fight week than earlier in the promotion. But a majority of boxing insiders were picking her to win.

Taylor is technically sound and was the naturally bigger woman. But Katie is fairly predictable as a fighter and doesn't use her size to wear down opponents. Nor is she a puncher. Her last seven bouts had gone the distance. And at age thirty-five (twenty-seven months older than Amanda), she appeared to have slowed a bit in recent fights.

"I'm preparing to be the best version of myself," Taylor said. "I don't think I'll have to do anything to reinvent myself. I'll go in there being myself and box the way I know I can box. I don't train to lose."

But to many, Serrano seemed a bit fresher than Taylor, a bit hungrier, and a southpaw to boot. Early in the promotion, Amanda had floated the idea of changing the bout from the traditional women's championship format of ten 2-minute rounds to twelve 3-minute stanzas. But that idea never gained traction.

Mike Griffin was the referee. For those looking for omens, Griffin had been the third man in the ring when Anthony Joshua defended his heavyweight belts against Andy Ruiz three years earlier at Madison Square Garden. That night, an undefeated icon fell. Would the same fate befall Taylor?

During the final pre-fight press conference, Jake Paul (who was backing Serrano) goaded Eddie Hearn (the lead promoter for the bout) into a million-dollar bet on the outcome of the fight. Hearn then promptly disavowed the wager, saying that it still had to be papered.

One thing that people agreed on was that everyone liked Taylor–Serrano as a fight. And its importance was obvious. Katie put the matter in perspective, saying, "This fight will be talked about for years and years. This isn't just for myself and Amanda. This is for the next generation of fighters. We are bringing the whole sport up with us. This is exactly the legacy that I want to leave. People laughed at me when I said I wanted to be an Olympic champion. They never would have believed this."

During the build-up to Taylor–Serrano, Hearn had proclaimed, "The world will stop to watch this fight." That was hyperbole. But on fight night, 19,187 fans (including four thousand who flew to New York from Ireland) packed Madison Square Garden, engendering a live gate of $1,450,180.

The atmosphere before the opening bell was akin to that of a World Cup football match with Taylor and Serrano carrying two of the world's most spirited fanbases into the ring with them. Serrano's partisans were loud and Taylor's were louder.

When the bell for round one sounded, it was clear that this was the biggest moment in the history of women's boxing.

Too often, mega-fights fall short of expectations. This one delivered. Sports fans know when they're being entertained. Taylor–Serrano was enthralling. Each fighter rose to the occasion. At times, the roar of the crowd was deafening.

Round one began with Serrano as the aggressor. Taylor tried to use the whole ring while Amanda tried to cut it off. Round two was more of the same with Katie showing lateral movement and Serrano dictating the pace. By round three, Amanda was fighting as though Taylor couldn't hurt her, but Katie seemed the stronger of the two in clinches. The crowd was so loud that, at the end of the stanza, Mike Griffin couldn't hear the bell. Things would get louder.

In round four, Taylor countered effectively at times and occasionally got off first. But she suffered a cut on her right eyelid. And in round five, the proverbial roof caved in on her. Serrano pinned Katie in a corner and unloaded. Taylor responded in kind. There was a deafening roar as the two women punched nonstop for virtually the entire two minutes. But now Taylor looked old. Amanda was dominating and relentless, battering Katie around the ring, staggering her on several occasions. The blood pouring from Taylor's nose was the least of her problems. She was taking a beating. As she walked slowly to her corner at the end of the stanza, she looked like a beaten fighter.

In round six, Serrano went for the kill. Taylor was fighting on heart. At that point, the hope from some Taylor partisans was simply that, win or lose, Katie would be able to finish the fight on her feet. "I knew I was going to have to dig deep and go to the trenches," she said when the bout was over.

In round seven, Taylor began to regroup. Serrano was still stalking. In round eight, Katie got her legs back and was again able to move laterally effectively. By round nine, Serrano's punches had lost some of their sting. And now Taylor was getting off first.

Round ten saw frenzied punching till the final bell with Taylor getting the better of it. When the battle was done, the warriors embraced, two women bloodied but unbowed, their faces bruised and swollen.

I thought Serrano won the fight. So did Benoit Russell, whose score was announced first—96–94 for Serrano.

The Queen is dead. Long live the new Queen.

Not so fast.

Glen Feldman's scorecard was read next—97–93 for Taylor.

And finally, Guido Cavalleri—96–93 for Taylor.

Clearly, Cavalleri didn't go into the fight with a pro-Taylor bias because he scored round five 10–8 in favor of Serrano despite the fact that there was no knockdown. Still, two of the judges gave only three rounds to Serrano. I think that was off the mark.

Serrano was gracious in defeat, saying, "Katie Taylor is a tough fighter. She's a strong champion, a warrior. She's Irish and she was able to withstand the power and come back."

Taylor responded in kind, stating, "We definitely got the best out of each other tonight; that's for sure."

Telling fans that a fight is for a belt doesn't mean that it will be a good fight. And just because a fighter has won a belt—or two or three—doesn't mean that he or she is a championship-caliber fighter. As Andre Ward observed, "A lot of people want to be great in this sport but they don't want to earn it."

Taylor and Serrano earned it. It's hard to think of two fighters who are more dedicated to their craft. And they were willing to go in tough by fighting each other; the best fighting the best.

It wasn't Ali–Frazier. But it was Taylor–Serrano.

As for what comes next, there's already talk of Taylor–Serrano II, to be contested in Ireland.

"Absolutely, we have to do this again," Taylor said in a post-fight interview. "It was an absolute war for ten rounds. Look what we've just done. I said before that, when you think Madison Square Garden, you think Muhammad Ali vs. Joe Frazier. But now everyone will be thinking of Katie Taylor vs. Amanda Serrano. She's a phenomenal fighter. A great, great person. It would be a privilege to fight her again."

But let's carry the Ali–Frazier analogy a bit further. Taylor–Serrano was a war. How much did it take out of each warrior?

Some of boxing's greatest fighters and best ambassadors for the sport become cautionary tales. The more that women's boxing advances, the more it will be plagued by the same problems that beset the men—including health and safety issues. In the not-too-distant future, will we have a generation of women fighters suffering from dementia pugilistica?

Earlier this year, Taylor acknowledged, "I definitely understand I can't do this forever, unfortunately, as much as I would love to. So many people have spoken about my retirement over the last few months. When I'm asked about it, I just answer politely. But on the inside, my stomach's churning."

Taylor's legacy has now been written. More fights will bring her more money but won't enhance her place in history. There's only one thing left for Katie to learn the hard way in boxing. And that's losing.

It will be tempting for Taylor to fight again, particularly in Ireland (where she has never fought as a professional). Her life as a boxer and her religious beliefs are the two things that she defines herself by most. The idea of stepping into the ring in front of tens of thousands of passionate fans at Croke Park in Dublin is alluring.

That said, Katie Taylor has opened doors that other women boxers will pass through in the years to come. Not only has she led her people to the promised land; unlike Moses, she has been allowed to enter it. I'd like to see her retire now. But she won't.

Don King—"How Are the Mighty Fallen"

Don King promoted a fight card on January 29, 2021, at the Seminole Hard Rock Hotel in Hollywood, Florida. But the more significant story is what happened before the fights began.

There was a time when King was the greatest showman outside the ropes that boxing had ever seen. Time and again, he promoted (and, with his persona, added value to) spectacles involving legends like Muhammad Ali, Joe Frazier, and George Foreman that are a treasured part of boxing lore.

Equally important, King was Black and from the streets. Rather than try to hide it, he stuffed it in people's faces.

King forced America to accept him as he was on his terms. We're not talking about an athlete, singer, or movie star who made his mark by entertaining people. We're talking about commerce and economic control. At his most powerful, he created magnificent events and made tens of millions of dollars for himself. He still stops any room he enters. But at age eighty-nine, he's no longer a force in boxing.

King is now a caricature of what he once was. His closest tie to power was on display on November 2, 2020 (one day before Election Day), when he issued a long, rambling press release that endorsed Donald Trump and proclaimed, "My fellow Americans, we must never forget that God is in the plan. We the people prayed to almighty God, asking him to give we the people, the American people, some type of relief from the excruciating pain of oppression brought upon them from the corrupt rigged system's establishment form of government. Almighty God answered we the people's humble prayers to him by anointing Donald J. Trump to become the 45th President of the United States of America. Vote Trump, for a man who is a non-politician, a man who's only obligation is to we the people and God. A man who is fearless, a man who could not be bought, bribed, intimidated or coerced, a man who is brave, courageous and bold. President Donald J. Trump, our spiritually touched, god-sent leader of faith and hope."

On the boxing side of the ledger, King's January 29 fight card grew out of a purse bid that was ordered by the World Boxing Association for a bout between Mahmoud Charr and Trevor Bryan.

The WBA, at present, is the most shameless of boxing's four world sanctioning organizations. Leading up to January 29, it had four heavyweight "champions." Anthony Joshua (the most notable of the group) is the WBA "super heavyweight champion." Robert Helenius is the WBA "gold heavyweight champion." Charr was the regular WBA "world heavyweight champion" by virtue of beating Alexander Ustinov in his most recent fight way back in 2017. Meanwhile, Bryan had last fought on August 11, 2018, when he beat B. J. Flores (a blown-up, thirty-nine-year-old cruiserweight) to claim the WBA "interim" world heavyweight title. Neither Charr or Bryan has ever beaten a world-class fighter.

The WBA ordered a fight between Charr (promoted by Global Sports Management) and Bryan (promoted by King) to determine a mandatory challenger for Joshua. When the Charr and Bryan camps were unable to agree on terms, the sanctioning body ordered a purse bid that was held on March 2, 2020. King won the purse bid with an offer of $2 million. The only opposition came from Global Sports Management, which bid $1.02 million. As the regular WBA champion, Charr was entitled to 75 percent of the winning bid (a projected payday of $1.5 million).

King's paperwork accompanying the purse bid said that the fight would likely be held on May 23, 2020, in Las Vegas, or on May 30, 2020, in Kinshasa, Qatar, or Saudi Arabia. No knowledgeable observer expected him to make good on the bid. There were several postponements, occasioned in part by the pandemic. Then the WBA demanded that King promote Charr–Bryan by January 29, 2021, or be declared in default of his promotional obligations. Things went downhill from there.

King announced that Charr–Bryan would take place at the Seminole Hard Rock Hotel with Beibut Shumenov vs. Raphael Murphy in a WBA cruiserweight title fight as a co-feature. Shumenov has fought once since May 2016. Murphy was knocked out in 2017 by Hugo Trillo (whose record at the time was 2–0–1). Then Shumenov–Murphy fell through and it was becoming clear that Charr–Bryan wouldn't happen either.

The root of the problem was twofold. First and foremost, it was obvious that, if Charr–Bryan went forward, it would be a financial disaster for King. He had a $2 million purse bid obligation for the main event plus undercard fighters to pay, travel expenses, and other costs. There would be no live gate because of the pandemic, no network license fee, and minimal pay-per-view buys. King simply didn't want to pay $1.5 million to Charr and $500,000 to Bryan.

Also, King preferred that Bryan fight an opponent who he controlled so, no matter who won, Don King Productions (DKP) would have the mandatory challenger for Joshua's WBA title under contract.

With these considerations in mind, King threw every roadblock possible in Charr's path.

When a WBA title fight goes to purse bid, each fighter's camp has the option of negotiating a contract with the winning promoter. If an agreement can't be reached, the WBA form contract will govern the event. King sent Charr a contract that was unacceptable to Mahmoud. In response, Pat English (Charr's attorney) sent King two contracts that had been signed by Charr. The first was the WBA form contract. The second was an amended version of the DKP contract. King had the option of signing either contract. Instead, he refused to sign either one (which was a breach of his purse-bid obligations).

King also refused to fulfill his obligation to help Charr get a P1 work visa to travel from Germany to the United States for the fight. On January 22 (one week before the scheduled bout), Charr went in person to a US consulate in Germany and, without paperwork from King, managed to get a visa to come to the United States. But without a signed contract from King, he couldn't get a P1 work visa. Thus, on January 27, Carl Lewis (an attorney for DKP) declared, "What they have is the equivalent of a tourist visa. So he's more than welcome to come to Florida, see the sights and take in all the attractions he wants. But as far as the fight, that can't happen without the proper documentation."

On January 24, while the visa controversy was unfolding, King filed a request for an exception with the WBA that would grant him relief from his purse bid obligation to Charr and authorize the sanctioning of a bout between Bryan and Bermane Stiverne (another King-controlled fighter) for the WBA world heavyweight championship. Charr, King suggested, should be designated as "champion in recess" because of his "unavailability."

That occasioned a scathing letter from Pat English who, on January 26, wrote to the WBA Championships Committee as follows: "The application by DKP for Bryan to fight Stiverne is based upon a lie. Mr. Charr is available and has done absolutely everything he was supposed to do. At this point, he has picked up his visa. He has taken two VADA [Voluntary Anti-Doping Association] tests. He has submitted his medicals. He has taken a Covid test so he can fly. The truth here is that King simply does not wish to reach into his pocket and pay the purses he committed to at the time of the bid."

Mahmoud Charr isn't the most sympathetic person one can cast in the role of an aggrieved party. His WBA title came about as a consequence of a deeply flawed process within the sanctioning body. Also, in 2019, a technical ruling enabled him to dodge a bullet after VADA reported a positive test result for the presence of epitrenbolone and drostanolone in his urine. But fighters have short ring careers. And King was putting the finishing touches on wasting a year of Charr's professional life.

Then things got truly bizarre.

On January 29 at 10:35 a.m. Eastern Time, Noryoli Gil of the WBA emailed a "resolution" from the WBA Championships Committee to eleven parties with an interest in Charr–Bryan. The resolution gave King everything he wanted. Based on the fiction that Charr had failed to fulfill his responsibilities under the WBA rules, the committee stripped him of his world title and declared him to be the WBA "heavyweight champion in recess." The resolution also requested that the WBA Ratings Committee include Stiverne in its ratings and authorized a fight between Bryan and Stiverne for the regular WBA "world heavyweight championship."

Prior to this ruling, Stiverne was unranked by the WBA, had been knocked out in his two most recent fights, and hadn't won a bout since 2015. He's forty-two years old.

Oddly, the resolution was dated January 26. More oddly, eighteen minutes after it was sent, the WBA sent a second email to the same parties that read, "Dear Sirs, Please disregard this communication, it is not valid and it was send [sic] by an involuntary mistake."

Then, at 1:26 p.m., yet another resolution (also dated January 26) was distributed. This resolution declared that King had "complied with the formalities required in the Purse Bid regulations" and restored the relief he had sought (designating Charr as "champion in recess" and declaring that Bryan–Stiverne would be for the regular WBA "world heavyweight championship").

The resolution also vacated the March 2, 2020, purse bid, but said that Charr would have the right to fight the winner of Bryan–Stiverne by May 30, 2021, pursuant to terms to be negotiated.

The WBA resolution ignored the fact that, after winning the March 2, 2020, purse bid, King had refused to sign the form WBA contract (as required by WBA rules). Had he signed the contract, it would have enabled Charr to get a P1 work visa.

Meanwhile, logistically, the January 29 promotion was in shambles.

This was to be King's first fight card as the lead promoter since August 28, 2015, when he promoted a four-bout card at the D Las Vegas Hotel & Casino headlined by Bryan vs. Derric Rossy for the "vacant NABF junior heavyweight" title. And there were questions as to whether he was up to the task.

The January 29 fight card had been styled by King as "Return to Greatness" and had an announced pay-per-view price of $19.99. But King—once the unquestioned master of promotion—did nothing to promote the event. No interviews. No promotional appearances. Nothing.

Distribution was also an issue.

King had an agreement in principle with In Demand to distribute the fight on cable, but it fell through because DKP couldn't meet In Demand's technical transmission requirements. DirecTV was already off the table. And when some would-be buyers went to DonKing.com during fight week to order the event, the first thing that popped up on the screen was a warning that cautioned, "This Connection Is Not Private. This website might be impersonating 'donking.com' to steal your personal or financial information. You should go back to the previous page."

That left FITE as King's only reliable pay-per-view distributor. But King dallied in signing their distribution agreement. Two hours before the fight stream began, FITE had only fifty-one advance buys.

Then came the hour of reckoning. The telecast began at 7:00 p.m. Eastern Time. The only way it would have been pay-per-view–worthy is if fans had been paid to watch it.

Once upon a time, King promoted events like Larry Holmes vs. Earnie Shavers at Caesars Palace with Ray Leonard, Roberto Durán, and Wilfredo Gómez on the undercard. But he isn't capable of putting the pieces of a big fight card together anymore. And it showed.

Don King Productions had announced that the telecast would include reruns of Larry Holmes vs. Gerry Cooney, the first fight between Julio César Chávez and Frankie Randall, and the rematch between Evander Holyfield and Mike Tyson. Oscar De La Hoya vs. Félix Trinidad was substituted for Holyfield–Tyson II at the last minute. All of these fights are available for free in their entirety on YouTube.

Bob Alexander hosted the event and provided blow-by-blow commentary for the live fights. Nate Campbell was the expert analyst. The live fights were dreadful.

Bantamweight Joahnys Argilagos won a four-round decision over Ernie Marquez (who now has one win in his last thirteen fights). Ring announcer J. D. Lyons announced the score with the incoherent proclamation, "All three judges score the fight exactly the same at 39-to-40." Then cruiserweight Johnnie Langston won a lopsided six-round decision over DeShon Webster (winless in his last five outings).

Shortly after ten o'clock, Lyons introduced Stiverne as "making his way to the ring." But Bermane didn't make his way to the ring. That left Alexander and Campbell to filibuster for twenty minutes and raised the issue of whether Stiverne might be engaged in a convivial discussion with someone about money.

Twenty minutes later, Lyons tried again.

"Once again, fight fans. Making his way to the ring . . ."

This time, Stiverne made an appearance followed by Bryan.

Lyons then began the in-ring introductions, only to be cut short by an unseen prompt, at which point he told the handful of pay-per-view viewers around the world, "I guess we're gonna do a national anthem. My apologies."

By this time, Lyons looked like a man who'd be happy if he never announced another Don King fight card again.

The fight that followed was abysmal.

Bryan and Stiverne looked as though they'd trained at Dunkin' Donuts. Each man weighed in at a fraction over 267 pounds. Trevor had fought his last fight at 236 pounds and now had a roll of flab hanging over the waistband of his trunks. Stiverne, whose best fighting weight was in the high 230s, looked pregnant.

It wasn't even a good club fight. Stiverne threw one punch at a time and never set anything up. Bryan was a bit busier. His jab (which wasn't all that good) was the difference. Choose your adjectives to describe the bout . . . messy, sloppy, lumbering, plodding.

By round eleven, Stiverne was gassed. Bryan hurt him with a right hand and dropped him twice. Soon after the second knockdown, referee Frank Gentile stopped the fight.

It's unclear how much each fighter will be paid. But neither fighter is expected to be happy with his purse. FITE is now projecting a total of under three hundred pay-per-view buys.

Don King was not seen live on camera or heard from during the telecast.

Four decades ago, Mark Kram wrote, "Don King is a man who wants to swallow mountains, walk on oceans, and sleep on clouds."

There was a time when King seemed capable of doing all of those things. But not anymore.

Another bad night for boxing.

The AB (Always Boorish) Hustle

Showtime served up a tripleheader from Mohegan Sun in Connecticut on February 20, 2021. The centerpiece was the newly reformed, more responsible, and more mature Adrien Broner who, six days earlier on Valentine's Day, told TMZ that his critics could "eat a dick and put gravy on it."

There was a time when Broner, now thirty-one, was regarded as having the potential to be a great fighter. He won belts at 130, 135, 140, and 147 pounds, which enabled him to be marketed as a "four-time world champion." But the titles were suspect in that there were always more credible champions in the same weight division at the same time. And his ring exploits were overshadowed by his outside-the-ring behavior.

Broner has a criminal record and history of other antisocial conduct that dates back to his teens. His transgressions have been well catalogued over the years. Bringing his resume up to date, the following highlights have occurred since he lost a unanimous decision to Manny Pacquiao on January 19, 2019 (Adrien's most recent fight prior to Saturday night).

1. On March 20, 2019, Broner posted a video on Instagram in which he took a social media feud with Andrew Caldwell to a new level and ranted, "If any fucking punk ass nigga come run up on me, trying to touch me on all that gay shit, I'm letting you know right now, if I ain't got my gun on me, I'm knocking you the fuck out. If I've got my gun on me, I'm shooting you in the fucking face. That's on God. I ain't playing with none of these niggas. I don't want that gay shit." Thereafter, Caldwell was granted a restraining order that prohibited Broner from coming within five hundred feet of him.

2. In April 2019, Broner pled guilty to misdemeanor assault and unlawful restraint after being charged with gross sexual imposition (a felony), misdemeanor sexual imposition, and abduction in conjunction with assaulting a woman in a Cleveland nightclub. He was

fined $1,000 by the court, required to reimburse the woman for $4,200 in medical bills, and sentenced to two year's probation. The woman then sued Broner and won an $830,000 default judgment. On November 2, 2020, Broner was jailed for contempt of court for failing to pay the judgment. He was released from jail two days later on the condition that the judgment would be paid out of the purse for his next fight.

3. At the February 21, 2020, weigh-in for the rematch between Tyson Fury and Deontay Wilder, Broner was removed in handcuffs from the MGM Grand Garden Arena by Las Vegas police officers after he refused a request by security personnel that he leave the premises. He had been previously banned from the MGM Grand because of an earlier incident.

4. On March 13, 2020, Broner was arrested in Miami, charged with DUI, and held overnight in a Miami jail.

5. Also in 2020, a Las Vegas court handed down a $4 million judgment against Broner in conjunction with a 2017 incident in which he knocked an individual named Carlos Gonzalez unconscious in a Las Vegas strip club. Broner was arrested after the incident and pled guilty to battery.

Hall of Fame trainer and ESPN commentator Teddy Atlas put things in perspective recently when he declared, "I don't expect people to be perfect. I expect them to be decent. Do you think I feel good being attached to a sport that puts Adrien Broner in the spotlight?"

As a fighter, Broner's primary value is now as an opponent for high-level A-side fighters. Prior to Saturday night, his ring record stood at 33 wins, 4 losses, and 1 draw. But he was winless in his most recent three outings. To maintain credibility, a fighter has to win now and then. And the last "then" for Adrien was on February 18, 2017, when he won a disputed split decision in his hometown of Cincinnati over journeyman Adrian Granados.

Initially, Broner was scheduled to fight Pedro Campa in his 2021 return to Showtime. Then Campa fell out because of a positive COVID-19 test and TBA was listed as the opponent. Often in boxing, TBA is more threatening than the adversary who actually steps into the ring on fight night. Enter designated victim Jovanie Santiago.

Santiago (14–0–1, 10 KOs) is a thirty-one-year-old native of Puerto Rico who had never fought a world-class fighter. Initially, the contract weight for Broner–Santiago was 140 pounds. Then Broner (who ballooned up last year to the size of a five-foot, six-inch cruiserweight) had trouble making weight. Two days before the bout, it was announced that Broner–Santiago would be contested at 147 pounds.

As the fight approached, Broner spouted familiar refrains: "I'm motivated again . . . I've rededicated myself to training . . . I'm more mature now . . . I'm staying out of trouble . . . I'm going to take over the sport." During a February 18 virtual press conference, he proclaimed, "I've had so many great performances and I'm looking forward to another great performance Saturday night. He [Santiago] is here because of me and everybody in this room is here because of me."

Justifying the matchup, Showtime Sports president Stephen Espinoza said of Broner, "He is still one of the most well-known, well-recognized, active fighters in the sport today. When you talk about recognition among casual fans and non-fans, he does have a level of awareness that brings people to his fights. He does not hesitate to take on quality opposition. People will watch and people will generally be entertained when Adrien Broner fights."

However, one might note that Broner has not been "active" lately (unless one considers his recent activity in strip clubs). This was his first fight in more than two years. Santiago (who was listed by BoxRec.com as the eighty-eighth-ranked junior-welterweight in the world) was not "quality opposition." And while Adrien has the captivating personality of a train wreck, his actual fights haven't been entertaining in quite a while.

Broner was a 7-to-1 betting favorite. He has skills (that he doesn't always use) and takes a good punch. And Santiago is essentially a club fighter.

It was a dreadful fight. Broner gave a stink-out effort (which is what fans have come to expect from him lately). Santiago did his best to take the fight to him. But Adrien made a concerted effort for most of the night to avoid engaging. Toward that end, he was aided by referee Arthur Mercante, who took away Santiago's inside game by prematurely breaking the fighters again and again when Jovanie was working at close quarters.

That led Showtime commentator Al Bernstein to declare, "A lot of breaks are happening in this fight when there's really no reason to break the fighters."

Mercante also chose to disregard Broner repeatedly shoving his forearm into Santiago's face and throat (which was Adrien's most effective inside weapon). And at the end of round four, Mercante deducted a point from Jovanie for a punch after the bell. That seemed a bit unfair since, as recounted by Bernstein, "Broner threw a punch after the bell and Santiago responded."

According to CompuBox, Santiago had an edge in punches landed in every round except the second (when each man landed six punches). Overall, Santiago outlanded Broner by a 207-to-98 margin.

So Santiago won. Right?

Wrong.

All three judges—Peter Hary (117–110), Tom Carusone (116–111), and Glenn Feldman (115–112)—scored the fight for Broner. That was a disgrace.

Giving the victory to Broner was bad enough. The margin of victory was unconscionable. As Paul Magno wrote two years ago, "Judges who err in favor of house fighters are a valued commodity. Whether there is some direct corruption or simply an embracing of useful idiotry is beside the point. The fact of the matter is that judges who tend to favor house fighters get consistent gigs and there's nothing that will get you left off the 'acceptable judges' list quicker than someone who takes a cushy high-profile judging gig but sticks a thumb in the eye of the business entity paying his salary."

After the bout, Broner spoke with Brian Custer of Showtime who noted that a majority of fans responding on Twitter as well as Steve Farhood (Showtime's unofficial scorer) had scored the bout in favor of Santiago.

"Fuck Twitter and fuck Steve Farhood," the newly reformed, more responsible, more mature Adrien Broner said.

Trainers Chepo and Eddy Reynoso drilled counterpunching and defense into young Canelo Álvarez. These lessons are serving him well as his career evolves.

Álvarez–Yildirim: Canelo's Journey Continues

Canelo Álvarez did what he was expected to do on February 27, 2021, at Hard Rock Stadium in Miami. The best fighter in boxing brutalized World Boxing Council mandatory challenger Avni Yildirim, forcing him to quit on his stool after three woefully one-sided rounds.

Yildirim, who came into the fight with a 21–2 (12 KOs, 1 KO by) record, is a poster boy for what's wrong with boxing's mandatory challenger system. The twenty-nine-year-old Turkish native, who lives in Istanbul, had never beaten a world-class fighter. The two times he stepped up in class, he was knocked out by Chris Eubank Jr. and lost a technical decision to Andre Dirrell. His most recent victory was a razor-thin majority decision over Lolenga Mock (an opponent in his mid-forties with fourteen losses on his ring resume). That was twenty-nine months ago. Two months before that, Yildirim beat a fighter with a 3–31–3 record.

But Canelo holds the WBC and WBA 168-pound belts and wants to unify the four major sanctioning body titles. To keep the WBC belt, he had to fight Yildirim.

Hard Rock Stadium seats close to 70,000 people for boxing, but attendance was capped at 15,000 because of the pandemic. In addition to being streamed live on DAZN, the card was available in the United States on traditional pay-per-view outlets.

There was the predictable chatter from Yildirim's camp that Canelo was underestimating his foe. Trainer Joel Diaz (who was working with Yildirim in California) proclaimed, "Avni may be an underdog but he doesn't care what anybody says. He's fighting for his country and he's going to shock the world."

Canelo paid lip service to the competitive merits of the fight, saying, "He's a strong fighter. He's fierce. He's always there, pressuring. At any moment, he's dangerous. This is boxing and one punch can change everything. It's not in me to underestimate anyone."

But there was a reason that Canelo was a 30-to-1 betting favorite. Yildirim was a big step down in the quality of competition after Canelo's three most recent outings (against Danny Jacobs, Sergey Kovalev, and Callum Smith).

"They're not giving me much of a chance," Yildirim acknowledged. "They look at me like it's impossible because, if you look at boxing in Turkey, there are not many successful Turkish boxers. Maybe in our history you may find some successful athletes. But our country is not famous for boxing."

Meanwhile, the always candid Tim Bradley (now an expert analyst for ESPN) put the fight in perspective, declaring, "Yildirim is a punching bag. He's one-dimensional. He doesn't have one-punch knockout power. He comes straight forward. His head is always in the middle. He leans forward over his front knee. Anytime he has stepped up his class of opponent, he's been destroyed. He looks terrible."

Elite athletes have an aura about them. Prior to the fight, Yildirim had proclaimed, "Canelo has never faced a true Turkish warrior." But Canelo has the carriage of a champion. And Yildirim has the presence of a club fighter.

Michael Buffer's ring introductions raised the energy level in the stadium. He's still the best in the world at what he does. Yildirim had to wait for seven minutes after entering the ring while a musical tribute to Canelo played.

The fighters had weighed in on Friday (one day before the fight). There was a public weigh-in for the cameras at 2:00 p.m. local time. The real weigh-in had been conducted six hours earlier behind closed doors with each man tipping the scales at 167.6 pounds. By the time the faux weigh-in occurred, both Canelo and Yildirim had gained roughly eight pounds.

Weight was the only thing about them that was equal. Canelo and Yildirim represent two distinctly different classes of fighter. Indeed, Avni had served as a sparring partner for Canelo when Álvarez was preparing for his 2018 rematch against Gennady Golovkin. His chances of beating Canelo in Miami were virtually nonexistent. And "virtually" disappeared when the bell rang.

According to CompuBox, Canelo outlanded Yildirim 16 to 1 in the first round. Then things got worse for Avni. Canelo started putting more into his punches and landing harder. A straight right hand dropped Yildirim in round three. He rose and Canelo battered him around the ring. Ironically, it was during this beating that Avni landed his only good punch of the night—a desperation left hook. Canelo walked through it with a look on his face that said, "Oh; you actually hit me. Now it's my turn again."

Sitting on his stool after round three, Yildirim had the look of a man who thought that it would be a good idea to stop the fight. That message was communicated to the powers that be and the fight was stopped. According to CompuBox, Yildirim landed a total of eleven punches in three rounds. Canelo landed six times that number. And trust me. Canelo's punches were harder. Much harder.

At age thirty, Canelo has compiled a 55–1–2 (37 KOs) record with many of his victories coming against quality opponents. He has continued to improve at an age when many fighters stop improving. Much of the credit for this goes to Canelo..He's a hard worker and a true professional. But credit is also due to Canelo's team as a whole and particularly to lead trainer Eddy Reynoso.

When asked to compare himself with Julio César Chávez (Mexico's most storied ring icon), Canelo has said again and again, "I want to make my own history."

He's doing just that. Canelo might not be as beloved as Chávez in his native Mexico. But he's starting to look like the better fighter.

Chris Arreola and the Andy Ruiz Rehabilitation Project

Thirty-one-year-old Andy Ruiz labored in obscurity for most of his ring career, plagued by a poor work ethic and a prodigious appetite. Then lightning struck. On June 1, 2019, he scored a shocking knockout upset over Anthony Joshua at Madison Square Garden to claim the World Boxing Association, International Boxing Federation, and World Boxing Organization heavyweight titles. But rather than build on his success, the 268-pound Ruiz ate more and trained less. Six months later in Saudi Arabia, weighing 283 pounds, he was outboxed by Joshua over twelve dreary rounds. In the ensuing weeks, he put on another 27 pounds to reach the 310 mark.

"I was depressed," Ruiz acknowledged later. "I was mad at myself because I knew I should have trained. I knew I should have done better. I'd been waiting for this moment my whole life. And once that moment happened, I went a little off the road. I started doing things that I thought I would never be able to do. I wasn't really focused on the [Joshua rematch]. I look back right now, and I'm like, 'Damn, man, if I would've stayed dedicated, if I would've stayed disciplined and do the right things that I was supposed to do.'"

Was Ruiz a one-night wonder? On May 1, 2021, in a fight that fell short of answering that question, he returned to the ring for the first time since losing to Joshua to fight forty-year-old Chris Arreola.

Arreola is one of the most likeable people in boxing. He has challenged for a version of the world heavyweight title on three occasions—against Vitali Klitschko, Bermane Stiverne, and Deontay Wilder. Each time, he was knocked out. Once upon a time, he was a very good fighter. He isn't anymore.

During the nine years leading up to Ruiz–Arreola, Chris had ten fights and won four of them. Most recently, on August 3, 2019, he'd lost a 118–110, 117–111, 117–111 decision to Adam Kownacki in a slugfest that brought his record to 38–6–1 with 33 knockouts. According to CompuBox, Kownacki hit Arreola in the head 291 times (out of 369 punches that Adam landed).

Unlike many fighters, Arreola means it when he says, "I bleed boxing. I put my whole self out there every time I fight."

That's all the more reason to be concerned about his continuing to fight.

Once upon a time, Arreola was the A-side in fights that Premier Boxing Champions impresario Al Haymon made for him. He was the guy that Haymon was safeguarding.

No more.

Ruiz–Arreola was about Ruiz. There was a lot of talk during the pre-fight build-up about "the new Andy" and the difference that training with Eddy Reynoso would make in his ring skills and conditioning.

"When we first met up," Ruiz said of Reynoso during an April 1 teleconference call, "it was like, 'All right, what do you want? What are we gonna do? Are you gonna be the same fighter like you were before? Or are you gonna take it to the next level?' I was like, 'You know what, Eddy. I wanna do whatever it takes for me to become a two-time heavyweight champion of the world.' That's when I made my decision. I was like, 'I'm gonna give all the discipline that I have, every sacrifice that I have to do. And having Eddy right here on my side, working together, changing all the stuff that I didn't do my last fight or ever, it just feels good. I do not wanna do the same mistakes I did before. Now I got my mind right."

Ruiz–Arreola was contested at Dignity Health Sports Park in California as part of a FOX-PPV telecast. For all the wars that Arreola has been through over the years, he has never beaten a world-class opponent. That wasn't going to change at age forty.

Ruiz weighed in at 256 pounds, 27½ pounds less than for the Joshua rematch. Presumably, he didn't just lose weight but also added muscle. "I'm not where I want to be at right now," he said at the final pre-fight press conference. "But I'm a lot better than where I was."

Arreola came in at a career low of 228½ pounds. "I've worked non-stop on defense with [trainer] Joe [Goossen]," he said when asked what would be different about this fight. "That's one thing we emphasized in this camp. Counterpunch and bring those hands back."

But a fighter doesn't learn new defensive skills in a six-week training camp at age forty. Ruiz was a 20-to-1 betting favorite.

On fight night, both fighters were warmly received by the crowd. Arreola has earned fan affection over time for the body of his ring work. Ruiz earned it with his knockout victory over Joshua.

The fight itself was more competitive and entertaining than most people thought it would be. Arreola is a professional. He came to win and had a big second round, dropping Ruiz with an overhand right before shaking him with a hook up top late in the stanza. He also started round three well, trading and getting the better of it. But Ruiz was the aggressor for most of the fight, stalking and outlanding Arreola in ten of twelve rounds.

Arreola was competitive. But Ruiz kept putting rounds in the bank. Andy came into the bout with a puncher's mentality, although he's not a particularly big puncher. He controlled distance and range well. His handspeed gave him a big edge. And he outworked Arreola for most of the night. Both guys wanted it and tested each other. Ruiz simply had more to work with. The judges scored it 118–109, 118–109, 117–110 in his favor.

"Honestly, man," Arreola said afterward. "Did he win? Fine. But don't tell me you're only gonna give me two, three rounds. Fuck that! I'm gonna be like Dr. Dre. All y'all can suck my motherfucking dick."

But the judges' scores were on the mark. Many of the rounds were close. But Ruiz won them.

Chris Arreola had close to two hundred amateur bouts. He has been hit in the head again and again over the course of forty-six professional fights by men like Vitali Klitschko and Deontay Wilder. According to CompuBox, he was hit in the head 125 times by Andy Ruiz. Enough is enough. The time to retire is now.

As for Ruiz, it's clear that Eddy Reynoso can get him into better condition than he was before. Let's see now how Andy's ring skills progress. Remember, he didn't do any better against Arreola on Saturday night than Adam Kownacki did twenty-one months ago.

Billy Joe Saunders was a stop along the way for the biggest star in boxing.

Álvarez–Saunders: Canelo Is on a Roll

Boxing is going through a difficult time. Fights between elite fighters are few and far between. Bogus "world championship" belts have devalued the sport. Contests involving social media influencers and exhibitions by long-past-their-prime former champions often get more media attention and fan support than legitimate fights. The negotiations to make Tyson Fury vs. Anthony Joshua (or fail to make it) have been an exercise in frustration. In the midst of all this, Canelo Álvarez gives boxing fans something to hold on to.

Canelo's credentials are a matter of record. His red hair was a much-publicized marketing tool early in his career. Because of that, some people were slow to give him his due as a fighter. But with victories over Gennady Golovkin, Sergey Kovalev, Danny Jacobs, Miguel Cotto, Shane Mosley, Erislandy Lara, and now Billy Joe Saunders en route to compiling a 56–1–2 (38 KOs) ring record, the thirty-year-old Álvarez has established himself as boxing's brightest star. Yes, he was outboxed by Floyd Mayweather seven years ago. But he was a young man then, still learning his trade.

Álvarez's quest for greatness continued on May 8, 2021, against Saunders at AT&T Stadium in Arlington, Texas.

Saunders, age thirty-one, hails from Hertfordshire in the United Kingdom and, prior to facing Canelo, had fashioned a 30–0 record with 14 knockouts. He won the WBO 160-pound belt in 2015 by majority decision over a faded Andy Lee but vacated the title after testing positive for oxilofrine (a banned performance-enhancing drug) prior to a scheduled 2018 title defense against Demetrius Andrade. One year later, he claimed WBO 168-pound honors by decisioning unheralded Shefat Isufi and followed with victories over the equally unheralded Marcelo Esteban Coceres and thirty-eight-year-old Martin Murray.

There are times when Saunders gets more attention for his conduct outside the ring than for fighting inside it. In 2018, the *Daily Mail* posted a video that showed him promising a woman 150 pounds' worth of crack (currency, not weight) if she performed a sex act on one of his friends and punched an innocent passerby. The woman's punch was captured on video. The sex act was not. In 2020, Billy Joe's boxing license was temporarily suspended by the British Boxing Board of Control after he posted a video on social media in which he demonstrated ways a man could beat his domestic partner while locked down during the pandemic.

Then, in February 2021, *Panorama* (the BBC version of *60 Minutes*) broadcast a feature on the ties between MTK Global (which advises Saunders) and Daniel Kinahan (the alleged leader of a $1 billion drug-trafficking empire). Former world champion and Irish icon Barry McGuigan was one of the few people willing to talk openly on camera about Kinahan. Thereafter, Saunders attacked McGuigan on social media, likening him to a rat and appearing to taunt McGuigan about the 2019 death of his daughter from cancer.

"Billy should just delete social media," his current promoter Eddie Hearn says. "Something happens and he tries to explain it and it gets worse and you're like, 'Ah, Billy, just leave it.' I can't babysit him. The stage of me holding his hand and trying to guide him through how to behave on social media and how not to behave has gone. It's too far for that now. He is what he is."

Canelo had won world titles at weights ranging from 154 to 175 pounds. Most recently, he'd seized the WBC and WBA 168-pound belts. Now he's on a mission to unify the four major 168-pound titles. Saunders was in the right place at the right time to get a big payday.

There was the usual pre-fight sniping during the build-up to the bout, most of it from the Saunders camp. Tom Saunders (Billy Joe's father) complained to Boxing Social that Hearn was siding with Canelo in the promotion and that there was "no loyalty" and "no trust" between the Saunders camp and the promoter. But promoters usually side with the fighter who's generating the big money for them. And let's not forget: Saunders left promoter Frank Warren in his rear-view mirror when the siren call of Matchroom and DAZN sounded.

Tom Saunders also complained about the size of the ring (he wanted twenty-four feet squared inside the ropes rather than the standard twenty). He even suggested that his son might pull out of the fight if he didn't get the ring he wanted. No one took that threat seriously. But Canelo went the extra mile, agreeing to a enclosure that was twenty-two feet on each side. According to Hearn, that was the largest ring Saunders had ever boxed in as a pro.

"I don't care, really," Canelo said. "I'm pretty sure he's never fought in a 24-foot ring. But if he wants all of the Cowboys Stadium, okay, I'll give it to him. Don't worry."

The final pre-fight press conference began with a video of Dallas Cowboys owner Jerry Jones reading a statement off a teleprompter in which he assured listeners that "fans who cannot be there can enjoy the fight live on D-A-Zone [sic]." The rest of the press conference was largely pro forma.

Saunders was undefeated in the professional ranks. But the odds were 6-to-1 in favor of the proposition that Canelo would change that. The six Brits that Álvarez had faced in the past—like most of his opponents— fared poorly against him. Matthew Hatton (L12), Ryan Rhodes (KO by 12), Amir Khan (KO by 6), Liam Smith (KO by 9), Rocky Fielding (KO by 3), and Callum Smith (L12) were all convincingly defeated.

Against that backdrop, Saunders (a southpaw who prides himself on being elusive in the ring) was expected to try to frustrate Canelo into making mistakes and avoid confrontations as much as possible.

Billy Joe put a bold face on things, saying, "You have to dare to be great. I believe I am the only one with the footwork, know-how, skillset, mindset, and brain to unlock that door in Canelo. Brain over brawn here. Brain wins this. Technical thinking wins this. I don't give a shit about Canelo Álvarez. Not two shits. I don't think Álvarez has faced a man with as much heart and determination to win as me. I've come here to take all of these titles and take them by storm. This will be the biggest upset in boxing history in certainly the last twenty years. I believe this is meant to be."

Mark Tibbs (who trains Saunders) cast a more measured light on Billy Joe's fight plan, saying, "We've got to slide and glide and not get drawn into what Canelo does and that's what it's all about with Billy Joe. It's about him being disciplined in what he's got to do and not locking horns and planting his feet because it won't work in our favor if we do that."

Meanwhile, Canelo spoke to the battle ahead, saying, "His style is very difficult. He is a lefty so that makes it even more difficult. But I am a fighter who has fought against all kinds of styles. I am ready for any style. I just have to work. It is a matter of having patience."

Demetrius Andrade was less diplomatic, telling writer Keith Idec, "Saunders looked like shit when he fought Martin Murray. He couldn't do anything. He really didn't dominate him in the way that he should have, the way somebody supposedly that good, that talented, should have done against Martin Murray. I just don't think Billy Joe has the steam to keep Canelo off him."

Still, Canelo–Saunders was a prizefight; Saunders has skills, and nothing is certain in boxing.

Canelo–Saunders was the sixth fight card contested at AT&T Stadium. Previous events had been headlined by Manny Pacquiao (twice), Errol Spence (twice), and Canelo. Ticket prices started at $40 and worked their way up from there.

The turnout on fight night was a tribute to Canelo's star power. The announced attendance was 73,126. That made it the largest crowd to attend a sporting event in the United States since the pandemic began in March 2020. More significantly, it was the largest indoor crowd ever for a boxing match in the United States, surpassing the 63,352 fans who attended the rematch between Muhammad Ali and Leon Spinks in the New Orleans Superdome on September 15, 1978. The crowd was loud and overwhelmingly pro-Canelo.

Once the bell rang, it was a champion versus a beltholder. My round-by-round notes follow:

> Round 1—Canelo likes to counterpunch. And Saunders isn't throwing anything for Canelo to counter, only stay-away-from-me jabs. Canelo working the body when he can.
> Round 2—Saunders using his jab a bit more aggressively. Canelo getting inside from time to time and landing to the body.
> Round 3—Saunders keeping Canelo at bay with his footwork and jab. Canelo comes on strong in the last thirty seconds of the round.

Round 4—Saunders looking for a formula that might win the fight, and he can't find it. Canelo fighting patiently, landing to the body when he closes the gap. Good left uppercut by Canelo. He's been looking for that punch.

Round 5—Saunders starts the round well, fades late. But he won the round.

Round 6—Saunders attacking a bit more.

Round 7—Saunders fighting as well as he can, but it's not good enough.

Round 8—Canelo landing hard body shots. Well-placed uppercut closes Saunders' right eye. The crowd is roaring. Canelo urges them on with a wave of his arm. Twice. Saunders in survival mode. He's getting beaten up.

After the eighth round, citing damage to Billy Joe's right eye, Saunders' corner stopped the fight. The judges had Canelo ahead 78–74, 78–74, 77–75 at the time of the stoppage. This writer gave Saunders the fifth and sixth rounds for a 78–74 margin in Canelo's favor.

More importantly, Saunders was clearly tiring. Canelo's body shots were taking a toll. With or without his damaged left eye, the rest of the fight was going to be ugly for Billy Joe.

"It was not as difficult as I expected," Canelo said afterward.

Meanwhile, the stoppage brought the issue of fighter safety into further perspective.

On November 28 of last year, Daniel Dubois had a narrow lead on the judges' scorecards when he took a knee and retired in the middle of round ten of a fight against Joe Joyce due to a badly swollen left eye. A post-fight medical examination revealed that Dubois had suffered a broken orbital bone and nerve damage—a condition that likely would have been exacerbated had the fight continued.

Supporters of the "go out on your shield" mentality criticized Dubois for his conduct. One of these critics was Billy Joe Saunders, who declared, "If my two eye sockets were broken, my jaw was broken, my teeth were out, my nose was smashed, my brain was beaten, I was not stopping until I was knocked out or worse. I don't agree with a man taking the knee and letting the ref count him out. Fighters get in that ring and we know what's on the line. Every fighter needs to understand and the fans need to understand that. Before I go on one knee, I'd like to go out on my back with my pulse stopped."

Talk is cheap.

Dubois is now scheduled to fight again on June 5. The decision to retire against Joyce may well have saved his career—and the eyesight in his left eye.

Saunders has now been diagnosed as having suffered "multiple fractures to the orbital area." He underwent surgery the day after the fight and will be out of action for the foreseeable future. Perhaps, in light of his experience against Canelo, Billy Joe will reconsider his own intemperate remarks with regard to Dubois.

Following a thirteen-month layoff occasioned by the pandemic, Canelo has now fought three times in less than five months. He's already the undisputed 168-pound champion. He just doesn't have all the belts yet. His current goal is to unify the four major 168-pound titles by defeating IBF beltholder Caleb Plant later this year. Should that bout take place, Plant will come to fight. But he won't win.

When boxing returned to Madison Square Garden after the pandemic forced a twenty-month layoff, it was overshadowed by a rap concert.

Triller at Madison Square Garden

On Tuesday, August 3, 2021, I went to the fights for the first time in seventeen months. The occasion was the inaugural TrillerVerz event at Madison Square Garden—a nine-bout card followed by a hip-hop "rap battle."

On July 1, it was reported that Triller would present twelve monthly shows at Madison Square Garden's Hulu Theater beginning on August 3. Each event would consist of a regular live boxing card followed by a TrillerVerz music battle. A subsequent press release stated that these events would take place on the first Tuesday of each month and be streamed on FITE.TV and other platforms.

Boxing is a vehicle of opportunity for Triller. The company is selling what it calls a "four-quadrant model" consisting of "influencers, legends, music artists and contemporary fighters." During the past year, it has sought to build its brand by blending the sweet science with contemporary urban music. Its greatest success to date was a November 28, 2020, event featuring an exhibition bout between Mike Tyson and Roy Jones paired with performances by Wiz Khalifa, French Montana, YG, and Snoop Dogg. Other Triller events have been less commercially successful.

The Garden gave Triller a good deal on rent for TrillerVerz and pushed for the involvement of a local promoter to oversee the boxing end of the promotion. DiBella Entertainment was hired to perform the nuts-and-bolts onsite duties. In return, it received slots on the card for four of its fighters—Mikkel LesPierre, Eric Walker, Ivan Golub, and Joe Ward.

Explaining the series, Ryan Kavanaugh (the driving force behind Triller) proclaimed, "It's about continuing to build our customers as well as to continue to deliver what they want. Pay-per-view is one way to make money but that is for big, big events. In the meantime, we need to build up our fighters and image. The idea is to have a series leading up to our big PPV events."

There are a lot of questions that can—and should—be asked about Triller, its financial underpinnings, its ever-changing business model, and

Kavanaugh. I'll be exploring these issues at a later date. This article is about a return to ringside after a long absence occasioned by the pandemic and what it felt like for this writer to be on the boxing scene again.

Tickets for the August 3 TrillerVerz show went on sale July 15 with five hundred tickets held in reserve as comps and for sale to the fighters and their camps. Within hours, every ticket available to the public had been sold. The music, not the fights, drove the promotion.

There was confusion surrounding the start time for the event. Initially, the media was told that the first fight would begin at 6:05 p.m. Then, on August 2, a 4:05 p.m. start time was finalized with a 7:00 p.m. start for the streaming portion of the fight card. The rap battle would commence around 9:30 p.m.

I arrived at Madison Square Garden at 3:45 p.m., the same time as Gerry Cooney. Gerry and I are friends and try to sit next to each other at fights. Toward that end, the first thing Gerry did on arriving at the theater was rearrange the seating labels on press row so we could sit together.

The specter of COVID-19 and its variants hung in the air. Media and spectators had been told in advance that, to be allowed entry, they had to be fully vaccinated and provide proof of having received their final dose no later than fourteen days prior to the event. All Madison Square Garden personnel on site had to be vaccinated. New York State Athletic Commission personnel were required to wear masks but there was no requirement that they be vaccinated. Everyone in the technical zone at ringside wore masks. Virtually none of the spectators were masked. With close to five thousand people in attendance by evening's end, it was a statistical certainty that some of the spectators were COVID positive.

Gerry and I wore our masks throughout the night. Security was tight, and I missed being able to move around freely from area to area to schmooze with friends.

The first fighters—junior-middleweights Nikoloz Sekhniashvili and Guido Schramm—entered the ring at 4:00 p.m. When the bell for round one sounded, there were two dozen spectators in the stands. Schramm won a unanimous decision. Then Robert Sabbagh decisioned an overweight, out-of-shape Cleveland Billingsly in a four-round heavyweight contest, and light-heavyweight prospect Matthew Tinker stopped sacrificial lamb Michael Rycraft in two rounds. There was little crowd response. Of course, there was little crowd.

Next up, flyweight Christina Cruz won her pro debut against Indeya Smith. BoxRec.com credits Cruz with a 93–39 amateur record and three knockout victories in 132 fights. It was hardly a surprise that the bout went the distance.

The best fight of the evening—on paper and in the ring—came next: Eric Walker (20–3, 9 KOs) vs. Ivan Golub (19–1, 15 KOs) in a welterweight matchup. Golub dropped Walker twice en route to a ten-round unanimous-decision triumph. Then light-heavyweight Joe Ward decisioned Tory Williams.

At 7:00 p.m., the Triller stream began with junior-welterweight Aaron Aponte knocking out Gerardo Gonzalez in the second stanza. The Theater was still two-thirds empty.

Then came the first co-featured fight of the evening, Chris Algieri (24–3, 9 KOs, 1 KO by) vs. Mikkel LesPierre (22–2–1, 10 KOs) at a 143-pound contract weight.

There was a time when Algieri was willing to go in tough. His career peaked in 2014 when he overcame two first-round knockdowns and a badly damaged eye to win a split decision over Ruslan Provodnikov and claim the WBO 140-pound title. But he lost by decision in his next outing when he was knocked down six times by Manny Pacquiao. Defeats at the hands of Amir Khan and Errol Spence followed. Since then, Algieri has sought out less threatening opposition. LesPierre met that criterion.

Early in the fight, it became clear that the bout was likely to go ten dreary rounds. And it did. Neither guy is a puncher. But Algieri was stronger physically, and LesPierre fought like he was just mailing it in. The final scorecards read 100–90, 100–90, 99–91 in Chris's favor.

Now the arena was filling up. But these were hip-hop fans, not fight fans. In essence, the fights were an opening act for the rap artists to follow.

Michael Buffer took over ring-announcing duties from Mark Fratto for the main event—Michael Hunter vs. Mike "White Delight" Wilson in what was styled as a ten-round WBA title-elimination bout. For the first time in memory, Buffer's classic intonation of "Let's get ready to rumble" failed to elicit a roaring Pavlovian response. This wasn't a boxing audience.

Hunter (19–1–1, 13 KOs) is a credible heavyweight. But he has fallen short each time he stepped up the level of competition.

Wilson, despite a 21–1 (10 KOs) record, was a safe opponent. One could make the case that he'd never even beaten a good club fighter.

Also, having weighed in at 224 pounds (26 more than for his most recent ring encounter), Wilson was clearly out of shape. He came to fight. And he's tough. But at a certain level, that's not nearly enough. In round four, with "White Delight" reeling like a heavy bag getting hit by a precision puncher, Hunter ended matters with a straight right hand up top.

At 8:30 p.m., a Madison Square Garden maintenance crew began breaking down the ring and setting up a stage for the music to follow. If Little Richard vs. Fats Domino had been on the bill, I would have hung around. But their voices were stilled long ago. And the idea of a TrillerVerz Rap Battle between The Lox and Dipset was of no interest to me. So I put away my pad and pen and went home.

Earlier in the evening, tickets for the event had been scalped on the streets outside the Garden and there were reports that some would-be spectators had tried to storm one of the entrances to the arena. As I was leaving the Hulu Theater, a security guard stopped me and cautioned, "You might want to take off your [press] credential so someone outside doesn't rip it off your neck."

"Sooner or later," Graham Clark wrote, "adversity catches up with every boxer who steps into the ring."

The End Game for Manny Pacquiao

Who would have thought that there would be a Manny Pacquiao fight and most people in boxing wouldn't care? That was the case on August 21, 2021, when Pacquiao fought Cuban expatriate Yordenis Ugás at T-Mobile Arena in Las Vegas for one of the WBA's many 147-pound belts.

Pacquiao (now 62–8–2, 39 KOs, 3 KOs by) is one of the most storied fighters in ring history. Two years ago, at age forty, he surprised a lot of people by outpointing Keith Thurman.

"It was a thrilling fight," Tris Dixon wrote afterward. "But Pacquiao goes beyond just that. Sure, the excitement is wonderful but watching an icon extending an already extraordinary legacy is something else. You feel like you're witnessing history and that you're a small part of it. That you are of the same era as one of these fighters allows you to feel a certain type of privilege. You were there."

But in truth, it's hard to know whether Pacquiao looked good against Thurman or Keith (who has won one fight in the past fifty-three months) looked ordinary. Either way, Manny's victory guaranteed that he would fight again.

Errol Spence (27–0, 21 KOs) was chosen as the opponent. Give Pacquiao credit. He has always been willing to go in tough. In this instance, most people in boxing believed, too tough. Spence, age thirty-one, is high on most pound-for-pound lists with a solid résumé highlighted by victories over Mikey Garcia, Shawn Porter, and Danny Garcia in his three most recent outings. Pacquiao, now forty-two, had been inactive for twenty-five months and scored one knockout in the preceding eleven and a half years.

Spence opened as a 4-to-1 betting favorite. Then the hype machine went into high gear.

"Manny has been training for his greatest victory," Freddie Roach (Pacquiao's trainer) said. "I've been studying Spence's tapes and going through what he does well and what he doesn't do well, And I think it's a good fight for Manny. I like the fight a lot."

Teddy Atlas, who speaks his mind candidly, declared, "It doesn't seem like a good idea for Manny. But you know what? That's part of the magic of Manny. He turns a lot of things that don't seem like good ideas into good ideas."

By late July, the odds had dropped to 2-to-1 in Spence's favor.

Then there was a problem. A big one.

On August 10, it was announced that Spence had suffered a torn retina in his left eye and would be replaced by Ugás, a thirty-five-year-old Cuban with a 26–4 (12 KOs) ring record. Ugás would enter the ring to face Pacquiao with an advantage in size. He was the naturally bigger man, having turned pro at 146 pounds compared to Pacquiao's 106. And at five feet, nine inches tall, he was three and a half inches taller than Manny. But Yordenis was best known not for any win but for losing a close decision to Shawn Porter twenty-nine months earlier. Pacquiao was a 7-to-2 betting favorite.

Prior to the bout, there was talk of Pacquiao being "the Tom Brady of boxing." But when the forty-four-year-old Brady takes the field, an offensive line averaging 300 pounds per man is protecting him. Half of the time that the game is in progress, Brady is sitting on the bench. And the average play isn't three minutes long.

Ugás fought a cautious fight. And Manny can't do what he once did anymore. His feet have slowed. He's no longer a pressure fighter. He can't dart in and out and frustrate (let alone brutalize) opponents by instantaneously recalibrating angles and following up with lightning-fast blows. He's no longer the destructive force that he once was.

It was a competitive fight and—because Pacquiao was involved—a moderately interesting one. But it wasn't a good fight. Pacquiao did nothing much. Ugás did nothing much a little better. The judges were on the mark with a 116–112, 116–112, 115–113 verdict in Ugás's favor. In truth, Abel Ramos put in a better effort against Yordenis last September than Manny did.

As for the future, Pacquiao likes to fight. But he's now an ordinary fighter. Ugás was the eighth man to beat him. If Manny keeps fighting, there will be more. His days as an elite fighter are gone. And night is coming on.

Outside the ring, Anthony Joshua carries himself like a champion.
Inside the ring against Oleksandr Usyk, he stumbled.

Oleksandr Usyk Upsets the Applecart

On September 25, 2021, Oleksandr Usyk won a unanimous decision over Anthony Joshua at Tottenham Hotspur Arena in London to claim the WBA, IBF, and WBO heavyweight titles. With that victory, Usyk follows in the footsteps of Vitali and Wladimir Klitschko to become the third heavyweight beltholder from Ukraine.

Joshua has an elegance about him. Unlike some heavyweights at the top of today's class, he seems rational and sincere when he speaks. "The world is cruel," he told Sky Sports a year ago. "You've got to have a thick skin. One minute you're on top of the world, and the next minute you're not. That's the name of the game we're in."

"A.J." has accomplished a lot in the past ten years. He won a gold medal in the super-heavyweight division at the 2012 London Olympics, became enormously popular in his homeland, and has earned tens of millions of dollars fighting. What he hasn't done is prove himself to be a great fighter. The promise that seemed to be there after he climbed off the canvas to beat Wladimir Klitschko in an enthralling spectacle before 90,000 screaming fans at Wembley Stadium in 2017 never fully blossomed.

The Klitschko fight changed Joshua. Instead of gaining confidence from walking through fire and prevailing, he seemed to be a more tentative and vulnerable fighter afterward. Less-than-scintillating victories over Carlos Takam, Joseph Parker, and Alexander Povetkin followed. Then promoter Eddie Hearn brought Joshua to America to showcase him at Madison Square Garden against the corpulent Andy Ruiz. Shockingly, Ruiz knocked A.J. down four times and stopped him in seven rounds.

Six months later in Saudi Arabia, Joshua gained a measure of revenge when he outboxed a grossly out-of-shape Ruiz to reclaim his belts. But A.J. hardly looked like a conqueror. A good jab doesn't just score points and keep an opponent at bay. It cuts; it hurts; it shakes up the opponent. Against Ruiz the second time around, Joshua threw a stay-away-from-me jab all night. As Jimmy Tobin wrote, it was as though he'd been transformed "from wild boar to truffle pig."

A cautiously fought victory over Kubrat Pulev followed. "It's easy to watch on YouTube and be confident," Joshua said afterward. "Easy to watch from the outside. But when you're in front of someone, actually in the ring, it's a completely different ballgame."

Usyk, like Joshua, won a gold medal at the 2012 Olympics (Oleksandr's was in the heavyweight division). He'd distinguished himself in the professional ranks by unifying the cruiserweight titles and had become the mandatory challenger for A.J.'s IBF belt by virtue of lackluster victories over Chazz Witherspoon and Derek Chisora.

Joshua was a 5-to-2 betting favorite. Usyk is a tricky southpaw who would be entering the fight with an 18–0 (13 KOs) professional record. But A.J. has heavy hands and a devastating uppercut. Twenty-two of his 24 victories had come by knockout. His chin is suspect but Oleksandr was deemed ill equipped to exploit that vulnerability. All one had to do was watch Usyk struggle against Witherspoon and Chisora to conclude that A.J. was too big a mountain for him to climb. There's a reason that there are weight classes in boxing.

At the weigh-in, Joshua was 20 pounds heavier than Usyk. It was, one observer opined, "a fight between a heavyweight and a wanna-be heavyweight." The greatest threat to Joshua seemed to be Joshua.

One day before the bout, A.J. was asked what would be next on his schedule after fighting Usyk. The assumption was that his next opponent would be the winner of Tyson Fury vs. Deontay Wilder (who are scheduled to fight on October 9).

"I've got a rematch clause if the worst happens," Joshua answered. "So, if I lose, I'm fighting Usyk again; the undisputed gets put on hold. If I win, I'll fight either one of them. If Fury wins, I'll fight Fury. If Wilder wins, I'll fight Wilder."

That answer was remarkable. Fighters often hype their opponent to build a promotion. But the phrase "if I lose" rarely escapes their lips.

On fight night, the atmosphere was electric. The 65,000-seat Tottenham Hotspur Arena had been sold out within twenty-four hours of tickets going on sale.

Joshua seemed to enjoy the fireworks and blaring music that accompanied his ring walk. It had been a long time since he'd fought before a large, roaring crowd in England. The stage was set. Then the fight started.

For Joshua loyalists, the contest was akin to opening a beautifully wrapped present on Christmas morning and finding bath towels inside instead of a much-desired stylish coat.

Usyk began cautiously, moving around the ring, throwing jabs like a pesky fly. A.J. looked clumsy and a bit befuddled. Oleksandr's southpaw style was giving him trouble. The proceedings brought to mind the advice that trainer Emanuel Steward gave to Lennox Lewis on the night that Lewis fought Ray Mercer. The plan that night had been for Lennox to outbox Mercer. Except the plan wasn't working. In the middle rounds, sensing that the fight was slipping away, Steward told Lewis, "Just fucking fight him." Lennox did as instructed and won a narrow decision.

Rob McCracken (Joshua's trainer) should have given A.J. the same advice. When A.J. went to Usyk's body (which was hittable), he seemed to hurt Oleksandr. But he didn't do it often enough. Instead of trading with Usyk, for most of the night Joshua seemed reluctant to let his hands go and looked less interested in hitting than concerned about getting hit.

Joshua came on a bit in the middle rounds but then relinquished control again. He needed to impose his size and strength on Usyk but didn't. He didn't fight like a heavyweight champion is supposed to fight.

As the bout progressed, Usyk suffered cuts above and below his right eye. A.J.'s nose was bloodied and there was a pronounced swelling beneath his right eye.

Usyk fought the final two rounds as though he needed them to win. Joshua fought the final two rounds like a beaten fighter and was in trouble at the final bell.

Give the judges credit for honest scoring. Their 117–112, 116–112, 115–113 scorecards in Usyk's favor were on the mark.

"This was the biggest fight in my career, but it wasn't the hardest," Oleksandr said afterward. "There were a couple of moments where Anthony pushed me hard but nothing special."

The loss to Andy Ruiz raised questions about Joshua. Joshua–Usyk answered them. A.J. is a good heavyweight, not a great one.

When the dust of time falls on a great fight, it becomes a classic.

Fury–Wilder III in Perspective

On October 9, 2021, at T-Mobile Arena in Las Vegas, Tyson Fury knocked out Deontay Wilder in the eleventh round of a sensational fight to put the finishing touches on their heavyweight championship trilogy.

It has been a strange dance between these two men. Less than a minute into round twelve of their first encounter on December 1, 2018, Wilder knocked Fury unconscious and shimmied to a neutral corner, having established his primacy in the heavyweight division. Or so it seemed. Somehow, Fury managed to beat the count and rise to his feet. Wilder couldn't finish. A minute later, Fury shook him with a clubbing right hand and Deontay was holding on to survive.

The rest is history. Fury–Wilder I was declared a draw. On February 22, 2020, they fought again. This time, Fury dominated from start to finish and stopped Deontay in the seventh round. Now these two men have engaged in a third fight—one that will be remembered as a classic.

Let's look at the framework that gave Fury–Wilder III its drama.

Wilder's performance in Fury–Wilder II was evocative of a playground bully who gets flustered when a kid who's tougher than expected decides to hit back. And like a bully, Deontay took the low road in the aftermath of his defeat. He should have said, "Tyson was the better fighter tonight. I got beat. There's a rematch clause. Next time, I'll kick his ass." Instead, he manufactured excuse after ludicrous excuse.

Initially, Wilder blamed the costume he'd worn into the ring—glitzy black body armor accessorized by a black mask adorned with horns and lit up by batteries—for his defeat.

"My last couple of outfits, they had no weight on it," he said. "It was more Styrofoam. This time around, we added different heavy things. The skulls, the rhinestones that was on there. There was a lot of things that were designed on there that made it very, very, very heavy. It had battery packs in the mask. When I first tried it on, I saw it had some type of weight to it. But during that time, you get so excited and you want people to see it. But we immediately started feeling, 'All right, we're gonna have to put this uniform on a certain amount of time before we go out, even if we had to delay it a little bit.' But our timing wasn't perfect.

"He [Fury] didn't hurt me at all," Wilder continued. "The simple fact is that my uniform was way too heavy for me. I didn't have no legs from the beginning of the fight. In the third round, my legs were just shot all the way through. A lot of people were telling me, 'It looked like something was wrong with you.' Something was. I knew I didn't have the legs because of my uniform. It weighed forty-some pounds with the helmet and all the batteries. I wanted my tribute to be great for Black History Month and I guess I put that before anything."

Now we know. The reason David defeated Goliath had nothing to do with David's sling and five smooth stones. It was all about Goliath's heavy body armor. Lest one forget, the Bible tells us that Goliath wore a tunic fashioned from hundreds of bronze scales, bronze shin guards, bronze plates covering his feet, and a heavy metal helmet. Boy, did that weaken Goliath's legs.

And by the way, keep in mind that Wilder said in a 2018 video that he trained regularly while wearing a forty-five-pound weighted vest.

Paulie Malignaggi put things in perspective when he observed, "This is where Deontay has had a problem in the last couple years. Nobody around him is honest anymore. Starting from the first Fury fight, somebody should have been like, 'Yo, playa; you didn't win that fight.' But now, just like the first fight where you said you got robbed and everybody's cheering you on, now you're saying after this fight, 'Yo, that thing was heavy. Man, that outfit was heavy.' Not one of your team has the balls to say shit. If everybody's just agreeing with you, a bunch of yes-men, you start to lose track of reality. Somebody in his team should've been like, 'Yo, you're gonna look like an idiot if you put that out there. Don't say that.' If you say, 'I didn't feel right on fight night,' say that. Don't say it was the outfit."

Then the excuses got worse.

In several social media posts, Wilder accused Fury of cheating. "I highly believe you put something hard in your glove," Deontay said. "Something the size and the shape of an egg weight. It's the reason why the side of my face swelled up in an egg weight form and it left a dent in my face as well. . . . You scratched flesh out of my ears which caused my ears to bleed. Why did my ear have scratches deep inside my ear? Because of your nails. It's so many different facts and proof that we have."

Here, one might note that, when a fighter's hands are wrapped before a fight, he makes a fist and his nails are tucked into the palm of his hand which is wrapped with gauze and tape and encased in a glove. There's no way a fighter can scratch the flesh out of an opponent's ear with his nails.

Next, Wilder targeted Kenny Bayless (one of the most respected referees in boxing), claiming, "The referee coming in the dressing room, I could feel his negative energy. His eyes looked like he took a cocktail drink before going into the fight. His energy felt like, 'I'm gonna do something to you, black man, but I've gotta do it. Fury didn't come to box. He came to really, really, really make the fight as dirty as possible. He was putting me in headlocks and still hitting me in the body, leaning over on me and still hitting me in the body. He came to fight dirty, and the referee let him get away with it. He elbowed me in my face too. He [the referee] acted like he ain't know what was going on. Either this motherfucker was drunk or he was part of it. Which one was it?"

But Wilder's ugliest accusations were aimed at his trainer, Mark Breland.

Breland is widely recognized as one of the most decent men in boxing and had trained Wilder from the start of Deontay's pro career. Under his tutelage, Wilder had been undefeated in his first 43 fights, scored 41 knockouts, and reigned as WBC heavyweight champion for five years. In round seven of Fury–Wilder II, Breland made the decision to halt the fight. Not only was Deontay taking a beating, the big punch that had always been his equalizer seemed to have been beaten out of him.

Initially, Wilder blamed Breland for making a good-faith error in stopping the fight.

"I am upset with Mark for the simple fact that we've talked about this many times," Deontay said. "It's a principle thing. As a warrior, as a champion, as a leader, as a ruler, I want to go out on my shield. If I'm talking about going in and killing a man, I respect the same way. I abide by the same principle of receiving. So I told my team to never, ever, no matter what it may look like, to never throw the towel in with me because I'm a special kind. I still had five rounds left. No matter what it looked like, I was still in the fight. I understand he was looking out for me and trying to do what he felt was right. But this is my life and my career and he has to accept my wishes. I still had my mind. I still knew what I was doing. Although I didn't have the legs, I knew how to move around the ring. It may look a certain type of way. But I'm never out of a fight because of my tremendous power. And I'd rather go out on my shield and my sword than anything."

But as time went by, Wilder moved to a more conspiratorial theory— that Breland had deliberately betrayed him.

"This motherfucker didn't even give me a warning," Deontay maintained. "In round seven, I'm getting myself back together and all of a sudden the towel is thrown in. They couldn't knock me out. They couldn't keep me down. It took a disloyal trainer to throw the towel in."

The accusations got worse.

"About fifteen minutes before going out to the fight," Deontay said in a rant on 78SportsTV, "warming up on the mitts, it was perfect, I felt great until I went to the ring. That transformation, I was drinking certain water and stuff, trying to keep myself hydrated. I just start feeling weird. My water was spiked, as if I took a muscle relaxer or something like that. It wasn't just the suit; my water was tampered with. This feeling here, it was a different feeling. It was like I had no control over my body. My legs was weak and stuff like that. I believe he [Breland] was part of it. He was the only one handling my water. He was the only one. I have strong sources.

"We know what the deal is," Wilder continued. "We know what's up, man. You would want to debunk something that we all have proof and evidence of. I told Jay [co-manager and assistant trainer Jay Deas], 'I believe Mark did something to the water.' I'm telling you; I know how I felt in the ring. That wasn't me. Now this is all coming out. He was definitely part of what was going on. If the shoe was on the other foot, they'd prosecute me. He's a bitch."

On October 2, 2020, it was publicly revealed that Breland's services had been terminated and that, in the future, Wilder would be trained by Deas and Malik Scott. Finally, in February 2021, Breland spoke out.

"A coach can only teach someone if they're willing to learn," Breland said in a social media post. "Deontay had become untrainable because he was at the point of, he knows more about boxing than all of us. I'm not a doctor. But I know blood coming out of your ears and dazed eyes could be a brain issue. And power comes from your legs, and his legs were gone. So I made a decision to stop the fight and I'd do it all again."

We live in age in which, if someone says something often enough and loudly enough, his or her supporters will believe it no matter how ridiculous and lacking in evidence the assertion is. Wilder's accusations were boxing's version of The Big Lie.

"All I can say is that he [Wilder] is mimicking Donald Trump," Bob Arum (Fury's co-promoter) said. "He likes to come up with conspiracy theories."

Asked about Wilder's allegations, Fury responded, "I think he has lost his marbles."

When Tyson Fury thinks that someone has lost their marbles, the chances are that more than a few marbles are missing.

★★★

The contracts for Fury–Wilder II contained a rematch clause. Thus, Wilder was entitled to an opportunity to avenge his defeat. But putting Fury–Wilder III together was easier said than done.

Each man was said to have been guaranteed $25 million for their second encounter. There was a widespread belief that Fox (which shared pay-per-view rights with ESPN) and Premier Boxing Champions (which promotes Wilder) had needed between 1.1 and 1.2 million buys in the United States to break even. But Fury–Wilder II only generated in the neighborhood of 800,000 domestic buys. Sources also say that Top Rank lost in excess of $5 million on the promotion.

Because Fury had won the second fight, the purse for Fury–Wilder III was to be divided 60–40 in favor of Team Fury. Tyson expected to make at least as much money from the third encounter as he'd made from the second (if not more). And Wilder didn't want to take a pay cut. But revenue expectations for Fury–Wilder III were inauspicious. This was the COVID era.

In autumn 2020, Team Fury announced that, since Fury–Wilder III hadn't occurred within the contractually mandated time frame, Fury planned to fight another opponent on December 5. In response, Shelly Finkel (Wilder's co-manager) said that Wilder was seeking mediation in an effort to ensure that Fury–Wilder III would take place before another fight for either fighter and that, absent a settlement, legally binding arbitration would follow. On November 15, Fury tweeted that his return to the ring would be pushed back to 2021.

Then talk turned to a proposed mega-fight between Fury and Anthony Joshua.

On March 13, 2021, Fury and Joshua signed provision of services agreements for a two-fight deal with Queensberry, MTK, and Top Rank (all on Fury's side of the table) and Matchroom (Joshua's promoter). Income from Joshua–Fury I was to be split 50–50 between the two camps. Income from the rematch would be split 60–40 in favor of the winner of the first bout. It was contemplated that the first fight between the two men would take place in June or July with Fury–Joshua II in November or December.

But it was an agreement in principle, not a finished deal. The site had yet to be determined. And more significantly, the money to finance the venture wasn't in place. There was a thirty-day window within which to finalize the contracts.

"I think that everybody is proceeding the way they should be proceeding," Bob Arum said. "When the fight will take place, where it will take place, that will work itself out. Right now, we've got a motherfucking pandemic. Everybody is stuck in the same thing, the coronavirus. The problem is, when can we schedule the fight and where. We're dealing with an element we have no control over. Who's going to put up money for a site unless they can attract people from the outside? Everybody is behaving appropriately except the pandemic."

And what would Arum say to boxing fans who were tired of waiting for Fury–Joshua?

"'Go fuck yourself,'" Arum answered. "'Find a life.' That's what I would say to them."

Things went downhill from there.

★ Matchroom CEO Eddie Hearn (on April 5, 2021): "July is the date. Really, I think end of next week it will be done. Talks have progressed extremely well and we're closing in on securing the venue and there will be an announcement in due course."

* Queensberry CEO Frank Warren (on April 9): "Hearn is the one who is dealing now with Saudi Arabia. We expect to know by early next week if the money there is real."

* Eddie Hearn (on April 22): "Some more exchanged final drafts, more calls tonight. It's as done as it can be. It's non-stop at the moment but it's happening. It's one hundred percent happening."

* Eddie Hearn (on April 26): "People doubted we would achieve the site fee. We have achieved that. Both fighters have signed the contract to fight. Both fighters have agreed to an offer from a site. It's never done until the ink is dry, but there are no obstacles to overcome except to finalize the paperwork and get it announced. I've not seen a fight fall through at this stage before."

* Bob Arum (on April 29): "It will take months for the Saudis to do their due diligence on such a huge deal. It is not just a site fee. There are ancillary demands from the Saudis stretching into the broadcast deals and other things. It could take months for it all to play out. It could even take until 2022 the way it looks right now. The fight in July or August is dead in the water as far as we are concerned. It is absurd what Hearn is saying, that it is a done deal."

* Eddie Hearn (on April 30): "The deal is agreed and we are waiting for the longform agreement to be signed. In the coming hours or days, they'll get a copy of the contract that's ready to go and they'll sign. Bob's ego is out of control. Let's all do our job."

* Eddie Hearn (on May 1): "Last night, we received the contract from the Middle East. All sides' lawyers have got to go through that and make sure they're happy with it. But we're all systems go. This fight is on. This fight is happening. I believe you'll get an announcement next week. You will get this fight next and you will get it for the undisputed world championship."

* Eddie Hearn (May 11): "August 7, August 14. It's a very bad secret that the fight is happening in Saudi Arabia. It's the same people we did the deal with for Andy Ruiz. That event was spectacular. As partners, they were fantastic, so we're very comfortable. We're ready to go."

* Frank Warren (on May 11): "I've seen Hearn has put something out today. It's just bullshit. I just don't get why he does this stuff. How many times has he announced this? I want the fight. But until it is signed, there ain't a fight."

OOPS!

As noted above, the contracts for Fury–Wilder II had provided for an immediate rematch. After losing to Fury, Wilder had exercised that right. Then, when Team Fury unilaterally declared that the rematch clause was no longer operative, Wilder sought mediation to resolve the issue. Ultimately, he took the matter to binding arbitration.

On May 17, 2021, Daniel Weinstein (the judge overseeing the arbitration) sided with Wilder and ordered that Fury–Wilder III take place before September 15.

"It was a shock to the system," Hearn declared on hearing the news. "This negotiation has been going on three, four months and we were always assured this wouldn't be a problem."

"Eddie Hearn has diarrhea of the mouth," Arum responded. "He can't stop talking and he doesn't think. In the contract, which Joshua signed and Fury signed, we specifically had a section talking about the arbitration and talking about the possibility that the arbitrator would order [Fury] to fight [Wilder]. So everybody knew about that. It's not a secret that it was in arbitration and that this was a possibility."

Either way, Fury–Joshua was dead. Thereafter, Fury–Wilder III was signed and scheduled for July 24 at T-Mobile Arena in Las Vegas. Almost immediately, the fighters began exchanging insults:

* Tyson Fury: "This guy is a glutton for punishment. He's an idiot. He got absolutely dismantled and smashed to bits in our last fight and he wants that all over again. He's telling people I cracked his skull, I injured his shoulder, I done his bicep. Yet he wants to get in there with me again. It's one of two things. He's absolutely crazy or he's a sucker for punishment. I'm knocking him out cold."

* Deontay Wilder: "My mind is very violent. We built a whole facility to commit a legal homicide. I cannot wait. When you contemplating and premeditating about harming a man and when you see that

person, what you've been thinking and what you've been feeling will come out. If your stomach can't digest what your eyes about to see, don't come to my fights. Don't watch my fights. Because I mean blood, and I'm out for blood."

* Tyson Fury: "Clearly, he's suffered his first mental breakdown. Not surprising, really. I injured him heavily. As well as the torn biceps he kept going on about, he ended up with a ruptured shoulder while I also gave him a cracked skull and two burst ear-drums. I smashed him to pieces. He felt like he'd been run over by an 18-wheeler. Make that a six-foot-niner. Then he lost the plot completely with all those mad allegations. He's had a lot of mental issues."

* Deontay Wilder: "My mentality is, you've been contemplating about hurting a person so bad, to the point you wanna disfigure him so his mother wouldn't even know who he was."

With that as background, the kickoff press conference took place on June 15 in Los Angeles. Wilder made a brief opening statement in which he proclaimed, "Time to cut off his head. Come July 24, there will be bloodshed." Fury responded, "He said all this last time. Decapitation, bloodshed, and all that. And we all know what went down there. Deontay Wilder's a one-trick pony. He's got one-punch power. We all know that. Great. But I guarantee you, he does not go past where he did before."

Thereafter, Wilder refused to answer questions at the press conference, letting Malik Scott answer for him. At the close of the festivities, there was a six-minute staredown.

Talking with reporters afterward, Fury said of Wilder's silence, "What's he gonna say? We've all heard enough of them excuses. Probably best he didn't speak because then no one could ask him any questions about why he's been saying all that stuff. So, probably good. Good idea, actually."

Thereafter, Wilder declared, "I'm looking forward to July 24, to show the greatness of me." He also analogized himself to Muhammad Ali, saying, "Deontay Wilder come along to take that same stand outside and inside the ring. It seem like it ain't enough. It seem like they have these buck-dancers that dance in our kind to go against us and try it down. But you can't buck-break me, man. I'm chosen. Ali is one of my idols in boxing, I appreciate to be compared to him, and I can see the comparison of what he stood for."

Here, it might be noted that this is the same Deontay Wilder who went to the White House for a photo op with Donald Trump in 2018 and, five years earlier, acknowledged assaulting a prostitute in a Las Vegas hotel room.

Fury has a history of irrational behavior and antisocial rants that have been well catalogued. In this instance, he seemed like the more stable half of the promotion.

Then there was a problem. A big one. On July 8, it was announced that Fury had tested positive for COVID and that Fury–Wilder III would have to be postponed.

"He got vaccinated in Miami," Bob Arum explained. "He got the first shot. And then he said he didn't want to get the second shot because he didn't want to get sick [from the vaccination] so close to the fight. So he got COVID instead."

In due course, Fury–Wilder III was rescheduled for October 9. Then, on September 25, the promotion (and boxing) received a jolt when Oleksandr Usyk outclassed Anthony Joshua to claim the WBA, IBF, and WBO heavyweight belts. Part of the buzz for Fury–Wilder III had been that the winner was expected to fight Joshua next in what would have been a mega-fight of the highest order. Now the pot of gold at the end of that rainbow was gone.

On September 28, responding to Wilder's threats to inflict bodily harm beyond the norm upon him, Fury took to social media and said, "I'm gonna smash your fucking face in, you prick. How about that for a fucking message."

As the clock ticked down to fight night, Fury continued to verbally savage his foe. Focusing on Wilder's claim that he had cheated to win their second encounter, Tyson proclaimed:

* "I don't really make much of the excuses. I think they just made him a weaker character and less of a man and less of a fighter. When you get beat, you get beat. Shake the man's hand and move on. Lots of fighters have lost. It's what they do after they lose that makes them who they are."

★ "He's very unstable at the moment. I'm not sure how I would react if I got absolutely smashed to bits like he did. But I guarantee it wouldn't be like this."

★ "Maybe we should have him weigh his costume before he walks to the ring in it so there can't be any excuses this time. It's been embarrassing for American boxing, really. You come up with excuses like this on the global stage with the world watching. It's absolutely pathetic."

★ "Acceptance is a hard thing because nobody wants to accept the truth. When I was an alcoholic, I didn't want to be told I was an alcoholic. I didn't want to be told I'm a fat bastard. It's almost like this little game in your own head where you don't want to know the truth even though you do know the truth. The moment that I accepted that I had to change and I had to get help and stop what I was doing, that's the moment I could step away from it all and start again. From what I'm hearing from this idiot here, he hasn't accepted what's happened to him."

Fury was a 5-to-2 betting favorite. But more than was usually the case, many insiders were reluctant to pick a winner. Or if they did, they hedged their pick a bit.

The case for Fury beating Wilder rested on the belief that Tyson was the better boxer technically; he was stronger mentally; he took a better punch; and twenty months earlier, he'd dismantled Deontay. Speaking of Wilder's performance in Fury–Wilder II, Teddy Atlas observed, "He showed that he doesn't know how to fight. He was exposed again for having no fundamentals, really none of the rudimental things that you need, usually, to be a top fighter."

Moreover, when Wilder dismissed Mark Breland, he could have accepted offers of assistance from experienced trainers. The fact that he chose Malik Scott and Jay Deas to train him (each of whom was already in his inner circle) indicated that Deontay planned to enter the ring with the same weapons and delivery system that he'd deployed in the past.

That said, it was strange to hear some of the same people who had once called Wilder the hardest-punching fighter in boxing history now saying that Deontay didn't have a chance.

Any heavyweight who hits as hard as Wilder hits has a chance.

Malik Scott was vocal in playing up his fighter. "He's not some big dumb guy who just throws a right hand," Scott said. "There's method to his madness. Deontay's IQ is very high. I watch him create, watch him put himself in position, set guys up into surgical traps. He is ten times more focused [now than he was before], training one hundred times harder. It's a violent camp. His mentality is very violent. This will be the best version of Deontay Wilder that you have ever seen."

Trainers always talk up their fighter's chances. But the prevailing view was that Wilder had used the preceding twenty months more effectively than Fury and would enter the ring in far better physical condition than Fury. Deontay would be in shape to go twelve hard rounds. Fury might not be.

Also, Wilder unquestionably was the harder puncher. And as Tris Dixon noted, "It wasn't about who he was beating [before] but how he was beating them. It was the inevitable knockout. You don't beat fighters like that if the only thing you have is a punch. That's not how the sport works. You need more than a few crumbs of talent. You need more than to be a one-hit wonder. You need to take your licks. You need to do the work. These fighters didn't just bow down before him, roll over and play dead. To get as far as he had, you can't just rely on Thor's hammer for a weapon. That was a gift but not the only thing that made him a champion."

Once the bell for round one of Fury–Wilder III rang, Deontay would have three strategies to choose from:

1. He could back up in the face of Fury's onslaught, in which case he'd lose.
2. He could move forward, throwing wild punches. But Fury is a good enough boxer that he'd be able to evade damage.
3. Deontay could work his jab (which is a good one), draw a line in the sand (the way Evander Holyfield did against Mike Tyson), refuse to back up from there, and throw his right hand when the opportunity presented itself.

At the final pre-fight press conference, Fury expressed confidence that he would win. But Tyson understood the risks involved. "Deontay Wilder is the most dangerous heavyweight out there," he acknowledged.

"Combine them all together and they don't make a danger like Wilder. So that's what I'm messing with. I'm playing with an atomic bomb, messing round, clipping wires. Every time you go into the ring with Deontay Wilder you're playing with that danger."

In sum, even though Fury–Wilder III might not turn out to be a difficult fight for Fury, it was a dangerous one. Tyson was expected to win. But. . . .

★★★

We live in a world in which there's frightening power in lies and wild accusations. No matter how irresponsible and blatantly false a statement might be, people who want to believe it will believe it. And social media enables its spread.

Within that milieu, there's something comfortingly honest about what happens in a boxing ring. The truth shows. Even if Wilder had won Fury–Wilder III, it wouldn't have justified his scurrilous allegations with regard to his knockout defeat in their second encounter. But Fury's performance on October 9 put a punctuation mark on the truth.

Fury is a massive man. He's six feet, nine inches tall and weighed in for Fury–Wilder III at 277 pounds (his heaviest fight weight ever). Wilder is two inches shorter and came in at a career-high 238. Fury's body evoked images of a slab of marbled beef. Deontay's looked as though it was plated with armor.

Wilder came out aggressively behind a hard jab in round one. He didn't land much but neither did Fury.

In round two, Tyson picked up the pace. "I'm going to go all guns blazing," he'd said before the bout. "Full-out attack." Now he made good on that pledge.

Essentially, Fury's fight plan boiled down to, "I'll hit you. If you hit me, so be it. We'll see who's standing when it's over."

That's quite a strategy for fighting Deontay Wilder. But that's what Tyson did. The two men were like giant mastodons battling for supremacy.

In round three, Fury dropped Wilder with an overhand right followed by a hard right uppercut. Deontay rose at the count of six, hurt, and referee Russell Mora gave him a few extra seconds to recover, asking

Deontay if he wanted to continue and instructing the fighter to walk toward him before the battle resumed. That was appropriate. The same process worked to Fury's benefit in round four when Wilder dropped him twice; first with a straight right to the forehead and then with a clubbing right hand behind the head.

"He caught me twice in the fourth round," Fury would say at the post-fight press conference. "But I was never like thinking like, 'Oh, this is over.' I was thinking, 'Okay, good shot. But I will get you back in a minute. And I did."

After the fight, some observers likened the battle to Ali–Frazier III and Holyfield–Bowe I. A more apt comparison would be the 1976 slugfest between George Foreman and Ron Lyle, when each man was dropped multiple times before Foreman prevailed on a brutal fifth-round stoppage.

Fury–Wilder III was enthralling. The two men fought like starving dockworkers battling for a sandwich on a pier. They mauled. They brawled. The bombs kept coming. They were slugging as much as boxing. Clearly, Fury was getting the better of it, landing hard clubbing blows. But every moment of a Wilder fight is high drama because—BOOM—Deontay has the means to end matters with one punch at any time.

They showed incredible heart, both of them.

In round ten, a roundhouse right put Wilder on the canvas for the second time. Deontay was exhausted but came back to hurt Fury at the end of the stanza. As Corey Erdman later wrote, "People that wounded, that tired, with eyes drooping and mouth dangling open, are only dangerous in the pro wrestling universe where fighters can power up and hit their signature maneuver out of nowhere. To watch that scenario play out in real life was nothing short of astonishing."

The carnage ended in round eleven. Wilder, bleeding from his mouth and left ear, went down face first after being hit with a right uppercut followed by a left hook and then a crushing right hand. Russell Mora didn't bother to count. It was over.

Fury won eight of the first ten rounds on my scorecard. The judges had it a bit closer (95–91, 95–91, 94–92) at the time of the stoppage. Give Fury credit. He didn't just get off the canvas. He got off the canvas and won.

Wilder left the ring before the result was formally announced—but not before a final lack-of-grace note.

"I'm a sportsman," Fury told ESPN's Bernardo Osuna in the ring during a post-fight interview. "I went over to show him support and respect, and he didn't want to give it back. So that's his problem."

At the post-fight press conference, Fury elaborated on that moment, recounting, "I went over to shake his hand and say well done. And he was like, 'No, I don't respect you.'" Tyson subsequently told IFL-TV, "I went to say well done to him, and he wouldn't have any of it. The man's a sore loser and a proper shithouse."

How good is Fury? It's hard to tell. We know he can take a punch. We know he has heart. His size and boxing skills would make him a formidable opponent for any fighter ever. But Tyson's reputation has been built in large measure on a lethargic victory by decision over an aging Wladimir Klitschko (who Anthony Joshua knocked out) and three fights against Deontay Wilder (who most definitely can punch but has limited boxing skills).

Fury deserves recognition as the best heavyweight in the world right now. Beyond that, he put the matter in perspective himself when asked at the post-fight press conference to assess his place among boxing's heavyweight greats.

"I can never fight people from the past," Fury answered. "I can only beat who's in my era. I don't like competing with fighters from the past because it's fantasy; it's not reality. And I wouldn't like to disrespect any of the former champions, even from when heavyweights were like 185 pounds. Let's just say I'm the lineal champion in my era. I can only beat the best of my day."

Canelo Álvarez is a champion. Caleb Plant was a beltholder.
There's a difference.

The Brutal Efficiency
of Canelo Álvarez

On Saturday night, November 6, 2021, Saul "Canelo" Álvarez scored an eleventh-round knockout over Caleb Plant at the MGM Grand Garden Arena in Las Vegas to secure the fourth and final belt in his quest to become the "undisputed" super-middleweight champion of the world.

Álvarez is widely regarded as the #1 pound-for-pound fighter in the world and boxing's brightest star. Three months ago, SportsPro (a London-based company) released a study that listed him as the fourth "most marketable athlete in the world" (behind Simone Biles, Naomi Osaka, and Ashlyn Harris). The next-highest-ranked boxer was Anthony Joshua at #75. The study was keyed to social media metrics. Canelo has close to 18 million followers on Facebook, Twitter, Instagram, and TikTok and, according to SportsPro, has generated more than 578 million impressions on these platforms.

In reality, the list is an indication of potential rather than true marketing power. For example, in 2020, SportsPro named Ryan Garcia as the twelfth "most marketable athlete in the world." LeBron James was designated as #24. Most people would rather have LeBron's marketing income than Garcia's.

Canelo, now thirty-one, turned pro at age fifteen and has improved steadily throughout his career. He entered the ring to face Plant with a 56–1–2 (38 KOs) record, the sole loss coming against Floyd Mayweather eight years ago.

"I didn't have the experience, the maturity," Canelo said earlier this year about that fight. "I wasn't the boxer I am today. Very different. That moment hurt a lot. But at that moment, I got to thinking, I'm not going to let this kill my dreams. Someday, I'm going to be the best boxer in the world. And now I am."

One might add that, at age fifteen, Canelo was held to a draw by a fighter named Jorge Juarez (who finished his career with an 8–27–3 record). Only an idiot would suggest that this "blemish" on Canelo's record diminishes his accomplishments as a fighter. The same is true of the loss to Mayweather.

Plant, age twenty-nine, came into the Canelo fight with a 21–0 (12 KOs) record and the IBF 168-pound belt around his waist. He has a compelling backstory focused on a hardscrabble upbringing in Ashland, Tennessee, and tells it with great drama.

Canelo wanted Plant's belt. He'd won his first 168-pound title (WBA) against Rocky Fielding in 2018 and added the WBC and WBO straps against Callum Smith (2020) and Billy Joe Saunders (2021). Becoming a unified champion appealed to him.

When Canelo–Plant was first announced, it was undetermined which network would host the pay-per-view telecast. Canelo had fought his most recent six fights on DAZN with Golden Boy and Matchroom as his promoters. This would be a Premier Boxing Champions card, which meant that FOX or Showtime would handle the pay-per-view and DAZN would be out in the cold.

Most boxing observers expected that FOX would get the nod (as it had with previous Premier Boxing Champions offerings like Fury–Wilder II and III, Pacquiao–Thurman, Pacquiao–Ugás, and Errol Spence's forays against Mikey Garcia, Danny Garcia, and Shawn Porter). But Showtime sent a "don't take us for granted" message to PBC impresario Al Haymon when it went into the Jake Paul business earlier this year, and Canelo–Plant wound up on Showtime Pay-Per-View.

Asked how he felt about changing promoters and networks, Canelo answered, "I just want to fight with everybody and have relationships with all the promoters and do the best fights out there. If I need to fight [on] Showtime with PBC, I'm good. If I need to fight [on] DAZN with Eddie Hearn, I'm good. I'm good with everyone, having a relationship with everybody."

That made sense. But there was one misstep that Canelo's team seemed to make in the negotiations for Canelo–Plant. And they'd made it before.

Plant's purse for fighting Canelo was reported to be $10 million. That number was negotiated in significant measure as a consequence of the purses believed to have been paid to Canelo's most recent five opponents—Danny Jacobs ($12 million), Sergey Kovalev ($12 million),

Callum Smith ($6 million), Avni Yildirim ($2.5 million), and Billy Joe Saunders ($8 million).

This is an area where Floyd Mayweather got it right. There came a time when Mayweather told the world that the belts were largely irrelevant. People were paying to see Floyd Mayweather. If a fighter wanted to fight Floyd, he stood in line and accepted a purse (generally between $1 million and $3 million) that left the lion's share and more for Floyd.

Canelo's most recent fight (against Saunders) drew 66,065 paying fans to AT&T Stadium in Texas. Plant's most recent fight was against Caleb Truax at the Shrine Exposition Hall in Los Angeles. Prior to that, he'd fought Vincent Feigenbutz at the Bridgestone Arena in Nashville. One might also note that Canelo's two fights against Gennady Golovkin in Las Vegas generated a combined live gate in excess of $51 million.

It has been widely reported that PBC guaranteed Canelo "nearly $40 million" to fight Plant (which was in line with previous guarantees to Canelo for his fights on DAZN). There's a school of thought that Canelo should be concerned with what he makes, not his opponents' purses. Still, $10 million for Plant seemed excessive. Had Caleb beaten Canelo, he might have become a $10 million fighter. He wasn't before they fought and he isn't now.

The promotion moved into high gear at the September 21 kickoff press conference in Los Angeles. Plant was introduced first and stood on stage facing the audience. Canelo came out next, stood beside Plant, and made a point of not standing in Caleb's space. Both men were wearing sunglasses. As prearranged, they then turned to face each other. Canelo took his glasses off. Plant moved into Canelo's space, put his hands behind his back, and started jawing. Canelo responded. Plant said something Canelo didn't like. Canelo gave Plant a two-handed shove to the chest, pushing him back. Plant came forward, slapped at Canelo with his left hand, and missed. Canelo countered with a quick jab that jammed Plant's sunglasses into Caleb's cheek beneath his right eye and drew blood, followed by a slapping right hand.

What caused the blowup?

Plant later said that it happened "because he's a bitch."

Canelo said Plant suggested that Canelo had sexual intercourse with his own mother and noted, "He can say whatever he wants to me but not to my mom. And he swing first. I just push him, but he swing first.

Then I do what I do."

Meanwhile, when it was Plant's turn to speak, he took the microphone and accused Canelo of being a "cheater."

In February 2018, urine samples taken from Canelo by the Voluntary Anti-Doping Association (VADA) had tested positive for clenbuterol, a banned substance. Canelo denied wrongdoing, and the amount of the drug in his system was consistent with the inadvertent ingestion of tainted beef. But a boxer is responsible for what goes into his body. Canelo agreed to a six-month suspension by the Nevada State Athletic Commission and paid $50,000 out of his own pocket for year-round VADA testing. There was no admission of wrongdoing on his part. But there was an acknowledgment that clenbuterol had been present in his system. Since then, Canelo has been tested more thoroughly by VADA than any boxer ever, always without complaint and never with an adverse test result.

"Did he get suspended for six months?" Plant asked rhetorically at the kickoff press conference. "Did he test positive? It's not a 'well, he said he is' and 'he said he ain't.' It's not up for discussion. It's not what I say. It's what the commission said. It's what the banned substance list said. I don't want this to be in our sport. There's no room for that in our sport. And you know, he got suspended for six months. So it is what it is. He's a cheater."

When it was Canelo's turn to speak, he looked directly at Plant and said in English, "I just want to say something. You are not on my level. And you will see November 6. You don't want to find out. I promise you. Thank you, everybody. I see you November 6. You know what I do."

PBC wisely skipped the ritual post-press-conference staredown. But thereafter, it sent out promotional material referencing the press conference itself as "epic" (presumably because of the altercation). "Epic" is a word that, in boxing circles, was once reserved for actual fights like Ali–Frazier III in Manila.

Plant was more measured than PBC in characterizing the physical confrontation between the two fighters. "It's boxing," he said. "How many times has that happened before us? How many times is that gonna happen after us? People make such a big deal out of that because it's a headline and a way for you guys to promote whatever videos you all are making or whatever for the fight. But it's just like, he pushed me; I got one on him; he got one on me; and that was it. I've been in worse scuffles than that. So, what's the big deal, really?"

Title unification was the marketing message during fight week.

"Only five male fighters in the history of boxing have accomplished becoming undisputed champion," Canelo said. "I want to be the sixth."

Canelo's big wins had come against Miguel Cotto, Gennady Golovkin, Danny Jacobs, Sergei Kovalev, and Billy Joe Saunders. Plant's big wins had been against José Uzcátegui, Mike Lee, Vincent Feigenbutz, and Caleb Truax. With that as background, Canelo was a 7-to-1 betting favorite.

Plant voiced optimism throughout the proceedings:

★ "I know that people don't believe me when I tell them I'm winning on November 6. All those people who tell me that I can't do something, you live believable lives and you do believable things. I promised myself that I was going to run this all the way to the top with no problem crashing and burning along the way. I set out to live an unbelievable life and accomplish unbelievable things. The people who doubt me are the reason that I'm here."

★ "I can't focus on what other people say about me. If I listened to the doubters, I wouldn't even be here. People are going to say what they're going to say. But I get the final say, and I can't wait to prove everything in the ring."

★ "The moment isn't going to be too big for me. The closer we get, the smaller the moment feels."

Meanwhile, Canelo predicted that Plant wouldn't last eight rounds and said, "I respect his skills. He's a good boxer. He boxes well. He's got a good fast jab, good combinations. He's tall, and it's going to be rough in the early rounds. It's not an easy fight. But I have the skills and I have the experience of being with fighters of all kinds of styles in the ring. I'm very confident that I can do it. Not confident in a bad way; just confident in what I know and what I can do. As the fight progresses, I am going to be able to get him out of there."

Still, this wasn't a computer game. Nothing in boxing is preordained. A fighter has to prove himself anew every time he enters the ring. And Canelo knew that.

Now a confession. I didn't watch the fight live. I'm a big Canelo Álvarez fan. But I don't like boxing's pay-per-view model. And with Anthony Dirrell vs. Marcos Hernandez (who now has two wins in his last seven fights) as the chief supporting bout, I decided I'd track Canelo–Plant through online reports and watch it on YouTube afterward rather than spend $79.99 to see it in real time.

At 11:30 p.m. eastern time, I went online to Boxing Scene to see where things stood. Dirrell had knocked out Hernandez shortly after 11:00 p.m. Most likely, it would be a while before Canelo–Plant started. I checked back at 11:50. There was still no indication that the fight had begun. I turned to ESPN.com and read that the ring walks were underway.

Back to Boxing Scene. Keith Idec scored round one for Plant and gave rounds two, three, and four to Canelo. ESPN was lagging behind on its scorecard but offered several sentences of commentary for each round that it scored.

At the end of eight rounds, Boxing Scene and ESPN each had Canelo ahead 78–74. . . . Then, at 12:39 a.m., Boxing Scene reported, "Canelo drops Plant with hard punches in eleventh and then finished him off with another series of big shots to knock Plant down and out with the fight being waved off by the referee."

Several minutes later, I saw the knockout on YouTube. On Sunday, I watched the entire fight on one of several YouTube postings.

Coming into the bout, Plant had seemed to think that his skills were sufficient that he could will himself to victory. That was a false hope.

Canelo has a will of iron too. And he's a professional. He always comes into fights in shape. He's a superb boxer, seamlessly blending defense with offense. He has a great chin. And now he has "man strength."

Canelo has carried his power with him—and then some—while moving up in weight. He carries his power late in fights. And trainer Eddy Reynoso brings out the best in him.

For most of Canelo–Plant, Canelo was stalking with Caleb in retreat. Plant tried to survive and score points when he could. But he was over-matched. Plan A wasn't working for Caleb, and there was no Plan B. Canelo was quicker. Canelo hit harder. Canelo's arsenal was more varied. Canelo took his time. He was disciplined and patient. As the fight wore on, his body work took a toll. Ultimately, he beat Plant into submission.

The end came in round eleven. A left hook followed by a brutal right uppercut (the most damaging blow in the sequence) and another left hook as Plant was sagging occasioned the first knockdown of Caleb's career. He stopped his fall by thrusting both gloves against the canvas and rose up.

"Do you want to fight?" referee Russell Mora asked.

"Yeah," Plant answered.

Caleb said it like he meant it. But he had nothing left. Canelo chased him around the ring, pinned him against the ropes, and knocked him down again with three crushing right hands—two up top and the third to the body as Plant was falling.

It was over.

After the fight, the fighters exchanged words of respect in the ring. Then Plant was taken to University Medical Center for observation.

Boxing fans have heard a lot in recent years about how Mexican fans have been slow to embrace Canelo in comparison with Julio César Chávez. In that regard, Canelo says simply, "I'm doing my history. Other fighters do their history. I don't want to compare myself to other fighters. I do things for myself, my history."

Over the past decade, Canelo has established himself as a great fighter. The Mexican people should be proud of him.

Shawn Porter had never been knocked out. Terence Crawford changed that.

The Meaning of Crawford–Porter

On November 20, 2021, Terence Crawford successfully defended his WBO 147-pound title with a tenth-round knockout of Shawn Porter before a sold-out crowd of 11,568 at Mandalay Bay in Las Vegas. It was a statement win for Crawford that boxing fans hope will pave the way for more and bigger career-defining fights in the future.

Crawford came into the bout recognized as one of the top pound-for-pound fighters in the world. His record stood at 37–0 with 28 knockouts. But at age thirty-four, he didn't have a defining fight on his resume. As Jimmy Tobin wrote after Terence's fourth-round stoppage of a faded Kell Brook last year, "No one seriously denies Crawford's talent, but no one seriously denies he is squandering it." Bart Barry noted, "Just because he has been near the top of abstract rankings for a couple years doesn't mean his reign has been a good one."

Crawford moved into the public eye with eleven fights on HBO during a fifty-month span that ended on May 20, 2017. The opponents were learning experiences, some more challenging than others. Terence did what he was supposed to do against them.

Then Crawford's activity level dropped. Over the next fifty-four months, he had only six fights. In the first—against Julius Indongo—he unified the four major 140-pound belts with an impressive third-round stoppage. But Indongo has now been knocked out in four of his last five outings.

After beating Indongo, Crawford moved up to 147 pounds and dominated a mix of past-their-prime names (Brook and Amir Khan) and marginal opponents (Jeff Horn, José Benavidez, and Egidijus Kavaliauskas). He'd been on the sidelines for more than a year before fighting Porter.

Why hasn't the superbly talented Crawford become a star?

For starters, the reality of boxing is that very few stars have been made since HBO dropped out of the business. One might ask why ESPN can't make stars in the sweet science? After all, ESPN has a much larger platform than HBO ever had. And it has money. In addition to advertising revenue and monthly payments from cable system operators, ESPN receives income from more than seventeen million people who subscribe to ESPN+. Within this framework, it pays Top Rank a reported $84 million annually in license fees for fights pursuant to a seven-year contract.

But long-term output deals with a promoter are often counterproductive for a network because they take away the network's biggest bargaining chip—the date. And they encourage the practice of fighters only fighting opponents who are under the same promotional umbrella (a practice akin to the inbred insanity that once accompanied members of royal families in Europe marrying their own cousins).

One key to HBO's success was that its boxing program was open to all promoters. That encouraged star-making fights. Indeed, one reason for the decline of HBO's boxing program was that there came a time when it forged an alliance with Al Haymon and gave Haymon's fighters preferential treatment in a way that wasn't in HBO's best interests and worked against the best fighting the best.

These forces came to a head for Crawford after his November 14, 2020, knockout of Kell Brook. Bob Arum (Terence's promoter) was asked by *The Athletic* about Crawford's future with Top Rank and, clearly frustrated, responded, "He's got to promote like [Teófimo] López does. He's got to promote like Shakur [Stevenson] does, like Mayweather did, like Pacquiao did. If he doesn't, then who the fuck needs him? He may be the greatest fighter in the world. But hey, I ain't going bankrupt promoting him. I could build a house in Beverly Hills on the money I've lost on him in the last three fights, a beautiful home. Nobody questions Crawford's tremendous ability. The question is, 'Does he pay the bills?'"

Four days later, Crawford responded during a SiriusXM interview. Some of his comments were confrontational. "It pissed me off because I'm one of the most loyal people," Terence said. "For him to say some foolish shit like that, it made me look at him a totally different way. Release me now and you don't have to lose money no more. I'm not a promoter. What am I? A fighter. I get paid to fight, I don't get paid to promote. He gets paid to promote. He's supposed to promote me. I always felt like I was set up from the jump so they didn't have to pay me the money that I deserved. I used to take pay cuts because I didn't care about the money. Now he's going to pay me more [than] the [contractual] minimum every single time that I fight because I deserve it. You're going to pay me what I'm worth."

But Crawford also struck a conciliatory note, saying, "I can't bash Bob Arum and Top Rank. They gave me the opportunity to accomplish everything in my career. I know deep down in my heart that Bob really is a good dude and he really did try everything possible in his will to get these fights I was asking for. I don't know what made him come out and say all of the negative stuff he said about me. I have a lot of things going through my head right now. I don't really like to talk about it because I'm not the kind of person to put my business in the streets. If I ever had a problem with Bob Arum and Top Rank, I always went to them. We may have a disagreement right now. We're going through some trials and tribulations, but we're gonna get it figured out. Top Rank is the company I am with right now, but who knows what the future may hold."

Money can soothe hurt feelings. But Top Rank built Oscar De La Hoya, Floyd Mayweather, and Miguel Cotto to superstardom, shepherded Manny Pacquiao through his glory years, and lost all of them to other promoters. That's the nature of boxing. So with time running out on its contract with Crawford, Top Rank matched Terence against Shawn Porter.

Porter had compiled a 31–3–1 (17 KOs) record that included victories over Devon Alexander, Paulie Malignaggi, Adrien Broner, Andre Berto, Danny Garcia, and Yordenis Ugás. But he'd lost his three biggest fights—against Kell Brook, Keith Thurman, and Errol Spence.

On the business side of things, Porter was promoted by Al Haymon (Arum's archrival in recent years). But Haymon was willing to cede control of Crawford–Porter to Top Rank. And Terence was likely to leave Top Rank once his contractual obligation to the promoter was fulfilled (which it now has been). So from Arum's point of view, why not make the fight?

Meanwhile, from Haymon's point of view, an upset would increase Porter's marketability. And let's not forget, Haymon would love to sign Crawford.

The build-up to Crawford–Porter was largely about Crawford. Porter is a class act and a good fighter who has always been willing to go in tough. But in terms of marketability, his ring losses had put a ceiling on how high he could climb.

There was also a question as to what Porter would bring to the ring on fight night. He'd fought only once in the preceding twenty-six months—an uninspiring win by decision over the justifiably unheralded Sebastian Formella. Indeed, some observers regarded Porter largely as a measuring stick for Crawford. Terence opened as a 4-to-1 betting favorite and the odds moved as high as 6-to-1. Yes, Porter was "always dangerous." And this was an opportunity for him to reboot. But at age thirty-five, could he compete with Crawford?

Terence thought not. "I respect everything that Shawn does," Crawford said at the final pre-fight press conference. "Shawn is athletic. He can box. He can bang. He can move around in the ring. He can cut corners and take angles. I'm just going to say that I do a lot of things better than Shawn."

When fight night came, Porter fought as hoped for, applying pressure as best he could. Crawford was simply better.

Terence is a complete fighter who shifts seamlessly from orthodox to southpaw. He now has "man strength" to go with his skills. He's no longer just a slick boxer; he's a puncher. With an attitude. And he keeps his strength as a fight wears on.

Porter fought well. The judges' scorecards were remarkably consistent. Each judge tallied each round the same except for round eight (which Steve Weisfeld and Dave Moretti scored for Porter and Max DeLuca gave to Crawford). After nine rounds, the cards stood at 87–84, 86–85, 86–85 in Terence's favor. But on a more primal level, Crawford had established his dominance.

The end came in round ten. Fifteen seconds into the stanza, a sharp right uppercut landed flush on Porter's jaw and dropped him to the canvas. Shawn rose at the count of three. Crawford went after him and connected with a crushing straight left followed by three more head shots of varying severity that downed Porter for the second time. This time, Sean was up at seven. Referee Celestino Ruiz was assessing the situation when Kenny Porter (Shawn's trainer and father) stepped onto the ring apron and stopped the fight.

"I understand my dad's position," Shawn said at the post-fight press conference. "I took too many shots right there, clean. And that's not what we do. It was bad defense, hands were down. Part of me wanted to get back and was careless. And then the other part of me was a little out of it and not able to defend myself quick enough."

Shawn then announced his retirement from boxing. Let's hope he stands by that decision.

Meanwhile, Crawford had some thoughts of his own that merit consideration:

* "Me as a fighter, a lot of people on the outside [say], 'Oh, I see this and I see that. I can exploit this kind of defense and do this with Terence Crawford.' Then, when they get in the ring with me, I'm totally different. Seeing something and being in the ring is two totally different things."

* "I look at most of the critics. They don't know much about boxing. They just go on what the next person saying or what they read and what they hear. They not going on they own boxing knowledge. So I don't really too much bother to care what critics say or how they view me and how they rate me."

* "A lot of people are born with the urge to win everything. That's me. Some people are born with more heart. You can't teach heart. You can't teach somebody to take punches. Some people are just born with natural ability and God-gifted skills. I believe that I'm one of them."

Don King redux.

"The Greatest Show on Earth" Comes to Warren, Ohio

On January 29, 2022, Don King promoted a six-bout card headlined by Trevor Bryan defending his faux "regular WBA world heavyweight championship" against Jonathan Guidry. The fights took place one year to the day after Bryan defended his belt with an eleventh-round knockout of Bermane Stiverne on a Don King card at the Seminole Hard Rock Hotel in Hollywood, Florida. One had to go back to a four-bout card at the D Las Vegas Hotel & Casino on August 28, 2015, to find another fight card with King as the lead promoter.

Once upon a time, King bestrode the boxing world like a Colossus. He was the driving force behind "The Rumble in the Jungle" in Zaire and packed 132,000 screaming fans into Azteca Stadium in Mexico to witness Julio César Chávez's destruction of Greg Haugen. Las Vegas casinos and historic venues like Madison Square Garden were his personal playpen.

But on January 29, King was promoting at the Packard Music Hall in Warren, Ohio—a facility that boasts of having 1,890 "sellable seats without obstructions" and 528 more with an obstructed view of the stage. And the seating capacity for the card fell short of those numbers because the ring was pitched in the center of the room.

The most entertaining thing about the pre-fight promotion was King. But his monologues tend to be less interesting now than before. The Don King of old might have styled this event as a "Fight for World Peace" and talked of staging it on the Russia–Ukraine border with Vladimir Putin and Vitali Klitschko as honored guests. Of course, with the Don King of old, the fighters might have been Muhammad Ali and George Foreman.

William D. Franklin (the mayor of Warren) issued a proclamation declaring that January 26 (three days before the event) was "Don King Day" in Warren. He also presented King with a plaque and told the promoter, "I am thankful to you, Mr. King, for letting us be the host of this great event seen by boxing fans worldwide. Who would have thought that Warren, Ohio, would be the host."

King responded, "We're going to have a sensational evening of boxing. It will give people a chance to have fun again. We are here to give you a moment of respite. Let's have some fun. No matter whether you are young or old, let the good times roll."

To his credit, King also addressed the issue of COVID head-on, telling fans who planned to attend, "It would be much better if you take the vaccinations and the shot, wear your mask and socially distance."

As for the heavyweight "championship" fight, Bryan's ring record was 21–0 (15 KOs). But no serious reckoning places him among the top big men in the world. And Guidry (17–0–2, 10 KOs) is a club fighter.

No one should blame Guidry for taking the fight. A thirty-two-year-old father of four, he has lived a hardscrabble life in Louisiana, eking out a living as a commercial fisherman and fighting for three-figure paydays when circumstances allow. His purse for facing Bryan was said to be $70,000. That was before the members of his team took their cut. He also received $10,000 for training expenses.

In the past, Guidry had fought a woeful collection of opponents. All but one of his previous fights had been in Louisiana in towns like Cut Off, Opelousas, Houma, Gretna, and Charenton with three appearances on undercards in New Orleans. He'd gone eight rounds once and a full six rounds twice. As for his amateur pedigree, he'd compiled a 2–4–1 (0 KOs) amateur ledger between 2007 and 2012. He's listed as five feet, eleven inches tall and had weighed in for his most recent fight at 263 pounds. Bryan was a 15-to-1 betting favorite.

King defended the choice of Guidry as an opponent, saying, "The whole essence of this card is opportunity."

Bryan suggested that any blame for Guidry's selection fall on shoulders other than his own. "I'm a fighter," Trevor explained. "When my promoter and manager say this is my next fight and who I'm fighting, all I can do is prepare and get ready for that."

Guidry addressed his presence on the card with the observation, "I've seen what they're saying, like 'who is Jonathan Guidry?' But it's just how things work. I have nothing to lose. I'm a nobody. But yesterday's nobody is tomorrow's somebody." Later, he told the media, "Not a lot of people can say they fought on a Don King card or fought on his show. I'm grateful that he's letting me fight on this show and fight for the world title.

Without him, I might still be on my shrimping boat or still be crabbing or something."

Tickets ranged from $550 down to $80. The pay-per-view price was $49.99. FITE (the most reliable distributor of the event stream) sold a meager eight hundred buys which, by extrapolation from past events, would place the total number of buys at roughly one thousand. Whatever the universe of resolutely hardcore boxing fans is in the United States, King and Bryan haven't tapped into it.

The undercard fights were dreadful. To fill time, viewers were shown the video of a twenty-year-old fight between Félix Trinidad and Mamadou Thiam (KO 3). King was visible for most of the evening, wearing his iconic "only in America" jacket that has faded and looks like a relic from another era. He appeared in the ring before the main event for a ten-count in honor of Las Vegas casino vice president Bob Halloran, who died earlier this year. Then Annette Blackwell (the mayor of Maple Heights, Ohio) read from a proclamation praising King for his character and good works.

Bryan, who has weighed in for fights as low as 200 pounds, had fought his last bout at a career-high 267. This time, he did himself one better, tipping (or was it toppling?) the scales at 268. He looked as though he'd trained in a fast-food restaurant.

Guidry came in at a pudgy 246 (a 17-pound reduction over his last outing).

When the bell rang, Bryan plodded around the ring, toying with Guidry for most of the contest. One of the few moments of drama came when Trevor's trunks started to slip beneath his stomach and off-camera adjustments were necessary. Finally, Bryan began letting his fists go a bit. But Guidry hung tough and Trevor couldn't put him away.

By round eleven, Bryan looked like he'd be content to cruise the last six minutes and win comfortably on points. But at that juncture, Guidry (who had a fighter's mentality if not the skills to go with it) began pushing the action. In round twelve, he pushed it too far, and Bryan dropped him seconds before the final bell. Poor camera work left viewers in the dark as to whether or nor Guidry beat the count. But the fight went to the scorecards, so one assumes that he did.

Judges Nathan Palmer (118–109) and Brian Kennedy (116–111)

scored the bout for Bryan. Steve Weisfeld (one of boxing's better judges) inexplicably had it 115–112 in Guidry's favor. Jonathan fought as well as he could. One hopes that Trevor can fight better.

Meanwhile, there's something noble, albeit poignant, about King's pursuit. He's ninety years old. His power is gone. But he keeps reaching for the brass ring and promoting.

Don Majeski (who has been in the sweet science for a half century as a match-maker, booking agent, writer, and more) is "a boxing guy." Majeski recently said of his identity, "Boxing is not something that we do. Boxing is something that we are. I came of age at a time when guys went to the gyms and hung out in the gyms with generations of boxing guys. Some of us made decent money. Most of us didn't. But we lived boxing. It was more than a job. It defined our lives."

A Club-Fight Card in Philadelphia

Prentiss Byrd worked as a trainer with Emanuel Steward at the Kronk Gym in Detroit from 1978 to 2001. Long ago, Byrd voiced the view, "Boxing has been dead for years. We're just walking through the graveyard."

I've written at length about the reasons for the decline of boxing in the United States. Phony championship belts, a pay-per-view economic model that separates fans from attractive fights, the failure of the sport's power brokers to make the fights that the public most wants to see, incompetent and corrupt officiating that mars the viewing experience (to say nothing of undermining the integrity of the sport).

In recent months, I've been involved in the making of a documentary that will examine the current state of boxing. On February 26, 2022, that project took me to Philadelphia to explore boxing through the prism of club fights.

There was a time when club fights were the lifeblood of professional boxing and the Blue Horizon in North Philadelphia was the most famous club-fight arena in the United States. *The Ring* called it "the number-one boxing venue in the world."

The building was constructed in 1865 as a row of three adjoining homes for the super-rich. In 1914, it was altered and became the Philadelphia home for a national fraternal lodge known as the Loyal Order of Moose. In 1961, the building was sold to a new owner who named it the Blue Horizon and, after further renovation, began hosting regular boxing shows. Marty Kramer, Herman Taylor, and Russell Peltz are among the promoters who made their name there. The arena closed in 2010 and is now awaiting redevelopment.

On arriving in the City of Brotherly Love on February 26, I went with the film crew to the Blue Horizon. The building is padlocked. A caretaker brought us inside. Prentiss Byrd's ghosts were in the house. Beyond that, it's difficult to describe what I saw.

The once-grand building where capacity crowds of 1,346 gathered for fights is now a monument to urban decay. A wreck, a ruin. Parts of it are structurally unsound. Clumps of plaster have fallen from the ceiling and litter the floor. The walls look like they've been torn apart by an explosion. Going anywhere inside requires walking through rubble. Twelve years of grime on the windows keep the sunlight out.

From that sad reminder of boxing's past, we went next to boxing's present.

The 2300 Arena is located in an industrial area of South Philadelphia beneath an overpass for Interstate 95. Built as a warehouse in 1974, it has been known at various times as Viking Hall, Alhambra Arena, The Arena, Asylum Arena, ECW Arena, and now 2300 Arena (a reference to its location at 2300 South Swanson Street). In recent years, it has been the site for weddings, bar mitzvahs, and other celebrations. After winning the Super Bowl in 2018, the Philadelphia Eagles received their rings in a private ceremony there.

The 2300 Arena is also home to club fights promoted by RDR Promotions (named for its founder, Rodney Rice).

Rice, age fifty-five, grew up in South Philadelphia. His mother was the rock of the family. His father (in Rodney's words) was "in and out of the home." Mostly out.

Rice is open about past mistakes. He fought a lot on the streets when he was young and, looking back on that time, says, "I had a lot of anger issues." From ages ten through fifteen, he was in a child guidance program at Children's Hospital of Philadelphia but was still "getting into bad things." There was a conviction for burglary. He was "moving toward drug dealing." Then "my sister, Dionne, pushed me into the Army."

Rice served in the military from 1988 to 1999, rising to the rank of staff sergeant. After leaving the service, he took a job with Terminix (a pest control company). "But I didn't know how to act out of the military," he acknowledges. "I got into drugs to cope. For a year, it was bad. I knew I needed help."

In 2000, Rice entered a drug rehab program. Then he returned to the pest control business. That was followed by a job in vector control with the City of Philadelphia. Since 2012, he has worked for the United States Environmental Protection Agency in its Inspector General's office. He balances the requirements of that job with the demands of his promotional company.

Rice's introduction to formal boxing began with sparring after he left the military ("I got my butt kicked"). Then he began helping trainers work with their fighters. After that, he says, "the evolution to being a promoter was natural for me."

RDR Promotions promoted two fight cards in 2020 and ten in 2021. The February 26 show was its first of 2022. Rice has a few fighters under contract. But for the most part, he fills out his cards with fighters who are independent or made available to him by other promoters on a fight-by-fight basis.

"I like building and rebuilding fighters," Rice says. "I love what I'm doing. The worst thing about the job is some of the people you have to deal with and the secrets you have to keep. I don't know where I'll go from here. There's no great plan. If I keep having fun, I'll keep doing it. If I'm not having fun, I'll stop."

Generic boxing doesn't sell well to the public at large anymore. That's why TV ratings are low for most bouts and arenas are largely empty during the undercard for big fights. But the sport has a hardcore fanbase, and RDR Promotions has tapped into it.

The 2300 Arena is a barebones facility with the feel of a former warehouse. It has a high ceiling, plain walls, and concrete floor painted black. Tickets for the February 26 event were priced at $150, $100, and $75. RDR's shows are building a following, in part because matchmaker Nick Tiberi makes pretty good fights and in part because each card has a half-dozen or so Philadelphia fighters who are ticket sellers. The shows are also available via pay-per-view stream on BXNG.TV for $19.95.

Greg Sirb (executive director of the Pennsylvania State Athletic Commission) does a hands-on job of overseeing combat sports in Pennsylvania—and for a fraction of what it costs to regulate boxing in nearby states like New York. Four hours before the bell for round one of the opening bout on February 26, Sirb was checking in fighters and their camps in addition to performing chores like carrying chairs into the technical zone at ringside for fighters' seconds to sit on between rounds during the fights.

Upstairs, sixteen fighters and their teams were crammed into two dressing rooms on the second floor. There was no music, just quiet conversation with each camp respecting the others' space. The vibe in the "blue" dressing room (which housed the underdog fighters) was far less optimistic than in the red.

At 6:40 p.m., the doors to the arena opened and the crowd began filing in. It was a good turnout. Most of the fans were in their seats when the first bout began at 7:20.

Watching a fight live from up close is different from what most fans experience in a big arena. The only way to get close to the ring at a big fight is to be a member of the media or a child of privilege with a thousand-dollar ticket. At club fights, the spectators are close to the action. They hear punches land and see the pain etched on a fighter's face. It's a unique experience that can't be fully understood unless one has been there.

The fighters on Rice's card were a mix of prospects, ticket sellers, and opponents. Being an "opponent" in boxing is one of the most painful, thankless jobs imaginable. Why do they do it? Wrigley Brogan answered that question several years ago when he wrote, "A few extra bucks, a chance to be admired for a few minutes, to be something uncommon, to know they have had a real life rather than a safe one."

The first bout of the evening was a mismatch between a local prospect, twenty-two-year-old Jabril Noble (2–0, 2 KOs) from Philadelphia, and Joseph Santana (0–4, 3 KOs by) from Providence. Rice is an advisor to Noble. Santana was a last-minute substitute after Darnell Jiles (who'd won once in nine fights dating back to 2008) fell out. Noble KO'd Santana at 2:01 of round one and, in an in-the-ring interview afterward, declared, "He was scared. He didn't want to fight. I want a better opponent next time than the one I just fought."

Bout number two was equally predictable. Edwin Cortes (1–0) fought Jerrod Miner, who was introduced to the crowd as "a seventeen-bout veteran." Miner's actual record (two wins in those seventeen fights) was left unspoken. Cortes prevailed on each judge's scorecard by a 40–36 margin.

That was followed by another mismatch. Nineteen-year-old Philadelphian Isaiah Johnson (3–0, 3 KOs), with whom Rice has a promotional contract, showboated before, during, and after his fight against Dieumerci Nzau, who lasted 72 seconds and has now lost twelve fights in a row.

Philadelphia boxing fans are knowledgeable. They understood what they were watching. Then they saw the sort of upset that makes going to club fights worthwhile.

Robert Sabbagh (3–0, 2 KOs) from Brooklyn was matched against North Carolinian Joel Caudle (8–6–2, 5 KOs, 2 KOs by) in a scheduled six-round heavyweight bout. Caudle, age thirty-one, is listed as five feet, ten inches tall and weighed in at 283 pounds. "Blubbery" doesn't begin to describe him. He'd lost his most recent five fights dating back to 2018. Sabbagh was expected to make it six losses in a row. But whatever Sabbagh might bring to the table, high-level boxing skills aren't on the list. Against Caudle, he seemed intimidated from the opening bell by the massive presence in front of him, took body shot after body shot, and never really fought back. His corner stopped the beating after four rounds.

Next up, twenty-five-year-old Dominique Mayfield (0–1, 1 KO by) from Philadelphia fought thirty-six-year-old Daryl Clark. Mayfield had been knocked out in the first round by a 3–11 fighter in his only other pro fight. Clark, from Houston, had a 1–1 record but that win came against a fighter who hurt his shoulder in the second round and had been unable to continue. Mayfield decisioned Clark by a 40–36, 40–36, 40–36 margin.

Mexican Oscar Barajas, who hadn't won since 2017 and had been brought to the 2300 Arena in the hope that he would lose to Philadelphian Jerome Conquest, turned the tables with a 58–56, 58–56, 57–57 majority decision triumph.

Then the third prospect on the card, twenty-eight-year-old cruiserweight Muhsin Cason (9–0, 6 KOs) from Las Vegas knocked out Louisianan Steven Lyons (winless in six fights dating back to February 2019) in five rounds.

Finally, the main event matched Ray Robinson (24–3–2, 12 KOs, 1 KO by) against Silverio Ortiz (37–28, 18 KOs, 6 KOs by). Robinson, age thirty-six and from Philadelphia, was once a prospect. But he couldn't beat the world-class fighters he faced and was winless in three bouts dating back to 2017. Ortiz, age thirty-nine, a last-minute substitute, had lost his last seven fights and 14 of 17 dating back to 2015. To be fair, the 14 guys Ortiz lost to during that stretch had a composite ring record of 230–13–5 at the time he fought them. He's a classic "opponent." KO 3 Robinson.

And that was boxing in Philadelphia on February 26, 2022.

In recent years, boxing has struggled in the United States.
But it's alive and well in England.

Tyson Fury vs. Dillian Whyte
in Perspective

On April 23, 2022, Tyson Fury scored a one-punch, sixth-round knockout over Dillian Whyte before 94,000 spirited fans at Wembley Stadium in London to retain his lineal and World Boxing Council heavyweight titles.

Fury, age thirty-three, entered the ring as the number-one heavyweight in the world by virtue of consecutive knockout victories over Deontay Wilder that brought his record to 31–0–1 with 22 KOs. He's a huge man (six feet, nine inches tall) with considerable flab around his waist that defies the contemporary notion of what an elite heavyweight's body should look like.

Whyte (now 28–3, 19 KOs) is thirty-four years old and had been knocked out previously by Anthony Joshua and Alexander Povetkin. His signature victories were against Derek Chisora (twice), Joseph Parker, and (in a rematch) Povetkin.

Whyte was entitled to fight Fury by virtue of being the WBC "mandatory" challenger. On December 7, 2021, the WBC ordered that a period of "free negotiation" of unspecified length begin in an effort to finalize a bout contract. But the parties were unable to reach an agreement. Thus, on December 30, the WBC announced that a purse bid would be held on January 11 and that the purse would be split 80–20 in Fury's favor. The bid date was pushed back several times amid rumors that Anthony Joshua (who'd lost his WBA, IBF, and WBO belts to Oleksandr Usyk last September and was contractually entitled to an immediate rematch) had been offered an eight-figure sum to step aside and let Fury–Usyk be contested immediately with a guarantee that Joshua would face the winner. Then, on January 26, Fury posted a video on Instagram scornfully reporting that Joshua had refused a step-aside package (A.J. probably did) worth $90 million (it probably wasn't) that would have allowed Fury to fight Usyk.

Ultimately, the purse bid was held on January 28. Queensberry Promotions (Fury's primary promoter) prevailed with a bid of $41,025,000. Matchroom Boxing (which had promoted Whyte's recent fights) bid $32,222,222. Under the terms of the purse bid, 10 percent ($4,102,500) of the total was designated to go to the winning fighter. The other 90 percent would be split on an 80–20 basis ($29,538,000 to Team Fury and $7,384,000 to Team Whyte). It's likely that Fury agreed to some sort of financial accommodation with Queensberry that allowed it to bid as high as it did. Meanwhile, Whyte was expressing dissatisfaction with the purse split.

"They keep going about the money and percentages," Fury told journalist Ron Lewis. "But this little shit is getting eight times more than I got when I beat Wladimir [Klitschko]. This sucker has done nothing but get chinned by a 45-year-old man [Povetkin was forty-one at the time]. He would be very sensible to take his money before he loses it. It is like this idiot has won the Euro Lottery."

On February 1, the WBC set a deadline of February 21 for signed bout contracts to be submitted to the sanctioning body. Whyte complied on the deadline day. Thereafter, he refused to attend the March 1 kick-off press conference in London because Queensberry was unwilling to augment its winning purse bid by giving him an upside on pay-per-view buys. That left Fury to tell the media, "The build-up to this fight will be fantastic because Tyson Fury versus his own shadow sells for sure."

Whyte also objected to the use of his photograph to publicize the fight, leading Frank Warren (Queensberry's primary owner) to declare, "This guy is getting thirty-two times the purse he got lodged by the WBC for his last fight. We're paying him good money. He's obliged to do certain things. Everything he doesn't do is going to be a problem afterward. Breach of contract is a breach of contract. He needs to show up and he needs to meet his obligations. He needs to do all the things that all boxers do when they're involved in big fights. Up to now, he has not done that. He's in breach."

On April 13, Whyte broke his silence with a brief post on social media that read, "I'm ready. I'm looking forward to seeing everyone on the 23rd of April. #LetsGooo!" That was followed one day later with a Zoom media conference call and the declaration "This is not the Tyson Fury show. Everyone is saying, Tyson Fury this, Tyson Fury that. He didn't sell out any of the fights with Deontay Wilder. This fight sold out because of me and Tyson Fury. We're both in the show together."

But by then, a shadow had descended over the proceedings. Daniel Kinahan (an Irish national currently living in Dubai) is widely believed to have been the controlling force behind MTK Global (the Dubai-headquartered fighter management company that managed Fury). On April 11, Kinahan (as well as six individuals and three companies he's believed to have done business with) was sanctioned by the Office of Foreign Assets Control of the United States Department of the Treasury for what the government says is his role as leader of the Kinahan Organized Crime Group.

Statements from various US officials read in part, "The Kinahan Organized Crime Group smuggles deadly narcotics, including cocaine, to Europe, and is a threat to the entire licit economy through its role in international money laundering. Criminal groups like the KOCG prey on the most vulnerable in society and bring drug-related crime and violence, including murder, to the countries in which they operate. The U.S. government will continue to use every available resource to dismantle these criminal networks."

Under United States law, all interests in the property of a sanctioned party that are in the United States or in the possession or control of people or entities in the United States must be blocked and reported to the US government. Moreover, government regulations generally prohibit all transactions within the United States that involve any property of a blocked party.

On April 14, MTK Global issued a statement that read, "MTK Global will comply fully with the sanctions made by the U.S. government against Daniel Kinahan. MTK parted ways with Mr. Kinahan in February 2017. He has had no interest in the business since then and will have no future involvement with us. MTK operates ethically, transparently and lawfully."

The MTK statement included a quote from MTK Global CEO Bob Yalen, who said, "MTK Global will take every measure to ensure the company and those who deal with it are fully compliant with the U.S. sanctions announced this week and take this matter extremely seriously."

That highlighted the question of why, if MTK and Kinahan parted ways five years ago, Yalen moved from the United States to Dubai (Kinahan's current home base) after assuming his position with MTK Global. Then, on April 19, MTK announced that Yalen had resigned as CEO "for personal reasons." That was followed the next day by an announcement that MTK was ceasing operations. In part, the MTK Global statement read, "As a business, we have faced unprecedented levels of unfair scrutiny and criticism since the sanctioning by the US Government of Daniel Joseph Kinahan. Since leading promoters have now informed us that they will be severing all ties with MTK and will no longer work with our fighters, we have taken the difficult decision to cease operations at the end of this month."

It's widely believed within the boxing industry that Kinahan was intricately involved in the operation of MTK Global throughout its existence and had the final say on all matters of substance involving MTK Global fighters. Indeed, Top Rank CEO Bob Arum recently told Yahoo! Sports that he paid $4 million in consulting fees to Kinahan ($1 million for each of Fury's last four fights in the United States, all of which were co-promoted by Top Rank) and that the money was sent to a company registered in Dubai.

If Kinahan had been tied to a major sport, his curriculum vitae would have led to his ouster long ago.

Four days before Fury–Whyte, Dillian failed to appear at a scheduled open media workout. One day later, he did participate in the final prefight press conference and, addressing his status as a 6-to-1 underdog, said, "This is one of those fights where I've been working on being adaptable. I'm going to have to adapt, make smart decisions when I need to, do what and how I need to do it. There's no strategy here. I just need to go in there and do my thing."

Fury had offered varying views on the impending battle during the build-up to the fight. At one end of the spectrum, he'd declared, "I'm gonna tell you the game plan. Straight out of the block, straight to the middle of the ring, push him back straightaway, big heavy artillery from round one and see how long he can take it. When I land a 'Lancaster Bomber' on his jaw, it's going to be over. That could be in round one or it could be in round six. I don't see it going past that. I will chop him to bits. I will smash his face right in."

But one had to consider the fact that Fury has accumulated considerable boxing mileage on his body in addition to abusing drugs, eating his way to obesity (Tyson says that, at one point, he weighed four hundred pounds), and struggling with depression for longer than he cared to recall. And Whyte is a world-class fighter. Thus, during fight week, Fury acknowledged, "A lot of people are underestimating Dillian Whyte, but not me. Dillian Whyte is a good fighter. He's big. He's strong. He's tough. He's game. He's got good power. He's knocked out a lot of men. He's got a lot of experience in the fight game. He's got a big left hook and a big right hand. Who knows? It could be me chinned on the night."

Fury's most recent five fights had been contested in the United States. Before that, he'd fought Francesco Pianeta in Northern Ireland on the undercard of Carl Frampton vs. Luke Jackson in August 2018. His most recent appearance in England had been in Manchester in June 2018 against Sefer Seferi on the undercard of Terry Flanagan vs. Maurice Hooker. But since then, Fury's victories over Deontay Wilder had significantly elevated his public profile. Their trilogy (and particularly their third fight) reminded people that boxing can be great. And Tyson has an outsized personality that has come to resonate with fight fans in the United Kingdom.

All of this made Fury–Whyte a historic event with seating at Wembley Stadium reconfigured to accommodate the largest crowd in the history of British boxing. Afterward, many commentators mistakenly claimed that the 94,000 fans constituted the second-largest crowd in boxing history, surpassed only by the 132,247 fans who witnessed Julio César Chávez's demolition of Greg Haugen at Azteca Stadium in Mexico City on February 20, 1993. But facts are facts. On September 23, 1926, Gene Tunney defeated Jack Dempsey in front of 120,757 fans at Sesquicentennial Stadium in Philadelphia. They met again 364 days later at Soldier Field in Chicago with 104,943 fans in attendance.

Fury's massive size compensates for his flaws as a fighter. When it was time to step on the scales, he weighed in at 264¾ pounds, 12 pounds less than he'd weighed for his third fight against Wilder. Whyte (a big man in his own right) came in at 253¼; pounds, 6 pounds heavier than for his last fight when he'd knocked out Povetkin.

The pre-fight spectacle ("Sweet Caroline" . . . the ring walks . . . flashing lights) was exciting. As with all fights, violence at a very primal level was about to be unleashed.

Fury was the clear crowd favorite.

Prior to the bout, Lennox Lewis had opined, "Only Tyson Fury can beat Tyson Fury right now. That means if he's not focused, if he sticks his chin out there, if he plays around, that's the only thing that can beat him."

But Fury didn't beat himself. He fought a strong, tough, measured fight.

Whyte (an orthodox fighter) fought the first round from a southpaw stance. Nothing much happened. But when a fighter deviates from what he usually does, it's often a sign that he doesn't think what he usually does is good enough to win.

In round two, Fury established his jab.

Whyte was a bit more aggressive in round three but to no avail.

In round four, things got ugly. Whyte suffered a cut above his right eye from a clash of heads, and there was a lot of illegal mauling on the inside with Dillian more of the transgressor.

"He tried to make it rough," Fury said afterward. "He was trying to manhandle me in there. But have you ever tried wrestling with a dinosaur before? I'm like a T-Rex in there, 270 pounds. It's difficult, especially when you're shorter and not as quick."

Each man fought cautiously in round five with Fury landing a bit more convincingly and continuing to control the action.

Then, late in round six—BOOM!!! Fury threw a jab followed by a right uppercut that landed flush on Whyte's jaw. Dillian went down flat on his back with his arms stretched out on the canvas above his head, struggled to his feet, and lurched forward. Referee Mark Lyson reached out to keep him from falling again and stopped the fight at the 2:59 mark. It was the right call. Given a minute to recover, Whyte might have been able to answer the bell for round seven. But it's unlikely that he would have lasted long.

According to CompuBox, Whyte landed only 29 punches over the course of six rounds while Fury landed 76. This writer scored all five rounds for Fury. To be honest, putting aside the enormous crowd and massive stakes involved, it was an ordinary fight with one memorable punch.

As for the future . . . Fury said before the bout that this would be his last fight. "I'm getting too old for this," he told the media during fight week. "I'm thirty-four this year. I've had everything to deal with, weight loss, up and down, alcohol problems, drug problems. I'm probably round about sixty when it comes to boxing years. Age catches up very quickly, so you've got to move over for the younger guys. I said to Klitschko all those years ago, 'You were a good champion in your day, but Father Time has caught up with you. You've got to move over for the younger guys coming through, give us a chance.' The mistake Wladimir made was he wanted to take on the next era of champions, and it didn't work out for him."

Then, four days after beating Whyte, Fury told Piers Morgan, "This is the truth, the gospel truth, nothing but the truth. I'm done. There will always be someone else to fight. The fans will always want more. They are always baying for more blood. But I don't have anything more to give. I always said that I wanted to walk away on top of the sport, and do it on my terms, and I didn't want to be the person who said, 'Well, I should have maybe retired two years ago.' No amount of material assets or money will make me come back out of retirement because I'm very happy. I'm healthy. I've still got my brains. I can still talk. I've got a beautiful wife. I've got six kids. I've got umpteen belts, I've got plenty of money, success, fame, glory. What more am I doing it for?"

If Fury does retire now and stays retired, all credit to him. But few people take his declaration seriously.

Meanwhile, in the aftermath of Fury–Whyte, there has been considerable hyperbole about Fury being on the short list of greatest heavyweights of all time. That's unsupported by the record to date.

Fury decisioned an aging Wladimir Klitschko to claim his first title in 2015 (a feat that Anthony Joshua bettered by knocking out Klitschko seventeen months later). Then, after a thirty-month absence from the ring, Tyson returned and worked his way back into shape with victories over Seferi and Pianeta. The trilogy against Wilder (a dangerous but flawed fighter) mixed in with wins over Tom Schwarz and Otto Wallin followed.

Fury has good boxing skills that are keyed to his size. When he sets his feet, he punches with authority. Against Wilder, he showed exceptional recuperative power after being whacked on the chin. He has made a remarkable comeback from drug abuse, obesity, and depression that left him contemplating suicide six years ago. Not one to shy away from touting his own ability, after beating Whyte, Tyson proclaimed,

"There's never been one who can beat me. Do you know why? I've got a 6-foot-9-inch frame, 270 pounds weight, move like a middleweight, hit like a thunderstorm, and can take a punch. I've got balls like King Kong, the heart of a lion, the mindset of the Wizard of Oz."

But the Wizard of Oz was a little man who relied on smoke and mirrors. And yes, Fury knocked out Whyte with a one-punch uppercut. But Povetkin didn't just knock out Whyte with a one-punch uppercut. Povetkin knocked Whyte unconscious. Joshua also knocked Whyte out with an uppercut, and Dillian didn't get off the canvas from that one either.

How would Fury have fared against Lennox Lewis, Vitali Klitschko, and other big men in their prime? We'll never know. But he's a fighting man worthy of the title "The Gypsy King." And he's the best heavyweight in the world right now.

*The biggest mistake people in boxing can make is to think
that their fighter is unbeatable.*

Dmitry Bivol, Canelo Álvarez,
and DAZN

On May 7, 2022, Rich Strike, an 80-to-1 longshot, turned Thoroughbred horse racing upside down by winning the Kentucky Derby. That night, Dmitry Bivol scored an upset of even greater consequence when he outboxed Canelo Álvarez at T-Mobile Arena in Las Vegas to earn a unanimous decision over boxing's reigning pound-for-pound king.

Álvarez (now 57–2–2, 39 KOs) is thirty-one years old. In recent years, he has been boxing's premier fighter, a magnet for high-rollers, and a massive pay-per-view draw. As Paul Magno recently wrote, "He has become the best in the world in a very old school way—by developing his game in the gym and adding respectable names to his resume."

At the start of this year, Canelo was also a promotional and network free agent. He'd fought six consecutive fights on DAZN with Golden Boy or Matchroom as his promoter and then jumped ship to fight Caleb Plant on Showtime-PPV under the Premier Boxing Champions banner. His victory over Plant was followed by spirited bidding for his services. PBC hoped to match Canelo against Jermall Charlo. Matchroom Boxing CEO Eddie Hearn was pushing Bivol as the opponent.

In late January, Eddy Reynoso (Canelo's trainer) opined, "I think a Charlo fight is more media-friendly. Charlo is a fighter that sells more, a fighter that more people follow. And because of that, it's a more attractive fight."

Also a less dangerous fight.

But DAZN was anxious to get back in the Canelo business. And Len Blavatnik (the Ukrainian-born multibillionaire whose exceedingly deep pockets finance DAZN) took an interest in Canelo. The two had lunch together in Miami last year the day after Canelo beat Avni Yildirim.

Also, on February 11, Charlo was arrested on a charge of felony assault (later dismissed) in Texas. That added an element of uncertainty to any Canelo–Charlo venture.

On February 26, it was announced that Canelo had signed a two-fight deal with Matchroom and DAZN. The first fight would be in Las Vegas for Bivol's WBA 175-pound belt in conjunction with Cinco de Mayo weekend. The second was provisionally scheduled for September 17 in conjunction with Mexican Independence Day weekend against Gennady Golovkin. Canelo's minimum purse for fighting Bivol was reported as $40 million with an even larger payday should he fight Golovkin in September. The contract was said to include an option in Matchroom's favor for a third fight against an unspecified opponent and an option for a rematch in Canelo's favor should he (ha ha—no way it will happen) lose to Bivol.

Bivol (now 20–0, 11 KOs) is five months younger than Canelo. He won the WBA 175-pound title in 2017 by knocking out the undistinguished Trent Broadhurst and had defended his belt seven times against largely pedestrian opposition. His previous six opponents had gone the distance against him.

After Canelo's choice of opponent was announced, there was some sniping that, in fourteen fights dating back to 2015, he'd faced only one Black opponent (Danny Jacobs). Charlo would have run counter to that trend.

Canelo–Bivol was Canelo's fifteenth fight in Las Vegas, where he has taken part in three of the five highest-grossing gates in state history. Álvarez was a 9-to-2 betting favorite. Those odds seemed long. Sergey Kovalev's reach and jab had given Canelo trouble when they fought in 2019. Bivol has a better jab than Kovalev and his footwork is far superior to Sergey's. Most likely, Dmitry would have been favored over all of Canelo's previous opponents with the possible exception of Golovkin.

"He has good power," Bivol said of Canelo. "He has good skills. He's a good fighter. But he's a man and he had a loss and draw. If you believe in your skills, if you're a good boxer, you could make him one more loss. I have enough to win this fight."

"I chose Bivol because he's a great fighter," Canelo said in response. "He's a fighter who fights at distance, good distance. He moves; he's fast for the division; he's strong. He's, for me, the best fighter at 175. I saw him many times. He knows what to do in the ring. He's a champion for a long time. I know what kind of fighter he is but I don't care. I'm in my prime and I have a lot of skills. I want to make history in my career and I'm gonna continue doing it with this guy."

★★★

I didn't watch Canelo–Bivol live on Saturday night. That might sound odd for a writer who would be writing about the fight. But it was a matter of principle.

I admire Canelo Álvarez as a fighter and a person. I've been in his dressing room in the hours before and after five of his biggest fights and hope to be there again in the future. But Bivol (who was born in Kyrgyzstan) is a Russian citizen and has lived in Russia since age eleven. I agree with Vitali and Wladimir Klitschko who voiced the view that, given Russia's brutal aggression in Ukraine, Bivol shouldn't have been chosen to fight Canelo. That denial, to me, would have been an appropriate extension of the economic sanctions currently in place against Russia.

DAZN and Matchroom took a contrary view. So did the world sanctioning organizations. On March 28, the WBA announced that it would sanction Canelo–Bivol for its 175-pound title (and the lucrative sanctioning fee that accompanied its sanction).

Two days later, after a trip to the Middle East that saw him whole-heartedly endorse Daniel Kinahan's involvement in boxing, WBC president Mauricio Sulaimán declared, "I'm glad that this fight is taking place and, when they are in that ring, they can show that boxing is far above politics. It is a sensitive issue because of what is happening, but we have also said that the boxers are not to blame for anything. I am happy that this fight is taking place. It has nothing to do with the conflict."

But sports are not "above politics." For the past century, sports have been very much a part of politics. Adolf Hitler weaponized the 1936 Olympics as propaganda for Nazi Germany. Sports boycotts were an important tool in the struggle to overcome apartheid in South Africa. The Saudi Arabian government is currently engaged in "sportswashing" at the highest level. Russian players will not be allowed to compete at Wimbledon this year because of the invasion of Ukraine.

Cinco de Mayo weekend celebrates Mexico's victory over the French Empire (another invading force) at the Battle of Puebla in 1862. The choice of Bivol as Canelo's opponent on May 7 was ill matched to that remembrance. I decided long ago that, as a personal protest, I wouldn't buy the fight on pay-per-view. After it was over, I watched it on YouTube.

Each fighter had weighed in on Friday within a shade of 175 pounds. Bivol likely weighed significantly more on fight night. At six feet tall, Dmitry enjoyed a four-inch advantage in height over Canelo with a commensurate edge in reach.

The Mexican and United States national anthems were sung in the ring prior to the fight but not the Russian anthem.

Before the fight, Bivol had said, "This is my chance to show all people my skills. And if I want to show my skills, I have to take the risks. This is a fight against the best fighter in the world, and you use everything. You have to risk every time when you see it. Not sometimes, every time."

That said, Bivol fought a cautious fight. There were few if any highlight-reel moments. Dmitry used deft footwork to maximize his advantage in size and reach and, with his jab, dictate the distance between the fighters for most of the night. Canelo was rarely able to land cleanly. When he did, Dmitry took the punches well. And because Canelo was unable to launch a sustained body attack, he was unable to wear Bivol down and come on strong in the late rounds as he often does.

Jack Blackburn (Joe Louis's trainer) was once asked to explain the key to boxing and answered, "If you get hit, hit the other fellow before he can hit you again."

Against Bivol, Canelo couldn't do that. According to CompuBox, he landed only 84 punches over twelve rounds and was outlanded in every stanza. The fight was reminiscent of his 2013 outing against Floyd Mayweather except, with Bivol, size was a more important factor than experience. Canelo could only do his best. And his best on Saturday night wasn't good enough against a highly skilled, bigger, equally deter-mined opponent.

The judges (Tim Cheatham, Dave Moretti, and Steve Weisfeld) scored the fight identically. Each one gave rounds one through four and round nine to Canelo for a 115–113 tally in Bivol's favor. Many observers felt that the judges were kind to Canelo with regard to rounds one through four.

The best move for Canelo now might be to say, "I'm at my best at 168 pounds; that's where I want to stay," and fight a long-talked-about third encounter with Gennady Golovkin in September. But that fight, if it happens, will be somewhat devalued commercially as a consequence of Canelo–Bivol. Alternatively, Canelo has a contractual right to an immediate rematch against Bivol and could exercise that right.

When asked if he wanted the rematch, Canelo responded, "Of course I do. It doesn't end like this."

That might not be a wise move for Canelo.

Meanwhile, apart from its merits as a fight, Canelo–Bivol was significant because of what it told boxing fans about DAZN.

On May 10, 2018, promoter Eddie Hearn and Perform Group CEO Simon Denyer announced a joint venture at a press conference in New York. Speaking about what was touted as a $1 billion, eight-year joint licensing agreement to provide content for DAZN, Hearn proclaimed, "We're here to change the game and elevate boxing to a new level for fight fans in America. We have the dates, the money, and the platform. We were dangerous without this. But with this money and this platform, omigod! We have by far the biggest rights budget in the sport of boxing and we're going to be ultra-competitive. We're going to put on the greatest shows with the greatest talent. This is a brand new era for boxing in the U.S. We're here and we mean business. We have money never seen before in the sport of boxing. If I fail here, I'm a disgrace."

DAZN tried to position Matchroom as the UFC of boxing and Hearn as Dana White. It didn't work. It's not enough to be a streaming network. A streaming network has to stream content that the public wants to see. The network that assured boxing fans that "pay-per-view is dead" isn't looking so healthy itself these days.

Last year, Hearn told IFL TV, "Our sport, our brand, needs to thrive. But you only do that by making the big fights and making the fights that people want to see. We cannot afford shit fights where fighters get a fortune but don't deliver for the broadcasters because they will kill the sport. I want to show how great boxing is. But we only do that by showing great fights."

Unfortunately, DAZN has given the public very few great fights. Nor (with the exception of raising Katie Taylor's profile in the United States) has it made any stars. If anything, it has taken already-made stars and made them smaller.

DAZN doesn't release subscription numbers. But SportBusiness.com has reported that the network lost $1.4 billion in 2019 and $1.3 billion in 2020. DAZN's boxing operation might be the biggest money-loser in the history of boxing.

Part of the problem has been that, when DAZN signed its multiyear deal with Matchroom, it made the same mistake that too many other networks make. It gave away its biggest bargaining chip—dates.

HBO Boxing was as good as it was during the glory years, in part, because Time Warner Sports president Seth Abraham resisted the temptation to align the network with one promoter. One of the key factors in the subsequent decline of HBO Sports was the decision by Abraham's successor to heavily align the network with Al Haymon.

DAZN would have been better served by launching as an open shop and forcing promoters to compete for its dollars. It might have taken a few years for the contracts that some promoters had with other networks to run out. But DAZN said it was in boxing for the long haul.

Now, four years after its launch, where is DAZN? Keith Idec of Boxing Scene answered that question when he referenced DAZN's schedule for early 2022 as "heavy on fights in England and short on meaningful fights in its underserved U.S. market."

Indeed, DAZN appears to have abandoned its plans to conquer America. Last year, DAZN Group chairman Kevin Mayer was interviewed by Alex Sherman on CNBC and asked, "Is there any avenue that you can foresee that would allow DAZN to be a bigger factor in the United States?"

"It's conceivable," Mayer answered, "in the future, theoretically, that DAZN could make inroads here. I just think that, for the time being and for the medium term, we really need to focus on Europe and Asia."

In addition to its reliance on Matchroom, DAZN has also done business with Golden Boy Promotions. It was Golden Boy that originally brought Canelo (as well as Ryan Garcia and Vergil Ortiz) to DAZN. But Matchroom will be DAZN's primary content provider for the foreseeable future. In June 2021, DAZN and Matchroom announced a five-year deal that calls for at least sixteen Matchroom fight cards in the United Kingdom to be available exclusively to DAZN subscribers in the UK and Ireland each year. These fights and other Matchroom offerings will also be shown on DAZN in the United States and other designated markets around the world.

More significantly, perhaps, DAZN has abandoned its previous pledge that boxing fans will see the best fights on DAZN for one low monthly subscription price.

As noted, DAZN streamed six of Canelo Álvarez's previous outings as part of its subscription package. Canelo–Bivol was a pay-per-view event that cost current DAZN subscribers $59.99 and was sold to others for $79.99.

Pay-per-view is dead?

"I'm not personally shirking away from comments we made about pay-per-view four years ago," DAZN executive vice president Joe Markowski said recently. "I'm not gonna try and pretend that was just a marketing campaign or I was just poking the bear. We're humble enough and honest enough to admit that we maybe, in hindsight, got that wrong. I'd be insincere if I said, 'You know, we were only joking about that.' We believed it at the time."

But there are questions as to whether DAZN's hybrid subscription-pay-per-view model will be any more successful than its previous business plan. Canelo's most recent fight (against Caleb Plant) generated an estimated 800,000 pay-per-view buys, showing that his economic appeal remains strong. But Canelo–Plant had the enormous CBS-Showtime platform to market the promotion. DAZN only has DAZN. Best estimates are that Canelo–Bivol engendered only 500,000 buys.

Canelo Álvarez was DAZN's standard bearer and the best hope to lead DAZN out of the wilderness. Let's face it. The outcome of Canelo-Bivol was not good for DAZN.

Thus, the following colloquy that's making the rounds:

Genie: I will grant you one wish.
Aladdin: I want to live forever.
Genie: I can't grant wishes like that.
Aladdin: Okay, I want to live until DAZN turns a profit.

There was other ring action in 2021 and 2022 worthy of comment.

Fight Notes

On April 10, 2021, Ebanie Bridges fought Shannon Courtenay for the vacant WBA world bantamweight championship. The fact that Courtenay–Bridges was a "world championship" fight is an embarrassment.

John Sheppard (who oversees BoxRec.com) reports that one out of every seven women's fights is for a sanctioning body belt, with "world" championships near the top of the pyramid. Indeed, Sheppard notes that boxing's world sanctioning bodies have created more women's "championship" belts than there are active women boxers.

Bridges entered her "world championship" fight with a 5–0 (2 KOs) ring record. But the caliber of her opponents was appalling. Taken in order, they were:

* Mahiecka Pareno, whose two career wins came against a woman named Jean De Paz (who has never won a fight)
* Laura Woods, whose only pro fight was against Bridges
* Kanittha Ninthim, who has lost twelve of thirteen fights
* Crystal Hoy, who has won one of eleven fights since 2010.
* Carol Earl, age forty-five, whose only career victories came against fighters with a composite ring record of 0–16.

So how did Bridges quality for a "world championship" fight? Well, Bridges is—shall we say—voluptuous with long blonde hair and given to wearing bikinis. As Boxing Scene recently reported, "There is more footage and photos found online of Bridges in bikinis than there are of her actual fights."

One might find further elucidation in statements that Bridges made recently to various outlets:

* "There's plenty of girls with more fights than me. The difference? It's the way I look. Let's be real. If I wore what everyone else wore, people wouldn't be interested. You can criticize me as much as you like. But if I looked plain, then you wouldn't even know this fight

was happening. People will tune in to see if this girl wearing lingerie can actually fight or is she just a model? This is an entertainment business. Everyone wears underwear at weigh-ins. Do you want me to wear a paper bag?"

★ "It doesn't matter what society thinks what you should be doing. If you want to do it, you just fucking do it. I won't hide the fact that I'm beautiful. What the fuck! I'm going to go over there and going to flex in my lingerie. I'm going to be who I am."

★ "Hey; for people who judge me on first sight, open your mind a little bit and maybe you can see that this girl is pretty fucking real even though she has fake tits."

Prior to fighting Bridges, Courtenay had compiled a 6–1 (3 KOs) record against mediocre opposition. Shannon isn't close to being a world-class fighter. But during the pre-fight promotion, she indicated that she took her trade seriously, saying, "I look at people like Katie Taylor that has done everything she could to raise the bar to allow women like me to fight for a living. And I don't like it being disrespected by not talking about the boxing, talking about what someone's gonna wear at a weigh-in. People like Katie Taylor didn't work her backside off to pave the way for women like me and you to be in this position to talk about underwear."

The fight itself was a pleasant surprise. Bridges was the physically stronger of the two women and the aggressor for most of the bout. Courtenay landed the cleaner punches but didn't hit hard enough to keep Ebanie off. A clash of heads in round two bloodied the scalp of each combatant.

Neither woman had a credible defense. A right hand wobbled Bridges in round five and began the process of closing her left eye. By round nine, the skin around it was a bulging purple mess and the eye was completely shut. At that point Ebanie couldn't see right hands coming, but Shannon lacked the power to put her away. It was a good, honest, low-level club fight.

The judges ruled unanimously for Courtenay by a 98–92, 98–92, 97–94 margin.

Ebanie Bridges has the right to present herself to the public the way she wants to. But for the WBA to sanction Courtenay–Bridges as a "world championship" fight shows how absurd WBA "world champion-ships" can be and why today's better women boxers don't get the respect they deserve.

★★★

I've written at length about the inadequacies of the New York State Athletic Commission. On June 11, 2022, these inadequacies were on display again.

Dakota Linger had been brought to Madison Square Garden from West Virginia as an opponent for heavily favored Josue Vargas. Forty seconds into round two, Linger rocked Vargas with a hard right hand. Josue staggered backward and fell to the canvas. Inexplicably, referee Ron Lipton ruled the knockdown a slip.

ESPN blow-by-blow commentator Bernard Osuna responded to Lipton's ruling with the declaration, "It's called a slip. Unbelievable! That was a right hand that hurt Vargas."

The action resumed. Linger threw three dozen unanswered punches, many of them blows to the head, that culminated in Vargas being blasted through the ropes. Rather than stop the fight, Lipton gave the obviously woozy Vargas a count and, when the fighter regained his feet, allowed the carnage to continue.

"Vargas is not all right," Osuna told a national television audience with urgency in his voice. "He's finished."

Twelve more unanswered punches followed with ESPN expert analyst Timothy Bradley shouting, "Omigod! Stop the fight! Stop the fight! Stop the fight! Stop the fight!"

Finally, several ringside personnel climbed onto the ring apron and ended the slaughter.

How bad was it? The *Mirror* (one of the United Kingdom's more popular news outlets) ran an article headlined "Boxing Referee Accused of Trying to Get Fighter Killed by Not Stopping Fight." That was hyperbolic. But undisputed world lightweight champion Devin Haney wasn't when he posted on social media, "This type of stuff will ruin a fighter forever."

It can also leave a fighter with permanent brain damage.

After the bout, Vargas was hospitalized for observation.

"It doesn't matter who the house fighter is," Timothy Bradley told this writer one week after the carnage. "It doesn't matter what the fans want to see. The referee has to stop that fight and he didn't."

The New York State Athletic Commission fails consistently to take corrective measures when confronted with poor refereeing and judging. Meanwhile, seven days later, not a single NYSAC commissioner or executive director Kim Sumbler attended the Artur Beterbiev vs. Joe Smith fight card at Madison Square Garden.

Is this New York governor Kathy Hochul's idea of good government?

★★★

Boxing is never easy. But Artur Beterbiev (now 18–0 with 18 KOs) made it look that way when he stopped Joe Smith (28–3, 22 KOs, 2 KOs by) in a 175-pound title-unification bout at the Hulu Theater at Madison Square Garden on June 18, 2022.

Beterbiev, age thirty-seven, was born in Russia and has lived in Montreal for more than a decade. All but one of his fights have been in Canada or the United States. He won the vacant IBF 175-pound title by knocking out the unheralded Enrico Koelling in 2017 and added the WBC belt to his collection by stopping Oleksandr Gvozdyk two years later. His other title defenses have been against Callum Johnson, Radivoje Kalajdzic, Adam Deines, and Marcus Browne. He's a dangerous fighter.

Smith, age thirty-two, had been widely regarded as a high-level club fighter. Then, on December 17, 2016, he knocked out fifty-one-year-old Bernard Hopkins in the final fight (and sole KO by) of The Executioner's illustrious ring career. That raised Joe's profile. But he lost two of his next three bouts (against Sullivan Barrera and Dmitry Bivol). Victories over Jesse Hart and Eleider Álvarez began the rebuilding process. On April 10, 2021, Smith won a majority decision over Maxin Vlasov to claim the WBO 175-pound belt. A January 15, 2022, stoppage of Steve Geffrard followed.

Beterbiev was a 7-to-1 betting favorite. Smith is at his best in the trenches but that's where Artur shines brightest. The conventional wisdom was that Joe would give it everything he had but that what he had wouldn't be good enough. His strengths as a fighter played into Beterbiev's. And everything that Joe can do in a boxing ring, Artur does better.

It was hard to find an impartial observer who wasn't picking Beterbiev to win by knockout. The prevailing view was that Smith wouldn't be intimidated but that he would be ground down and beaten up. Artur is a champion and top-level fighter. Smith was a beltholder who wanted to become a champion. There's a difference.

There were no surprises on fight night. Smith came out aggressively at the opening bell, determined to live or die with what he does best. Beterbiev responded in kind. He knocked Joe down toward the end of round one and twice more in the next stanza with a barrage of punches that were like ocean waves crashing against the shore. Words like "obliterate" and "demolish" come to mind. He also thoroughly outboxed Joe in addition to outpunching him. Referee Harvey Dock appropriately stopped the bout with Smith on wobbly legs at 2:19 of the second round.

★★★

Vasiliy Lomachenko continued his sojourn through boxing with a unanimous-decision victory over Jamaine Ortiz at Madison Square Garden's Hulu Theater on October 29, 2022. But there were signs that his magic wand might be less magical than before.

Lomachenko is thirty-four years old. Throughout his career, he has combined captivating ring skills with a willingness to go in tough. But when Vasiliy went up to 135 pounds in search of greater challenges and more lucrative paydays, he lost some of the competitive edge that he enjoyed over fighters at lower weights. Two years ago, Teófimo López brought him down to earth with a 119–109, 117–111, 116–112 performance.

Ortiz (16–0–1, 8 KOs) was considered a safe opponent. Jermaine had decisioned Jamel Herring in his last fight. But nothing on his résumé suggested that he'd pose any problems that Lomachenko couldn't solve. Vasiliy was a 20-to-1 betting favorite.

"I'm not his promoter," Lomachenko said when asked about the apparent disparity in skills between the two fighters. "I'm not his trainer.

I'm not thinking about if this step up is too much for him or not."

Lomachenko, who is a Ukrainian national and member of his country's territorial defense battalion, was also reluctant to comment on a range of issues relating to the war in Ukraine. "I am a bad judge of politics," he said. When asked specifically about the propriety of Russian athletes such as Dmitry Bivol and Alex Ovechkin being allowed to compete in the United States, he answered, "I'd have to know more about their personal circumstances to comment on those situations."

The October 29 fight card was constructed around Lomachenko, with Top Rank using his presence to fulfill contractual obligations to seven other fighters who are at various stages of development in their respective ring careers and to build them for the future. All seven emerged victorious. None of their opponents came to lie down. But when two men fight and one is better than the other, the better fighter usually wins. And when one fighter is much better than the other, "usually" changes to "almost always."

Lomachenko has never been a fighter who strikes fear into the hearts of opponents by blasting them out with overwhelming power. He relies on speed, reflexes, conditioning, and a keen boxing mind to outbox them.

Fighters who rely on preternatural reflexes and speed get old at a younger age than their brethren. Vasiliy's age is now showing.

The twenty-six-year-old Ortiz fought aggressively in the early going and, at times, appeared to be the quicker of the two fighters. After six rounds, he was even on two of the judges' scorecards and leading 58–56 on the third. Then Lomachenko's craftsmanship and conditioning turned the tide. Referee Charlie Fitch did a good job, letting the fighters fight out of clinches and only inserting himself in the proceedings when necessary. One might note here that Vasiliy is no longer the amateur standout who had trouble dealing with roughhouse tactics in his ambitious early days as a pro. He now knows, and is willing to employ, some of those tactics himself.

The 117–111, 116–112, 115–113 decision in Lomachenko's favor was a good one.

★★★

On November 22, 2022, Broadway Boxing returned to its geographic roots with a fight card at the Edison Ballroom on Forty-Sixth Street just off Broadway near Times Square.

Broadway Boxing is the creation of Lou DiBella. Twenty-five years ago, HBO bestrode the sweet science like a Colossus and DiBella was its point person on boxing. Then Lou left the network. He hoped to build a roster of elite fighters, make deals with TV networks on their behalf, and outsource a lot of the nuts-and-bolts work to third-party promoters. But circumstances forced him to become a promoter himself.

DiBella's original vision for Broadway Boxing was based on the belief that New York had a lot of talented young fighters coming out of the amateurs and that small fight cards on a regular basis were necessary to accommodate them. His inaugural Broadway Boxing show was contested at the Crown Plaza Hotel on November 21, 2003. Emmanuel and Joshua Clottey were featured in separate bouts. John Duddy, in the third fight of his pro career, knocked out Leo Laudat on the undercard.

As Broadway Boxing grew, fighters like Vitali Klitschko, Gennady Golovkin, Sergio Martínez, Paulie Malignaggi, and Andre Berto starred in its events and HBO televised the action on *Boxing after Dark.*

But promoting is hard. HBO pulled back and eventually left boxing altogether. DiBella didn't have a network propping him up the way that Premier Boxing Champions (Showtime and Fox), Top Rank (ESPN), and Matchroom (DAZN) do. Nor did he have a foolish investor who was willing to drop millions of dollars on his shows. For a while, Lou had the lifeline of being the promoter of record for PBC. But that time is long gone.

"If I added up all my Broadway Boxing shows," DiBella said recently, "I'm probably down well over a million dollars over the past twenty years. I've made money on about twenty percent of the shows and lost money on the other eighty percent. Usually, I just hope to break even. But when things go right, these shows build my fighters for other platforms. It's a loss if you never get the money back. It's an investment if you do."

DiBella's most recent Broadway Boxing show in New York had been at Terminal 5 on December 5, 2019. Mary McGee won the IBF women's 140-pound title that night but Lou took a big hit financially.

"The venue was too hard for most people to get to," DiBella says, looking back on that night. "The tickets just didn't sell. It's hard to find a venue in Manhattan, let alone near Broadway, that works. Losing Roseland and B.B. King's [both of which hosted numerous Broadway Boxing cards but were in buildings that were torn down] really hurt."

November 22 marked the 117th edition of Broadway Boxing. Roughly one hundred of these shows have been in New York.

"Good club fights have become prohibitively expensive to promote," DiBella says. "And it's a horrible time to be doing club shows in New York. Everything costs more here. Hotel rooms cost more. Meals cost more. The commission's medical and insurance requirements are the same for the Edison Ballroom as they are for shows at Madison Square Garden and Barclays Center, and they cost a fortune. But I promised myself that I'd do a show in New York before the end of the year."

Jay and Alan Wartski are brothers who love boxing and have been involved with the sport for decades. Alan operates the Edison Ballroom.

"I asked Alan if he could cut me a break to help make the show economically viable," Lou recounts. "Alan told me that the Tuesday and Wednesday before Thanksgiving were open, and here we are. I'm going into this knowing that I'll lose money. The Edison Ballroom will seat about five hundred people on fight night. If I sell out, I'll lose money. But I'm doing this to make a statement I just want everyone who's there, including me, to have a good time."

There was a party atmosphere at the Edison Ballroom on fight night. DiBella was a gracious host as he worked his way around the room. The best ringside VIP tables cost $3,750 for ten people and included dinner with an open bar. Further away from the ropes, the same amenities could be had for a lesser price. A limited number of tickets without dinner or drinks were available for $125.

Lou changed boxing when he was at HBO and, after he left the network, boxing changed him. "I used to love being in boxing," he says. "It was my life's dream to work in this sport. I was a huge fan. I had incredible enthusiasm. A lot of that is gone now. Not all of it, but a lot."

"I'm viewing this show as a test," DiBella continued. "Not a test of will I make money on it, but a test of the concept of having VIP tables, a good dinner, and an open bar. If I sell the room out and people say, 'This was great; when are you doing it again?' we can go from there."

The first bout began at 7:20 p.m. Most of the crowd, incentivized by dinner, was there for the early fights. The food was good. The sight lines were excellent. The one thing missing was good fights. Clarence Booth tested Mykquan Williams in the main event before fading in the late rounds. But none of the fights caught fire. The A-side fighter won every bout and the action was less than compelling. Many of the spectators had left by the time Williams–Booth started.

DiBella is in the International Boxing Hall of Fame for his work at HBO and as a promoter. He has an eye for making good fights. One week before the show at the Edison Ballroom, he said, "Broadway Boxing has had our share of clunkers but we've also had our share of great fights."

Given Lou's track record, one can expect Broadway Boxing to have its share of great fights in the future. But this show was a clunker.

★★★

On December 10, 2022, Top Rank promoted a seven-bout card at Madison Square Garden designed to showcase and develop some of its young fighters. The one I was most interested in watching was Jared Anderson.

There's an allure to heavyweights. But in today's world of careful matchmaking and hype, it can be difficult to know who's the real deal and who isn't. Also, there's the caveat from Mark Kriegel, who wrote, "The typical American heavyweight has become a guy who already has failed as a ballplayer. Boxing was not his first sport. He has been recycled."

Anderson has a solid amateur background as a boxer. He's listed as six feet, four inches tall and weighs 240 pounds. He turned pro in 2019 and entered the ring on December 10 with 12 knockouts in 12 fights against opponents whose records were better than they were. He sits patiently through interviews and answers questions politely but has a guarded (sometimes condescending) attitude toward the media. "They'll pick you apart," he says, adding, "They don't understand what it is to be a fighter because they've never experienced it.

"There's nothing good about getting hit in the face," Anderson noted during a sit-down before the final pre-fight press conference. "But that's how I provide for myself and my family."

One presumes that punching someone else in the face is more to his liking.

Anderson had fought at Madison Square Garden once before, knocking out Oleksandr Teslenko in the second round in December 2021. This time, the opponent was Jerry Forrest in Jared's first scheduled ten-round fight.

Forrest (who entered the ring with a 26–5, 20 KOs record) had two losses and two draws in his most recent four outings. But he'd been stopped only once (by Gerald Washington nine years ago); fought to a draw against Mike Hunter and Zhilei Zhang; and went the distance in losing to Kubrat Pulev, Carlos Takam, and Jermaine Franklin.

In other words, Forrest wasn't going to beat Anderson (a 20-to-1 favorite). But he was viewed as a credible measuring stick for Jared's power and staying power given the fact that Anderson had gone past the second round only three times in his career and never past round six.

At the final pre-fight press conference, Anderson was the epitome of style. He wore charcoal-gray slacks, a light-gray sport jacket, black turtleneck, and black loafers accessorized by a white-gold Cuban necklace embedded with diamond fragments and Cartier sunglasses with buffalo-horn temples. The glasses are listed on Cartier's website for more than $3,000.

For his ring walk—in a markedly contrasting image—Jared wore a blue Santa Claus suit with white faux fur and a mask from *The Grinch Who Stole Christmas*. His trunks were blue with white faux fur and cut in a manner that would have done Héctor Camacho proud.

All of that was irrelevant once the fight began.

Forrest came out firing in round one and Anderson fired back. Before long, Forrest was pinned in a corner, taking a hellacious beating. He simply had nothing to keep Anderson off. Jared threw more than a hundred punches in round one, most of them "power" punches in the truest sense of the word. And he mixed them well, going to the head and body with brutal efficiency. There were no knockdowns, but it warranted being scored a 10–8 stanza. After more of the same in round two, referee David Fields stopped the slaughter at the 1-minute, 34-second mark.

Forrest is a journeyman nearing the end of his run. But Anderson handled him the way a legitimate prospect should and then some.

Boxing's elite heavyweights are getting on in years. Deontay Wilder is 37, Oleksandr Usyk 35, Tyson Fury 34, and Anthony Joshua 33. At age 23, Anderson represents the next generation. How will his skills evolve? How will he respond when his will is truly tested? It will be a while before we know the answers to those questions. Meanwhile, he's a formidable prospect and entertaining to watch.

★★★

Many boxing fans consider Julio César Chávez's March 17, 1990, knock-out of Meldrick Taylor his most memorable fight. It was particularly memorable for me because I watched it on television in Indonesia sitting on a sofa next to Muhammad Ali.

In 1990, Sony sponsored a week-long series of events in Indonesia and invited Muhammad to Jakarta as a guest of honor. I was researching a biography of Ali and came along for the ride.

"Super Show '90" featured music and boxing. Kool and the Gang performed in concert. There was a fight between former heavyweight champion Tim Witherspoon and a heavyweight from Kansas named Greg Gorrell. Larry Holmes did double duty, boxing in an exhibition against James Tillis and singing in the Grand Ballroom of the Sahid Jaya Hotel.

Ali was in good spirits throughout the trip. He'd been to Indonesia once before, in 1973 when he cruised to a twelve-round decision over Rudi Lubbers. Recently, his designation as "the greatest heavyweight of all time" had been questioned by those who thought that Mike Tyson might be greater. But on February 11, 1990—five weeks before Chávez–Taylor I—Buster Douglas had knocked out Tyson in Tokyo.

Earlier, Ali had said about Tyson, "He's predictable, the way he moves his head. He has fast hands, but he's slow on his feet and my hands were faster than his. The way to beat Tyson is with a fast jab, a hard right hand, and if he hits you, you have to be able to take a punch."

Minutes after Tyson was knocked out in Tokyo, my telephone rang and a voice asked, "What do you think people will say now when someone asks them who was greater, Mike Tyson or me?"

Chávez–Taylor I was the kind of fight that boxing fans were privileged to see in an era when the best fought the best. Chávez, the WBC 140-pound champion, entered the ring at the Hilton Hotel in Las Vegas with a 68–0 record. Taylor, a former Olympic gold medalist, held the IBF 140-pound title and was undefeated in 25 fights.

There was a fifteen-hour time difference between Jakarta and Las Vegas. Muhammad and I watched the fight live on television in his hotel suite on Sunday morning. It was an international feed with Bob Sheridan as the blow-by-blow commentator. Scoring the fight, Ali and I had Taylor comfortably ahead in the eleventh round. Then. . . .

Fade to black. . . . The show had run long and the satellite time that Don King Productions reserved had expired.

Muhammad and I went down to the hotel dining room to eat lunch, assuming that Taylor would win a decision. Toward the end of our meal, TV executive Arnie Rosenthal came into the room and told us he'd heard that Chávez had won on a twelfth-round knockout.

Later that week, Ali and I watched the end of the fight when it was replayed on Indonesian television. With 15 seconds to go in round twelve, Chávez caught Taylor in a corner and dropped him with a hellacious right hand. Meldrick rose at the count of four. Referee Richard Steele looked into his eyes, asked "Are you okay?" and, not waiting for a response, stopped the fight. There were four seconds left on the clock. The official time of the stoppage was 2:58 of round twelve.

Taylor was hurt. But given the time left on the clock, it's unlikely that Chávez would have been able to hit him again. He certainly wouldn't have had time if Steele had waited for Meldrick to answer his question or instructed him to "walk toward me." Also, in 1990, a fighter could be saved by the bell ending the final round. So even if Taylor had been dropped a second time, he would have won the fight.

Thus it was that Bob Sheridan proclaimed, "There will be some controversy here."

Adding to the controversy, judge Chuck Giampa had Chávez ahead by a point at the time of the stoppage. Dave Moretti (108–101) and Jerry Roth (107–102) had more credible scorecards, each of them favoring Taylor.

Richard Steele defended the stoppage, saying, "I'm not the timekeeper and I don't care about the time. When I see a man who has had enough, I'm stopping the fight."

Ali had a different view.

"Stopping the fight was wrong," Muhammad told me after we watched the replay. "That little Black boy from Philadelphia fought his whole life to get to where he was. And the referee took it all away from him."

Every now and then, a fighter who changes the narrative in boxing comes along.

George Dixon

George Dixon was boxing's first Black world champion.

"For a decade leading into the twentieth century," Jason Winders writes, "few Black men were as wealthy and none were more famous. To a Black culture cementing its first national heroes, Dixon was the single-most significant athlete of nineteenth-century America. He fought constantly as a professional—maybe against a thousand opponents in his lifetime. While most were exhibitions against rather faceless foes, a hundred or so of those bouts were chronicled by both Black and white presses. A half dozen came to define an era."

In *George Dixon: The Short Life of Boxing's First Black World Champion, 1870–1908* (University of Arkansas Press), Winders gives readers a well-researched, well-written, entertaining account of this remarkable man.

Dixon was born on the outskirts of Halifax, Nova Scotia, on July 29, 1870. Quite possibly, one of his grandfathers was white. Sometime in the 1880s, the Dixon family moved to Boston.

Dixon fought his first fight at age sixteen. A year later, Winders notes, "he was just a kid. Thin lead weights slid into his shoes between his bare feet and leather soles so he could climb above one hundred pounds and legally be allowed to compete. He had the body of a boy—thin, gangly, with arms slightly longer than his diminutive frame should have allowed. At first, he fought at 108 pounds. As the years went by, he developed into a genuine bantamweight and fought at 112 pounds. Then he went up to 116 pounds, then to 118, and then to 122, all apparently without suffering any loss of skill."

There are few visual images of Dixon in combat. Contemporaneous written accounts suggest that, at his peak, he had remarkable defensive skills, excellent timing, superb footwork, an uncommon ability to judge distance, and an educated left hand. He was blessed with courage, patience, the ability to endure punishment, and an iron will. His training regimen was sophisticated for its time.

A handful of fights were of particular importance in Dixon's storied ring career. On June 27, 1890, having journeyed across the Atlantic Ocean, he knocked out British bantamweight and feather-weight champion Nunc Wallace in Soho, England. That raised his profile exponentially. Nine months later in upstate New York, Dixon knocked out Cal McCarthy in a rematch of a 1890 draw to claim the American portion of the featherweight crown. Then, on July 28, 1891, in San Francisco, he knocked out Australian bantamweight champion Abe Willis.

"His bout against Willis," Winders writes, "would solidify Dixon as the greatest fighter—not just Black fighter—of his division in the world. With this victory over Willis, George Dixon became the undisputed world bantamweight champion, the first Black man to earn a world box-ing title. And it all happened before his twenty-first birthday."

Then, for good measure, Dixon knocked out Fred Johnson, the newly crowned British featherweight champion, in Brooklyn on June 27, 1892. That further solidified his kingdom.

These triumphs came at a time when boxing was becoming ingrained in America's national consciousness. The *Police Gazette,* with a weekly cir-culation that ran as high as 400,000 copies, was America's most popular tabloid magazine. Editor Richard K. Fox relied heavily on the sweet science to sell the publication. In 1889, roughly 60 percent of its head-lines dealt with boxing. Now, with Dixon at his fighting peak, the *Police Gazette* called him "the greatest fighter—big or little—the prize ring has ever known."

Winders puts the importance of those words in context: "Perhaps today we read over words like 'slave' and 'master' too easily. But the mind-set that fueled centuries of this thinking did not die with the stroke of the Great Emancipator's pen. It was deeply embedded in American culture. Just a generation before the Dixons arrived in the United States, the Black body was nothing more than a tool of labor, an expensive shovel or plow horse used and abused by a white master. Now a Black man was asserting his manhood by way of sport, beating white men with his near-bare hands, rising to heights higher than any man his size no matter what color. Dixon stood as champion, inspiration, among the wealthiest and best-known men in the country. More than a fighter, Dixon came to represent hope."

That said, in truth, Dixon regarded his celebrity standing as belonging more to himself than to Black America. "In the ring," Winders writes, "he was a hero to the Black man. But he lived in a white world rather contentedly." Dixon's manager, Tom O'Rourke (who took half of Dixon's earnings), was white. Dixon was married to O'Rourke's sister. Dixon was widely admired for his ring skills. But equally important to the narrative, he was not regarded as a threat. "Much of his widespread acceptance," Winders notes, "hinged on his smaller-than-normal stature." And despite being married to a white woman, he had always "known his place" in society. Tom O'Rourke, Winders recounts, was often "quick to make mention of that in the press."

In all his research, Winders was able to find only one instance in which Dixon was reported as speaking publicly about his meaning to Black America.

On May 22, 1891, Dixon was honored at the Full Moon Club in Boston's West End, the center of the city's Black community. Speaking to an audience of mostly young Black men, he declared, "I have always tried to do my duty. I have never yet entered the ring but that I was conscious that I was not only fighting the battle for myself alone, but also for the race. I felt that, if I won, not only credit would be given to me, but that my race would also rise in the estimation of the public."

"This moment," Winders observes, "among the thousands of mentions of Dixon in the press of the day, is an outlier. Never again in the reporting did he speak about a 'duty' to his race. Certainly, his actions in the years that followed were not in line with what Black America expected—or needed—from him. Never political or bombastic, rarely confrontational or rebel-rousing, Dixon never embraced his race duty more publicly than this moment."

In September 1892, Dixon further solidified his importance when he participated in a historic three-day fight festival called "The Carnival of Champions" at The Olympic Club in New Orleans.

On September 5, Jack McAuliffe knocked out Billy Myer to retain the world lightweight crown. More famously, on September 7, James J. Corbett dethroned John L. Sullivan to claim the heavyweight championship of the world. In between these two fights—on September 6—Dixon defended his world featherweight crown against Jack Skelly.

Prior to the Civil War, New Orleans had been the slave-trading capital of the United States. Now, a Black man and a white man were exchanging blows there. And the battle was waged before spectators of both colors.

"Among the earliest arrivals for the Skelly–Dixon bout," Winders writes, "were Black spectators for whom a large section on one of the upper general admissions stands had been set apart. It was a first for the club—an amazing sight in the heart of the former Confederacy. Among the crowd of two hundred Black men were prominent politicians and regular men lucky enough to snag a ticket. Five thousand people had filled the arena. City councilman Charles Dickson, a prominent member of the Olympic Club, welcomed Dixon into the ring and then warned the crowd that the upcoming contest was between a Black man and a white man in which fair play would govern and the best man win." Dixon knocked out Skelly in eight rounds. His fame and the adulation for him would never peak that high again.

The Carnival of Champions showcased Dixon in a way that he hadn't been showcased before. "Until that moment in New Orleans in September 1892," Winders observes, "Dixon was an insulated fighter. Then he landed in the middle of forces already in motion, forces still lingering from the after-effects of slavery and the Civil War. All of those forces would gain strength that summer and continue through Dixon's lifetime as societal forces shifted to a more aggressive approach toward limiting Black opportunity. Shielded from those forces for years, Dixon would soon experience them head-on without the protection of the white world in which he inhabited. The Carnival of Champions was not a moment when George Dixon changed the world. It was the moment when Dixon left his sheltered existence and became part of it."

"Immediately after the Dixon-Skelly bout," Winders reports, "Olympic Club members regretted pairing the two." Olympic Club president Charles Noel publicly stated, "The fight has shown one thing, however, that events in which colored men figure are distasteful to the membership of the club. After the fight, so many of the members took a stand against the admission of colored men into the ring as contestants against white pugilists that we have pretty well arrived at the conclusion not to give any more such battles. No, there will be no more colored men fighting before our club. That is a settled fact."

In the same vein, following Dixon–Skelly, the *New Orleans States* editorialized that there was "inherent sinfulness" to interracial fights and complained that "thousands of vicious and ignorant negroes regard the victory of Dixon over Skelly as ample proof that the negro is equal and superior to the white man."

Meanwhile, as the forces of repression were pushing back against gains made by Black Americans during the Reconstruction Era following the Civil War, Dixon's ring skills were eroding. In addition to competing in official bouts, he was fighting in hundreds upon hundreds of exhibitions as part of traveling vaudeville shows.

"In advance of the troupe arriving in town," Winders recounts, "a notice was posted that fifty dollars would be given to any person who could stand up before Dixon for four rounds. During these engagements, Dixon met all comers and often fought [multiple opponents] irrespective of size in the same night—an immeasurable toll on his small frame." A newspaper in West Virginia noted, "Dixon is meeting too many lads in his variety show act. His hands cannot certainly be kept in good condition with such work. He has used them so much in these four-round bouts that they are no longer the weapons they were."

As for official fights, Winders reports, "Noticeable cracks in Dixon's once spotless technique were developing. Dixon's speed was waning. His punches were no longer beating his opponent's attempts to block. His grunts were louder and more emphatic as blows that would once find empty space were now landing squarely on his face."

Lifestyle issues were also becoming a problem. Again, Winders sets the scene:

> When it came to New York City at the turn of the twentieth century, Manhattan's Black Bohemia embodied the newer and more daring phases of Negro life. On these streets, visitors found a lively mix of vice and vitality with clubs packed nightly with free-spending sporting and theatrical people, as well as those hoping to catch a glimpse of those famous patrons. The area had become a national symbol of urban depravity, noted mainly for its gambling houses, saloons, brothels, shady hotels, and dance halls that stayed open all night. And while few boxers of this period were residents of New York City, they all found their way to Black Bohemia.

Dixon began to frequent Black Bohemia and, by the time he became a regular, he was bleeding money into the district's many establishments. The ponies got some; George couldn't resist craps; and then there was booze to be bought at high prices for everybody. And he drank. Dixon would tear off $5,000 as his share of a win and it would disappear, one way or another, in a few days.

"Dixon got rid of his money faster than any fighter I ever knew, except myself," John L. Sullivan noted.

Dixon lost his featherweight title to Solly Smith in 1897 but regained it the following year. Then, on January 9, 1900, he fought Terry McGovern at the Broadway Athletic Club in New York. McGovern administered a brutal beating. The fight was stopped by Dixon's corner in the eighth round.

"I was outfought by McGovern from the end of the third round," Dixon acknowledged afterward. "The blows to my stomach and over my kidneys were harder than any I ever received. I entered the ring as confident as ever, but after going a short distance, I discovered that I was not the Dixon of old. My blows, although landing flush on my opponent, had no effect."

After Dixon–McGovern, *The Plaindealer* (a Black newspaper in Topeka, Kansas) editorialized, " The race has no gladiator now to represent it. We are in darkness, for Dixon's light has been put out."

On March 30, 1900, less than three months after losing to McGovern, Dixon opened a saloon called the White Elephant in the heart of the Tenderloin District. He was a poor business manager and his own best customer. Prior to fighting McGovern, he'd said that the McGovern fight would be his last. It wasn't.

The White Elephant failed and Dixon kept fighting. Over the next six years, he engaged in 77 official bouts, the last of them on December 10, 1906. According to BoxRec.com, he won only 13 of these encounters. Overall, BoxRec.com credits him with having participated in 155 recognized boxing matches with a final ring record of 68 wins, 30 losses, and 57 draws. In Dixon's era, when a fight went the distance, there was often no declaration of a winner.

Meanwhile, Dixon began drinking more heavily. As Winders writes, "He increasingly celebrated his victories with or drowned his troubles in alcohol. That led to numerous confrontations with police. His personal demons were clashing with public sentiment toward Blacks in the wider society. His celebrity no longer shielded him. In public, he was prone to violent outbursts and fits of rage. In private, he was beholden to his own dark vices. Few Black men were as pitied, and none named more frequently from public square and pulpit as a cautionary tale of modern excesses."

In due course, Joe Gans succeeded Dixon as the most famous and successful Black boxer in the world. After defeating Battling Nelson on September 3, 1906, Gans made a show of publicly offering Dixon a job as head bartender at a hotel that he owned in Baltimore. But the job never materialized.

"I never heard anything from Joe about going to Baltimore," Dixon said later. "I guess he was advertising his show when he said that. But his hotel would sure look good to me right now"

"It isn't what you used to be," Dixon told an interviewer. "It's what you are today. The men who followed me in the days of prosperity can't see me when I am close enough to speak to them."

On January 4, 1908, Dixon was admitted to Bellevue Hospital in New York.

"He was wasted and worn," Winders writes. "To the doctors, he famously said he had 'fought his last fight with John Barleycorn and had been beaten.' His condition became worse and continued sinking. He died at 2 p.m. on January 6, 1908. He was thirty-seven years old. His funeral service in Boston was the largest funeral gathering for a Black man in the history of the city."

Winders has done an admirable job of recounting George Dixon's life. He places people and events within the context of their times and brings names in dusty old record books to life. He writes well, which is a prerequisite for any good book; does his best to separate fact from fiction; and is sensitive to the nuances of his subject. He also avoids the pitfall of describing fight after fight after fight, focusing instead on the ones that mattered most. Readers are transported back in time to the Olympic Club in New Orleans for the three-day Carnival of Champions in 1992. Dixon's sad beating at the hands of Terry McGovern in New York in 1900 is particularly well told.

Winders also performs a service by stripping away the myth of Nat Fleischer as a reliable boxing historian.

"Much of Dixon's story," Winders writes, "has been left in the hands of Fleischer. Although he is an icon to many, not all are enamored by Fleischer's ability to recount the past. His research and record keeping leave much to be desired. His biographies and record books are rife with errors."

Winders then approvingly quotes historian Kevin R. Smith, who labeled Fleischer's best-known writing about Black boxers (the five-volume *Black Dynamite* series) as "heavily flawed," called some of his other offerings "downright ludicrous," and declared that Fleischer was "unabashed in his use of poetic license, making up sources and fictionalizing events when unable to unearth the true facts."

Less than a year after Dixon died, Jack Johnson journeyed to Australia and dethroned Tommy Burns to become the first Black man universally recognized as heavyweight champion of the world. "Historians want to start with Johnson," Winders writes, looking back on that moment. "But why not Dixon? By ignoring him, we have lost the point where the story of the modern Black athlete in America begins."

One reason many chroniclers start with Johnson is that so little about Dixon is known. "Historians," Winders acknowledges, "have placed Dixon at the forefront of boxing pioneers, but they often don't seem to know why, beyond a few lines related to his ring résumé. . . . Outside of some isolated examples, sport history and Canadian history—indeed, Black history—rarely celebrate his accomplishments. There is an odd silence in his isolation. . . . Dixon . . . sits tantalizingly, even frustratingly, close to us—just over a century ago. Surely his life should be too recent to be lost to time already."

Winders has done his part—and then some—to save us from that loss. *George Dixon: The Short Life of Boxing's First Black World Champion, 1870–1908* is as good a biography of Dixon and portrait of boxing in that era as one is likely to find.

Every woman in boxing today can trace part of her success to Christy Martin.

Christy Martin: *Fighting for Survival*

More than any other fighter, Christy Martin was responsible for legitimizing women's boxing in the public eye. She was also a closeted gay woman married to a man who physically and psychologically abused her for years before stabbing her multiple times, shooting her in the chest, and leaving her for dead on their bedroom floor. *Fighting for Survival,* written with Ron Borges and published by Rowman & Littlefield, is her story.

Martin was born in Mullen, West Virginia, on June 12, 1968, and grew up in the coal-mining town of Itmann. Her father was a miner. "All you need to know to understand the limits of Itmann," Martin writes, "is your cellphone won't work there."

When Christy Salters (her name before she was married) was six, she was sexually molested in the basement of her parents home by a fifteen-year-old cousin who forced her to perform oral sex on him. Other than her future husband, she didn't tell anyone about it for thirty-seven years.

She was a troubled adolescent. "I started associating drinking with popularity," she acknowledges. "I was running around with thirty-year-olds when I was still a teenager. I sold speed to friends of my parents. I was a bad kid doing things I shouldn't have done."

She was also gay.

Christy had sex with a girl for the first time when she was thirteen. In high school, she ventured back and forth between the sexes.

"I wasn't together at the time when it came to totally understanding my own sexuality," Christy acknowledges. "Can I be straight if I try? Should I be who I am or try harder to please everyone else? You doubt sometimes the direction you're going. Other times, you're totally sure. I'd been with men and women in high school so I'd say I was bi-sexual at that time. But to me, being in a relationship with a woman was easier. It was always where I was most comfortable."

"In towns as small as Itmann and Mullens, people talk," Christy continues. "I knew they wondered about me. It is exhausting hiding who you are from your family and your friends and the world around you.You're always afraid someone knows the truth.You may tell yourself you don't care. But if you really didn't care, you wouldn't be hiding what you're doing or what you're feeling, would you?"

Coming out wasn't an option. Christy's mother was vehemently homophobic, a view shared by many people in that corner of the world. "Put it this way," Christy says. "You weren't coming out in Itmann, West Virginia. Not unless you were planning on leaving the same day."

Then, to further complicate matters, Christy got pregnant at age twenty-one. Chris Caldwell had been her "sort of boyfriend" since they were in fifth grade. As the years passed, they saw each other from time to time.

"One night," Christy remembers, "we went out as friends, had a few drinks, and had drunken sex. I was in love with Bridget [her girlfriend of the moment], so why did that happen? I was selfish, that's why.There's no other explanation. I never told my parents. I didn't want the added pressure of them saying they'd raise the baby while I finished school, which I know my Mom would have done."

So she chose to have an abortion.

"It's one of those things that will always bother me," Christy writes. "But it's the decision I made. I still feel guilty about it. But I made a choice and I had to move forward."

Meanwhile, Christy found safe haven in sports. Despite being only five feet, four inches tall, she excelled in basketball, averaging 27 points and six rebounds per game during her senior year of high school. In her junior and senior seasons, she was designated first team All-State.

"I had a pent-up rage inside about having to hide that I was gay from the world as I knew it," she recalls. "You're so angry that you can't be who you want to be and you can't change who you are.You're trapped and it makes you mad without understanding what you're really mad about. In sports, it's acceptable to be overly aggressive so you can let some of those emotions out in a safe place.At times it even gets rewarded."

That led to boxing.

"I'd been going to Toughman shows for years with my friends and family," Christy reminisces, "and always wondered what I'd do if the bell rang and I found myself standing all alone in one corner of the ring."

Then, at age nineteen, she saw a poster inviting women to participate in a "Mean Mountaineer" tournament.

"That," Christy recalls, "is how, on October 1, 1987, I found myself standing in the wings at the Raleigh County Armory wearing a pair of 16-ounce boxing gloves and leather headgear, waiting to try something I knew nothing about."

But Christy Salters had an advantage over the other women in the tournament. "Many of them were muscular," she remembers. "They looked stronger than me. But I was in better condition and I was an athlete. Most of them were just tough girls."

Christy won her first fight by decision and, the next night, came back for more. In the finals, she knocked out an opponent who was heavier and five inches taller with a single punch.

"She wasn't staggering around and kind of woozy," Christy recounts. "She was out and the crowd went into a frenzy! It was awesome. I could feel the adrenaline rush from the crowd, and that was it for me. I was hooked on boxing. The first thing I thought of when they gave me the champion's jacket and the $300 [prize] was, 'When's the next one?'"

Soon, a boxing ring was one of the few places where Christy felt safe.

"I won't sugarcoat what boxing is about," she writes. "You don't find too many well-adjusted prizefighters. We all have our demons, something driving us to run toward pain when human nature says run away. You don't find many fighters who weren't spawned out of some kind of dysfunction. If you're normal, whatever that means, you're not likely to choose a sport that involves getting hit in the face."

But Christy continues, "I loved boxing more than anything in my life. The ring was where I could be me. In the ring, who I chose to love didn't matter. I felt able to get out my frustrations and the anger that was locked up inside me. It was okay for me to go in there and be as aggressive as hell and as competitive as I wanted to be. They might laugh at us on the way into the ring. But if we fought hard and did some damage, they'd cheer us on the way out. They didn't care if you were gay or straight. Whatever it was that drove you to fight was fine to the people watching as long as you could fight. I just wanted to be a boxer. It became all that mattered to me. For too long, I didn't have control of anything but the 20-by-20-foot area inside those ropes. Maybe that's why I loved it in there so much."

On September 9, 1989, at age twenty-one, Christy turned pro. "Women's boxing was not yet a truly legitimate sport," she acknowledges.

"It was still a freak show, but at the time I didn't give it a thought. I just wanted to fight."

Soon after, her promoter suggested that a man named Jim Martin become Christy's trainer. On March 20, 1992, Christy Salters and Jim Martin were joined together as husband and wife. Much more on that later.

By the end of 1993, Martin had 19 wins as a pro against a single loss and 1 draw. Then she was brought to the attention of Don King, who signed her to a contract calling for five six-round fights a year at $5,000 a fight. Prior to that, she'd been making roughly $500 per fight and her biggest purse had been $1,200.

Christy's inaugural fight with King was a first-round knockout of Susie Melton on January 29, 1994. Five more victories followed. Then, on December 16, 1995, King matched her against a sacrificial lamb named Erica Schmidlin who was making her pro debut. As expected, Martin won on a first-round knockout. That night marked a turning point because Christy's bout was on the undercard of Mike Tyson vs. Buster Mathis Jr.

Martin fought on Tyson undercards six times. Those fights, she says, "were my stepping stones to a world I never knew existed—the big-time side of boxing." Tyson, she writes, was "like a magic carpet ride for me, providing a platform to show my skills and a huge audience that turned me into someone I never thought I could be."

After destroying Schmidlin, Martin defeated a no-hope opponent named Melinda Robinson and then Sue Chase (who would end her career with a 1–23–1 record). The Chase fight was significant because it was on the undercard of Félix Trinidad vs. Rodney Moore at the MGM Grand in Las Vegas and was televised by Showtime—the first time that a fight between women boxers aired nationally in the United States. That was followed by a first-round knockout against another no-hoper named Del Pettis.

Then, three weeks later, everything changed. On March 16, 1996, Christy was matched against an Irish boxer named Deidre Gogarty on the undercard of the rematch between Mike Tyson and Frank Bruno on Showtime-PPV.

Christy was a natural 135-pounder. Two hours before the weigh-in, Gogarty (who would finish her career with 8 wins in 13 fights) weighed 124.

After stuffing rolls of quarters into her bra, socks, and underwear, Deidre tipped the scales at 130.

A 60–53, 60–53, 59–54 beatdown followed. But Martin was about to become famous, not because she won but because Gogarty broke Christy's nose. It gushed blood throughout the fight. Writing for the Associated Press, Ed Schuyler later called it "the most lucrative bloody nose in the history of boxing."

"That fight," Christy says, "turned in a matter of seconds from being an event that was being laughed at and ridiculed in the arena to one that absolutely thrilled people who were watching. That drippy nose and the uniqueness of the story of the husband-and-wife fighting team [by that time, Jim Martin was Christy's husband] turned me into a national phenomenon."

In the weeks that followed, Christy appeared on dozens of national television shows and was on the cover of *Sports Illustrated*.

"You could not get any bigger in the world I was inhabiting than to be on a *Sports Illustrated* cover," she writes. "And there I was, staring back at myself from every newsstand in America. You dream about some things, but other things are so big you don't even think about them happening because just the thought would be ridiculous. That's what being on SI's cover was for me."

After beating Gogarty, Martin defeated Melinda Robinson for the second time followed by a first-round knockout of Bethany Payne. Then she signed a new contract with Don King calling for a minimum purse of $100,000 per fight. All told, she fought 27 times over the course of eight years with King as her promoter. Writing about a memorable moment in their relationship, she reveals, "Don did try to proposition me once in Venezuela at a WBA function. I asked him to go into another room because I needed to talk to him and he came on to me. After he made his pitch, I laughed and told him I only wanted to fight my way to the top. He started cackling and said, 'You're already at the top.' Then he came to hug me and poured his drink down the back of my dress."

After leaving King, Christy fought eleven times over the course of ten years. But the good part of her career was over. Her record in those 11 fights was 5 wins, 5 losses, and a draw. Age and a higher level of opponent caught up to her.

The worst of the defeats was a fourth-round stoppage at the hands of Laila Ali in 2003. Laila was six inches taller than Christy and outweighed her on fight night by at least twenty pounds. Christy's announced weight of 159 was as phony as Deidre Gogarty's had been seven years earlier. Why did she take the fight? For a $400,000 purse. And to use her word, she was "massacred." The fight ended when she took a knee and chose not to rise before the count of ten.

Looking back on that night, Christy writes, "I was totally embarrassed and ashamed. I'll never get over it. I'd be more accepting of losing to her if I'd been knocked out or took a beating for six more rounds. To quit on my knees is not who I was."

Virtually all boxer autobiographies focus on a fighter's ring career. This one does it better than most. But what separates *Fighting for Survival* from other fighter autobiographies is the horrifying nature of Christy's life outside the ring coupled with the brutally honest way in which she recounts it.

When Ron Borges met with her to discuss the possibility of their working together, one of the first things he told her was, "I'm not interested in working on a dishonest book."

Neither was Christy. Later, as she began opening up about the horrors of her life, Borges counseled, "You don't have to tell me everything bad that happened."

But she did.

"I've never dealt with anybody who was more open about her life than Christy Martin," Borges says. "There were times when we had to stop because the memories overwhelmed her. I don't think I could do what she did with me. But Christy really believes that she survived the murder attempt and everything that came before it as part of a larger plan. And her goal now is to reach as many victims of abuse as possible."

Christy's decision to marry Jim Martin (her trainer) was a watershed moment in her life. He was twenty-four years older than she was. Why did a gay woman marry a man old enough to be her father?

"I have to admit, I was intrigued by him and his boxing stories," Christy writes. "Now that I'm free and looking back thirty years, it makes no sense. But when I remember the girl I was then, a naïve kid from Nowhere, West Virginia, I can understand what I did. I wasn't attracted to him. I was never passionate about him. The night Jim Martin proposed to me, I was ill-prepared to do what would have been best. I wasn't strong enough to declare to the world who I really was.

"When we first got married," Christy continues, "I was still a little confused about my sexuality. Deep inside, I knew I was gay. I spent a lot of years trying to figure out how I felt about that. But the longer we were together and the better I understood who I really was, the more it weighed on me. So there I was; a closeted gay woman athlete in a sport that barely existed with a boyfriend older than my Dad. All my passion came out in the gym because there was none at home. We got along all right in those days because we had boxing in common and that was our main focus. I'd say, in those years we were married, I was really asexual. It got to the point where I didn't care about sex at all. I wanted to be in love with someone but I replaced that desire with a love for boxing."

Christy's rise to stardom after the Gogarty bout threatened to upend the applecart.

"I was now a gay woman in a phony marriage suddenly under the microscope that is the American hype machine," she recalls. "Thankfully, it was the American hype machine before social media. I have a lot of things to be thankful for. And the absence of things like Instagram, Twitter, Facebook and the like back then are some of them because, had they existed, I would have been 'outted' long before Jim put a bullet in my chest and destroyed my hiding place."

Also, Christy reminds readers, "Part of the boxing sell for us was that I was a married woman, trained and managed by her loving husband, so how could I be gay?"

The deception came with a heavy price attached. Christy says that, without her knowledge, her husband skimmed large amounts of cash off the top of her fight purses. There were what she describes as "almost daily emotional beatdowns." And at times, Jim was physically abusive. "But when the abuse is mostly emotional manipulation," she explains, "you see it differently. You question what you can do to fix things. You start to think he's right about you. You're the problem. It often takes a long time before you realize who the victim really is. That's the kind of emotional control someone can have over you. You know you should leave, but you're ashamed of the situation you're in and afraid of the consequences if you go.

"A lot of women end up in similar situations to the one I was in," Christy continues. "We stay out of fear, out of obligation, out of believing it's all we deserve. The brave ones don't stay. But would an openly gay female get the same chances I got if I wasn't hiding who I really was? I hadn't seen anyone who did, and I wasn't about to risk it all to find out. I was a lesbian locked in a sham marriage designed to protect me from a sporting world I'd come to believe would never accept me as I was. [So] you compromise. You lie. You hide. You try to fit into a world that isn't your own creation. You accept things you never thought you'd accept. You replace boxing for love and try to equate financial success with personal happiness."

It didn't work.

Writing about her husband, Christy states, "Protecting his wife never factored into his thinking. I was just a human ATM machine to him. He kept telling me I'd become a star and make him a lot of money but until that happened we needed another way to supplement what the fights brought in. And Jim came up with quite a solution. He wanted me to fight men in their hotel rooms. He said he'd heard there were guys who got off on it and they'd pay me to beat them up. When he first suggested it, I hollered at him, 'Bitch! Get a job!' But it didn't take him long to convince me to do it, like he did with so many things I wish had never happened.

"The first time was in a hotel room in Fort Lauderdale," Christy remembers. "I'm in this guy's room, ready to fight, and all he kept trying to do was grab me and hold while I beat the bejesus out of him. The guy seemed to like it. Go figure. When it was over, we took his money and left. I felt like a prostitute must feel the first time. I felt dirty. I knew that hadn't been about boxing. It was a sex thing from the start for the guy. I said I'd never do it again. But of course, I did. When you need money and all you have to do is go punch some guy around in his hotel room, it's easy to find an excuse to do it again. The second time, it was easier to accept. I still didn't feel right about it but you find ways to justify it. I told myself, whatever it is for the guy, it's just boxing to me. Every time I did something like that, I left a little piece of myself back in that room. A piece of my dignity had disappeared."

Christy's unhappiness and confusion caused her to cross over other lines of propriety as well. Prior to fighting Andrea DeShong, she labeled her opponent a "dyke bitch."

"I said what I said," Christy admits. "I should never have done it. But I did." Making matters worse, she later told DeShong, "I'm going to put something on you that your girlfriend can't get off."

"It was another part of my self-destruction," Christy acknowledges. "I paid a price for those kind of statements and still do to this day with some people in the gay community."

She also got into a fistfight with a woman in a parking lot and wound up paying $30,000 to settle a lawsuit that arose from the incident.

Worse, she got hooked on cocaine.

"My whole life, I'd been against using drugs," Christy writes. "I tried marijuana in high school but I didn't like the high. Same with speed. Tried it. Didn't like it. So I stuck with drinking to excess instead. But as my life and my career unraveled, so did my resolve. One night, Jim came home with a baggie and dropped it on the table in front of me. He said that a fighter announced he was done with cocaine and there was the proof. I took the bait. The bag sat there for a day or two, looking at me. I didn't care about myself and I hated Jim and what my life had become. What did it matter if I tried cocaine just once? I was alone the night I finally grabbed that baggie and opened it. I snorted a line and it was like the first time I knocked someone out and the crowd went crazy. I loved the feeling it gave me. At first, I only did it on Friday nights and weekends. Pretty soon, it was Mondays too. Then it became every day. It took a month until it had me. Pretty quickly, I'd do anything for coke. Jim would do it occasionally with me but mostly it was me, alone in the house. I was also taking pain pills for all the injuries I'd had in boxing and drinking, too. I overdosed so many times I should be dead. Basically, if I was awake in those years, I was high."

Christy was hooked on cocaine for more than three years. Then, through the muddle that her mind had become, she had an epiphany.

"I was walking through my house, high, when I saw my reflection in a mirror and stopped dead in my tracks. I thought, 'You really look like an addict.' At that moment it hit me. What was looking back at me wasn't Christy Martin. It wasn't the Coal Miner's Daughter. It wasn't the WBC world super-welterweight women's champion. It was a drug addict. That's what I'd become. I immediately went and did a line to try and erase that thought but it wasn't the same. By the next day, I'd decided things needed to change and I had to be the one to make the change. That day, I realized if I bent over and did one more line of cocaine, I'd do it until I was dead."

Then Christy told Jim that she was going to leave him.

"Five days later [on November 23, 2010]," she writes, "stone cold sober, I was lying on my bedroom floor with a bullet in my chest, stab wounds all over my body and blood everywhere. I was finally free, if I didn't die first."

Jim Martin was tried and convicted of attempted murder in the second degree and sentenced to a minimum of twenty-five years in prison. He won't be eligible for release until 2035.

After recovering from the attempt on her life, Christy had two more fights and lost both of them. She also suffered a stroke while in the hospital undergoing surgery for a broken hand after the first of those two encounters.

"I stayed in ICU for a week," she recalls. "When I finally left, I couldn't walk right, talk right, or see right. My words were slurred and I had double vision which remains a problem for me at times to this day."

She needed a cane to get around. But she was allowed to fight again. "The California State Athletic Commission [which oversaw the bout] didn't have a clue," she notes.

But *Fighting for Survival* has a happy ending. Martin has steered clear of cocaine for more than a decade. And in 2017, she married Lisa Holewyne. Their marriage is unique. Couples sometimes fight. But on November 17, 2001, Christy and Lisa had fought each other at Mandalay Bay in Las Vegas with Christy winning by decision.

"I was one hundred percent sure I wanted to spend the rest of my life with Lisa," Christy writes. "And five years later, nothing has changed. I was surer of that than anything in my life, including my decision to give over my life to boxing. I still love boxing but it isn't my first love anymore. Lisa is."

Fighting for Survival is written the way Christy fought. Straightforward and don't hold anything back. It goes beyond being a boxing book and is as honest as any autobiography I've read.

There's an art to capturing another person's voice, and Borges has it. One never gets the feeling that he's putting words in Martin's mouth.

Rather, he's helping her organize her thoughts and putting them on paper. There's no need to over-sensationalize. The fact are lurid enough.

Christy is active today in working to combat domestic violence. She also promotes fights in North Carolina, South Carolina, and Florida. Summarizing her journey, she writes, "Let's be clear about one thing. Trust and believe when I tell you, this is not a victim's story. Although a lot of folks might see it that way, it is not a victim's story at all. It's a survivor's story." And she adds, "I'm not looking for a pity party for Christy Martin. A lot of things that happened in my life before I was free to be me were great and I wouldn't trade them for a different path because this is the path I had to walk to be who I am today. All I'm saying is, you don't have to go as far down that road as I did to be free."

In Carlos Acevedo's eyes, "There was nothing wholesome
about Tommy Morrison."

The Duke: The Life and Lies of Tommy Morrison

Tommy Morrison was born in Gravette, Arkansas, on January 2, 1969, and lived in Oklahoma for most of his life. He fought in countless toughman contests, had three organized amateur bouts, and turned pro in 1988. Over the next seven years, he compiled a 45–3–1 (39 KOs, 3 KOs by) ring record, the high point of which was a 118–109, 117–110, 117–110 decision over George Foreman in 1993 to claim the vacant WBO heavyweight throne.

In Foreman's next fight, he knocked out Michael Moorer to annex the WBA, IBF, and lineal heavyweight titles. In Morrison's next fight, he was knocked out by Michael Bentt in the first round.

Morrison's other losses were brutal "KOs by" at the hands of Ray Mercer and Lennox Lewis. During the course of his career, he knocked out faded versions of James Tillis, Pinklon Thomas, Joe Hipp, Carl Williams, and Razor Ruddock. As a postscript, between 1996 and 2008, he scored stoppages over three particularly inept opponents after having been diagnosed as HIV positive. He died in 2013 at age 44.

The Duke: The Life and Lies of Tommy Morrison by Carlos Acevedo (Hamilcar Publications) chronicles Morrison's life.

"Morrison," Acevedo writes, "came from a broken home. He was a secondhand son, passed from here to there, from nowhere to nowhere bound, wherever he would stick. His father was abusive. His mother once beat a murder charge. His brother would spend fifteen years in prison for rape. And Tommy? His mother first made him use his fists when he was five years old."

"I was the guy your parents warned you about in high school," Morrison cautioned.

The Duke is divided into two parts. Part I deals with Morrison as a fighter. His early ring record was fashioned against a collection of hopeless opponents. Then Bill Cayton took over as lead manager and Tommy graduated to a higher grade of stiff. Cayton built Morrison brilliantly as an attraction. He propagated the deceit that Tommy was a distant relative of movie star John Wayne and was instrumental in landing Morrison the role of Tommy Gunn in *Rocky V*. Cayton also used his skill and economic power to ensure that Morrison was featured on high-profile boxing telecasts.

At times, Morrison struggled in the ring. "He was," Acevedo writes, "especially susceptible to right hands. And when he opened fire, he often did so squared up to his opponent which made him a big target and left him exposed to counterpunches." Moreover, Morrison trained less rigorously than he should have and burned the candle at both ends. "Let's put it this way," Cayton said. "Tommy Morrison makes Mike Tyson look like a monk."

But as Acevedo notes, "Morrison worked the body with zeal, often doubling up hooks with either hand after landing to the rib cage. His signature right-to-the-body-right-uppercut combination was both lethal and often unexpected. In close, Morrison could surprise an opponent from either side with damaging shots. There was also the undeniable potency of his left hook. And Morrison showed the kind of heart often lacking among his peers. Morrison was someone who had to be nailed to the canvas before he lost."

It was inevitable that Morrison would come to be spoken of as a "Great White Hope." To his credit, he did his best to avoid making race an issue. "It's kind of sad," he told the *Kansas City Star*. "To be honest, it's a big advantage being white. There aren't that many white fighters around. But I'd prefer to stay away from that because it's racist."

By 1991, Morrison had run his record to 28–0 with 24 knockouts. Then Cayton matched him against Ray Mercer for the WBO heavyweight title. It was a mistake. For three rounds, Morrison dominated the action, pounding the granite-chinned Mercer with sledgehammer blows. Then Tommy ran out of gas and, in round five, was knocked unconscious.

Undeterred, Cayton rebuilt Morrison's credibility, matching him in fights that resulted in seven wins and a draw over the next seventeen months. That led to a $2 million payday against George Foreman in a 1993 bout for the WBO heavyweight title that Mercer had vacated after beating Morrison. Fighting against Foreman with uncharacteristic caution and in excellent condition for one of the few times in his career, Tommy emerged victorious.

The world was now Morrison's oyster. He had a belt and was a big name in the heavyweight division. A deal was made for a title unification bout against Lennox Lewis that would pay Tommy a minimum purse of $7.5 million. But first, Morrison wanted an interim fight against a walk-over opponent in Oklahoma. The walkover opponent was Michael Bentt.

KO by 1.

"All fighters reach a peak," Acevedo writes. "A point at which the rigors of training and the punishment received in the ring combine to break them down. For some fighters, particularly aggressive ones such as Morrison, short peaks are the rule. [After the Bentt fight], it was clear that Morrison was beyond his best days. Over the span of two years, from October 1993 to October 1995, he was knocked down ten times. And Morrison compounded these issues with a torrid nightlife, a lax attitude toward training, and a dependency on steroids that likely had an adverse physical effect on him."

Ah, yes. Morrison's night life.

Part II of *The Duke* deals with Tommy's life outside the ring. In his later years, he would use cocaine, crystal meth, Adderall, and Special K. In the early 1990s, he was a drinker. And alcohol fueled his temper.

"Morrison," Acevedo writes, "was the kind of drunk who would pick fights in public and reject outright the concept of a designated driver. He could also become violent when under the influence."

A drunk Morrison slashed an exotic dancer with a broken beer bottle in Kansas City. She sued. According to John Brown (Morrison's co-manager), the case was settled for $100,000.

Morrison pled guilty to simple assault and public intoxication in conjunction with another incident and was fined $310. He was also arrested and pled no contest to two misdemeanor counts of assault and battery stemming from an altercation at a party given by Tammy Witt (the mother of his son, Trey). In that instance, Morrison received a sus-pended sentence, was fined $600, and ordered to perform thirty hours of community service.

But the drinking was nothing compared to the women.

"In the wake of *Rocky V*," Acevedo recounts, "Morrison had become what John Brown called a 'Bimbo Magnet.' At the peak of his stardom, between the premiere of *Rocky V* and his upset loss to Michael Bentt, he lived out an adolescent fantasy that might have been the rudimentary plot of a teen sexploitation film. His life was truly a wild one. Wherever Morrison went, he trailed yearning women behind him. They shadowed him at personal appearances, before fights, after fights, in lobbies, restaurants, bars, and clubs. Few celebrities, even minor ones, spend their nights partying in Kansas City or Jay [Oklahoma] or Iowa. But Morrison had little interest in the bright lights of New York City or Los Angeles. The local whirlwind he created in small towns was more than enough for him."

"His attraction to women was more than anything you can imagine," Bill Cayton told a reporter for the *Vancouver Sun*. "He was a womanizer beyond anything I've ever known."

"It was unbelievable," Morrison said to *Sports Illustrated*. "It was all right there. You could feed yourself as fast and as much as you wanted."

Then everything changed. For the worse.

Much worse.

On February 10, 1996, Nevada State Athletic Commission executive director Marc Ratner announced that, for medical reasons, Morrison had been scratched from a fight card scheduled for the MGM Grand Hotel & Casino that night. Ratner declined to specify what the medical issue was. Five days later, at a press conference held at the Southern Hills Marriot Hotel in Tulsa, Oklahoma, Morrison addressed the issue with candor and grace.

"First of all, I'd like to thank everybody for being here today," Morrison said. "I'm sorry that I couldn't be here in person on Monday when Tony [promoter Tony Holden] informed you of what the present situation was. At that time, I felt it was more important to be with my family. Since that time, I've taken action to have more extensive tests run. I was informed just a little while ago that those tests do in fact confirm that I have tested positive for the HIV virus. There was a certain point and time in my life that I lived a very permissive, fast, reckless lifestyle. I knew that the HIV virus is something that anyone could get, but I also believed the chances were very, very slim. I thought that the real danger of contracting this rests in the arms of those who subject themselves to certain types of lifestyles—addicts who share needles, people who practice a homosexual lifestyle. I honestly believed that I had a better chance of winning the lottery than contracting this disease. I have never been so wrong in my life. To all my young fans out there, I'd ask that you no longer see me as a role model but see me as an individual who had an opportunity to be a role model and blew it. Blew it with irresponsible, irrational, immature decisions; decisions that one day could cost me my life."

That was laudable. But within seven months, Morrison had pivoted 180 degrees. He had come to believe that HIV was a hoax and that the drugs developed to fight it were, in fact, designed to kill patients. In Acevedo's words, "like so many other fanatics, [Morrison] ignored facts and substituted intuition for verifiable science."

Now Morrison had a different view of his own medical condition. "I don't have a lot of confidence in all this medication," he said. "I've chosen not to take it. See, I don't think that HIV causes AIDS. Some of the research I've read and some of the doctors I've talked to—there are still a lot of unanswered questions. It hasn't been proven scientifically to my satisfaction that HIV leads to AIDS. It's the medication that's killing people. You unravel the little piece of paper in the bottle and you read about the side effects and they match identical with the symptoms of AIDS. HIV's never been proven to cause AIDS. HIV ain't never killed anybody."

Thereafter, Morrison repeatedly denied that he was HIV positive. But as Acevedo notes, "A lawsuit [instituted after Morrison's death] brought to light dozens of documents revealing medical records that repeat over and over the fact that Tommy Morrison had HIV. These records include prescriptions, credit card statements, test results, memos from physicians, expert testimony, even psychiatric intake notes. The evidence that Morrison had been living with HIV for years is overwhelming."

The end game for Morrison was long and ugly, marked by alcoholism, drug abuse, and uncontrolled aggression. But as Acevedo states, "Nothing about his carnal lifestyle—reckless, aimless, remorseless, seemingly bottomless—is as shocking as the willingness of dozens of women to risk a potential death sentence by sleeping with the most famous carrier of HIV outside of Magic Johnson."

In Acevedo's eyes, Morrison was now a menace to society.

He was also a bigamist, having married two different women (Dawn Freeman and Dawn Gilbert) in 1996. He would marry for a third time in 2011, two years before he died.

Meanwhile, again and again, Morrison was getting arrested. Twice in 1997 on charges ranging from driving under the influence to carrying a loaded firearm while under the influence of intoxicants. On December 20, 1997, he was sentenced to six months in prison (later reduced to thirty days). The following year, he was arrested again, this time for driving under the influence, destruction of private property, running a red light, and driving with a revoked license. In 2000, he pled guilty to myriad charges and was sentenced to ten years in prison with eight years suspended. He was released after fourteen months.

Morrison also subjected himself to cosmetic surgery that amounted to self-mutilation. As recounted by Acevedo, "In June 1999, Morrison underwent a series of surgeries for chest and biceps implants in Tulsa with nightmarish results. When the last procedure was over, Morrison and Landon [a friend] checked into a motel for a brief recovery period. That was where Dawn Gilbert found Morrison, looking like the creation of a Hollywood-style mad scientist."

Landon told Gilbert that the doctor had used implants for the biceps rebuild that appeared to be shin guards bought from a sporting goods store. "As disturbing as his new implants were," Acevedo notes, "the most shocking part of his appearance was the multiple tubes that now protruded from his body, each attached to one of the four bags surrounding him. Tubes came from each armpit and each bicep, and the bags contained a yellowish gunk and blood."

Yet bizarrely, Morrison continued to fight. On November 3, 1996 (less than nine months after first testing HIV positive), he'd been allowed to enter the ring in Tokyo and scored a first-round knockout over Marcus Rhode. Then, after a decade-long absence, he returned to boxing and stopped two no-hope opponents in West Virginia (2007) and Mexico (2008).

All the while, his mind was rotting away.

"When he was only in his mid-thirties," Acevedo writes, "Morrison was already exhibiting classic signs of pugilistic dementia. Slurred speech, forgetfulness, scattered thoughts, a scanty attention span. He increasingly suffered from paranoia. His IQ was measured at 78, which placed Morrison on the borderline for mental disability. Anyone who had heard Morrison speak after fights or read his interviews knew that he was an eloquent young man capable of expressing himself in complex sentences. By the time he hit rock bottom, that was no longer the case."

Morrison, Acevedo continues, "also suffered from the burnout effect of methamphetamines. And in the early 2000s, he was diagnosed with HIV-related encephalopathy. Combined with his career as a prizefighter, these afflictions left him with a tenuous grip on reality. ESPN interviewed Morrison in 2000 while he was serving out a term in a Texarkana lockup for a variety of drug-related charges. In his orange prison garb, Morrison looked like he had just returned from a week-long crank binge in Arkansas swampland. He was heavy-lidded; some of his teeth were missing; he spoke haltingly; many of his answers were rote; his hair had thinned into a wispy comb-over. And he seemed delusional."

Fast-forward to 2011. Morrison was arrested twice more on charges that included felony possession of controlled substances and misdemeanor possession of paraphernalia for use. Acevedo recreates what followed:

"The sports world is shocked to see the latest mug shot of Tommy Morrison, an image that seems to foreshadow death. Only forty-two years old, Morrison resembles a vagrant who has just returned from a harrowing ordeal. A video of his court appearance is even more disturbing. Morrison looks like a cross between a confused little boy and a senile old man. He is haggard, ashen, bewildered."

At that point, the criminal justice system applied what Acevedo calls "pragmatic mercy."

"Simply put," he writes, "Morrison is unfit for prison. He is, by then, unfit for anything. In less than two years, he will be dead."

In evaluating *The Duke*, one should begin with a thought from Acevedo himself, who cautions, "Any biographical narrative is bound to raise questions of veracity. The life of Tommy Morrison more so, perhaps, because of how much of it took place in half-light. Toughman contests, club fights in Wichita and Great Falls, orgies in rattletrap motels, stints in jail and prison, and night crawling with tweakers from crash pad to crash pad across the Southeast. By nature, Morrison seemed drawn to subterranean pursuits."

That said, Acevedo writes well. His tale moves briskly through Morrison's life from his hardscrabble origins to his self-destructive end. The recounting of Morrison's ring career doesn't have the depth and nuance of some of Acevedo's earlier writing about boxing. And there are times when he gives Morrison less credit than Tommy might deserve as a fighter.

But *The Duke* comes to life in Part II. The material dealing with Morrison's spiral into oblivion outside the ring is powerfully written and informative. Acevedo shows here that he's a very good writer.

When Marvin Hagler first walked into Goody Petronelli's gym, the trainer told him, "No matter how good you become as a fighter, you'll still get hit. No one likes to get hit because it hurts, and you're not gonna like it either."

The SuperFight:
Marvelous Marvin Hagler vs.
Sugar Ray Leonard

Sugar Ray Leonard and Marvin Hagler were two of the greatest fighters of all time. On April 6, 1987, they met in the ring at Caesars Palace in Las Vegas in one of the most anticipated fights ever. *The SuperFight* by Brian Doogan (published by Brian Doogan Media) revisits that historic encounter and puts it in context.

"Leonard," Doogan writes, "was Ali's successor, the most charismatic, bankable, and virtuoso exponent of his trade. The standard-bearer for his sport. Apolitical with multicultural appeal, courted by corporate America, championed by the TV networks, paraded and fawned over on the chat show circuit. The cool acceptable face of a dark, squalid, ultimately indefensible profession."

Or phrased differently, as Mike Tyson put it, "Ray Leonard was a pitbull with a pretty face" who became the highest-paid athlete of his time.

Hagler loved the craft and hated the business of boxing. His early years were spent in riot-torn Newark, New Jersey. His mother moved the family to Brockton, Massachusetts, where Marvin dropped out of high school after fathering a son. Trained and managed by Goody and Pat Petronelli, he earned his championship by cutting a wide swath through the middleweight division.

"Hagler has done everything you could ask of a champion," Hall of Fame great Archie Moore said after Marvin (or, as he was legally known by then, "Marvelous Marvin") destroyed Thomas Hearns over three of the most enthralling rounds in boxing history. "He's fought one top contender after another and beaten them all. I rate him right up there with Sugar Ray Robinson. He's a hard hitter with both hands. And he's cruel in the ring, like a great fighter must be."

Hagler was hard-working, disciplined, and honest. Pure fighter, if there is such a thing. "His aura," Doogan observes, "spoke for him."

"I've gotten meaner since I became champion," Hagler noted. "They're all trying to take something from me that I've worked long and hard for years for. And I like the feeling of being champ."

For most of their respective ring careers, Leonard and Hagler plied their trade in parallel universes, dominating the welterweight and middle-weight divisions. The thirteen-pound weight differential between them was considered too wide to bridge. From time to time, Ray dangled the possibility of a super-fight in front of Marvin in the manner of Lucy pulling the football away from Charlie Brown in the *Peanuts* comic strip of that era. But he was toying with Hagler. And over time, Marvin's resentment grew, fueled by the disparity in purses between them.

Mike Trainer was a constant throughout Leonard's ring career. Ray trusted the attorney to look after his business interests, and Trainer did so brilliantly.

Hagler's purse for his first pro fight was forty dollars. Leonard, the darling of the United States boxing team at the 1976 Olympics, made $50,000 for his pro debut. He earned $1 million for his first title opportunity against Wilfred Benítez. Hagler's first title challenge was against Vito Antoufermo on the undercard that night. Marvin was paid $40,000. And he got screwed by the judges, who ruled the bout a draw.

Four fights later, Hagler earned a second title shot, this time against Alan Minter, who he stopped in three rounds. Marvin's purse that night was $150,000. Meanwhile, Leonard was paid $17 million for two fights against Roberto Durán (a loss avenged in an immediate rematch) and $12 million (equal to more than $35 million today) for knocking out Thomas Hearns.

"No one," Doogan writes, "wanted to take a look beneath the mask that was Sugar Ray, the ATM machine for family and friends, the all-American and international star, [But] to Hagler, he was always 'pretty boy'—a description the middleweight king spat out with contempt. The antithesis in almost every respect of the spartan blue-collar outsider who, by overwhelming force of will, climbed the ranks to establish himself as the feared ruler of the sport's red-light district."

Five months after beating Hearns, Leonard disposed of Bruce Finch in three rounds. Then he suffered a detached retina and left boxing, only to return in 1984 to fight Kevin Howard. Howard knocked Ray down— the first time in Leonard's career that he'd been on the canvas. Ray prevailed on a ninth-round stoppage that brought his record to 33–1. But he'd looked mediocre, and the assumption was that his days as an elite fighter were over.

Meanwhile, Hagler was becoming increasingly marketable with victories over Durán and Hearns elevating him to superstar status. On March 3, 1986, he added to his laurels by stopping John Mugabi in eleven rounds.

But against Mugabi, Hagler seemed to be slipping a bit. And outside the ring, for the first time, he was growing ambivalent about fighting.

At the same time, Leonard was getting an itch that he had to scratch. Commenting during the telecast of Hagler–Hearns, Ray acknowledged, "I would be lying if I told you I didn't envy those two men up there right now. There is a lot you don't miss in boxing. You don't miss the roadwork while the rest of the world is sleeping. You don't miss all the hype, all the promotion. But you do miss moments like these. You miss the feeling that, for a little time, the whole world is looking at you and the guy you are fighting. You miss the fact that, for a few days of your life, you're at the dead center of the world."

Offers for Hagler vs. Leonard were forthcoming. Despite Hagler's ebbing desire, it was a fight that Marvin had to take. Bob Arum, who would promote the bout, said as much when he declared, "If Leonard decides not to accept the offer, I think Marvin would be delighted. He really and truly doesn't want to fight Leonard. He's doing it to protect his reputation."

Eventually, a deal was reached. For only the third time in his ring career, Leonard would be on the short end of a purse split. Leonard–Benitez and Durán–Leonard II had been the first two instances. This time, after all the revenue streams were added up, Team Hagler would take home roughly $20 million while Leonard's end would be $12 million.

But in exchange, Leonard received several significant concessions. The fight would be twelve rounds, not fifteen. It would be contested in a twenty-foot ring. The fighters would wear ten-ounce gloves instead of eight. And because Ray had previously suffered a detached retina, the fighters would wear thumbless gloves.

"I'm not coming back to have a career," Leonard said. "I've had a career. I want Marvin."

Hagler was a 7-to-2 betting favorite.

In the preceding five years, Leonard had fought once—his unimpressive outing at 149 pounds against Howard. Now he'd be fighting the dominant middleweight of his time and one of the greatest fighters ever.

Previously, Emanuel Steward (who trained Thomas Hearns) had opined, "A Hagler–Leonard fight would be a fraud on the public. It would be another Larry Holmes–Muhammad Ali show. A hoax."

The sporting press was in accord:

* Hugh McIlvanney (*The Observer*): "I think it's ludicrous that Sugar Ray should be able to come back after one fight in more than five years—nine very unimpressive rounds—and step into a world championship fight. We all love Sugar Ray. He possessed everything essential to the great man's fighting armoury. Superb technique, speed, fluency, imagination, punching power, and a strong chin. And behind his dazzling good looks and the readily summoned charm, there was the remorselessness of a street fighter. But what is being said about him now by his admirers relates mainly to what he was. I think he is more memory than substance."

* Jim Murray (*The Los Angeles Times*): "You look at Sugar Ray Leonard and you want to take him to lost-and-found and buy him an ice cream cone until you can find his mother and father. You look at Marvelous Marvin Hagler and you wonder where the police are when you need them. If this is a contest, so is a train wreck."

* Tom Boswell (*The Washington Post*): "Hagler is the embodiment of the fighter we don't want Leonard to fight. Hagler hurts you. He changes you. Permanently."

"If he's foolish enough to step in the ring with me, I'm foolish enough to rip his eye out," Hagler said ominously. "Nobody is going to want Leonard when I get through with him. I'm gonna rip his brains out. Ray says he'll use strategy. But I'll be using something called punching. This guy is just a pretty boy."

Sixty of sixty-seven writers polled on site predicted that Hagler would win, fifty-two of them by knockout.

"It was almost like we were going to a hanging," HBO commentator Barry Tompkins later reminisced. "That was the mood in the air that week in Las Vegas. People thought there's no way Ray Leonard can win this fight and, essentially, we're about to watch an execution."

"Maybe I don't hit as hard as Marvin, but I hit consistently," Leonard offered in response. "If I'd always heeded everybody's advice, I would have stayed in school and never boxed."

Hagler was thirty-two years old. Leonard was thirty. In 1987, that was getting on in age for a fighter.

Earlier in his career, Leonard had battled an addiction to cocaine. Now that was behind him. Hagler, by contrast, had dabbled with cocaine after beating Hearns. Except with cocaine, it's hard to just dabble.

More to the point: prior to fighting Leonard, Hagler had said, "For me, the fight with Tommy was World War I. This fight is World War II." But when the bell for round one against Leonard rang, Marvin didn't fight like it.

Richard Steele (who refereed Hagler–Leonard) later recalled, "I saw something different about Hagler. He wasn't himself. As the fight unfolded, I began to realize he was trying to be a boxer instead of the fighter he really was. His 'destruct and destroy' mindset was what got him to be the great fighter, the great champion he was. But Leonard had won the mental battle. He got Hagler to change his style."

Most notably, Hagler gave away the first three rounds by fighting from an orthodox stance instead of his usual southpaw stance. That would cost him dearly.

Equally important, Barry Tompkins later revealed that, before the fight, Leonard had confided in him, "I'm going to tell you how you beat Marvin Hagler. You've got to fight three times a round for fifteen seconds. At the beginning of the round, in the middle of the round, and you have to do it again at the end of the round. And you'll steal the fight."

When it was over, Dave Moretti scored the bout 115–113 for Leonard. Lou Filippo favored Hagler by a 115–113 margin. The deciding vote was cast by Jo-Jo Guerra, who seemed to have trouble understanding what he'd been watching and cast the deciding tally 118–110 in Leonard's favor. Guerra's scorecard cast a stench over the proceedings. Had he scored the bout 115–113 for Leonard, the verdict would have been less controversial.

For the record, I scored Hagler–Leonard twice—once in a theater watching on closed-circuit TV and later viewing a replay on television. Each time, I scored the bout a draw.

"The truth is really simple," Hagler said bitterly afterward. "And everybody knows it. Leonard didn't come to fight. He came to run all night. With the politics, I knew if Leonard stayed on his feet, I was probably gonna lose. And he ran and survived."

But Leonard wasn't trying to win a war. He was trying to outpoint an opponent and win a prizefight. As Doogan states, "Whatever the vagaries of the scoring, the reality is Hagler was unable to make good on his vow while Leonard, against all odds, continued to execute his battle plan."

Hagler never fought again. He retired and stayed retired, moving to Italy and landing roles in four action films.

"You always need to have another road ahead of you," Marvin said of his new life. "If you ever feel it's done, then it is done and you're done too. You've always got to keep reaching and striving."

Leonard, it turned out, was more of a junkie for boxing than Hagler was. Having engineered one of the greatest comebacks in boxing history, Ray would fight five more times over the next ten years, ending his illustrious career on losses to Terry Norris and Héctor Camacho, both of whom did to him what people had thought Hagler would do.

The SuperFight is a good book. Brian Doogan did his homework conscientiously. He writes smoothly and fashions compelling portraits of Leonard and Hagler, bringing both men to life. He recounts the key fights in each man's career leading up to their April 6, 1987, encounter and also their lives outside the ring, including Leonard being sexually abused multiple times as an adolescent, Ray's troubled first marriage, and the descent into cocaine that almost destroyed his life.

Hagler's life is similarly explored. One of many whimsical details Doogan recounts that caught my eye is the recollection of Robbie Sims (Marvin's half-brother) who says of their childhood years, "Every day, he made sure I made my bed, cleaned my side of the room, put my shoes away and the dirty clothes in the dirty-clothes bag."

Hagler succumbed to an apparent heart attack at age sixty-six on March 13, 2021 It's a tragedy that he died as young as he did.

*Hagler–Leonard was preceded by Hagler vs. Thomas Hearns—
a fight known simply as "The War."*

Hagler–Hearns and Three Rounds
for the Ages

It's a line in boxing's record book: April 15, 1985—Marvelous Marvin
Hagler vs. Thomas Hearns at Caesars Palace in Las Vegas—KO 3.

Hagler–Hearns was marketed as "The Fight" and later became known
as "The War." The combatants, United Press International reported,
fought like men fought "before the discovery of fire or the invention
of the wheel." "The way it turned out," famed sportswriter Jim Murray
wrote, "we'll all have nightmares for weeks."

Reminiscing about the first round, Larry Merchant recalled, "It was
as though you couldn't breathe for those three minutes. There'd been
an electric buzz around the fight all week, but people were expecting a
traditional boxing event. Once it started, there was a new story and the
realization that this was something they'd never seen before."

Don Stradley revisits this epic fight in *The War: Hagler–Hearns and
Three Rounds for the Ages* (Hamilcar Publications). His work comes on
the heels of Brian Doogan's book, *The SuperFight*, which chronicles the
historic encounter between Hagler and Ray Leonard two years later. In
some respects, the books cover similar terrain. But *The War* stands on its
own as an excellent recounting of a landmark fight—"boxing as it appears
in our imagination," Stradley writes, "wild and unbridled."

The War gives readers the usual biographical details about Hagler and
Hearns.

Hagler, Stradley recounts, was "the eldest child in a fatherless family
of seven, an introverted lonesome boy, likely to sit alone on his fire escape,
playing with pigeons and injured animals. At fourteen, he dropped out
of school and went to work in a toy factory to help support the family."

Hearns, Stradley tells us, "dropped out of Detroit's Northeastern
High School during his senior year to pursue boxing full-time. His amateur career had taken him around the country and to Asia and Europe.

But his schoolwork suffered; he'd been required to repeat eleventh grade."

Stradley also sprinkles in lesser-known facts. Writing about the collection of animals (including a macaw, a bulldog, and a cougar named Atomic) that Hearns maintained on his estate, Stradley reports, "There was the crazy night when Hearns wanted to prove he was indeed quick as a cat and started shooting his right hand in the vicinity of Atomic's head. The animal whirled, opened its mouth, and clamped down on his fist. Horrified that his moneymaking knuckles might be damaged, Hearns had to choke the cat with his left hand to get his right hand out of its mouth. Hearns bled all over his expensive home."

As for Hagler, Stradley writes, "Alex Wallau, executive producer at ABC Sports, allegedly told Hagler's camp that, if he wanted to be known as 'Marvelous,' he should go to court and make it official. This was typical of the way Hagler was treated at the time. ABC never had a problem calling Ray Leonard 'Sugar Ray,' but wouldn't call Marvin 'marvelous.'"

There's a long section in the book—maybe too long—on the difficulties encountered in making the fight, which was first announced for May 24, 1982. There's also an entertaining recreation of the fourteen-day, twenty-one-city pre-fight publicity tour when the promotion finally got off the ground.

Stradley hits his stride in describing the scene in Las Vegas in the days leading up to the fight. Al Bernstein told him, "Las Vegas was on fire that week. The event took on a life of its own. During that period, Las Vegas was in transition. It was between the Rat Pack era and the corporate era. And Las Vegas was not a respected place. People thought of Las Vegas as an absurd cliché, some cornball place your uncle went to." But that week, Bernstein continued, "you could feel the energy flying through the air. I really believe Hagler–Hearns put Las Vegas over the top."

The scene on fight day is particularly well told. A few samples:

* "Hector Camacho occupied a spot by the Caesars Palace swimming pool in nothing but some gold jewelry, blue sneakers, and a leopard-skin slingshot bikini. Trying to snatch a bit of spotlight for himself, the twenty-two-year-old Puerto Rican lightweight burst into a loud rendition of Madonna's hit from the previous fall, '*Like a Virgin*.' While Camacho sang and strutted, artist LeRoy

Neiman sketched him. When Neiman presented the finished drawing, Camacho asked him to pencil in more muscles."
★ "There was certainly reason to believe the Las Vegas casinos would've
preferred a Hearns victory. The money being dropped on Las Vegas
that week wasn't coming from Boston. It was Hearns's followers
coming down from Detroit. So of course, Las Vegas wanted Hearns
to come back again and again. Hearns brought the high rollers. It
was all Detroit street money."

And there was Pete Hamill's take on the scene: "They came piling
out of cabs and airport limousines: cartoon Detroit pimps, overdone fancy
ladies, bi-continental drug dealers weighed down by chains, medallions
and Rolexes. They were here for Hearns and Hagler. But Sinatra was
at the Golden Nugget for two nights so you could also see second-rate
hoodlums from the East. All wandering through the neon wilderness of
girlie shows, ninety-nine-cent breakfasts, and the pervasive intoxicating
apparatus of gambling."

Hagler was thirty years old. Hearns was twenty-six. Marvin had been
an early 6-to-5 favorite. By fight week, those numbers were reversed.
Eventually, the odds wound up even.

Hagler preferred the traditional fifteen-round championship distance
to the newly implemented twelve-round limit but pledged to "put fifteen
rounds into twelve." Asked about the fact that many people were picking
Hearns to win, Marvin said simply, "We all have our ideas about this fight,
but only Tommy and me can get at the truth." As for Hearns's prediction
that he'd knock Hagler out in the third round, Marvin responded, "He
says he'll knock me out in three because he can't count past three."

The fight was contested on a Monday evening. Closed-circuit television was the driving economic force behind it and, in those days, most
theaters were unavailable for boxing on Saturday night. Saturday was
"movie date" night. The weigh-in, as was standard practice back then, was
held at 8:00 a.m. on the day of the fight.

Hagler's fight plan was simple.

Tony Petronelli's father managed Hagler and his uncle trained Marvin.
"We were not training for a boxing match," Tony told Stradley. "We
wanted a street fight. We knew Hearns was a gunfighter and he'd trade

punches with you. So it was all a matter of whose chin would hold up. We knew Marvin had one of the best chins ever, and Hearns wasn't known for having a great chin. The plan was to have Marvin jump all over him. It wasn't a gamble."

"This fight comes down to who can take the hardest shot, who can take the most punishment," Hagler prophesied.

The War unfolded accordingly. Hearns broke his right hand in round one. After that," Stradley writes, "Hagler was fighting to do damage, while Hearns was fighting to survive." The end came with a minute left in round three and Hearns no longer able to defend himself.

Al Michaels and Al Bernstein handled the closed-circuit commentating duties. Barry Tompkins and Larry Merchant called the fight on a tape-delay basis for HBO.

"They both left everything they had in the ring," Merchant said later. "They poured everything in their minds and bodies into their fight. Those eight minutes transformed Hagler from a terrific pro into a star and one of the great middleweights of all time."

As for the fact that there was no rematch, Merchant observed, "I can't imagine a rematch being as good. It's a beautiful picture that has been framed and can't be duplicated. That was the way it was supposed to be. That's the way it stands."

The saga of Hagler–Hearns is a good story and Stradley tells it well. *The War* ends with a nod to the future. Hagler–Hearns made Hagler vs. Ray Leonard inevitable. But there's also a poignant nod to the past.

Hours after Hagler–Hearns ended, Wallace Matthews (who covered the bout for *Newsday*) was introduced to Sugar Ray Robinson, who was suffering from dementia and would die four years later at the much-too-young age of sixty-seven. They chatted briefly and the greatest fighter who ever lived asked Matthews, "Did I ever fight those guys?"

Marvin Hagler adjusted well to life after boxing. Sadly, that life was too short.

Marvelous Marvin Hagler:
In Memoriam
(1954–2021)

Marvelous Marvin Hagler, who was universally respected within the boxing community and was one of boxing's greatest champions, died suddenly on March 13 at age sixty-six.

Usually, there are warning signs before a great fighter dies. He's old. Or he's relatively young but in failing health. Newspapers dust off their obituaries. The end is near.

There was no such warning here. The news came in a post on Hagler's official fan club page signed by his wife, Kay, that read, "I am sorry to make a very sad announcement. Today, unfortunately, my beloved husband Marvelous Marvin passed away unexpectedly [near] his home here in New Hampshire. Our family requests that you respect our privacy during this difficult time."

No cause of death was announced. TMZ later reported, "One of Hagler's sons, James, tells TMZ his father was taken to a hospital in New Hampshire earlier on Saturday March 13 after experiencing trouble breathing and chest pains at home. We're told about four hours later the family was notified he'd passed away."

Hagler came up the hard way. Most fighters do. He was born in Newark, New Jersey, on May 23, 1954. His mother moved the family to the blue-collar town of Brockton, Massachusetts, in the wake of the 1967 riots that devastated Newark. Marvin started boxing in Brockton and was discovered in a local gym by Goody and Pat Petronelli—brothers who would train and manage him throughout his career.

Hagler's creed was simple: "Anytime, any place, in anyone's backyard." He turned pro on May 18, 1973, fought his entire career at middleweight, and compiled a 62–3–2 (52 KOs) record over the course of fourteen years. He fought with a withering seek-and-destroy style and was as relentless in training as he was in fights. He seized the middleweight throne with a third-round knockout of Alan Minter in London in 1980 and successfully defended it twelve times. His most notable victory was a third-round stoppage of Thomas Hearns in a nonstop slugfest that's widely regarded as one of the most thrilling fights in boxing history. The only blemish on his record that he didn't avenge by knockout was a loss by decision to Sugar Ray Leonard.

After the Leonard fight, Hagler (one month shy of his thirty-third birthday) walked away from boxing. He moved to Italy, learned Italian, and played the hero in grade-B action movies. He was a boxing success story—a great fighter who retired in good health with money in the bank and stayed retired.

One anecdote speaks volumes. Flying home from Las Vegas after an eight-figure payday, Hagler called his wife on the telephone. Phones on planes were a novelty in those days and were activated by using a credit card. Marvin spoke with his wife for about a minute before telling her, "I got to hang up now. I don't know how much this thing costs."

How good a fighter was Hagler?

Six years ago, I conducted a poll to rank the greatest middleweights of modern times. The contenders were limited to the post–World War II era and did not include fighters like Stanley Ketchel and Harry Greb because there isn't enough film footage available to properly evaluate them.

The nine fighters under consideration, listed alphabetically, were Nino Benvenuti, Gennady Golovkin, Marvin Hagler, Bernard Hopkins, Roy Jones, Jake LaMotta, Carlos Monzón, Sugar Ray Robinson, and James Toney. The panelists were asked to predict the outcome of every fight had each of these fighters fought the other eight in a round-robin fantasy tournament.

Twenty-four experts participated in the ranking process. They included matchmakers, trainers, fighters, historians, and media representatives ranging from Teddy Atlas and Russell Peltz to Bruce Trampler and Mike Tyson. The electors were to assume that both fighters in each fight were at the point in their respective careers when they were able to make 160 pounds and were capable of duplicating their best 160-pound performance.

The incomparable Sugar Ray Robinson finished in first place. Hagler beat out (or one might say "beat up") the other contenders to finish as the #2 ranked middleweight of modern times.

Putting matters in further perspective, I once asked Bernard Hopkins how he would have fared against Sugar Ray Robinson.

"Sugar Ray Robinson at 147 pounds was close to perfect," Hopkins answered. "But at middleweight, he was beatable. I would have fought Ray Robinson in close and not given him room to do his thing. He'd make me pay a physical price. But at middleweight, I think I'd wear him down and win."

And how did Hopkins think he would have done against Hagler?

"Me and Marvin Hagler would have been a war," Bernard responded. "We'd both be in the hospital afterward with straws in our mouth. We'd destroy each other. My game-plan would be, rough him up, box, rough him up, box. You wouldn't use judges for that fight. You'd go by the doctors' reports."

There came a time in Hagler's ring career when he decided that he should be introduced at fights and referenced in the media as "Marvelous Marvin Hagler." But as Muhammad Ali learned after changing his name from Cassius Clay, the boxing world isn't always compliant in matters of nomenclature. Finally, after being introduced without the "Marvelous" at one fight too many, Hagler went to court and legally changed his name to Marvelous Marvin Hagler.

Hagler was a true champion in and out of the ring. He earned the right to be called "Marvelous."

Everything that Nico Ali Walsh does in boxing is viewed through the prism of his grandfather's legacy.

Some Thoughts on Watching Nico Ali Walsh Fight

On December 11, 2021, twenty-one-year-old Nico Ali Walsh won a majority decision over Reyes Sanchez on the undercard of Vasiliy Lomachenko vs. Richard Commey at Madison Square Garden.

I was a guest at the wedding decades ago when Nico's parents got married. And I knew his grandfather well. Nico's grandfather was Muhammad Ali.

Nico grew up watching videos of fights with Muhammad by his side. "His favorite fighter to watch," Nico remembers, "was himself." And while people who lived through Ali's glory years were saddened by Muhammad's physical decline, Nico had a different perspective.

"My grandfather was having physical problems by the time I was born," Nico recalls. "Slow, soft-spoken; that was how I was used to seeing him. That was the only Muhammad Ali I knew. So his condition wasn't as hard for me to accept as it was for some people. In fact, I remember watching tapes of him when he was young and saying to myself, 'Wow! Who is that guy?'"

Nico had his first amateur fight at age nine and participated in close to thirty bouts over the course of ten years. Then he decided to try his hand at professional boxing, which led to a meeting with Bob Arum at Top Rank.

Mike Joyce (Nico's uncle, who is also his manager) took the lead at the meeting on Nico's behalf. Joyce is a Chicago attorney and understands both the sport and business of boxing. His mission is to protect Nico as best he can within the realities of the sweet science. Nico and his parents (Rasheda and Robert Walsh) were also at the meeting.

Nico, it was explained to Top Rank, wasn't focused on belts. He wouldn't be boxing with the expectation of becoming a great fighter. He would be boxing because he wants to challenge himself, experience the core of what his grandfather experienced in the ring, and fight in places with connections to his grandfather.

"Doing what my grandfather did makes me feel closer to him," Nico says.

Nico made his pro debut on August 14 in Las Vegas (where Muhammad Ali fought seven times). His opponent was a South Carolinian named Jordan Weeks who came into the bout with a respectable 4–1 record and had been chosen for his lack of ring prowess. The fight was heavily hyped because of Nico's lineage and was covered by worldwide media outlets such as the *New York Times* and CNN.

ESPN televised the bout and made a point during its telecast of saying that Nico was wearing trunks that Everlast had made for his grandfather. Indeed, blow-by-blow commentator Joe Tessitore spoke so reverentially of the trunks that one might have concluded they were a relic on par with the Shroud of Turin.

However, according to Craig Hamilton (the foremost boxing memorabilia dealer in the United States), Everlast made hundreds of trunks with the same Ali label. Their manufacture started circa 1973, and many of the trunks never reached Ali. They were siphoned off for resale by members of Muhammad's entourage or given to third parties by Everlast. Also, Nico weighed in for his pro debut at 162 pounds. And from 1973 on, Muhammad fought at weights ranging from 212 to 236 pounds. Boxing trunks aren't one-size-fits-all.

Nico, in his pro debut, knocked Weeks out in the first round.

"He's fighting to keep the Ali name alive," Tessitore gushed.

Let's get real. With or without Nico's ring career, the Ali name will live forever.

After his pro debut, Nico journeyed to Atlanta (where his grandfather knocked out Jerry Quarry in 1970 and lit the cauldron at the 1996 Olympic Games). This time, the opponent was thirty-six-year-old James Westley (a novice with one pro bout on his ring résumé). Nico did some effective body work against Westley and hit hard enough to do damage against a fighter without much of a punch or chin. There were two knockdowns. KO 3.

I met Nico for the first time when he was at Gleason's Gym for a light workout three days before fighting Sanchez at Madison Square

Garden. People whose judgment I trust had told me that he's a nice young man. They were right.

Nico has a fighter's nose and doesn't look at all like his famous grandfather. With his graceful movement and lithe frame, he could pass for a ballet dancer.

Muhammad Ali fused his own father's loud, bombastic behavior and his mother's loving sweetness into one cosmic personality. Nico exudes his grandfather's gentle side. He likes people, and people like him. He's unfailingly polite and has a kind word for everyone he meets. "I don't have a problem inflicting pain when I'm in the ring," Nico says. "It's part of the job. But other than that, I try to be nice."

Nico seems sincere when talking about his long-term goals. "I love boxing," he says. "I'm passionate about boxing, but it's not my life. I want to do something with my life that makes people feel good about themselves."

He's also intellectually curious and has one semester remaining as an undergraduate at the University of Nevada, Las Vegas where he's majoring in business entrepreneurship. While in New York for the Sanchez fight, he juggled fight preparation with online exams in marketing, business law, and geology.

Pressed for more about himself, Nico volunteers that he values alone time and likes to do his own thing. "And in some ways," he adds, "I'm an old soul." Bolstering the truth of this latter statement, he points to his workout playlist, which includes songs by Frank Sinatra, Elvis Presley, the Beatles, the Temptations, Little Richard, and Bobby Vinton.

Hall of Fame matchmaker Bruce Trampler confirms the point, noting that watching Nico in the gym was the first time he ever saw a fighter working out to the tune of "Red Roses for a Blue Lady."

Like his grandfather, Nico is a practicing Muslim. He takes his religion seriously.

"I don't drink, smoke, or party," he says of his lifestyle. But there's a twist.

"After my grandfather died," Nico explains, "I wanted to honor him in my own way, so I got several tattoos that paid tribute to him. As a Muslim, I shouldn't have tattoos. So I'm not a perfect Muslim."

Muhammad Ali fought three times at the "old" Madison Square Garden on Eighth Avenue between Forty-Ninth and Fiftieth Streets in

Manhattan. Nico would be fighting Sanchez in the current MSG, which opened in 1968 and hosted Muhammad on five occasions (including the historic "Fight of the Century" against Joe Frazier fifty years ago).

Lomachenko–Commey was a hard sell. The arena, which seats 20,000 for boxing, was configured for half that number. The announced attendance on fight night was 8,555.

Sanchez had a 6–0 (2 KOs) ring ledger. But those numbers were deceiving. His previous opponents had a composite record of 4 wins against 21 losses at the time he fought them. And he's from Kansas. Boxing in Kansas is like mountain climbing in London.

Nico has reasonably fast hands. But he doesn't move his head enough (particularly when punching) and brings his jab back low. Watching him hit the pads with Mike Joyce at Gleason's Gym, the sound I heard was a pop, not a whack. He's trained by Sugar Hill, which might not be a good fit. And he doesn't have the hunger or wellspring of anger that can fuel a fighter to be great.

Top Rank has matched Nico against opponents who shouldn't be able to hurt him. But every opponent that Nico fights is motivated to beat Muhammad Ali's grandson. And "hurt" is a relative term in boxing. As Joyce notes, "Even a powder-puff puncher can hurt you."

Once Nico vs. Sanchez began, it was clear that Sanchez had limited physical gifts and only basic boxing skills. But those skills were more than Nico's first two opponents had to work with. Nico went headhunting in round one. In round two, he opened Sanchez up by going to the body and followed with hurting blows up top. But in round three, the tide turned. Nico tired and got hit in the head by punches he shouldn't have been hit with. Right hand after right hand. A lot of them. It was painful to watch. I'm sure it was painful for Nico, too. Then, in round four, Sanchez tired and stopped throwing his right hand with conviction.

I scored the bout 39–38 in Nico's favor, calling the last round even. Alan Nance gave the fourth round to Sanchez, making his scorecard a draw. Robin Taylor gave the final stanza to Nico for a 39–37 verdict in his favor. Then came the shocker. James Kinney gave every round (including the third) to Nico.

This isn't the first time that viewers have seen Kinney embarrass boxing with his scorecard. When Joe Smith fought Jesse Hart on ESPN last year, two of the judges were on the mark, scoring the bout 98–91 and 97–92 for Smith. Inexplicably, Kinney's scorecard favored Hart.

Teddy Atlas once addressed the issue of bad scoring in boxing with the observation, "It's a terrible situation when the best I can say for some of these judges is that they're incompetent. Because the other alternative, if they're not incompetent, is that they're corrupt."

The fewer fights that James Kinney judges in the future, the better.

What lies ahead for Nico in boxing? Continuing the theme of his fighting at sites identified with his grandfather, there's talk of fights in London, Louisville, Miami Beach, and Chicago. Zaire and the Philippines aren't on the list, but Saudi Arabia would like a piece of the action.

Meanwhile, let's state the obvious. Nico is twenty-one years old. One month after Cassius Clay turned twenty-two, he defeated Sonny Liston to claim the heavyweight championship of the world. We're talking about two vastly different levels of boxing.

Nico reveres his grandfather's legacy. He understands which one was Muhammad and which is Nico. But there's another matter to consider when contemplating Nico's ring future—brain damage.

Boxing is like cigarette smoking. People know that it's bad for them, but some people do it anyway. Safe boxing is an oxymoron. All boxers get hit in the head in fights and while sparring.

Getting hit in the head leads to brain damage. The only question is "how much?" Every punch to the head carries with it the potential to cause serious damage. Permanent damage.

Think for a moment about the distortion of a fighter's face that we see when we look at a photograph taken from the optimum angle at the exact moment a hard punch lands.

When Nico boxes, he inflicts brain damage on his opponents too.

After watching Nico's fight against Sanchez live from ringside, I watched it again on television the following morning. I counted 25 blows to Nico's head in round three alone.

It would be a tragedy if, at some time in the future, Nico's physical condition were to mirror that of his famous grandfather.

Nico will be protected as well as a fighter can be protected by his management team and promoter. Top Rank knows how to build a fighter, commercially and in terms of his ring prowess. Sanctioning bodies will bend over backward to find belts that Nico can fight for. He'll be well paid. Close decisions are likely to go his way. That said, I agree with Mike Joyce who, three days before Nico's fight against Sanchez, told me in Gleason's Gym, "If I had my druthers, we'd call it a day after this fight."

Whenever Nico fights, my heart will be in his gloves. But I'd rather that he not fight again. Muhammad Ali sacrificed so much at the altar of boxing—more than enough to obviate the need for sacrifices by any member of his family in the years to come.

★★★

Note to the reader: The original plan was for Nico to have a handful of fights leading to a big payday somewhere in the Middle East followed by his retirement from boxing. Then things began to change. Mike Joyce dropped out of the management team and Bob Walsh (Nico's father) took over. "Nico has the bug," Bob told me. And Nico added, "When I was little, I said I wanted to be a world champion like my grandfather. But it was like saying I wanted to be a comic book superhero. Now it's attainable. It's real."

On October 29, 2022, Nico fought on the undercard of Vasiliy Lomachenko vs. Jamaine Ortiz at Madison Square Garden. Billy Wagner (his carefully chosen opponent from Montana) had toughman skills. Nico staggered him with a jab in round one that, judging by the blood, broke Wagner's nose. Thereafter, he controlled the fight with his jab en route to a unanimous-decision triumph. But Nico got hit with punches that a good boxer shouldn't get hit with. And he'll get hit with more of them as his career unfolds.

In recent years, Oscar De La Hoya has gone through some hard times. This column was reminder of his importance to boxing.

Oscar De La Hoya: An Appreciation

No fighter gets out of boxing unscathed.

No fighter goes into boxing unscathed either.

For much of his life, Oscar De La Hoya has struggled with demons outside the ring and in it. He has battled substance abuse, been betrayed by people he trusted, and faced other formidable challenges that are a matter of public record. He emerged from the 1992 Olympics at age nineteen with a gold medal in the lightweight division and became known worldwide as "The Golden Boy." But he was more complex than people imagined and bruised easily on the inside. His life was often far from golden.

As an adolescent, De La Hoya built his life around boxing. "There was a time when I was fourteen or fifteen," he later reminisced, "when I realized that someday I could make a living from boxing. At that point, I began to focus more on boxing than on school."

He won his first pro title at age twenty-one. The world was his oyster, or so it seemed. He was so fresh and young. Dr. Margaret Goodman conducted her first pre-fight physical with Oscar that year. "I remember asking him how many years he would fight," Goodman recalls. "He told me, 'I am going to retire at twenty-six.'"

He was ten years off the mark.

Fighters are paid for their marketability (which is different from their ability although the two are often entwined). De La Hoya was the right man in the right place at the right time. Initially, the powers that be in boxing embraced him as "the anti-Tyson." Then he benefited from the absence of a true heavyweight champion that the sport could rally around.

He loved the limelight and the big event. His nineteen fights on pay-per-view generated 13,850,000 buys.

153

"A lot of people think I had everything handed to me on a silver platter," De La Hoya said when he was in his prime. "People see the actual fight and say, 'Wow, he won all this money in one night.' But it's not that easy. People don't realize how many sacrifices I've had to make over the years. It was a long road to where I'm at now. One of the things that bothers me most is that very few people really understand what it means to be a fighter. It's not easy being an athlete, especially at this level, and on top of that, being a fighter."

He was always willing to go in tough. De La Hoya had ten fights against men who were subsequently inducted into the International Boxing Hall of Fame. That number will rise as more of Oscar's opponents such as Manny Pacquiao enter the hallowed halls in Canastota. BoxRec. com lists him as having fought 26 times against men who were current or former world champions and winning titles in six different weight classes.

One gauge of celebrity status is name recognition. Like Madonna Ciccone and Oprah Winfrey, De La Hoya became a first-name phenomenon.

In his glory years, Oscar was a superb ambassador for boxing. He mattered to people who didn't care about the sport. He was their window onto the sweet science. And when they looked at him, the view was good.

De La Hoya talked with fans, posed for pictures, and signed autographs. "It's tiring sometimes," he admitted. "I'll be out on the street with my wife. We'll just want to be alone and people will come over to me constantly. But when it doesn't happen, if I go somewhere and no one comes up to me, I miss it. So I guess you can say that I love it, I hate it, and I can't live without it."

He was clean-cut with no tattoos or body piercings. Men admired him; teenage girls adored him. He was conscious of the image he projected and worked a room as well as anyone. Many high-profile athletes arrive at functions, sit at a table surrounded by bodyguards, and talk only with people they already know. Once Oscar arrived, he moved from person to person, saying hello to everyone.

He was a crossover star of the highest order. One could check off the boxes . . . Olympic gold medal . . . movie-star handsome . . . bilingual. And he could fight.

Oscar was also a symbol of Hispanic American empowerment.

In creating Golden Boy Promotions, De La Hoya leveraged his marketability as a fighter to become more successful as a promoter than any fighter before or since. He was the principal shareholder in Golden Boy Sports and Entertainment Group, which had five subsidiaries: (1) Golden Boy Promotions; (2) Golden Boy Management, which represented fighters; (3) Golden Boy Television and Film, which produced programming; (4) Golden Boy Videos, which owned visual rights to fights including his own; and (5) Golden Boy Music, which owned the rights to CDs and music videos.

Golden Boy Real Estate Group owned a large stake in an office tower in downtown Los Angeles and a minority interest in a second office tower in New York. Golden Boy Corporate Holdings had an interest in CPK Media, which gave it a stake in *La Opinion* (then the largest Spanish-language daily in the United States) and *El Diario– La Prensa* (the nation's oldest Spanish-language newspaper). De La Hoya also had endorsement contracts with Visa and Nestlé and a licensing deal for his own line of clothing.

And, oh yes. Oscar owned a 25 percent interest in the Houston Dynamo soccer club that he sold last year for a sum reported to be in excess of $50 million.

We live in an age when people—particularly young people—tend to be oblivious to what happened and who made it happen in an earlier time. They should understand that Oscar De La Hoya's importance radiated far beyond boxing. In and out of the ring, he lit up the sky when he was young.

In Praise of Larry Holmes

I'm a big Larry Holmes fan. I met him in 1984 shortly after I began writing about boxing. We chatted briefly and I felt a fan's excitement at being in his presence. Over the years, I've been with him on numerous occasions. He's unpretentious with a certain nobility about him, which is fitting because he's boxing royalty.

Holmes was born in Cuthbert, Georgia, in 1949 and grew up poor in Easton, Pennsylvania. He turned pro in 1973 and, in effect, had two ring careers. In the first, he was heavyweight champion of the world with a 48–0 record and defining victories over Ken Norton, Earnie Shavers, and Gerry Cooney sandwiched around the sad dismantling of an aging Muhammad Ali. In the second—with Father Time diminishing his skills—Holmes lost his title by decision to Michael Spinks, came out on the short end of a highly questionable verdict in a rematch, and was stopped by Mike Tyson (the only "KO by" in Larry's 75-bout career).

Holmes had a nasty right hand and one of the best jabs in boxing history. Derek Bryant (who sparred with Larry) said of that jab, "I never saw it coming. I only saw it going back." But there were times when Holmes over-committed on the jab and lifted his chin when he threw it. That left him vulnerable to a well-timed counter-right (as Earnie Shavers, Renaldo Snipes, and Tyson demonstrated). Each of those men knocked Holmes woozy. And each time, Larry got up.

"First you get up," Holmes explained. "Then you worry about whether or not you're all right."

He knocked Shavers and Snipes out.

Most experts put Holmes on the short list of great heavyweight champions of all time. One way or another, he found a way to beat people up.

He has also been a good citizen and avoided the pitfalls that some elite athletes fall prey to. There are no newspaper accounts of Holmes being arrested with a gun or Holmes sexually assaulting a woman. Indeed, one night over dinner, Larry told me, "All these athletes and celebrities and other people who force themselves on women; there's no excuse for that. 'No' means no. Anybody can understand that. 'No' is the first word you learn after 'mama' and 'dada.'"

It wasn't all smooth sailing between Larry and myself. In 1990, while conducting research for a biography of Muhammad Ali, I traveled with Ali to Indonesia, where among other things, we attended a Larry Holmes singing engagement at the Sahid Jaya Hotel in Jakarta. Afterward, I wrote a concert review that appeared in *The National* and was less than complementary. Larry telephoned and screamed at me for forty-five minutes. Part of me was honored. I told myself, "Larry Holmes, one of the greatest fighters of all time, thinks my writing is important enough to spend forty-five minutes on the phone with me." And part of me was worried: "Larry Holmes, one of the greatest fighters of all time, is really pissed."

For almost a year after that, Larry refused to speak to me. Then he decided he would say hello but not shake hands. But beneath his gruff exterior, Larry is a softie at heart. Eventually, he forgave me. Subsequently, we went on a multi-city tour together, hosting a series of cocktail receptions with Angelo Dundee on behalf of Punch Cigars. We've appeared jointly on TV shows. In 1999, Diane Holmes (Larry's wife) invited me to a surprise party to celebrate Larry's fiftieth birthday at a restaurant that he owned in Easton.

I have fond memories of that night, the most enduring of which is Larry's response when he walked into the restaurant and everyone shouted "Surprise!"

Larry stared in astonishment. Then he went over to the bar and announced that, from that point on, the food was free but people at the party would pay for their own drinks.

Surprise! Like the rest of us, Larry likes money.

"The best thing about being a fighter," Larry has said, "is making money. Why do football players play football? For the money. Why do basketball players play basketball? For the money. Why do baseball players play baseball? For the money. I didn't fight to entertain people. I fought to get paid. Nobody was allowed to punch me in my face for free."

I asked him once, "Suppose you could travel back in a time machine and fight any heavyweight champion in history. Who would you want to fight?"

"If the money is the same," Larry answered, "tell me which one is the worst fighter, and that's the guy I want to fight."

Larry always spoke his mind.

"I always told the truth as I saw it," he says. "That's the way I am. Some people don't like it, but I call things the way I see them. If I'm wrong, I can say I'm sorry afterwards."

Another time, when I asked Larry to evaluate his place in boxing history, he responded, "To me, I'm better than Ali ever was. I'm better than Joe Louis ever was. In my opinion; my opinion. And I have the right to say that about myself."

If Larry at his best fought Ali at his best, I'd pick Ali. But it wouldn't be a walk in the park. And if they fought ten times, Larry would win some of them.

Years ago, Larry told me, "None of us is promised tomorrow. If I go twenty-five more years, that's a blessing. But if I don't, I've done my thing."

He's still doing his thing. And he deserves this special issue of *The Ring* devoted to his accomplishments. The nicest thing for me about writing this column is that it gives me the chance to tell Larry how much I like him and how much I appreciate what he has meant to boxing.

According to the powers that be at Madison Square Garden, Jake Paul vs. Hasim Rahman Jr. would have been the 1,750th fight card held at the fabled arena. It's safe to say that, when Joe Louis, Rocky Marciano, Sugar Ray Robinson, and Muhammad Ali plied their trade at "The Mecca of Boxing," they didn't envision Jake Paul.

Jake Paul, Boxing, and the Fight that Wasn't

No sport honors its past more than boxing does. And no sport does more to disrespect it.

On August 6, 2022, social media personality turned boxer Jake Paul was expected to fight Hasim Rahman Jr. in the big arena at Madison Square Garden. The scheduled event was heralded by massive publicity. The headline bout and key supporting contests (most notably, Amanda Serrano vs. 25-to-1 underdog Brenda Karen Carabajal) were to be televised in the United States on Showtime-PPV and in the United Kingdom by DAZN.

Then the walls came tumbling down.

There have always been circus-like sideshows in boxing. In the 1800s, John L. Sullivan fought all comers in cross-country tours. More than a century later, adult glamour model Jordan Carver and adult film star Melanie Muller did battle in Düsseldorf, Germany, over four heated rounds made notable by the fact that Michael Buffer served as ring announcer for the contest.

Muhammad Ali squared off against Antonio Inoki and Lyle Alzado. Chuck Wepner faced Andre the Giant. Mark Gastineau and Jose Canseco tried their hand at ring combat. Danny Bonaduce (*The Partridge Family*) fought Barry Williams (*The Brady Bunch*). Manute Bol exchanged punches with William "the Refrigerator" Perry. Tonya Harding took on Paula Jones. Joey Buttafuoco (lover of Amy Fisher a/k/a "the Long Island Lolita") traded blows with Chyna (who was billed by the World Wrestling Federation as "The Ninth Wonder of the World," Andre the Giant being #8).

But these events were sideshows. The difference now is that the side-shows are becoming boxing's showcase events. More and more, trash boxing is how the sport is being portrayed by the powers that be and perceived by the general public.

Enter Jake Paul, whose videos have engendered hundreds of millions of views on social media platforms.

Paul is a twenty-five-year-old entertainer with various antisocial acts on his résumé. On April 9, 2021, a twenty-four-year-old woman named Justine Paradise (a "TikTok star" with more than 500,000 followers of her own) made a more serious allegation when she posted a twenty-minute video on YouTube in which she accused Jake of sexually assaulting her at his Los Angeles home in 2019.

"Sex is very special and very important to me," Paradise said in her post. "Normally, everybody respects me when I don't want to do sexual things, so I thought that it was fine if I went in his room. I thought it would be fine to kiss him because I thought he would stop if I didn't want to do anything else."

But according to Paradise, Jake then grabbed her face, forced her to perform oral sex, and touched her in inappropriate places. More specifically, she stated that "Jake Paul fucked my face without consent. I couldn't tell him to stop. He just shoved himself in me. He didn't ask for consent or anything. That's not okay. On no level at all is that okay. Just because I let you kiss me and I let you hold my hand and I let you dance with me in your room, that doesn't give you the right to come in my mouth."

As of July 30, 2022, more than 1.9 million people had viewed Paradise's YouTube post. Paul has denied the allegations through counsel and in his own Twitter post.

In 2018, Jake ventured into boxing with an amateur fight against another social media personality named Deji Olatunji. Talking with Teddy Atlas about that encounter earlier this year, Jake (who shares a January 17 birthdate with Muhammad Ali) recalled, "I was sick of doing YouTube and sick of the entertainment industry. As time progressed, I realized it wasn't who I was. And when I got the opportunity to box another YouTuber, I picked up the gloves and began training the next day and fell in love with the sport. When I won my first fight, that was the best feeling and the most accomplished I've ever felt."

Sixteen months later, Jake turned pro. Since then, he has put together a 5–0 (4 KOs) ring record with victories over Ali Eson Gib (another social media personality), Nate Robinson (a retired NBA player), Ben Askren (a retired MMA combatant), and Tyron Woodley (another retired MMA combatant who Jake fought twice). None of these men had boxed professionally before and none have boxed professionally since.

When Jake began boxing, he brought his social media following with him. That made him marketable. Unlike many of today's highly paid fighters, he can generate the revenue from ticket sales and pay-per-view buys to cover his paycheck without suckering a gullible investor or ill-informed television executive.

He's also athletically gifted or he wouldn't have been able to accomplish what he has done in the ring so far. He has been learning the fundamentals of boxing and worked to become a better fighter. At this point, he's certainly better than a Golden Gloves novice.

But a lot of people are offended by the fact that Jake is being packaged as a boxing star. Elliot Worsell (writing for *Boxing News*) likened his ring outings to "fast food sold at premium prices" and observed, "Jake Paul's pull has little to do with the quality of the matchup and everything to do with Paul himself who has made a career out of being the center of his own universe. Boxing fans, or at least some of them, struggle to understand this. Yet Jake Paul fans not only understand it but are so conditioned to it being normal they will never even so much as question it. To them, so long as Jake Paul is seen wearing boxing gloves and throwing punches in a boxing ring, he is, with no hint of irony, a professional boxer. It doesn't matter how he looks in the process of throwing those punches. Nor does the identity and fulltime occupation of the person receiving them matter. All that matters as far as they are concerned is that Jake Paul is now a boxer because Jake Paul says he is now a boxer. He has achieved all this not by dazzling us with his boxing skills but instead by simply being a famous character. He found a sport happy to place cash above principles and realized fairly quickly that being a famous character in a sport lacking any sort of character will open doors and also woo promoters and television networks, even the ones feigning interest in the sport's integrity."

Meanwhile, people in the boxing community had started to press the issue of when Jake would box a real boxer. To satisfy that demand, he signed to fight Tommy Fury at Madison Square Garden on August 6.

Fury, age twenty-three, is known largely as Tyson Fury's half-brother. He was undefeated in eight fights with four knockouts. But all one needed to know about his record was that Jake represented a step up in competition. Tommy's first five opponents now have a composite ring record of 12 wins against 242 losses with 5 draws. And his next three opponents were nothing to write home about.

Then, with the August 6 date in place, Fury fell out. On June 29, one day before a planned kickoff press conference in New York, he was refused entry onto a flight from London to New York because his ESTA (Electronic System for Travel Authority) document was denied.

"I have no clue why I'm not allowed to travel to the USA," Fury said in a social media post." But there was informed speculation that the denial was a consequence of dealings between the Fury clan and Daniel Kinahan (who has been sanctioned by the United States Department of the Treasury for what the government says is his role as the leader of an international drug cartel known as the Kinahan Organized Crime Group).

On July 6, Jake announced that Fury had been dropped as his opponent. One day later, he revealed on social media that his new opponent would be Hasim Rahman Jr.

It's often said that a fighter whose record is padded has beaten "the usual suspects." Rahman (the 31-year-old son of former heavyweight champion Hasim Rahman Sr.) had a 12–1 (6 KOs) ring record. But it was built against opponents who had lost to the usual suspects.

Paul–Rahman was scheduled for eight rounds at a 200-pound contract weight with the weigh-in to be held one day in advance of the fight. The contract further provided that Hasim would not be allowed to weigh more than 215 pounds at a second weigh-in to be conducted the following morning. Jake's weight for his five previous pro outings had ranged from 189 to 192 pounds. Rahman turned pro in 2017 at 234 pounds, had fought as high as 269 (February 2021), and weighed 224 for his most recent bout on April 29, 2022. Making the 200-pound cruiserweight limit was expected to be a challenge for him.

There was some sniping about Rahman's purse for the fight, which a reliable source says was between $250,000 and $500,000 (probably closer to the first number). One day before the July 12 kickoff press conference at Madison Square Garden, Jake told MMA Hour, "Hasim Rahman Jr., actually right now, is trying to renegotiate his contract. He signed a contract last week for ten times more than he's ever been paid for any one of his fights, and now he's trying to renegotiate. He already signed on the dotted line, and now he's trying to go back and be like, 'Well, I'm not going to fight.' So who knows if this fight is even going to happen because we're not going to pay him more money. He's not worth it. So it's unfortunate, man. Don't fumble the biggest bag of your life, dumbass."

Jake also distinguished himself by telling the *New York Times*, "I have the best [sparring sessions] when I eat candy before because it has all the glucose in it and the muscles and stuff burn the sugar and the glucose. So I'm eating, like, Nerds Gummy Clusters, SweeTarts Ropes, Sour Patch Kids. Those are some of my favorites."

Not exactly Novak Djokovic's diet regimen.

Hasim Rahman Sr. began the July 12 kickoff press conference at Madison Square Garden on a respectful note, saying, "Jake is a real fighter and we respect that. But he's moving too quick."

Jake then interrupted with the thought, "I'm ending that whole-ass legacy that your family got" and followed with, "It's bring-your-kid-to-work day."

That led Rahman Jr. to proclaim, "I'm here to end this facade that he's calling a career. I sparred this man [two years ago] with one hand. I didn't even use my right hand [Hasim had been instructed to throw only jabs in the sparring session]. And he turned his back and ran from me. I'll be using two hands when we fight."

Things degenerated from there with Jake calling Rahman "stupid" and a "pussy motherfucker" before adding, "Nobody knows who the fuck you are. Two days ago, you had five thousand Instagram followers. My mom has more followers than you. You're not worth shit."

In the midst of it all, Madison Square Garden executive vice president Joel Fisher told the assembled media that the Garden was "incredibly honored" to be hosting Paul–Rahman.

That left open the question of who would win. Jake was a 2-to-1 betting favorite. But the odds were somewhat skewed by the ardor of his social media followers. There's something to be said for the experience of boxing against, and being hit by, real boxers. Hasim had that experience. Jake didn't.

Team Rahman was hoping the fight would play out like the 1995 encounter at Madison Square Garden when Mitchell Rose (a "real" boxer with a 1–7–1 record) was brought in as a sacrificial lamb to be slaughtered by Eric Esch a/k/a "Butterbean" (a hard-punching, undefeated, 300-pound novelty act). Rose totally outclassed Butterbean and stopped him in the second round.

Greg Cohen had promoted Rahman since Hasim's first pro fight and provided his fighter's services pursuant to a standard provision of services agreement to Holden Boxing LLC (which Most Valuable Promotions—Jake's promotional company—was using as promoter of record for the fight).

"We're being treated like the C-side in this promotion," Cohen acknowledged. "We know our role. But that's okay. There's no rematch clause and no options. Winning will make everything sweet."

That said, the feeling among boxing insiders was that Rahman wasn't as good as many people thought he was and Jake might be better than traditionalists were giving him credit for being.

There was talk of Hasim having had a hundred amateur bouts in addition to his professional outings. But BoxRec.com (which admittedly is incomplete when it comes to recording amateur fights) listed Rahman's amateur record as 9 wins against 12 losses with zero knockouts. And according to BoxRec, the guys he beat in the amateurs had 21 losses in 35 fights at the time he fought them.

Rahman's chin was suspect. Jake could whack a bit. Experience might teach a fighter how to avoid getting hit, but it can't teach a fighter how to have a chin.

Hasim's stamina was also an issue. In his most recent outing, he'd won the first four rounds against James McKenzie Morrison before running out of steam and being stopped in the fifth stanza.

In sum, people who know boxing didn't know who would win.

"I feel like I'm representing boxing," Hasim said. "It would be embarrassing if I lost to this clown."

But Jake took a contrary view, telling the *New York Times*, "I'm going to go out there and show the world that I'm a professional boxer."

Then everything fell apart.

Eight days before the fight, the New York State Athletic Commission (which had been subjecting Rahman to periodic weight checks) demanded that the contract limit be raised to 205 pounds out of concern that any weight loss beyond that could endanger Hasim's health. Jake agreed to the change and, on the morning of Saturday, July 30, Rick Torres (Jake's attorney) texted Greg Bloom (the attorney for Team Rahman) advising him of the change and asking that Rahman execute documents memorializing the contract revision.

"Please note," the text read, "that time is of the essence and it is imperative that this Amendment and Acknowledgement be duly executed by GCP [Greg Cohen Promotions] and Rahman and returned to us before 11:59 ET tonight or we will announce cancellation of the event first thing tomorrow."

In response, Rahman engaged in some ill-advised brinkmanship. Hoping to raise the weight limit even higher, he said that he was unwilling to weigh in below 215 pounds. Shortly after 8:00 p.m., rather than wait until the 11:59 p.m. deadline, Jake's team pulled the plug on the fight.

The following day, Rahman acknowledged in an Instagram post that he'd agreed to the 200-pound limit but said that his body "simply would not let me do it."

After that, there were dueling declarations regarding who was to blame for the cancellation. Rahman claimed that he hadn't irrevocably refused to make the 205-pound weight limit and that Jake was afraid to fight him. MVP attacked Rahman for deceit and lack of professionalism.

All of this leads to leads to the questions: (1) Why didn't the promotion wait until the 11:59 p.m. deadline to cancel the fight, and (2) If Rahman was out as Jake's opponent, why didn't the promotion simply find another opponent? Last-minute substitutions are common in boxing at the club-fight level. And Paul–Rahman was always about Jake.

One theory is that ticket sales for the fight were lagging and, once Rahman indicated he wouldn't fulfill his contractual obligation, MVP decided to walk away from the promotion because a half-empty arena would have hurt Jake's brand.

Nakisa Bidarian (Jake Paul's business partner) has stated that the cancellation "had zero to do with ticket sales" and that tickets were selling well. But when asked by this writer how many tickets had been sold for the August 6 card, Madison Square Garden (which is loath to give out misinformation) declined comment.

There's also a question regarding a statement that Jake made at an April 15, 2021, press conference prior to fighting Ben Askren when he told the media, "I've gone and gotten brain scans and have early signs of CTE."

In reality, CTE can't be diagnosed until after a person has died. But taking note of that comment, the New York State Athletic Commission had asked Jake to submit extensive medical information (including an MRI) as a prerequisite to licensing him to fight on August 6. Let's see if Jake's next fight is scheduled for New York.

Meanwhile, what does all of this mean for boxing?

First, give Jake credit for getting in the ring and fighting. "All I'm doing," he told Teddy Atlas earlier this year, "is putting in the work and trying to get better and fighting tougher opponents each time."

Jake should be judged as a fighter based on what he does in the ring. But let's take a look at what he represents—the trend toward what I referred to earlier in this article as "trash boxing."

Jake recently told Marc Raimondi of ESPN, "I wanted to bring my fanbase that was a digital fanbase [to boxing]. Now there's sixty million of them who are boxing fans."

But if Jake Paul played eighteen holes of golf in a pay-per-view match against a local club pro, would that bring more fans to golf? I doubt it.

When people go to a sanctioned toughman contest or illegal underground fight, they understand that they're not watching professional boxing at a world-class level. But the current wave of celebrity boxing is muddying the waters and taking people into an Alice-in-Wonderland world that blurs the lines between what professional boxing is and isn't.

When Seth Abraham was president of Time Warner Sports, he turned down a pitch from Vince McMahon to televise professional wrestling because he felt it would undermine the credibility of HBO's boxing franchise. Showtime has had no such qualms about heavily promoting Jake Paul.

It's just a matter of time before the World Boxing Council or some other sanctioning body creates a special belt for Jake or finds a vacant title that he can fight for against an inept foe.

When boxing fails for years to make Terence Crawford vs. Errol Spence and has been unable to give fans a unified heavyweight champion for decades, it shouldn't be surprised when trash boxing seeps into the void.

Soon after DAZN jump-started the recent wave of trash boxing, Paulie Malignaggi declared, "I don't want this sport to get to the point where you say 'boxing' and the random person you think of will be Logan Paul or Jake Paul rather than Anthony Joshua or Canelo. There's not going to be an audience for the real world-class fighters if they keep doing this."

Or as Elliott Worsell recently wrote, "If Jake Paul is considered good for boxing without actually boxing a boxer, what does that say about boxing? It says, I suppose, that nowadays it's not the skills that matter but the hype."

★★★

Note to the reader: On November 19, 2022, Hasim Rahman Jr. returned to the ring against Greg Hardy (a former NFL football player with one professional fight on his resume). Hardy knocked Rahman down in the second round and won a unanimous decision.

"I'm a fighter," Anthony Joshua said after losing his rematch against Oleksandr Usyk. "I'm not a normal person. To be a fighter is a real different mindset and lifestyle—especially to be a good fighter."

Usyk–Joshua II and the Hour of Reckoning

Boxing is the most basic of all sports. Two men engage in a fistfight. But the August 20, 2022, fistfight between Oleksandr Usyk and Anthony Joshua came with a lot of baggage attached.

The bout was contested at the King Abdullah Sports City Arena in Saudi Arabia under the patronage of Crown Prince Mohammed bin Salman, whose authoritarian government has a dismal record on human rights and was complicit in the murder of *Washington Post* journalist Jamal Khashoggi.

Usyk was a standard bearer for the Ukrainian people, who are struggling to survive Vladimir Putin's brutal aggression. And as the winner of the fight, Oleksandr is now in position to claim a mind-boggling payday for fighting Tyson Fury.

There was a time when it seemed as though Anthony Joshua would be the face and future of boxing. After winning a gold medal in the super-heavyweight division at the 2012 Olympics, he turned pro and annexed the WBA, IBF, and WBO crowns. His career peaked in 2017 with a thrilling eleventh-round conquest of Wladimir Klitschko before 90,000 frenzied fans at Wembley Stadium in London. He was charismatic, gracious, and likable; a superstar ascendant.

But the Klitschko fight took something out of Joshua. Lackluster victories over Carlos Takam, Joseph Parker, and Alexander Povetkin followed. Then promoter Eddie Hearn brought him to America to enhance his global appeal and matched him against 20-to-1 underdog Andy Ruiz. Ruiz knocked Joshua out in the seventh round. That was the extent of the effort to market A.J. in America.

Six months later, Joshua decisioned a grossly out-of-shape Ruiz in a rematch. That was followed by a victory over trial horse Kubrat Pulev.

But A.J. looked like a belt-holder in those fights, not a champion. Then, in September 2021, he fought Usyk for the first time.

Usyk had enjoyed an impressive run in unifying the four major cruiserweight belts before moving up to heavyweight where the big money lies. The transition did not start well for him. In his first two fights at heavyweight, Usyk looked ordinary against a shopworn Chazz Witherspoon (who hasn't won a fight since 2019) and struggled en route to a 117–112, 115–113, 115–113 decision over Derek Chisora (who has lost three of four fights since 2019).

But when Joshua–Usyk I came, Usyk outboxed the bigger, stronger, harder-punching man by a 117–112, 116–112, 115–113 margin and had A.J. in trouble at the final bell. Joshua didn't complain about the judges' decision. He didn't blame his corner, the referee, or some form of skul-duggery. He was the epitome of class.

"It was a tough fight," A.J. said. "It wasn't my night. Well done to my opponent. I'm not a sulker. I'm not going to go home tonight and be crying about it because this is a long process. This is not like one fight and I'm done. When I was walking back through the tunnel after the fight, I just said to myself, 'I'm ready to get back to the gym. I'm ready to put that work in. I've got to take it as a great lesson and build on that situation. I'll get back to the drawing board and get it right the next time when we go again."

The threshold issue with regard to Usyk–Joshua II was whether the fight would happen at all.

Usyk is a Ukrainian citizen. Following Russia's invasion of Ukraine in February of this year, he joined his country's territorial defense force.

Vitali and Wladimir Klitschko were elite heavyweights during their boxing days. Vitali held the WBC heavyweight title and is now mayor of Kyiv. He's one of the two most recognizable figures in rallying the forces of resistance in his homeland against Vladimir Putin's brutal war. Ukrainian president Volodymyr Zelensky is the other.

Wladimir, who once held the WBA, IBF, and WBO belts, returned to Kyiv from the United States to stand as a symbol with his brother.

After weighing the issue, the Klitschkos decided it was in the best interests of the Ukrainian people for Usyk to fight the rematch against Joshua.

"A very important message could be carried through an event like this," Vitali said of the fight. "We do not know if in three months we will exist. I have plans to speak to Oleksandr Usyk to give him advice, to have some special messages that he can put out there."

"There are pros and cons, and it's a hard decision to make for Oleksandr Usyk," Wladimir added. "But to have the Ukrainian flag raised and our anthem played and one of our ambassadors of our country out there in the world with the right mindset could be more positive than negative."

In late March, Usyk left Ukraine to train in Poland.

"It was a very difficult decision, extremely difficult," Alexander Krassyuk (Usyk's Ukrainian promoter) said. "But the announcements he can make to the public through what he does is just extraordinary. You can't lose that chance. The whole world is going to be sitting and watching this fight. He is not fighting for himself. He's not just fighting for his personal legacy. He's fighting for the whole country. He's fighting for the whole democratic world."

"I really didn't want to leave our country," Usyk acknowledged. "I didn't want to leave our city. But at one point, I went to the hospital where soldiers were wounded and getting rehabilitation from the war. And they were telling me to fight for the country inside the ring and you're even going to help more for our country instead of being here fighting in Ukraine. A lot of my close friends are still in the country. I'm in touch with them every day. I ask them how are they feeling? Are they in a safe place? I want to live there and, right after the fight, I'm going back to Ukraine."

"The world's wrongs," Jimmy Tobin once wrote, "are not righted because one fighter bludgeons another." Still, it was clear that the outcome of Usyk–Joshua II would resonate with the Ukrainian people. As a condition of making the fight, Usyk stipulated that the bout be televised free of charge on Ukrainian state TV.

Meanwhile, a site had to be chosen.

Joshua–Usyk I had been contested at Tottenham Hotspur Arena in London. The 65,000-seat venue sold out within twenty-four hours of tickets going on sale. But the economics of boxing have changed in recent years. Sold-out soccer stadiums and Las Vegas casinos are at a disadvantage when competing against Middle Eastern oil money.

On June 19, it was announced that Usyk–Joshua II would be contested in Saudi Arabia on August 20. That was in line with efforts by the Saudi government to enhance its image through "sportswashing."

Writing about the negative response to Phil Mickelson and other pro golfers participating in the Saudi-sponsored LIV Golf International Series, Pulitzer Prize–winning journalist Paul Krugman addressed the claim that the golfers were being victimized by a "media/cancel culture." In so doing, Krugman declared, "If getting paid big bucks to provide favorable P.R. to a regime that deals with critical journalists by killing them and dismembering them with a bone saw doesn't merit cancellation, what does? The rise of cancel culture seems much less important and ominous than the rise of sellout culture. More and more people at the top of our social hierarchy appear willing to do anything for anyone as long as the money is good enough."

It's easy to tell someone else not to make as much money as they can. In this instance, Saudi interests paid a reported $77 million for all rights to Usyk–Joshua II. That said, fighting in Saudi Arabia was hardly in line with Usyk's "pro-democracy" message. Particularly in light of the fact that, on March 19, 2022, the Saudi government announced that it had executed eighty-one people that day for what the Saudi Ministry of Interior said were "heinous crimes."

Joshua's 2019 rematch against Andy Ruiz had also taken place in Saudi Arabia. Asked about the issue of sportswashing at the June 21, 2022, kickoff press conference in Jeddah for Usyk–Joshua II, A.J. responded, "I don't know what that is. I'm here to win the heavyweight champion of the world. I like Saudi. I think Saudi's good. I'm having a good time here. I'm treated really well. All that allegation stuff, for me, I'm not caught up in any of that stuff. I'm here to have a good time, mix with the local people, bring entertainment to Saudi."

Eddie Hearn (Joshua's promoter and the architect of Usyk–Joshua II) voiced a similar view, telling the assembled media, "It feels fantastic to be back. We're delighted to bring what is the biggest fight in the heavyweight division, one of the biggest fights in world boxing, to the Kingdom. We've heard a lot about the growth of boxing here in Saudi Arabia, something that is very important to us as fans of the sport. It's amazing to bring huge high-profile fights to The Kingdom."

The fight was billed as "Rage on the Red Sea." The promotion kept talking about the bout being for THE heavyweight championship of the world. But right now, Tyson Fury wears the crown. Usyk–Joshua II was for some belts.

There was only modest buzz for the event in the United Kingdom and less in the United States. Having sold virtually all rights to Usyk–Joshua II to Saudi interests, Matchroom (Hearn's promotional company) had limited incentive to spend its own money on promotion.

On July 7, it was announced that Sky Sports had purchased rights to broadcast the bout in the United Kingdom and that the fight would be available on a pay-per-view basis on Sky Sports Box Office. That was an embarrassment for DAZN, which, on June 13, 2022, had announced a "landmark deal" pursuant to which Joshua would become a "global brand ambassador, special advisor to, and shareholder in, DAZN Group" and that his "future fights" (no number or time frame was announced) would be streamed on DAZN platforms throughout the world. It wasn't until six days before the bout that a plan to stream Usyk–Joshua II on DAZN in countries other than the United Kingdon, Ireland, Ukraine, and MENA (a group of countries in the Middle East and North Africa) was finalized.

It's not unreasonable to think that the memory of Jamal Khashoggi had a chilling effect on coverage of the event by onsite journalists.

In early March, Joshua had announced that he was replacing Robert McKracken as his head trainer with former assistant trainer Angel Fernandez. Then, on May 30, the public was told that Robert Garcia would serve as A.J.'s lead trainer for the fight.

Age wasn't expected to be a factor. Usyk is thirty-five; Joshua is thirty-two.

Joshua had been a 5-to-2 betting favorite in their first encounter. Usyk was a 2-to-1 favorite the second time around.

A lot of people had thought it would be a mistake for Joshua to take an immediate rematch against Andy Ruiz. But A.J. did, and it was the right decision. The difference here was that the loss to Ruiz was widely regarded as a fluke. A change in strategy coupled with Ruiz coming in grossly out of shape tilted the playing field for the rematch in A.J. favor.

But Usyk's victory over Joshua hadn't been a fluke. And unlike Ruiz, Usyk was expected to be in good shape for the rematch. If A.J. were to win, a new fight plan was in order. He'd tried to outbox Usyk in their first encounter. To win the rematch, he'd have to be more daring, not more cautious. He'd have to rely on his own superior strength, size, and power.

Joshua acknowledged as much, saying:

* "The fight with Usyk, in my mind, was going for twelve rounds. That was my game plan because I thought I could compete with him as a boxer. That's how he became champion. So the goal now is to go back to basics and go for the knockout."

* "One of my strengths is my power. But I always wanted to go down that path of being a clean boxer, hit and not get hit. You need to have good defense. But I moved away from the ferocious side of boxing where I knew I could hit and stun people. I am looking forward to getting back to that."

* "I know I can be better than that night. It's easier to say than it is to do. But within my heart and soul, my brain and body, I truly feel I've got a lot more to give. I'm angry at myself and the only way I can be in a better place is to get myself right by going out there and performing."

* "Styles make fights, and [in Joshua–Usyk I] I adopted the wrong style. That's not to say I'll go out there and swing like a madman. But I have to go out there and hurt the guy and take his soul to the point where he wants to give up. That's all I have in my mind at the minute—that one track and to stay on course and take this guy to places he doesn't want to go."

But the case for an Usyk victory was equally compelling.

"I have never made any loud or bright speeches," Oleksandr said. "To become world champion, all I did was work hard in my training camp and gym. That's what I am going to do until the day of the fight. I don't think about him or what he is going to do, whether he has a new tactic or a new trainer. I really don't care. I am just thinking about myself. We learned about each other in the first fight. We have had enough time to study each other. The last bout will be continued, round thirteen, round fourteen, round fifteen, however long the fight will last. I know that he will be different this time. But so will I."

Tickets for the event went on sale on July 20 and were priced from 20,000 Saudi riyal ($5,400) down to 375 Saudi riyal ($101).

The opening bout on the telecast matched Ramla Ali (born in Somalia but now living in England) against a pathetically overmatched Crystal Garcia Nova in the first professional fight ever between women in the Saudi Kingdom. Earlier in the week, Ali had hosted a women's boxing clinic and praised Saudi Arabia as a "very progressive" country.

That earned a rejoinder from Felix Jakens (head of Priority Campaigns and Individuals at Risk for Amnesty International UK) who declared, "The reality for women in Saudi Arabia is that they face serious discrimination in marriage, divorce, inheritance and child custody. In recent years, Saudi women who have been brave enough to call for reforms in the country have been jailed, tortured and completely silenced. There's nothing even faintly progressive about Saudi Arabia's human rights record. This fight is yet more sportswashing as Saudi Arabia tries once again to distract from its appalling human rights record."

Garcia had a "what am I doing here" look on her face during the fighter introductions and was stopped less than a minute into the first round.

"I got to be honest," DAZN commentator Chris Algieri said after the stoppage. "That was pretty embarrassing."

Usyk–Joshua II began as a cautiously fought tactical encounter. Joshua (who enjoyed a 244- to 221-pound weight advantage) started out as the more aggressive fighter. But Usyk is a well-schooled southpaw and hard to hit. There was tension because of the stakes involved. But for the first eight rounds, there wasn't much action. Joshua was boxing well, and his size plus the spectre of his power kept Oleksandr from getting untracked. Had the fight been in Las Vegas, there would have been boos.

But those boos would have turned to cheers in the late rounds as the action increased and the drama built. Joshua had been putting body shots in the bank. And they took a toll.

In round nine, Joshua opened Usyk up by going to the body again and then scored repeatedly up top. It was a dominant round. Usyk was fading.

And then Usyk did what a great fighter does. He came out aggressively in round ten and turned the tide. It was a championship round in the truest sense.

CompuBox is an inexact metric. But here, the numbers told a tale. CompuBox credited Joshua with outlanding Usyk 28 to 9 in round nine (24 to 8 in power punches). In round ten, Usyk reversed those numbers (39 to 10 in punches landed with a 32 to 9 advantage in power punches).

Very often, the first thing a fighter loses isn't his reflexes or legs. It's the will to walk through fire to win. Ever since he walked through fire to beat Wladimir Klitschko, Joshua has appeared reluctant to do it again. Usyk summoned up what he needed to do to win. Joshua couldn't.

Both men were tired in rounds eleven and twelve. And both men dug deep. Usyk dug deeper.

I thought that Usyk clearly won five rounds and Joshua four with three rounds up for grabs. The judges ruled in Usyk's favor by a 116–112, 115–113, 113–115 margin.

After the fight, Joshua was on an emotional rollercoaster.

Infuriated by the decision, he took hold of the WBA and *Ring Magazine* belts, dumped them out of the ring, and confronted Usyk, demanding, "How did you beat me!" He then stormed angrily out of the ring, was persuaded to return, commandeered the microphone, and made a disjointed, rambling speech that included:

* "Usyk, one hell of a fucking fighter. Let's give him a round of applause. That's just emotion. If you knew my story, you would understand my passion. I ain't no fucking amateur boxer from five years old that was an elite prospect from a youth. I was going to jail. I got bail and started training my ass off because, if I got sentenced, I wouldn't be able to fight."

* "The fucking passion we put into this shit, man. This guy, to beat me tonight, maybe I could have done better, but it shows the levels of hard work he must have put in. So please, give him a round of applause as our heavyweight champion of the world. Woo! Motherfucker!"

* "I'm not a twelve-round fighter. Look at me! I'm a new breed of heavyweight. All them heavyweights—Mike Tyson, Sonny Liston, Jack Dempsey. 'Oh, you don't throw combinations like Rocky Marciano.' 'Cause I ain't fuckin' fourteen stone; that's why! I'm eighteen stone and I'm heavy! It's hard work! This guy here is a phenomenal talent. We're gonna cheer for him three times."

That was followed by five (not three) "hip-hip hoorays," after which Joshua started discussing Ukraine, concluding with, "I ain't never been there. But at the same time, what's happening there is—I don't know what's happening, but it's not nice at the end of the day."

Later, at the post-fight press conference, Joshua was a model of decorum. Asked about his earlier odd remarks, he explained "I was mad at myself. I said, 'I got to get out of here [the ring] because I'm mad.' When you're angry, you might do stupid things. But then I realized, 'Oh, shit; this is sport. Let me do the right thing, come back.' And I just spoke from the heart. [Boxing] comes at a big cost. It will never break me but it takes real strength for it not to break you. And tonight, there's a little crack in the armor because I took a loss. You saw me upset."

Asked if he was proud of himself for the fight he'd put up against Usyk, A.J. answered, "It's really really hard for me to say I'm proud of myself. I'm upset, really deep down in my heart."

Then he broke down in tears.

But no moment said as much about Joshua's character as his response when asked, "Do you feel you earned respect back tonight?"

"From who. Who am I trying to earn respect from?"

"The public."

"It's not my business what they think of me," Joshua responded. "Do you know what people should respect me for? When I meet them, greet them, shake hands. 'Yes, please; no, thank you.' Don't respect me because of the fights and the belts. That isn't what makes a man or a woman. It's your character and how you treat people. That's how I want to earn respect."

It's incumbent, of course, to put all of this in perspective.

First, let's not confuse Usyk with Sugar Ray Robinson. He has been the best cruiserweight of this era. But he struggled at heavyweight against Chazz Witherspoon and Dereck Chisora. And it's hard to know how much of his success against Joshua is attributable to A.J.'s shortcomings. Remember, Joshua has now lost three of five fights over the past forty-seven months.

In all likelihood, Tyson Fury will end his "now you see me, now you don't" retirement posture and fight Usyk for all four major sanctioning body belts at some point in the not-too-distant future. That leads to a final thought.

Boxing has the worst infrastructure of any major sport. It's an unwieldy mess with parts that are largely incompatible with one another. There are multiple "world champions" in most weight divisions— a practice that confuses fans and dilutes the meaning of the word "champion." The business has an economic model that puts its showcase events behind a paywall, creating a barrier between the sport and would-be fans.

Contrast boxing with the National Football League in the United States. The weekend of January 22–23, 2022, offered the most exciting two days of football in NFL history. The best were playing the best. All four divisional playoff contests (which were seen on free television) were decided by a score on the last play of the game. Icons like Tom Brady and Aaron Rodgers were defeated. A new generation of stars asserted themselves. The last second heroics of Patrick Mahomes and Josh Allen are now part of sports lore. And it culminated in the Los Angeles Rams beating the Cincinnati Bengals in the Super Bowl three weeks later.

Boxing hasn't had a universally recognized heavyweight champion since Lennox Lewis retired in 2004. Imagine if it took the National Football League two decades to organize a Super Bowl.

Prior to fighting Gennady Golovkin for the third time, Canelo Álvarez was asked if he thought Golovkin was the same fighter he'd fought before. "I don't know," Canelo answered. "I'm going to find out."

Canelo–Golovkin Lite

After two exciting, action-filled fights, Saul "Canelo" Álvarez and Gennady Golovkin ended their rivalry on September 17, 2022, with a fight that was evocative of flat beer. Canelo retained his WBC, WBA, IBF, and WBO 168-pound titles by unanimous decision. But the drama of their earlier encounters was missing.

Canelo and Golovkin had met in the ring twice before. The consensus in boxing circles was that Gennady deserved the decision in their 2017 confrontation. But the judges scored the fight a draw in a ruling tarnished by Adelaide Byrd's ludicrous 118–110 scorecard in Canelo's favor.

"I did my job in the ring and the judges didn't," Golovkin said afterward.

Canelo prevailed on a 115–113, 115–113, 114–114 majority verdict in their 2018 rematch.

Golovkin's subsequent ring appearances were limited to victories over Steve Rolls, Sergiy Derevyanchenko (a questionable decision), Kamil Szeremeta, and Ryota Murata. Meanwhile, Canelo rose to greater heights, beating Rocky Fielding, Danny Jacobs, Sergey Kovalev, Callum Smith, Avni Yildirim, Billy Joe Saunders, and Caleb Plant to solidify his claim to boxing's pound-for-pound throne.

Then, on May 7, 2022, Canelo fought Dmitri Bivol in a bid for the WBA light-heavyweight title. It was a bridge too far.

"Success," Jimmy Tobin wrote, "taught Alvarez that his style made even larger men skittish. It cowed them, then broke them. He had no reason to expect otherwise."

But against Bivol, "otherwise" came to pass.

Great fighters of the past, even in their prime, had losses on their record because they went in tough again and again. Muhammad Ali lost to Joe Frazier in Ali–Frazier I. Ray Leonard lost his first fight against Roberto Durán. Max Schmeling beat Joe Louis in their inaugural encounter.

Canelo had established himself as boxing's brightest star. But against Bivol, he came up short, losing a 115–113, 115–113, 115–113 decision.

"When the sport's pound-for-pound king is upset," Corey Erdman wrote afterward, "it will entice discussions of whether the fighter's status was ever deserved at all. It's important to remember what this fight was—a brilliant fighter daring to venture well above his optimal fighting weight in search of a challenge. Canelo could have remained at 160 or 168 and found plenty of opponents who would have been unable to test him whatsoever. Instead, he chose one of the best light-heavyweights in the world, precisely because he was a difficult opponent. Five-foot-eight longtime super-welterweights are not supposed to beat prime top-level light-heavyweights no matter how high up on the pound-for-pound list they may be."

"Like most fighters with greatness in mind," Paul Magno added, "Canelo extended himself a bit too far and felt the pushback from reality. If anything, it should be commended that he even made this effort. Beating Bivol would've been beyond impressive. It didn't happen. So we all move on."

Moving on meant Canelo–Golovkin III—the final installment in a rivalry that began with good feelings and expressions of mutual respect but had turned sour.

Golovkin was resentful of the judges' decision in Canelo–Golovkin I. That resentment became full-blown antagonism five months later when urine samples provided by Canelo to the Voluntary Anti-Doping Association while he was readying to return to the ring tested positive for clenbuterol, a banned substance. The amount of the drug in Canelo's system was consistent with the ingestion of tainted beef. But a boxer is responsible for what goes into his body. Álvarez agreed to a six-month suspension.

Golovkin savaged Canelo for the presence of clenbuterol in his urine.

"It's not meat," Gennady said when the finding was announced. "Canelo's team are using these drugs and everybody's trying to pretend it's not happening. This guy, he knows. This is not his first day in boxing. Check him on a lie detector and then we can find out everything."

Since then, Canelo has been tested more thoroughly by VADA than any other boxer ever, always without complaint and never with an adverse test result. That said, one month before Canelo–Golovkin III, Gennady was still keying on the issue.

"I'm not that kind of person who's going to belittle any athlete's achievements," Golovkin told the *Orange County Register*. "And Canelo's achieved a lot. But there are questions about how he did that and what he used. I did not say something just because I just came up with it. There are lab results. When asked, I said, 'Yes, I believe that he cheated.' And if somebody in his team didn't like my words, I believe it's their problem."

Then, for good measure, Golovkin added, "Many Mexicans love me. And nobody in Kazakhstan loves Canelo."

Needless to say, Canelo was displeased with Golovkin's comments.

"He said I was dishonest, that I was a cheater, that I was a shame to my country," Álvarez noted at the Canelo–Golovkin III kickoff press conference. "He's an asshole. He really is. He pretends to be a nice guy. Then, in other places, he talks a lot of shit. Be a man and say what you want to say. I don't pretend to be some other person. I don't say things in another place, then come here and pretend to be someone else. He always says I am scared and running away when I am fighting the best guys out there and he's fighting Class D fighters. I don't know why he's surprised this fight is personal for me. I hope he's taking it personal too. He's going to need it."

Golovkin sought to moderate the dialogue as the fight approached.

"I don't feel any hatred toward him," Gennady said. "This is a sport. To me, he's just an athlete, just another human being, just a boxer. If you have something against your opponent, you display it during the fight. When the fight is over, you hug each other, you shake hands, and you put everything past you. Whatever differences we have, we will meet in the ring and resolve them."

"Do you think he dislikes you?" a reporter asked Canelo.

"Of course," Canelo answered. "But I don't care."

Canelo–Golovkin III, like its predecessors, was contested at T-Mobile Arena in Las Vegas. Their first two fights had generated live gates of $27,059,850 and $23,473,500 with pay-per-view buys in the United States numbering 1.3 million and a little more than 1 million, respectively. But those fights had been on HBO-PPV with HBO's cachet and marketing muscle behind them. By contrast, Canelo–Golovkin III was on DAZN-PPV.

DAZN executive vice president Joe Markowski (one of the architects of DAZN's financially disastrous boxing program in the United States) sought to paint a bright picture at the kickoff press conference when he declared, "The intrigue from the public has remained, one hundred percent. You can use any metric you want to look at, from a social media perspective, from a media perspective."

But in truth, Canelo–Golovkin III had passed its optimum sell-by date. And DAZN has failed to build an effective marketing platform in the United States. Best estimates are that Canelo–Bivol (on DAZN PPV) engendered 300,000 fewer buys than Canelo vs. Caleb Plant (which was a Showtime-PPV venture). Three days before Canelo–Golovkin III, more than 7,000 tickets were unsold.

Golovkin had never entered a fight before as an underdog. He was a 2-to-1 betting favorite over Canelo in their first two encounters. This time, Canelo opened as a 3-to-1 betting favorite and the odds rose to 4-to-1 as fight night approached.

Many observers thought the 168-pound contract weight would favor Canelo. His most recent six fights had been contested at super-middleweight or higher while Golovkin had fought at middleweight for his entire career. But Canelo began his career at 139 pounds (21 fewer than Gennady). And the 168-pound contract weight spared Golovkin the wear-and-tear that making 160 pounds would have imposed on his body. Thus, age was expected to be more of a factor than weight.

Gennady is no longer the fresh-faced young man who fought in the United States for the first time a decade ago. He's forty years old. Canelo is thirty-two. That's a significant difference. Johnathon Banks (Golovkin's trainer) sought to downplay the issue saying, "I think the media gives too much attention to his age. Some fighters can perform into old age and some can't. Golovkin still looks great."

But forty is forty.

Also, there was a widespread belief that Canelo had improved as a fighter since the two men met in the ring for the second time four years ago.

"He is a really good fighter, one of the best I've fought," Canelo said of Golovkin. "No doubt of that. He earned his titles. But I think he's going to be surprised how much I've improved. My resistance, my strength. That will definitely surprise him."

Golovkin minimized those considerations. Asked about Canelo's power at 168 pounds, he responded, "All my opponents knew how to punch. Canelo is a very difficult opponent. But as you see [from the Bivol fight], he loses too.

"I don't want people to think that the result of the third fight is going to erase the results of the first two," Gennady added. "This is a different time, different weight category. The first two fights went into history already. So any outcome of the third fight should not affect the memory of the first two and should not erase what happened there."

But for Canelo, there was a link. Canelo–Golovkin III was a "must win" fight in terms of his legacy. If he lost to Golovkin, it would cast a shadow over his performance in their first two encounters and lead to the conclusion that Gennady (with his otherwise unblemished record) was the better fighter all along.

Canelo–Golovkin III was expected to be an entertaining encounter between two future Hall of Fame fighters. Unfortunately, once the bell for round one rang, it didn't evolve that way. Canelo was fighting for money and glory. Golovkin looked like a man who was fighting for the money.

There was little sustained action. During the first half of the bout, Canelo moved forward, fighting patiently with a measured attack and piling up points. He was the hunter. Golovkin (who once ground up opponents) fought like a fighter who didn't believe in himself. He avoided confrontations and looked for openings rather than trying to create them. He did nothing to change the flow of the fight.

There are times when a fighter has to take imprudent risks and expose himself to increased punishment as his only hope for avoiding defeat. That was the situation Gennady found himself in during the second half of the fight. And while he did pick up the pace a bit, he never took the risks that he must have known he needed to take in order to win.

Most ringside observers gave Canelo the nod by a wide margin. I scored the fight 117–112 (8–3–1 in rounds) for Canelo. The judges turned in a surprisingly close 116–112 115–113, 115–113 verdict in his favor.

"This fight was more tactical, like chess," Golovkin acknowledged afterward. "Today, Canelo was better."

Canelo–Golovkin III was disappointing from an aesthetic point of view. It was also a financial disaster for DAZN. The streaming service guaranteed Canelo a reported $45 million for the bout and Golovkin $20 million. But the $64.99 pay-per-view price in the United States alienated many of DAZN's monthly subscribers who had signed up on the promise that fights like this would be seen at no extra cost. And non-subscribers in the US were asked to pay $84.99.

Reliable reports state that the fight engendered between 550,000 and 575,000 buys in the United States (hundreds of thousands of buys below DAZN's break-even point). DAZN sought to put a good face on things, issuing a press release that declared, "The Canelo vs. GGG III fight night saw a global audience in the millions with more than 1.06 million buys generated worldwide including PPV and DAZN subscriptions." But these numbers indicate a meager half-million "buys" (including pre-existing subscriptions) outside of the United States. And many of these buys were in countries where the purchase price for a pay-per-view fight is minimal.

There's an old proverb dating to the sixteenth century that counsels, "A fool and his money are soon parted." DAZN's principal owner Len Blavatnik isn't a fool. But his company is parting with a lot of money.

Larry Goldberg didn't have to promote a professional boxing match.
But he wanted to.

A Promoter's Pro Debut

The phrase "pro debut" is often heard in conjunction with fighters. But promoters make pro debuts too. On October 13, 2022, at Sony Hall in the heart of Times Square, Larry Goldberg made his pro debut.

Goldberg, age forty-five, grew up in and around Atlantic City, where he fell in love with boxing. He has an internet-marketing background and, in 1997, founded BoxingInsider.com. In the past, he'd promoted amateur fight cards. Now he was going pro.

If Goldberg's pro debut had been in Montana or Kansas, it might have been similar to his amateur experiences. But it was in New York. Promoting a professional fight card under the best of circumstances is like herding twenty cats across a football field while a game is in progress. When promoting in New York, think fifty cats.

The New York State Athletic Commission has more rigorous protocols for promoters than any other state. For example, the fighter medical insurance required in New York costs $1,645 per bout. That's $9,870 for a six bout card. Line item costs such as hotel rooms for fighters and their teams are also higher in New York than elsewhere.

Virtually everyone wants something for free when dealing with a promoter. Promoting a fight card can be analogous to planning a six-figure wedding on a five-figure budget.

"It's my first show," Goldberg acknowledged during fight week. "There's so much to do. I'm learning and I'm making some mistakes. I'll lose some money; I hope not too much. But it's a start."

Sony Hall is a difficult venue for a boxing promotion. Finding space for changing rooms, medical examinations, and other requisite areas is a task unto itself. Because of the building's configuration, it costs more than the norm to bring the ring in and out.

Goldberg was promoting the October 13 event in association with DiBella Entertainment.

"Larry knows that he can't make money in Sony Hall," Lou DiBella noted. "But he's learning the ropes. It's like a graduate course in promoting. And it costs money to get an education."

One might be forgiven for likening Goldberg's "education" to a diploma from Trump University. The tuition is high, often without much hope of a meaningful return. Ultimately, boxing maven Eric Bottjer was brought in to help the promotion with compliance issues and other matters.

"Eric was a life-saver," Larry said afterward. "I don't want to think about what might have happened without him."

Goldberg put together his own production team and arranged for the fights to be streamed live on BXNG.TV with Randy Gordon and Gerry Cooney handling the commentary. He hired a round-card girl on the morning of the fights. Matt Competello (who Larry worked with in the amateurs) was brought in as the ring announcer.

The New York State Athletic Commission had limited the number of fights that would be allowed on the card to six because of the cramped quarters in the back of the house. Ticket prices ranged from $102 to $325.

One fight fell out when a fighter who, Goldberg says, agreed to a $3,000 purse refused to get on a plane and come to New York unless his purse was increased to $5,000. That left Larry with only five fights. And he had to pay the $1,645 insurance fee for the cancelled fight because it had already been bonded.

Heather Hardy was Goldberg's headline attraction. Several opponents for Heather fell out. And for good measure, it rained on fight night, which threatened to put a damper on last-minute ticket sales.

Dave McWater (the 2020 Boxing Writers Association of America "manager of the year") manages Ivan Golub, who was in the second bout of the evening. Sitting in Sony Hall before the fights began, McWater reminisced about his own experience as a promoter.

"Years ago," McWater recalled, "I backed Don Elbaum on a show in Connecticut. Don assured me that we'd sell 5,000 tickets. About an hour before the first fight, I went to the box office and we'd sold 259. After that, I decided I'd be better off managing than promoting."

Then the gods smiled on Goldberg. Walk-up sales were better than expected. Sony Hall nearly sold out. The venue was jammed.

The seating was chaotic with close quarters everywhere from ringside to the standing-room area by the bar. But all of the sightlines were good.

The ring canvas was gray, not powder blue, and the ring ropes were black. The overhead lights were dimmer than the norm. All of that, when combined with the unusually close quarters, gave the evening an old-time fight-club feel.

The fights moved smoothly from one to the next without the long delays occasioned by the demands of bigtime television.

Fight #1 saw Petros Ananyan (16–3–2, 7 KOs) face off against Paulo Cesar Galdino (12–6, 8 KOs) in a super-lightweight contest. Neither man had much defense and both men got hit a lot. But Ananyan hit harder and Cesar got hit more often, leading to a sixth-round stoppage. The fight was notable because Freddie Roach was in Ananyan's corner and the venue was set up in a way that waiters with plates full of chicken tenders and fried calamari kept walking in front of the trainer while rounds were going on. "I did wonder what the fuck was going on," Roach said afterward.

Ivan Golub (20–1, 15 KOs) vs. Wesley Tucker (15–3, 9 KOs, 1 KO by) was the second bout. Golub was arguably the most accomplished fighter on the card. But the big ticket sellers were Heather Hardy, Nadim Salloum, and Andy Dominguez Velasquez, so the last three slots were reserved for them.

Tucker is a club fighter. During the preceding five-and-a-half years, he'd lost three times to other club fighters and won once. In round two, he scored a knockdown when he tagged Golub and Ivan's gloves touched the canvas. But then Wesley tired and morphed into a human punching bag. His corner stopped the carnage after four rounds.

In fight #3, Andy Dominguez Velasquez (7–0–0, 6 KOs), a good flyweight prospect, knocked down Ricardo Caraballo (7–1, 2 KOs) two minutes into the first stanza. Ricardo rose on wobbly legs, and virtually everyone in the arena except Sparkle Lee could see that he was in no condition to continue. Unfortunately, Lee was refereeing the fight. So Caraballo took more unnecessary concussive blows to the head before he was knocked down again and the fight ended.

Fight #4 featured Nadim Salloum (8–1, 3 KOs) vs. Jorge Leandro Capozucco (4–0, 3 KOs). Salloum, age twenty-eight, was born in Lebanon

and now lives in Brooklyn. He's a ticket-seller, having developed a significant following in the Lebanese American community. His ring skills aren't
as good as his marketing. That said, Leandro only had one punch—an
arcing overhand right that landed more often than it should have because
Salloum has a porous defense. But Salloum also had a more varied arsenal
and more power than Leandro. Referee Steve Willis stopped the fight in
round six.

Then it was time for the main event—Heather Hardy (22–2, 4
KOs) vs. Calista Silgado (20–15–3, 15 KOs, 3 KOs by). Hardy (who
moved from 126 to 135 pounds last year) had lost her last two outings by
decision against Amanda Serrano and Jessica Camara and hadn't won
a boxing match since 2018. Silgado was competing at 118 pounds as
recently as May of this year and had lost four of her most recent five
fights. Her one victory during that stretch came against a woman who
has had two fights in her entire ring career and been knocked out in
both of them.

Silgado had flown to New York from Miami and arrived at 11:30
on Tuesday night. She weighed in on Wednesday, fought on Thursday,
and flew back to Miami on a 5:00 a.m. Friday flight. Such is the life of
a B-side fighter.

Hardy–Silgado was scheduled for six two-minute rounds. Once the
fight began, it was clear that Heather's reflexes have slowed noticeably
since her prime years. Calista looked old and tired and had powder-puff
fists. It wasn't a hard fight to score. Two judges appropriately ruled 58–56
in Hardy's favor. One judge gave Heather all six rounds and shouldn't be
assigned to judge again without extensive retraining.

Hardy is forty years old. Her defense has always been suspect. She's
tough and has a fighting spirit. But that alone doesn't cut it in boxing,
particularly at age forty. The punches add up for women fighters as inexorably as they do for men. Now would be a good time for Heather to
stop fighting.

At evening's end, Goldberg's father (who was at the show) told him,
"Congratulations! This was your second bar mitzvah."

So . . . where does Larry go from here?

He came out of the promotion with his honor and reputation intact.
He lost some money but not as much as he feared he might.

"I'll be able to sleep well tonight for the first time in two months," Goldberg said when the show was over. "I can't believe this worked out as well as it did because it could have gone really bad. I was petrified that things out of my control would go wrong. I've got a lot to digest. But now that I know how the sausage is made, it should be easier for me next time. Next time, I'll know how to save money on hotel rooms and airfare and all the other things that add up. I'd like to promote at Sony Hall again. I think I can make the numbers work and turn a profit there. I'd like to promote a fight card in Atlantic City. That's one of my goals. Maybe I'll turn Boxing Insider into a streaming platform. There's so much to think about."

Meanwhile, give Goldberg credit for loving boxing and putting his money where his heart is.

In the ring, Deontay Wilder evokes images of a raptor from Jurassic Park.

The Return of Deontay Wilder

Deontay Wilder, as expected, confirmed his status as a major player in the heavyweight division with a one-punch, first-round knockout of Robert Helenius at Barclays Center on October 15, 2022.

Wilder, age thirty-six, had fought twice in the preceding thirty-four months and been knocked out each time by Tyson Fury. Those fights showed that Deontay is exciting to watch, brave, and tough. They also showed that, while he takes a good beating, he doesn't take a particularly good punch. And his defensive skills, such as they are, are rooted in his offense.

In some ways, Wilder's irrational, mean-spirited response to his first defeat against Fury caused as much damage to his image as Fury's fists did. After that loss, Deontay claimed that the costume he'd worn during his ring walk was too heavy and had robbed him of his strength. Then, without evidence, he accused Fury of fighting with loaded gloves and referee Kenny Bayless of either being drunk on fight night or taking part in a conspiracy against him. Finally, again without evidence, he claimed that Mark Breland (his trainer at the time) had tampered with his water bottle and prematurely stopped the fight.

All of that ran counter to the narrative that Premier Boxing Champions (Wilder's promoter) was trying to build in support of the notion that Wilder is a role model. After Deontay's second loss to Fury, in the pursuit of image control, PBC issued a statement in his name that read in part, "I would be lying if I said that I wasn't disappointed. But after reflecting on my journey, I now see that what God wanted me to experience is far greater than what I expected to happen. We didn't get the win, but a wise man once said the victories are within the lessons. I would like to congratulate Tyson Fury for his victory and thank you for the great historical memories that will last forever."

That was preferable to the diatribe that had followed loss number one. But then, when asked by Brian Custer during a September 2022 interview whether he would consider a rapprochement with Fury, Wilder replied, "Nah, never, because I know the truth behind that. I don't condone cheating and shit like that. I know that no matter what people say. You got analysts that say, 'If he did have something in his glove, why did you not go to the authorities?' Why the fuck would I go to the authorities when I have an opportunity to release my own energy and put my hands up on him in the possibility of trying to kill him and get paid millions of dollars doing it. Okay, go to the authorities and they lock him up. Then what's next? That's it. We proved our case. Nobody getting fed. What justice has that done? That don't make no sense."

In sum, people have grown accustomed to strange ramblings from Wilder. Indeed, in a February 2022 podcast with Byron Scott, Deontay addressed his decision-making process regarding his ring future with the advisory, "I'm thinking about doing Ayahuasca [a psychedelic tea that originated in South American religious rites]. That's gonna be my decision-making process. Boxing's put a bad taste because of what it's done to me. It's dangerous, politics, cheating."

Here, one might note that Healthline reports, "Those who take Ayahuasca can experience symptoms like vomiting, diarrhea, feelings of euphoria, strong visual and auditory hallucinations, mind-altering psychedelic effects, fear, and paranoia. Some experience euphoria and a feeling of enlightenment while others go through severe anxiety and panic."

Sounds like a plan.

Then, in May, Wilder announced during the unveiling of a statue in his honor in his hometown of Tuscaloosa that he would fight again and proclaimed, "I'm coming back on popular demand because that's all I've been hearing from high and low. From homeless people all the way up to millionaires. You feel me? It's just been an amazing feeling. So many people reaching out, telling me it's important because, without an American, heavyweight boxing really isn't exciting."

Later, Deontay augmented that sentiment to include, "I knew that I had to come back because I motivate and inspire so many around the world. What really got me back to this point was like, damn, the world really needs me."

The designated victim for Wilder's comeback fight was Robert Helenius. Born in Sweden, now living in Finland, Helenius had compiled a 31–3 (20 KOs) ring record marked by two victories over Adam Kownacki and marred by stoppage losses at the hands of Gerald Washington and Johann Duhaupas. During the Wilder–Helenius promotion, he was hyped as "Finland's finest" (which is a bit like being a snowball's warmest).

Helenius had never beaten a world-class fighter and wasn't about to start on October 15. If one were to take a computer and design a perfect opponent for Wilder to stop in two rounds or less, Robert would be the guy. Years ago, I described him as having the movement of a stalagmite. Now thirty-eight years old, he has since gotten slower and easier to hit.

Wilder had sparred with Helenius numerous times preparatory to fighting Tyson Fury. That experience confirmed that Helenius was a "safe" opponent. Very safe. This would be a payday for Deontay, not a test.

Neither Wilder or Helenius attended the August 30 kickoff press conference at Barclays Center, addressing the media electronically instead. Later, Deontay declared, "October 15 is the return of the king. My second reign is going to be filled with joy and excitement for me and those who support me." Wilder also advised, "I want to get back to the big fights and to giving the fans what they want to see. I'm doing it for the people this time."

One might question whether charging $74.99 to see Deontay fight Helenius on pay-per-view was doing it for the fans or to the fans.

With eleven bouts on the card, October 15 promised to be a long night at Barclays Center. The first fight was scheduled to begin at 5:00 p.m. The four-bout pay-per-view telecast didn't start until nine o'clock. The early undercard bouts were contested in a virtually empty arena and distinguished by the fact that, in one of them, both fighters (Keeshawn Williams and Julio Rosa) wore pink trunks.

In the first pay-per-view bout of the evening, Emmanuel Rodríguez dominated Gary Antonio Russell throughout the fight. Then, in the latter stages of round nine, Russell headbutted Rodríguez, who suffered a cut beneath his right eye and fell to the canvas, stunned. Rodríguez appeared to be in no condition to continue. But inexplicably, referee Benji Esteves (who has Magomed Abdusalamov vs. Michael Perez and Arturo Gatti vs. Joey Gamache on his refereeing résumé) allowed the fight to go on. Fortunately, there were only fifteen seconds left in the round. Rodriguez survived those seconds, after which Nitin Sethi (chief medical officer for the New York State Athletic Commission) stopped the bout. The fight went to the scorecards because it had been terminated as the result of a headbutt (ruled "accidental" by Esteves—a questionable determination) and Rodriguez won a lopsided unanimous decision.

Then Frank Sanchez stopped Carlos Negron in round nine of a predictably one-sided fight that referee Ricky Gonzalez stopped at precisely the right time. That was followed by the co-featured bout of the evening—Caleb Plant vs. Anthony Dirrell in a fight styled by the WBC as a 168-pound title-elimination contest.

One year ago, Plant had a 21–0 record with 12 knockouts and was the IBF 168-pound beltholder. Then he learned the hard way via knockout defeat that Canelo Álvarez is better than Caleb Truax, Vincent Feigenbutz, and Mike Lee (the guys Plant had successfully defended his title against). Dirrell is seven years older than Plant. Eight years ago, he held the WBC 168-pound belt before losing to Badou Jack in his first title defense.

At the August 30 kickoff press conference, Dirrell had played the role of loudmouthed instigator, calling Plant a pussy, et cetera, and so forth. That behavior continued through the final pre-fight press conference. Plant took it all in stride, saying, "I definitely feel there's a lot of jealousy there. I don't give a fuck about what he says. That don't mean nothing to me. When I beat him, it will be because I'm better than him. But he already knows that."

Plant was an 8-to-1 betting favorite.

The fight began with Dirrell, the quicker man, looking to counter. Plant kept trying to get untracked and make something happen but couldn't. Dirrell fought a chippy fight, fouling repeatedly in the clinches. That should have earned a warning followed by a point deduction but didn't. Finally, in round eight, Plant took matters into his own hands and threw Dirrell to the canvas during a clinch.

Meanwhile, Dirrell had slowed down and was posturing more than fighting. The boos from the crowd were raining down.

In round nine, the boos turned to BOOM!

Plant hooked to the body and followed with a hook up top that landed flush on Dirrell's jaw, rendering Anthony unconscious.

Immediately after the knockout, with Dirrell still out cold, Caleb pantomimed shoveling dirt onto his grave.

Bad feelings between the two? Absolutely! Dirrell shot off his mouth throughout the promotion as though he were to have the final word on the subject. He didn't.

Then it was time for the main event. Wilder was a 7-to-1 betting favorite. His presence at the top of the card made the evening a happening even if Wilder–Helenius didn't shape up as a competitive fight. That said, ticket sales had been slow. It took steep discounts and a lot of freebies to fill in the lower regions of Barclays Center. No celebrities were shown on the big overhead screen at ringside.

It should also be noted that no sport other than boxing starts its signature competitions a half-hour after midnight. Fans who had arrived at Barclays Center when the doors opened had spent more than eight hours in their seats when the bell for round one of Wilder–Helenius rang.

They didn't have to wait long afterward.

Wilder is a vicious puncher with an aura of menace about him. Opponents know that he wants to hurt them, short-circuit their brains. And with a single punch delivered at any time, he can do it. His record (now 43–2–1 with 42 KOs) stands testament to that.

This was the first time since 2019 that Wilder had fought someone other than Tyson Fury. It had to be a relief for him to see an opponent other than the Gypsy King standing across the ring from him when the bell for round one sounded. Helenius had promised to bring his A-game. And maybe he did. But the fight was about Deontay, not Robert.

Helenius moved forward clumsily at the opening bell behind a pawing jab that he brought back slowly and low. Wilder bided his time; waited until Helenius leaned forward head first while overreaching with a lunging left to the body that fell short; and closed the show with a compact right hand that landed smack in the center of Robert's face at 2:57 of the first stanza. Referee Michael Griffin didn't bother to count. Helenius was unconscious before he hit the canvas.

A lot of people in boxing think that, other than Tyson Fury, Deontay Wilder is the best heavyweight in the world today. I'm one of them.

*On a night when Deontay Wilder fought Robert Helenius
in Brooklyn and Devin Haney fought George Kambosos in Australia,
two women earned the spotlight.*

Claressa Shields Did What
She Had to Do to Win

Years from now, historians will write that 2022 was the year when women fighters emerged as a significant force in boxing. Much of that history will key on the April 30 fight between Katie Taylor and Amanda Serrano that delivered ten exciting rounds fought at a high skill level before a roaring sold-out crowd at Madison Square Garden. On October 15, an all-women fight card at the O2 Arena in London built upon that platform.

The October 15 card was co-promoted by BOXXER and Salita Promotions in association with Top Rank, streamed in the United States on ESPN+, and televised by Sky Sports in the United Kingdom. Originally scheduled for September 10, it was postponed out of respect for the Royal Family following Queen Elizabeth II's death on September 8.

Alycia Baumgardner outpointed Mikaela Mayer in the first co-featured bout on October 15 to claim the WBC, IBF, and WBO 130-pound belts. But the fight that resonated most with the public and had the most historical significance was Claressa Shields's unanimous-decision triumph over Savannah Marshall for the WBC, WBA, IBF, and WBO 160-pound titles.

Shields, now twenty-seven, won a gold medal in the middleweight division at the 2012 London Olympics (the first year that women's boxing was an Olympic sport). Four years later, she repeated that achievement at the Rio de Janeiro Olympics as the capstone on a 77–1 amateur record. Since then, she'd won 12 out of 12 professional fights and accumulated belts in three weight divisions. She entered the Marshall bout with the WBC, WBA, and IBF 160-pound titles.

Claressa is also given to unrealistic statements, such as telling TMZ, "I spar with men. I drop men. I beat men up all the time. They may be stronger than me, but their boxing ability isn't like mine. I think I can beat up Keith Thurman. I really do. GGG, he's older now. I could give GGG a run for his money."

To put that comment in context, Shields has scored one knockdown and two stoppages in six years as a pro.

Marshall, age thirty-two, was also 12–0 in the professional ranks but with 10 knockouts. She'd won the WBO 160-pound belt in 2020 and engendered considerable comment when she rendered Femke Hermans unconscious with a brutal left hook in round three of their April 2, 2022, encounter.

It was Marshall who dealt Shields the sole loss (amateur or pro) in Claressa's sojourn through boxing—a 14–8 decision at the 2012 AIBA Women's World Championships. Shields was seventeen at the time; Marshall was twenty-one. Later that year, Savannah lost in the first round of competition at the London Olympics to Marina Volnova of Kazakhstan (who Shields defeated in the second round). In 2016 in Rio de Janeiro, Marshall lost in the second round of competition to Nouchka Fontijn of the Netherlands (who Shields defeated in the gold-medal bout).

There was some trash-talking at the July 5 kickoff press conference. Marshall told the assembled media that the fight was taking place in the UK "because Claressa doesn't sell a ticket" and added, "I've knocked out people you went ten rounds with. That's all you need to know. I'm a better fighter. I'm not just going to beat you. I'm going to hurt you. See you on September 10, babe."

"I don't hate nobody," Shields responded. "But I do have a huge dislike for her. My grandma told me not to use the word 'hate,' so I won't use it."

Leading up to the scheduled September 10 fight, Shields was the more loquacious of the two fighters:

* "Her beating me in 2012 before the Olympics was the fluke of her career. I've never seen something like this in boxing before, someone who lives off of an amateur win for ten years. It's like they're trying to erase everything I've done in the past ten years because I have been dominant in boxing for a decade, since I was seventeen. I won the Olympics. I won it again. I turned pro. I won titles. And it's like, 'Wow! It's still not enough for you guys.'"

★ "If her game plan is to try and stand there in the middle of the ring
   and to out-bang me, she going to be sleeping. If her game plan is to
   be smart and try to box, move, she'll last a bit longer. If it has to be
   a war, it's going to be a war that I win. If it's going to be a boxing
   match, I'm going to win the boxing match. And if it has to be both,
   I'm prepared to do it all."

★ "To all of you that are doubting me, just make sure you apologize
   after the fight. Say, 'We were wrong. You're the best and we respect
   you,' and that you respect my hard work and my accomplishments."

Meanwhile, Marshall had her own take on the impending battle,
saying, "I'm going to take her into deep water and drown her in
the Thames."

Then everything changed. On September 8, Queen Elizabeth died,
ushering in a period of unprecedented national mourning. The British
Boxing Board of Control ruled that the fight card would be postponed.

"I'm sad about the fight being postponed," Shields acknowledged.
"But I'm a big girl and I understand that the Queen of the country passing
has an entire country mourning. Whatever the decision, I'm respectful of it."

Marshall seemed to take the postponement harder, telling Sky Sports
that she went to Buckingham Palace with a sister and a friend to pay
respects before adding, "I had a week off, and I needed it. I felt emotion-
ally drained. I didn't get out of bed for a couple of days after. I was trying
to be positive but I was disappointed. I was upset, the 'it always happens
to me' kind of vibe."

In due course, the card was rescheduled for October 15. Ten days
before the bout, the WBC announced that it had created yet another belt
to add to the many baubles that it bestows on fighters; this one a specially
crafted "Elizabethan Belt" (purple, not green) that would be given to the
winner of Shields–Marshall.

When fight week arrived, some of the buzz that swirled around the
original September 10 date had dissipated. But anticipation was still high.

Peter Fury (who trains Marshall) said of Shields, "She's got fast hands,
she's good defensively, and she's good with counters. She puts flurries
together well. With her feints, she makes fighters hesitant. Before they
know it, she's in range and teeing off on them with her quick hands."

As for his own charge, Fury noted, "She's got the ability to switch people's lights out, and that's a different sort of power than most."

Meanwhile, Shields remained the more quotable of the two fighters, offering a range of thoughts:

* "I'm not worried about Savannah Marshall. Nobody was ever running from her. Nobody was ever scared to come over here and fight her. We said, 'Let's do it. And you better punch as hard as you say you can. Because if you don't have any punching power, it's going to be a hard night for you.'"

* "She's going to try to come out there and land a big shot. That's really all I see. But it's a boxing match. I may get hit in there. But if she thinks she won't get hit, then she's mistaken. If she thinks she is a better boxer than me, she's mistaken. I'm going to adapt and do whatever I have to do to win and make the fight easy. She can't outbox me. She's not very skilled."

* "I really feel in my spirit that I am going to knock Savannah Marshall out. This is going to be my statement fight. She's not going to be able to handle my shots."

This was the first time that a women's bout had headlined a fight card at the O2 Arena. In keeping with that theme, all eleven bouts on the bill showcased women fighters. The first nine were expected to be relatively easy outings for promoter favorites. Shields–Marshall and Mayer–Baumgardner were another matter.

Mayer, age thirty-two, came into her fight with a 17–0 (5 KOs) ring record. She'd won the WBO and IBF 130 pound belts by decision over Ewa Brodnicka (in 2020) and Maiya Hamadouche (2021) and defended them successfully by decision over Jennifer Han earlier this year. Baumgardner, age twenty-eight (12–1, 7 KOs) annexed the WBC 130-pound belt with a surprise knockout of Terri Harper last year.

Mayer was a 5-to-2 betting favorite. The women "had to be separated" during a fight-week interview on Sky Sports, again at the final pre-fight press conference, and once more at a post-weigh-in staredown, proving that women fighters can act as silly as the men.

When fight night arrived, the hostilities between them were more muted. Baumgardner prevailed on a 96–95, 96–95, 93–97 split decision, and ESPN commentator Tim Bradley opined, "The next time they do it, I want to see more action."

Shields–Marshall was far more fan-friendly and a classic confrontation between boxer and puncher.

The women had three common opponents—Sydney LeBlanc, Hannah Rankin, and Femke Hermans. Shields outpointed all three without losing a round on any of the judges' scorecards. Marshall (in her pro debut) won every round against LeBlanc, stopped Rankin in seven rounds, and, as previously noted, knocked Hermans unconscious.

The stakes were high. Whoever won would be elevated to legitimate stardom. Shields was a slight betting favorite. An enthusiastic sold-out crowd of 20,000 witnessed the action.

Once the bell for round one sounded, Marshall kept coming forward, firing punches for the entire night. Shields was respectful of Marshall's power but understood that the only way she could keep Savannah off was to hurt her. Claressa didn't run. She fired back and often fired first.

A ten-round firefight followed.

Shields was the better boxer, faster, and pulled the trigger more quickly than Marshall did. She was also the more accurate puncher.

Marshall showed more boxing skills than she had in previous fights. Her most effective blows were hooks to the body. And she wasn't above using her forearms, shoulders, and elbows on the far side of the rules when she and Shields were fighting inside. Claressa didn't complain. She just fired back.

It was an action fight from beginning to end. Shields showed more fire and firepower than she had in previous outings. She had to in order to win. Each woman gave it everything she had. Both dug deep in the second half of the fight.

The judges' 97–93, 97–93, 94–94 verdict in Shields's favor was on the mark.

Crawford, Avanesyan, Spence, and BLK Prime

On December 10, 2022, Terence Crawford knocked out David Avanesyan in the sixth round of a fight promoted in Crawford's hometown of Omaha, Nebraska, by a virtually unknown company called BLK Prime. The promotion was destined from the start to lose millions of dollars and seemed to make no sense from a business point of view. The organizers have a track record of—shall we say—questionable business dealings. And the fight that fans wanted to see was Crawford vs. Errol Spence, not Crawford–Avanesyan.

Let's dissect the mess.

Crawford is a complete fighter. He can box. He can punch. He transitions seamlessly from orthodox to southpaw and is equally effective from either stance. When he beat Julius Indongo at 140 pounds in 2017, he became the first champion to hold all four major sanctioning body belts in any weight class since 2006. He has been a fixture at or near the top of pound-for-pound lists for years. The only thing missing from his résumé (which now shows 39 wins with 30 knockouts in 39 fights) is a signature win over another elite fighter.

Spence has long been the logical opponent for Crawford to fight. But the boxing business isn't logical. As Carlos Acevedo wrote, "Boxing rarely yields to the wishes of the public. In the real world, fans would be the equivalent of consumers and no company in its right mind would ignore, much less insult, its customer base. Most companies are interested in developing a quality product and maintaining some kind of relationship with their clientele, who have purchasing power behind them. But promoters are impervious to market forces because market forces, for the most part, do not exist in boxing. It hardly matters if a ticket sells, a Nielsen point is produced, a pay-per-view is ordered. All a promoter needs to do is bend the ear of a network executive [or gullible investor], preferably one with little interest in quality control, and—voila!—he is flush. This is the business model to end all business models."

Spence has consistently put a damper on prospects for Crawford–Spence. "Me and Terence Crawford are on different sides of the street," Errol said in 2019. "He's just signed with ESPN. I don't fight for ESPN. I fight for Showtime or Fox. Terence Crawford has got to come across the street."

"There's no such thing as 'across the street,'" Crawford responded. "Back in the day, you never heard fighters say 'across the street.' What street? This is boxing. Everybody fights everybody."

Then, this year, Crawford's contract with Top Rank expired and he became a promotional free agent. It was an ugly parting with Terence suing Top Rank for alleged racial bias and breach of contract. The claim of racial bias seems unfounded and legally frivolous. Not having seen Crawford's contract with Top Rank and a full accounting with regard to his fights, it's impossible to voice an opinion with respect to the contract claim.

Regardless, the major impediment to making Crawford–Spence had been removed from the mix. Or so it seemed. The problem was that Premier Boxing Champions impresario Al Haymon (Spence's de facto manager) continued to take negotiating positions that worked against making the fight.

More specifically, Haymon wanted Crawford to fight Spence on a percentage basis with no minimum guarantee. And according to Crawford, PBC refused to insert a clause in Terence's contract that would have required financial transparency to ensure that he got an honest accounting.

Remarkably, Crawford was amenable to fighting without a guarantee. That's how badly he wanted to fight Spence. But the lack of transparency was a sticking point.

"I never heard of a fighter ever taking zero guarantee in a fight," Terence said in a November 1 Instagram Live session. "That is something that's new to me, but that's something that I was willing to do to make this fight happen. I told him, 'All right, cool; I'll take no guarantee. I'll take the less end of the money. Whatever it is you want, I'll take it because that's how much confidence I got that I'm gonna beat that man. So even though I knew I was getting fucked, I just wanted a little transparency. I said, 'Okay, if I'm gonna bet on myself, then I want a little transparency.' I wanna know things that's gonna affect my check. I wanna see if the numbers add up to what they tellin' me. It's just simple to me. To think that a person would go in a business with a person and this person would tell them, 'Oh, well, I'm not gonna tell you how much we really made, but I'm gonna just give you this. You just gotta trust me.' Come on, now. It don't make no sense."

Here one might note that asking a fighter of Crawford's magnitude to fight with no guarantee and without full transparency sounds like a page out of Don King's old playbook.

Crawford also maintained that, at one point in the negotiations, two hedge funds offered to pay guaranteed purses of $25 million each to him and Spence but that, in his words, "Al told me straight up, 'I'm not letting anybody touch this fight.'"

Maybe the hedge fund money was real. Maybe not. If it had been put in escrow, that wouldn't have been Crawford and Spence's problem. Then again, if the money had been put in escrow, Crawford and Spence would have had transparency. They would have known exactly how much money was there to be divided between them.

Bottom line: It appears as though Crawford wanted the fight and Team Spence didn't. "I believe in my abilities and I believe in myself," Terence said. "Errol Spence, he can't say the same."

Then the earth shifted. Attorney John Hornewer had been negotiating Crawford–Spence with Haymon and Showtime Sports president Stephen Espinoza on Crawford's behalf. On October 20, Hornewer got a telephone call from Team Crawford telling him to stop. Later that day, Hornewer learned from news reports that Crawford and David Avanesyan had signed contracts to fight each other on December 10 at CHI Health Center in Omaha.

Avanesyan (Russian born and now living in England) has beaten some good fighters but not any very good ones. One of his losses came by stoppage at the hands of Egidijus Kavaliauskas (who Crawford knocked out).

Crawford–Avanesyan was funded and streamed by a little-known subscription video-on-demand service called BLK Prime and was also available on traditional outlets. It was publicly stated that Crawford's contract called for him to receive a $10 million purse with half of that amount having been placed in escrow as of October 20. This might have been an accurate number. More likely, it was an exaggeration for the sake of publicity and ego.

How did the deal come about?

"These people [BLK Prime] came out of the woodwork," Frank Warren (Avanesyan's promoter) told this writer. "I have no idea who they are. They contacted us through the fighter. George [Warren's son and CEO of Queensberry Promotions] and [Queensberry event manager] Andy Ayling put the deal together. And I can assure you; there's no way in the world that David would be going to the United States unless his money was safeguarded."

"It is what it is," Crawford said after the deal was announced. "I'm moving forward with my career. I agreed to everything that I needed to agree to get that fight [Crawford–Spence] made. But there's only so much I can do. Al told me, 'Well, you take this fight or you got nothing.' I don't know like the type of caliber of people that he been dealing with. Like, what do you really expect? You expect me to be disrespected, ran over, stepped on, and just sit there and just take it. We're gonna turn up with BLK Prime. We gonna do our thing. They turnin' boxing around, man. All the biggest fights going through them. They the new wave. You wanna fight this guy, you wanna fight this guy. They gonna make it happen."

Okay. . . . So what is BLK Prime? As noted above, it's a video-on-demand service. As of this writing, it charges $3.99 per month for content exclusive of pay-per-view events. It's hard to think of a promotional company about which so little is known that appeared on the boxing scene in conjunction with a fight of this magnitude.

The driving force behind BLK Prime appears to be Desmond Gumbs, who has been on the fringe of the entertainment business for years and is alleged in various internet postings to have left a trail of unpaid creditors in his wake.

Gumbs is also listed as the athletic director and head football coach at Lincoln University—a private school in Oakland, California. According to Wikipedia, Lincoln is on the US Department of Education's Federal Student Aid (FSA) List of Institutions on Heightened Cash Monitoring.

"Heightened Cash Monitoring," Wikipedia explains, "is a step that FSA can take with institutions to provide additional oversight for a number of financial or federal compliance issues, some of which may be serious and others that may be less troublesome. The list notes 'severe findings' for Lincoln University."

In addition, a November 1, 2018, report from an online publication called *Record Searchlight* ties Gumbs to a motel called Market Street Manor that the Shasta County (California) District Attorney's office said was purchased in April 2017 by Desmond and Chandler Gumbs through a company called Earl Freddy Invest C LLC.

In a news release, District Attorney Stephanie Bridgett declared, "The Market Street Manor has become a hub of crime and violence in our community and it is a public nuisance. I cannot permit this business to continue violating the law without consequences." The news release also referenced "deplorable living conditions" in the motel including the allegation that some rooms were "infested with rats, mice and bedbugs" and Bridgett's claim that "the Gumbses' ownership is putting a strain on law enforcement and affecting neighboring businesses."

A company in the United Kingdom called BLK Prime Limited is registered as a property management business and lists Desmond Gumbs as a director. BLK Prime G LLC is listed by Bizapedia as a California limited-liability entertainment company whose filing status has been "suspended" by the Franchise Tax Board for failure to meet state tax requirements.

These are not good credentials.

Crawford, as noted, said that his purse for fighting Avanesyan would be $10 million. That was far above market value and considerably more than Terence received for recent fights against Jose Benavidez Jr. ($3.5 million), Amir Khan ($4.8 million), Egidijus Kavaliauskas ($4 million), Kell Brook ($3.5 million), and Shawn Porter ($6 million).

"I already got half of my money," Crawford told Brian Custer several weeks before the bout. "And I'mma get the other half before I even step in the ring, like a week before or so. That way, I don't have to worry about if they have the money or they don't or have to go through all those hoops on getting paid. My money is already secured."

Avanesyan's purse was $550,000 with no option clause should he win the fight. The contract also called for him to receive partial payment had the fight fallen through due to no fault on his part. Avanesyan's purse was held in escrow by attorney Leon Margules. The final payment to the escrow fund was due on December 5 and was received by Margules on December 9.

Expenses for the promotion, if Crawford had in fact contracted for $10 million, were expected to total close to $12 million. Where would the revenue to cover these costs (or even a $5 million purse for Crawford) come from?

Tickets for the event were priced from $500 down to $50. In a best-case scenario, the promotion could hope for a live gate of $1 million to $2 million. The other substantial revenue stream would come from pay-per-view buys. But Crawford has never been a pay-per-view draw. "His marketability," Bob Arum has observed, "didn't measure up to his ability. Terence's numbers on PPV have always been dreadful."

Crawford vs. Shawn Porter generated a dismal 135,000 pay-per-view buys. And that was with two talented "name fighters" competing against each other and ESPN's marketing muscle behind the promotion. BLK Prime had no marketing platform to build on.

By way of comparison, ESPN's main Instagram page has 24.2 million followers. BLK Prime's main Instagram page is credited with 47,000.

Moreover, Crawford–Avanesyan would be airing opposite the Heisman Trophy presentation followed by a Top Rank card featuring Teófimo López on ESPN. Best estimates were that Crawford–Avanesyan would generate well under 50,000 buys.

On November 28, 2022, BLK announced that Crawford–Avanesyan would be distributed on pay-per-view through traditional cable and satellite outlets by Integrated Sports and streamed by BLK Prime and PPV.com for $39.95. Protocol Sports Marketing was chosen to market and distribute worldwide media rights (excluding the United States and Canada).

In an effort to bolster the promotion, thirty-seven-year-old Cris Cyborg was added to the card in a four-round lightweight boxing match against Gabrielle Holloway (another MMA fighter who engaged in two boxing matches six years ago and lost both of them).

Todd Grisham was brought onboard to handle the blow-by-blow commentary with Paulie Malignaggi and Antonio Tarver beside him.

CHI Health Center seats 17,000 for boxing. The announced crowd for Crawford–Avanesyan was 14,630. The undercard was undistinguished.

The television production suffered from a lack of multiple camera angles. Crawford (a 12-to-1 betting favorite) knocked Avanesyan unconscious with a highlight-reel left-uppercut-right-hook combination in the sixth round.

And a thought in closing. . . .

Four decades ago, a man named Ross Fields (who adopted the alias "Harold Smith") formed a company called Muhammad Ali Professional Sports and, with Ali's consent, began promoting fights. Smith paid outlandish purses to fighters and MAPS hemorrhaged money until it was revealed that the source of his funding was $21 million ($73 million in today's dollars) that had been embezzled from the Wells Fargo Bank of California.

BLK Prime's boxing venture might be on the up-and-up. But it's worth remembering what Bob Arum said about Harold Smith's promotional activities way back when.

"I am totally bewildered," Arum stated, "why anybody would go into boxing ventures for the purpose of losing substantial sums of money. They are paying double and triple what other promoters could afford to pay and remain solvent. How they do it and why is a mystery. Where does the money come from?"

York Hall is an important part of the fabric of British boxing.

Reflections on a Night at York Hall

Bethnal Green in London is widely viewed as the spiritual home of modern boxing. Daniel Mendoza, the most scientific and accomplished fighter of his time, whose championship reign extended from 1792 to 1795, lived there. So did many of his fighting brethren.

In the centuries that followed, there were small fight clubs all over London. Most of them have disappeared. But York Hall in Bethnal Green still exists. For many British fighters, competing there is a rite of passage. Lennox Lewis, Tyson Fury, Anthony Joshua, Joe Calzaghe, Ricky Hatton, Carl Froch, and David Haye all fought in York Hall early in their respective careers. But the venue is better defined by the thousands of anonymous fighters who plied their trade within its walls.

"It's a place that's frozen in time," Tris Dixon said recently. "In summer, it's hotter than hell. In winter, it's brutally cold. The changing rooms are a disgrace. And it's wonderful. If you're a boxing fan with a bucket list, York Hall has to be on it."

I've been to a lot of fights in my life, but only once before in England and that was twenty years ago. On September 16, 2022, I went to the fights at York Hall.

I'd arrived at Gatwick Airport south of London on September 15 and stepped into a world of celebration and mourning. One week earlier, Queen Elizabeth II had died. Very few people work until age ninety-six, but the Queen did. In 1926 (the year she was born), the British empire was the largest in human history, encompassing 25 percent of the earth's land surface. The British flag flew in India, much of Africa, and two dozen other countries around the globe. Elizabeth's seventy years on the throne saw massive geopolitical change. Her reign intersected with the terms of sixteen prime ministers and fourteen presidents of the United States. She was a living symbol of unity in a fractured world.

The days that followed the Queen's death were part tradition, part religious rite, part carefully calibrated political theater, and part personal mourning. People queued up for hours on end in a line that stretched for miles to file past her coffin in Westminster Hall. The weather played a role in bringing out the crowds. The temperatures were comfortable with no rain and a gentle breeze.

One might ponder the fact that Queen Victoria ascended to the throne in 1837 and reigned for sixty-three years. Elizabeth II served as Queen for seventy. England has had a woman as its monarch for 133 of the past 185 years. Now, barring unforeseen tragedy, the crown will pass from Charles to William to George. It will be many years before a woman reigns again.

York Hall opened in 1929 in a ceremony presided over by the Duke and Duchess of York (later King George VI and his queen). It originally housed a public Turkish bath that is now an upscale spa. The hall began hosting fights in the 1950s and was renovated in 2005. The surrounding neighborhood is undergoing gentrification but still has one of the highest crime rates in London.

Waiting for the doors at York Hall to open, I thought back to my previous experience at the fights in England. On December 15, 2001, I was at the Wembley Conference Centre in London. The undercard included a nineteen-year-old welterweight named Matthew Macklin in the second pro fight of his career and twenty-one-year-old Enzo Maccarinelli. But the fans had come to see a man from Australia named Justin Rowsell be fed to a young lion named Ricky Hatton. The lion devoured his prey in two rounds and everyone went home happy (with the exception of Team Rowsell). Decades later, I remember the energy in the arena that night and the frenzy that accompanied Hatton's "Blue Moon" entrance as though it were yesterday.

The doors to York Hall opened at six o'clock and I went inside. The arena offers a more intimate setting than one might expect from a facility that accommodates 1,200 fans for boxing. A low-hanging balcony looms over the ring with two rows of seats on opposite sides of the balcony and four rows of seats at the back end.

York Hall is where ring announcer David Diamante called his first fight in the United Kingdom. "It's a special place," Diamante says. "I love it. Walking into York Hall is like walking back in time. It's an old building, grit and grime, bare bones, no amenities. It's not glamorous but it has soul. There's not a bad seat in the house. The ghosts are there. And the fans make it even more special. These are real fans. They don't get all dressed up. They're not there to be seen. They're there for the fights. They're rabid and knowledgeable."

"On fight nights," British boxing writer Gareth Davies told me, "the hall is an absolute bear pit, a cauldron of fire with magic dust in the air."

BoxRec.com has records for 690 fight cards that were contested at York Hall dating back to 1967. This would be the twenty-first card held there in 2022. In a nod to fate, Frank Warren (who promoted Ricky Hatton vs. Justin Rowsell) was the promoter on September 16.

Warren, whose blue eyes rival those of Frank Sinatra, has been promoting fights since 1981. "In the old days at York Hall," he recalls, "if it was a good fight, people would throw money into the ring. But health and safety stopped the practice because they were afraid the coins would hit someone in the eye or something like that."

"The old days" are referred to a lot in boxing. When boxing was boxing—as the saying goes—ticket sellers were matched against each other in neighborhood fight clubs. Now, as Matt Christie recently wrote, "We're left with too few contests that actually pit a developing fighter against a developing fighter. In the home corner, you have the ticket seller, the point of interest, the all but preordained winner, versus the away fighter who is not supposed to have his or her arm raised. The script is written long before the opening bell and, consequently, it's very rare that the away corner gets a single victory.

"Going all out and trying to win is rarely encouraged," Christie added with regard to the "away" fighter. "If they do win, they might find that they won't be invited back to the away corner for a while so their earnings are at risk. Furthermore, anyone who has spent time in and around the small hall scene in Britain will have heard journeymen being told to go easy on certain fighters in the name of education for the up and comer, teach him a few things but don't embarrass them. The problem with this is that professional boxing has become a glorified popularity contest."

Warren takes issue with Christie's appraisal—at least as far as his own shows are concerned. "A lot of these fighters are young," the promoter says. "They're learning their trade. They don't have man-strength yet. Too many hard fights early would be bad for them physically and in terms of their development as fighters."

Regardless of how one views the issue, the fans at York Hall on September 16 got their money's worth.

The first four fights went as expected. The red corner was the designated "winners" corner. Blue was for the presumptive losers. The fighters' records told the tale.

Pro debut vs. 1–2 . . . 6–0 vs. 3–17 . . . 5–0 vs. 3–37–2 . . . 1–0 vs. 3–18–1.

Some of the opponents waited for the opening bell with a look that said, "This will be painful." And they fought like their objective was to avoid confrontations, last the distance, pick up a paycheck, and go home.

Others came to win.

In the fifth fight of the evening, there was a surprise. A big one.

Frank Arnold (a popular super-featherweight with a 9–0–1 record) stepped into the ring to face Brayan Mairena (a Nicaraguan citizen living in Spain who had lost 30 of his last 31 fights).

Now it's 30 of 32.

Mairena landed repeatedly up top in round one.

"Keep your composure, Frank," Warren shouted from ringside. "Keep your hands up."

As the bout progressed, Mairena kept pressuring his foe. He wasn't there to serve as a learning experience. In round three, he knocked Arnold down and pummeled him around the ring. Only the bell saved the favorite from destruction.

That would have been a good time to stop the fight. But Arnold's corner and the referee allowed the bout to continue. Bad choice. Just past the two-minute mark of round four, an overhand right sent Arnold plummeting to the canvas where he landed face first, unconscious, with a sickening thud. He lay there for a frighteningly long time with an oxygen mask over his face before rising on unsteady legs and being helped from the ring.

It was a reminder to the sold-out crowd that anything can happen in boxing and, also, just how dangerous boxing is.

Order was restored in fight number six when 3–0 decisioned 1–19.

That was followed by a spectacular fight. Cruiserweight Ellis Zorro (14–0, 6 KOs) swept the first four rounds against Dec Spelman (18–5, 9 KOs), punctuated by a brutal body shot in round four that put Spelman on the canvas and appeared to end the bout. But Spelman survived and started putting hurt on Zorro in the next stanza. In rounds six and seven (the seventh being one of the best back-and-forth rounds I've ever seen), he had Zorro in trouble. Zorro's face was a bloody mess. He appeared to be out on his feet. There was doubt as to whether he'd be able to answer the bell for round eight, let alone survive it. But Spelman was too tired to make anything more happen. Zorro prevailed by a 77–74 margin.

Next up—Royston Barney-Smith (2–0) vs. Paul Holt (8–14, 2 KOs), 6 rounds, junior lightweights.

Barney-Smith is an eighteen-year old southpaw with a good amateur pedigree and charisma. His first two fights as a pro had been wins by decision over fighters who, as of this writing, have zero wins in 23 fights. Holt was expected to provide more of a challenge. He didn't. A crushing overhand left that landed flush in the jaw ended matters at the 36-second mark of round one.

"This is a building step," Barney-Smith said afterward. "Like for a LEGO. I want to build a castle."

He's the sort of fighter that Frank Warren can build well.

At that point, the crowd stood for a minute of silence in honor of the Queen.

Elizabeth II wasn't a boxing fan. But she did something that no other British monarch ever did. She bestowed knighthood on a professional boxer. When Henry Cooper retired from the ring, he was the most beloved fighter in the history of British boxing. Later, he was instrumental in raising millions of pounds for charity and served as a spokesperson for the National Health Service in a campaign that encouraged people age sixty-five and older to get flu shots. In recognition of his contributions to society, Queen Elizabeth conferred knighthood upon him in 2000.

The crowd stood respectfully for the tribute.

Then came the main event. Denzel Bentley (14–1–1, 13 KOs) vs. Marcus Morrison (25–5, 16 KOs). Twelve scheduled rounds for Bentley's British middleweight title. Rounds one and two were a slugfest with lots of give and lots of take. By round three, Bentley had established his dominance. In round four, the referee appropriately called a halt to what was becoming a harrowing destruction.

The best performances of the evening were turned in by Bentley and Barney-Smith. But the two fights that stand out most in my mind are Arnold vs. Mairena and Zorro vs. Spelman.

Arnold was hurt. But no one stopped the fight. Again and again, he was blasted with punishing blows to the head before he succumbed. On some primitive level, it was less troubling to me that it was Arnold who was knocked unconscious rather than the underdog Mairena. Attribute that, if you will, to some misguided notion of fairness on my part. But the beating that Arnold took on September 16 might change his brain forever.

Zorro vs. Spelman was a "great" fight. Each man was on the brink of oblivion at different times during the bout. And each man came back to turn the tide. That leaves me to reflect on what it means when a fight is "great"—two fighters mercilessly pounding each other, inflicting lasting damage on one another.

Mairena, Arnold, Zorro, and Spelman asked questions of each other in the ring and also questions about boxing. If someone cares about fighters, these questions have to be asked.

Curiosities

As William Wordsworth wrote more than two centuries ago,
"The Child is father of the Man."

Boxing through Young Eyes

My uncle died in early October 2021. As per his request, he was cremated and the family converged in New York at the end of the month for the interment of his remains. Reece Chapman (my thirteen-year-old great-nephew) lives in Montana and was here for the ceremony.

There was a time when boxing was a bonding force between generations. Fathers and sons sat down in front of a television set and watched *Gillette Friday Night Fights* together. The first fight I went to was the 1965 bout between Floyd Patterson and George Chuvalo at the "old" Madison Square Garden on Eighth Avenue and Forty-Ninth Street. Patterson was on the comeback trail after consecutive first-round knockout losses to Sonny Liston and beat Chuvalo on a 8–4, 7–5, 6–5–1 decision.

My uncle took me to that fight.

Reece's three favorite sports to watch on television are football, basketball, and boxing. The closest he'd been to a live professional fight was when I brought him to Gleason's Gym before the pandemic and he saw two fighters sparring. On October 30, 2022, Top Rank promoted an eight-bout card at the Hulu Theater at Madison Square Garden. Reece had never been to a fight. I decided to bring him.

Not many people who go to a fight sit close enough to the ring that they can see the anger, fear, hurt, and other emotions that cross fighters' eyes. Television cosmetizes the violence. Sitting in the press section, there's no filter. Either a person is drawn to the spectacle or repulsed by it.

Reece is a people person with empathy for others. I wondered how he'd process the reality of boxing. I asked Top Rank media relations director Evan Korn if Reece could be credentialed for the October 30 fight card. Evan said yes, and event access manager Katie Neff helped implement the plan.

Reece and I arrived at Madison Square Garden on fight night at 6:40 p.m. Our seats were second row center in the ringside press section.

The arena was virtually empty. Most of the eight bouts had a clear favorite. Top Rank has two matchmakers—Bruce Trampler and Brad Goodman— who are on the short list of best matchmakers ever. I explained to Reece that a big part of their job is to select opponents for fighters that Top Rank is trying to build. Each fight should be a learning experience for the favorite and end with a "W" on his record. Some fighters are handled with more care than others. Some need less protection than others.

Reece took his status as a credentialed member of the media seriously. Over the next four-and-a-half hours, he would fill an old spiral-bound HBO Boxing notebook I'd given him with eleven pages of notes.

The lights went on and rap music played as the first boxers made their way to the ring. Viewed from our vantage point, the ring ropes seemed suddenly evocative to me of horizontal prison bars.

At 7:10 p.m., the bell for round one of the first bout sounded. Kasir Goldston (3–0, 1 KO) vs. Marc Misiura (2–1, 1 KO). Misiura's two wins had come against opponents with 1 win in 13 fights. Against Goldston, he was aggressive until he got hit, at which point he opted for a less confrontational strategy. Later in the fight, he got chippy and lost a point for an intentional head butt. The judges' scores were 40–35, 40–35, 40–35 in Goldston's favor.

Fight #2—Ray Cuadrado (1–0, 1 KO) vs. Michael Land (1–3–1, 1 KO). Land was game but didn't have the skills to compete. Cuadrado won a 40–36, 39–37, 39–37 decision.

Fight #3—Jahi Tucker (4–0, 2 KOs) vs. Jorge Rodrigo Sosa (3–2, 3 KOs). Sosa was tough. But tough is different from good. In round two, Tucker started putting a beating on him. Sosa was taking too many clean punches and getting hurt. At 2:18 of the stanza, referee Shawn Clark stopped the bout.

Three fights down, each one ending as expected.

Now the arena was filling up. The crowd was becoming part of the drama.

Fight #4—Pablo Valdez (4–0, 4 KOs) vs. Alejandro Martinez (2–1–1, 2 KOs). How did Martinez get to 2–1–1? His previous opponents had compiled a composite ring record of 6 wins, 70 losses, and 1 draw. That's how.

Valdez was a heavy favorite. But as Lennox Lewis once observed, "A punch in the face; that changes everything. All the things you practiced can suddenly stop working."

In round two, Martinez staggered Valdez and had him holding on. Thereafter, Martinez was the hunter and Valdez was the hunted. At the end of round four, the ropes kept Valdez from going down but referee Eddie Claudio failed to call a knockdown. Claudio also warned Valdez about holding multiple times but failed to take a point away long after a deduction seemed warranted. If Claudio's work left something to be desired, the scoring of the judges was worse—a 59–55, 59–55, 57–57 majority decision in Valdez's favor.

"What?" Reece said in disbelief. "That's crazy."

In other words, a thirteen-year-old attending his first fight card ever saw Valdez–Martinez more clearly than the judges.

Now Reece was into the scene.

"It's really cool," he told me. "How fast the fighters' hands are; how focused they are; the way they move around the ring."

Fight #5—Matthew Gonzalez (12–0, 8 KOs) vs. Dakota Linger (12–5, 8 KOs). All of Linger's wins had come in West Virginia or North Carolina. In the previous three years, he'd won twice and suffered five losses. The wins came against DeWayne Wisdom (1 win in his last 38 fights) and Darel Harris (2 wins in his last 23 outings).

Twelve–0 from New York City vs. 12–5–2 from Buckhannon, West Virginia. Guess who won.

Wrong.

Linger came out throwing punches with the sophistication of a toughman contestant and kept throwing. Everyone in the arena could see the punches coming except Gonzalez.

When a young fighter is pressured, either he forgets what he has learned about boxing or he uses it. Gonzalez forgot. The result was a totally entertaining, all-action brawl between a boxer and a toughman in what devolved into the equivalent of a toughman contest. The crowd cheered loudly for much of the bout and was on its feet at the end. The judges ruled it a majority draw—a reasonable verdict, although the nod could have gone to Linger.

"I've never see anything like this," Reece said. "This is really really cool."

Fight #6—Jonathan Guzman (24–1, 23 KOs) vs. Carlos Jackson (17–1, 11 KOs) brought the fans back to earth. Eight technically fought rounds. Guzman was the more passive of the two. Jackson tried periodically to pick up the pace, but Guzman had the skills to blunt his attack. When it was over, Jackson was on the long end of a 78–74, 77–75, 75–77 decision.

Then came the co-feature bout—Carlos Caraballo (14–0, 14 KOs) vs. Jonas Sultan (17–5, 11 KOs). Things got interesting in a hurry when Sultan (a decided underdog) knocked Caraballo down with a right upper-cut in round two (Reece's first official knockdown). He did it again in round three but was badly hurt himself in round four.

The action got even better from there. It was a sensational, brutal, back-and-forth fight. By round eight, Caraballo was unloading, landing shot after shot to Sultan's head. The carnage continued in round nine with cries of "stop the fight" reverberating through the air. Then, out of nowhere, Sultan dropped Caraballo again with a left hook.

All told, Caraballo was knocked down four times and Sultan once. Each man suffered more damage than a fighter should. It was a legitimate fight of the year candidate with all three judges scoring the bout 94–93 in Sultan's favor.

"WOW!" Reece said. "WOW! WOW! WOW!"

The last fight of the evening—Jose Zepeda (34–2, 26 KOs) vs. Josue Vargas (19–1, 9 KOs)—was memorable in its own way. Zepeda had come up short in two previous title opportunities and is best known for a fifth-round knockout of Ivan Baranchyk in an exciting slugfest that was the Boxing Writers Association of America's 2020 "fight of the year." Vargas was stepping up his own level of competition to take the bout. At the Friday weigh-in, the fighters' camps had gotten into one of those stupid shoving matches with punches thrown at the close of the staredown. Now it was time to fight for real.

Midway through round one, Zepeda smashed Vargas to the canvas with a perfectly timed overhand left that landed flush. Vargas rose on wobbly legs, and Zepeda finished him off at the 1:45 mark of the stanza.

Maybe someday, years from now, Reece will remember that I took him to his first pro fights.

★★★

When Shakespeare wrote, "The first thing we do, let us kill all the lawyers," he wasn't thinking about Mike Heitner.

Mike represented Top Rank for decades and was as good as any contract lawyer in the business. Hundreds of championship fights bore his imprint. He was also one of the nicest people in boxing.

One of pleasures that came with going to a Top Rank press conference or a Top Rank fight was the opportunity to sit and chat with Mike. He died suddenly in his sleep on October 19 at age 82. A lot of people who were at Madison Square Garden this week missed him. I was one of them.

As a writer, I take pride in having contributed to the history of The Ring.

The Ring at 100

A.J. Liebling wrote, "It is through Jack O'Brien that I trace my rapport with the historic past through the laying-on of hands. He hit me, for pedagogical example, and he had been hit by the great Bob Fitzsimmons from whom he won the light-heavyweight title in 1906. Fitzsimmons had been hit by Corbett, Corbett by John L. Sullivan, he by Paddy Ryan with the bare knuckles, and Ryan by Joe Goss, his predecessor who as a young man had felt the fist of the great Jem Mace. It is a great thrill to feel that all that separates you from the early Victorians is a series of punches on the nose."

Like Liebling's punches on the nose, *The Ring* binds boxing history together. I felt that very strongly twenty-five years ago when I attended the magazine's seventy-fifth Anniversary Dinner in Atlantic City. Countless ring greats were in attendance. Ali–Frazier III was honored as the "best fight" during *The Ring's* existence. The "best round" was the opening stanza of Hagler–Hearns. "Best knockout"—Ray Robinson's one-punch KO of Gene Fullmer. "Best trainer"—Eddie Futch.

The most important award was "best fighter." The nominees were Joe Louis, Henry Armstrong, Muhammad Ali, and Sugar Ray Robinson. Ali had been told in advance that Robinson would be the honoree. He wanted to pay tribute to Sugar Ray but was unable to attend and asked that I read a poem in his absence:

A CONCESSION SPEECH OF SORTS
TO SUGAR RAY ROBINSON

BY MUHAMMAD ALI

Sugar Ray was handsome. But I'm more than handsome; I'm pretty
Sugar Ray was clever. But I'm smart and witty
Sugar Ray was a fighter I always admired
But if Sugar Ray ever fought me with all my dancing, by the end of round
*   two he'd be tired*
Pound for pound; you can argue about who's best for days

Aw, give it to Ray; he invented the phrase
Calling him pound-for-pound is easy to see
As long as you remember, The Greatest is me

Now, twenty-five years later, *The Ring* is celebrating its hundredth anniversary. Very few magazines reach that age. Well-established institutions like *Time Magazine* (first published in 1923) and *Sports Illustrated* (1954) have yet to reach the century mark.

The first issue of *The Ring* was published in February 1922 under the guidance of Nat Fleischer.

"You have to remember the era we're talking about," historian Randy Roberts says. "In 1920, the Walker Act legalized boxing in New York. In 1921, Jack Dempsey fought Georges Carpentier in New Jersey in front of eighty thousand fans, which was the largest crowd in America to witness a sporting event up until that time. Dempsey–Carpentier was also the first world championship fight broadcast blow-by-blow on radio. This is the beginning of modern boxing. And one year later, *The Ring* comes along, takes boxing out of the hands of the *Police Gazette*, and becomes the sport's most important publication."

Fleischer was sometimes careless with facts. And he was known to tilt editorial coverage to favor certain fighters. But over time, *The Ring* became known as "The Bible of Boxing."

At age ninety-one, Jerry Izenberg is almost as old as *The Ring*. "We've both endured through good times and bad," the dean of American sportswriters says. "I like to think that I've done some good writing about boxing. And *The Ring* was once enormously important. Boxing owes the idea of 'pound-for-pound' to *The Ring*. Long before today's sanctioning bodies tarnished the word 'champion,' the Ring belt was boxing's most prestigious title. And before the internet came along, *The Ring Record Book* was essential for anyone who wrote about boxing."

As for the value of early issues of *The Ring*, boxing memorabilia dealer Craig Hamilton notes, "The first issue of *The Ring* has value as a collectible. In good condition, it's worth about $2,500. Other issues from 1922 are worth $300 to $400 each. Once you get to the 1940s, the value drops considerably because so many copies are available. Depending on the cover subject and condition, they sell for twenty to forty dollars each. And the market goes down from there."

In 2010, Hamilton bought a set of bound copies of *The Ring* from 1922 through 1987 at auction for $4,125. "That was a steal," he says. More recently, he brokered the sale of a collection of bound issues from 1922 through 2019 for $15,000. That was a generous price.

"There was a time when the cover of each issue of *The Ring* was designed around an original painting," Hamilton adds. "Most of them were oil on canvas and some of them are quite nice. The original paintings for some of those covers sell for as much as six or seven thousand dollars each. That's if you're talking about Jack Dempsey, Joe Louis, or Sugar Ray Robinson."

But forget about dollars. Let's give the last word about *The Ring* to the people most important to the magazine—the fighters.

George Foreman is one of boxing's most respected elder statesmen. *The Ring* was forty-six years old (less than halfway through its journey to date) when Foreman won a gold medal in the heavyweight division at the 1968 Olympics in Mexico City.

"Boxing matches were on TV," George recalls. "But in those days, a clear broadcast was rare and hardly ever seen in color. And forget about close-ups of the boxer's face. When I saw my first *Ring Magazine,* I was thrilled to see boxers in the real. *Ring Magazine* made them human beings I could touch, heroes I could imitate. I started going to the newsstand monthly, looking for the next issue of *Ring*, looking for myself somewhere. In 1968, a line or two started to appear. That was special to me."

And Sugar Ray Leonard adds a thought. Leonard—regarded by many as the greatest fighter since the original Sugar Ray—looks back on his years in boxing and says, "*Ring Magazine* gave me more than just boxing news. It gave me confidence in myself. To be on the cover of *Ring Magazine* meant I'd finally made it!"

★★★

Note to the reader: The November/December 2022 issue of *The Ring* (which was mailed to subscribers in October) came with the advisory that, after one hundred years, *The Ring* would no longer publish a print edition.

As noted above, the inaugural issue of *The Ring* appeared in February 1922. To put that date in perspective, Calvin Coolidge was president of the United States. John F. Kennedy was four years old. For the first time in his illustrious career, Babe Ruth no longer took the mound as a pitcher. Rocky Marciano had yet to be born. There were no fights on radio or television because there was little radio and no television.

In the century that followed, *The Ring* chronicled boxing history, sometimes better than anyone else. But without an inspirational change in vision, the print edition was no longer economically viable.

The Ring says that it will maintain an online presence through RingTV. com. But there's a special feel to paper. It's sad that *The Ring* as boxing fans knew it for a century is no more.

Some whimsical thoughts on boxing.

Fistic Nuggets

Boxing fans have heard "Sweet Caroline" a lot lately. It's played just before the main event at all Matchroom Boxing fight cards. When Tyson Fury fought Dillian Whyte for Queensberry Promotions in front of 94,000 screaming fans at Wembley Stadium, "Sweet Caroline" was an integral part of the pageantry. The song has become a universal sports anthem, which is counterintuitive since the lyrics have absolutely nothing to do with sports.

"Sweet Caroline" was written and first sung by Neil Diamond in 1969. It was a good year for music. The Beatles, the Rolling Stones, the Doors, the Fifth Dimension, Elvis Presley, Stevie Wonder, Bob Dylan, Glen Campbell, Johnny Cash, Kenny Rogers, and Simon & Garfunkel were all on the best-seller charts. Motown was in full bloom. 1969 was also the year that Frank Sinatra recorded "My Way."

"Sweet Caroline" climbed to #4 on the Billboard 100 list. Four decades later, before singing the song at a fiftieth-birthday party for Caroline Kennedy, Diamond maintained that he'd been inspired to write it by an old magazine photo of the former president's daughter. Then, in 2014, he abandoned that fiction and said he'd written it for Marsha Murphy (his wife in 1969) but that he'd needed a three-syllable name to go with the melody.

Music has been part of sporting events since 1887 when Notre Dame played Michigan in football and the Fighting Irish band attended the game. Since then, sports musical traditions have permutated and grown.

"Sweet Caroline" entered the realm of sports in 1996 when the NFL Carolina Panthers began playing it at home games—a practice that has continued in Charlotte ever since. The Boston Red Sox first played it at Fenway Park in 1997. A Red Sox employee named Amy Tobey (who was responsible for ballpark music) aired it over the public address system for a friend who'd just given birth to a baby named Caroline. Thereafter, it was played sporadically at Fenway Park until 2002 when it became a permanent part of the soundtrack during the eighth inning of all home

games. After the 2013 Boston Marathon bombing, Neil Diamond journeyed to Boston and led the crowd at Fenway Park in singing the song.

Over the years, numerous college bands have incorporated "Sweet
Caroline" in their song rotation. The Northern Ireland national football
team played it during a post-match celebration after beating England in
2005 and has played it at home games ever since.

The tradition has now spread its wings. Earlier this year, hundreds of
thousands of people sang "Sweet Caroline" at the NFL draft in Las Vegas.

The playing of "Sweet Caroline" constitutes a feel-good moment.
Like most shared music, it fosters a sense of belonging to a group. And
the crowd becomes part of the drama, making its own contribution to
the lyrics:

Hands, touching hands
Reaching out, touching me, touching you
Sweet Caroline
  Whoa-oh-oh!
Good times never seemed so good—
  So good! So good! So good!

For those onsite, the experience is akin to the bonding power of
Michael Buffer's "Let's get ready to rumble." So let's give the final word
on "Sweet Caroline" to the great man himself.

"I love it," Buffer says. "When that song is played, it turns the fans on
and lets them know that what they've been waiting for is here. I make
a living getting the crowd up for the main event, so I appreciate what it
does. Anything that gets the crowd going like that is good."

★★★

THINGS YOU'LL NEVER HEAR IN THE
MEDIA CENTER BEFORE A BIG FIGHT

★ "There's no need for a written contract. Ryan Kavanaugh gave me
his word that the deal is one hundred percent solid."
★ "My wife and I asked Adrien Broner to babysit for our children."
★ "I just made a new will and named Don King as the executor of
my estate."

★ "I was impressed by how calmly Lou DiBella defused the crisis."

★ "If this goes wrong, Al Haymon won't be able to show his face around here."

***

"The bigger they are, the harder they fall" is one of boxing's most endearing adages.

It came from Budd Schulberg's novel—*The Harder They Fall*—which was based on Primo Carnera and made into a feature film starring Humphrey Bogart. Right?

Wrong.

Okay. Let's try again.

It was Bob Fitzsimmons who coined the phrase in a newspaper interview prior to fighting James Jeffries, although accounts differ as to whether it was before their 1899 fight at Coney Island or their 1902 rematch in San Francisco.

Strike two. . . . One more strike and you're out. You'd better ask Adam Pollack for help.

Pollack is an Iowa attorney who has written a series of groundbreaking biographies about boxing's early gloved champions. He traces the phrase back to John L. Sullivan.

More specifically, as recounted by Pollack, Mike Donovan (a former fighter turned boxing instructor) said of Sullivan in 1884, "He can settle any man in the world, and the bigger the man against him, the better it is for him. I was with him in Hot Springs when they picked a terrible big fellow for him to knock out. I felt of this fellow at the hotel, and I tell you he was something immense. He had the broadest shoulders of any man I ever saw, was as hard as iron, and weighed about 240 pounds. I told John of the kind of a fellow he had to meet. 'Is he a big fellow?' says John. 'You can bet,' says I. 'He's a stunner.' 'Then the bigger he is, the harder he'll fall,' says John. Well, he knocked that big fellow out in just two punches."

Eight years later, prior to fighting James Corbett, Sullivan was reflecting on his ring career and said that Herbert Slade (a 200-pound New Zealander) was among the "gamest" fighters he'd ever fought. But, Pollack notes, the Great John L added, "Slade had the disadvantage that all big men have that I have met with. The bigger they are, the more heavily they fall."

Of course, they only fall hard if you can knock them down.

Desperate people do desperate things.

Grimmish

Grimmish by Michael Winkler (Westbourne Books) is a strange book. And an intriguing one. The book focuses on a one-year period in 1908–1909 when boxer Joe Grim toured Australia engaging in fights. Winkler describes his writing as "experimental non-fiction." Experimental fiction with a factual underpinning would be more accurate.

Grim (né Severio Giannone) was born in Italy in 1881. His family came to the United States when he was ten. Fighting was in his nature. He was famed in his day for the ability to endure punishment and being virtually impossible to knock out.

BoxRec.com credits Grim with 179 known bouts between 1899 and 1913 resulting in 17 wins, 33 losses, 6 draws, and scores of "newspaper" defeats. He entered the prize ring well over three hundred times and was battered by myriad opponents whose names have been lost to history, and also by Bob Fitzsimmons, Joe Gans (twice), and Jack Johnson. During and after his ring career, he was committed to facilities for the treatment of mental health issues. He died in Philadelphia Hospital for Mental Diseases in 1939 at age fifty-seven.

Winkler views Grim through the eyes of a first-person narrator and a man who may or may not be the narrator's much older uncle. The book opens with a pseudo-review by the author himself that functions as a preface, foreword, introduction—call it what you will.

In this opening, Winkler warns readers of "the question of authenticity and the impossibility that this presentation of Grim will bear much or any connection to the flesh-and-blood fighter Joe Grim. The inclusion of extracts from contemporary newspaper accounts," he adds, "lends context, although less tenacious readers may find they impede progress. There is no narrative arc, close to zero love interest, skittish occasional action, incident rather than plot."

All true. And I might add that there are passages in *Grimmish* involving a talking goat where I had no idea what Winkler was trying to accomplish.

That said, through a collection of fragments and vignettes, Winkler crafts a compelling impressionistic portrait of Grim.

"Joe Grim," he writes, "reminds us of where the bounds of the normal are drawn, and stands conspicuously and spectacularly outside that compass. Without obstacle, without evasion, without contradiction."

Other thoughts advanced by Winkler include:

* "Grim's philosophy in its entirety—or more than a philosophy, which implies a distance between self and thought however small; his tao, his raison d'etre, his self—was simply this: I can take more punishment than they can deliver."

* "Grim withstood hundreds of blows every fight. He was a one-off, the ultimate boxing outlier. But his metier was resilience rather than resistance. He absorbed and accepted. His contests changed in a profound sense, becoming not about winning or losing, but hinging on whether or not he could endure the punishment meted out. And on that score he invariably triumphed. Grim became a spectacle rather than a fighter, but he was popular and he made a living."

* "There was always a third person in the ring, but the role of the referee was neutered by Grim's resilience. The crowd had paid, quite explicitly, to come and see if Grim could endure the beating, and no referee had the imprimatur to stop that fun."

* "Try picturing a baseball bat swung with great force into your exposed ribs, under the armpit. Try to conceive of a well-aimed mallet landing erratically just above your left ear, and you with no means to stop it. Imagine these things are happening to you in front of a crowd baying like starved dogs. Imagine a single vicious punch to your face, and then multiply it by many hundred, and then think of the cheering that each punch drags from thousands of jeering onlookers. Then we have some gesture towards understanding Grim."

Winkler also recreates Grim's voice:

* "I think of myself as a travelling artiste. The crowds love me, and then they speak of me once I've gone, and that adds value to my days on the planet, somehow."

★ "In that boxing time, I am outside of time. Six rounds, three minutes each, and in that span I belong to that span only. There is no
connection to clock time, to earth time. And that is how I live, with
and for those ripped out portions where time has no dominion. Six
three-minute rounds, five one-minute breaks, twenty-three minutes
that are as long as you need them to be, or they can be devoid of
time altogether."

★ "I stand in front of the hardest hitting men on the planet, and then
the promoter still tries to fuck me sideways on fight payments as I
make my way home. It is a pitiful racket and I have been in it too
long, and I have no other path ahead, and that is that is that."

★ "I worry that I am outside the scope of nature. I am not just at the
edge of my species, but over the margin. I do not belong. I worry
that one day my fighting might end, and that without the pain I
will have no map to find myself."

Pain—"the rich realm of pain," Winkler calls it—is a recurring theme
throughout *Grimmish*. At the beginning of the narrative, Winkler concedes, "The sustained depiction of physical violence is likely to alienate
some, while others may weary of the defiant wallowing in the sludge of
masculinity. [But] there is likely to be a readership, however small, that
finds within these covers something sincere and worthwhile."

This pain isn't confined to the prize ring. There are tales in *Grimmish*
of men mutilating each other with hot poker irons in tests of will and the
ability to endure pain. Other fragments include:

★ "What is the thing we call pain? It is something that captures the
attention of the sufferer but otherwise has no meaning. It makes
no sound, has no colour or smell, occupies no physical space. And
yet at its most extreme, pain becomes the only thing of which the
sufferer is aware, bigger for the victim in that instant than any object
in the universe."

★ "Some might think that the glory of pain is that it teaches you things.
And I say as one who might know, if there is enough of it then pain
is just pain. A lot of pain is a lot of pain, and it is not a friend and
not a teacher and not a guide and not a redemption. It is just pain."

★ "My audience wants to travel with me on a pain journey, so I give them as much as they need. And for the rest, I block blows, I absorb the force of punches through my neck and spine, I stall and distract, I allow myself to be knocked down in order to intensify the spectacle and to wear some extra seconds off the clock. It is a show, and my body is the stage and the instrument, and that is why they pay, and that is how I get to eat well and put money in my name into the bank."

And some parting thoughts from *Grimmish:*

★ "Interesting what humans will pay for, what we actually like. When James Corbett went to England, they wanted to entertain him and their idea was to take him to a rat pit and have a champion bulldog kill a thousand rats in a thousand seconds."
★ "Anybody can learn to box. But to fight, it is different."
★ "There's a trick to life. I think you'll find it, even if you have to wait until you're very old. Just keep looking. You'll probably get there in the end."

If you're intrigued and want more, read *Grimmish.*

*Two decades ago (with help from Clement Clarke Moore), I wrote
"A Christmas Eve Visit from George Foreman." In 2022, I updated
that version for contemporary times.*

A Christmas Eve Visit
from Tyson Fury

IN THE BEGINNING

'Twas the night before Christmas at the start of this poem
The Gypsy King's family was happy at home
Tyson sat next to his children and missus
Full of good cheer and giving out kisses

There was happiness, laughter, contentment, and love
Then came a crash on the roof up above
Followed by moaning and groaning . . . "Oh, my!
I've broken my leg," they heard Santa Claus cry.

Tyson brought Santa Claus down from the roof.
"Oh, what a blunder! Oh, what a goof!
Oh, what a mess," Santa Claus wailed.
Then Santa's rosy-red pudgy cheeks paled.

"Can't travel," said Santa. "My leg hurts real bad.
Children all over the world will be sad.
No presents this Christmas, that's how it will be.
It's the worst thing that ever has happened to me."

"Oh, this is terribly sad," Tyson cried.
"It will bring heartache to children worldwide
There has to be something that I can do
To help in this moment of crisis for you?"

Then Tyson sat Santa Claus down by the fire
And stared at the flames as they rose ever higher.
He furrowed his brow ever deeper in thought
And clenched his big fists as he did when he fought.

He clenched them so hard that his face turned bright red
And a great inspiration came into his head
"I've got it," he said. "I know what I'll do.
I'll deliver the presents and pretend that I'm you."

"There's a problem, said Santa. "You're a really big fellow.
And your suit looks like draperies from a bordello
Children will tremble and cry out in fright
If they stay up till midnight and see you tonight."

"Nonsense," said Tyson. "I'm a big cuddly chap.
Children are eager to sit on my lap."
"All right," said Santa. "But before you deliver
There are rules to be followed if you're the gift-giver.

"Now and then someone will make a request.
I've got a long list of which presents are best.
As a substitute Santa, please take my advice.
Bring this list with you and read it through twice."

Then Santa gave Tyson a long list to read
So Tyson would understand how to proceed
'Twas a task for a King; it would take him all night.
But Tyson was certain that he'd get it right.

SANTA'S LIST

Gennady wants judges who see things his way
Terence wants Errol with no more delay
Claressa wants one more fight just like the last
Don King would like to go back to the past

Both of the Charlos want love and respect
Eddie Hearn wants to see Queensberry wrecked.
Frank Warren would like Eddie Hearn to be quiet
DAZN would like someone to come in and buy it

Triller would like to pick up a quick buck
Lou DiBella has asked for a change in his luck
A.J. requested a future that's sunny
All of the sanctioning bodies want money

Probellum asks that we solemnly pray
That people forget all about MTK
And Deontay fervently hopes that it's true
That he'll never again have a fight against you

Adrien Broner wants less time in jail
Andy Ruiz wants less weight on the scale
Amanda Serrano wants Katie again
For a payday as big as they give to the men

Michael Buffer would like boxing fans to all rumble
Most people want Pretty Boy to be humble
Joe Joyce now lusts for a big money fight
And Dillian would like to end each bout upright

Jake Paul has written that he's in distress
He'd like to know how he got into this mess
And musicians would like to hear more songs divine
Like Hatton's "Blue Moon" and "Sweet Caroline"

Sky Sports would like Ben Shalom to succeed
Ring 8 wants cash to help fighters in need
Paco wants favors too many to mention
Gareth A. Davies wants lots of attention

Conor Benn says as a fighter he's clean
And wants no more talking about Clomifene
Clean fighters want to see more funds for VADA
Whose testing is light-years ahead of USADA

Gervonta wants Ryan. And Ryan wants him
But the chances of that really happening are slim
And no surprise here; Top Rank wrote in to say
It wants everyone to do all things its way

Canelo wants more belts to put round his waist
And the memory of fighting vs. Bivol erased
Lennox would like to be able to claim
That he knocked you spark out in a video game

Fans everywhere would like more fights for free
With only the megafights on pay-TV
The fans also want to see judges who score
Like an impartial jurist instead of a whore

Matt Christie wants good health for all of the fighters
And a much bigger budget to pay for his writers
And here's a request made to Santa's chief elf
Al Haymon wants all of the toys for himself

IN THE END

On Christmas Eve, Tyson did just what he said
With toys piled high on the back of his sled
He went 'round the world in the spirit of joy
Giving out presents to each girl and boy

It made him feel good, and the part he liked best
Was wherever he went, to the East or the West
To the North or the South, lower or higher
Children left cookies and milk by the fire

He thought all the sweets were a wonderful treat
He ate every one, a remarkable feat
And I heard Tyson say when he came home that night,
"My stomach is stuffed, and my pants are too tight."

Issues and Answers

Boxing is being strangled by an environment in which anything goes.

The Script for Lamar Odom vs. Aaron Carter

The sweet science is being inundated by a wave of "trash boxing." YouTube personalities, social media influencers, and long-past-their-prime ring greats are capitalizing on the confusion created by hundreds of "championship" belts created by the world sanctioning bodies and the void resulting from the failure of the boxing establishment to make entertaining matchups with the best fighters fighting the best.

There have always been circus-like sideshows in boxing. The difference now is that the sideshows are becoming boxing's main event. Trash boxing is how the sport is being portrayed to the general public with paydays ranging from minimal to millions of dollars.

On June 11, 2021, former NBA basketball player Lamar Odom squared off against rapper Aaron Carter in the main event of an Official Celebrity Boxing card at the Showboat Hotel in Atlantic City. The event was available on pay-per-view through FITE for $29.99. Bovada (an online sports-betting site) listed Odom as a −400 favorite. The odds on Carter were +250.

The event was marketed to the public as a legitimate fight. Prior to it, Odom told TMZ, "I'm prepared. I don't know who he's sparring against, but I know my gym is full of guys that can fight and I've been sparring with and I have a really good trainer. He's been talking shit, but I'm gonna put him to sleep early. I asked his girlfriend yesterday, 'Which round do you want to wake him up in?'"

Retired UFC star Chuck Liddell, who served as referee for the confrontation, told TMZ, "I just wanna see how Odom is gonna fight Aaron. I'll let them fight to some extent. Obviously, it's a celebrity fight. I'm not gonna let him get too hurt. I'll protect either one from either of them no matter who's getting hurt. We don't want them to get hurt, but you gotta let them fight. People are paying to watch you fight. You're getting paid to fight. You wanna make some money, you gotta fight."

THE UNIVERSAL SPORT 239

But that was hype. In reality, the fight took place pursuant to a script that was submitted in advance to the New Jersey State Athletic Control Board. In other words—despite the existence of a betting line and the manner in which the event was marketed to the public—the fight was "fixed."

Odom–Carter was promoted by Damon Feldman, a former Philadelphia fighter who crafted a 9-and-0 record in a four-year career that ended in 1992. His first eight opponents had a composite ledger of 8 wins against 50 losses. His last opponent had lost 10 of 12 previous fights. Give Feldman some credit for knowing what it means to be in a boxing ring.

In 2011, as reported by the *Philadelphia Inquirer* on March 8, 2011, Feldman was sentenced to two years' probation after pleading no contest to charges that he had fixed fights and promoted fights without a license in Pennsylvania.

More trouble followed. According to an April 29, 2020, article by Jack McCaffery of 21st-Century Media, Feldman was incarcerated for thirteen months ending in December 2017 after a plea deal tied to charges of domestic violence that had been lodged against him. As recounted in a May 22, 2018, article in *Philadelphia Magazine*, the charges stemmed from an incident that occurred at the home of a woman who Feldman had previously been romantically involved with. The woman, who was bleeding profusely, told police that he had punched her several times in the face. Feldman told police that there had been a physical altercation between them and that the woman was injured when he threw her off of his back, causing her to fall down the stairs. The physical evidence was inconsistent with Feldman's statement.

Feldman promoted his first "celebrity boxing" event in 2008. Over the years, his promotions have featured the likes of Tonya Harding, Paula Jones, and Joey Buttafuoco. "My dream," he has said, "is to do a fight with Sylvester Stallone. If I could make money promoting regular fights, I would. But I can't, so I'm doing this."

That brings us to the June 11, 2021, encounter between Lamar Odom and Aaron Carter.

Odom is six feet, ten inches tall. He played in the NBA for fourteen seasons, seven of them with the Los Angeles Lakers. From 2009 to 2016, he was married to Khloe Kardashian.

In October 2015, Odom was found unconscious in a Nevada brothel after ingesting a combination of cocaine, alcohol, and other drugs. As reported by the *Los Angeles Times*, he suffered six heart attacks and twelve strokes. He's now forty-one years old.

Carter, a thirty-three-year-old rapper whose music career has been in decline in recent years, has struggled publicly with substance abuse and other issues.

Odom–Clark was scheduled for three ninety-second rounds with headgear. Paulie Malignaggi, Ice-T, and Coco provided the pay-per-view commentary. Multiple websites—many of them respected boxing and MMA outlets—reported on the encounter as though it were a real fight.

Sam Quinn of CBSSports.com wrote, "On Friday night, we saw one of the most anticipated celebrity boxing matches of the year. On paper, the fight looked like a mismatch. The 6–0 Carter is almost a foot shorter than Odom, and the difference in their weight and reach is similar. Odom has physical gifts that the rest of us simply don't and he showed it in knocking Carter out."

Mark Lelinwalla of DAZN News reported, "Despite giving up 10 inches in height, 64.5 pounds, and 11 inches in reach to Odom, Carter enjoyed early success with a barrage of lefts and rights that connected to his taller, larger opponent's head in the opening round. However, Odom got his bearings, went to the outside, and placed a right jab-left hook combination which dropped Carter. The pop star of the 90s didn't have his legs under him and wisely held on to survive the round. But he wouldn't make it against Odom much longer. The second round had Odom spinning Carter around and around before delivering several unanswered lefts to drop the singer once again. Special guest referee Chuck Liddell began counting, as Carter indicated that he was no longer fit to continue."

Nick Selbe of *Sports Illustrated* recounted, "The stoppage occurred in the second of the fight's three, 90-second rounds, as Carter failed to put up much defense against Odom's flurry of punches."

One might ask, "Where was the New Jersey State Athletic Control Board in all of this?" After all, the NJSACB is charged with regulating combat sports in New Jersey. And as earlier noted, Odom–Carter was marketed to the public as a legitimate boxing match. Odds on the outcome were posted on gambling sites such as Bovada. Normally, this would place the event within the purview of the NJSACB.

The answer is that the New Jersey State Athletic Control Board didn't have jurisdiction over the event because it wasn't a "real" fight. It was scripted entertainment.

Celebrity Boxing (Feldman's promotional company) represented to the NJSACB that Odom–Clark was "scripted," not a combat sports competition. Thus, it was no more subject to regulation by the NJSACB than professional wrestling is.

Further to that point, in advance of the event, NJSACB asked Celebrity Boxing to send it a copy of the script. On May 23, the promotion emailed the script to Deputy Attorney General Nick Lembo (who oversees legal matters for the NJSACB). Once the script was received, NJSACB commissioner Larry Hazzard was advised by the attorney general's office that he had no jurisdiction over the event.

In mid-June, this writer learned about the existence of the script. On June 30, pursuant to the New Jersey Open Public Records Act, I filed a request for documents from the Office of the Attorney General of the State of New Jersey. More specifically, I asked for "All documents relating to the June 11, 2021, boxing exhibition at the Showboat Hotel featuring Lamar Odom and Aaron Carter, including but not limited to any script for the main event."

On July 2, my request for documents was denied in its entirety by the Custodian of Records for the Attorney General's Office. Three grounds were listed for the denial:

1) "The event referred to in your request was not subject to the regulatory purview of the State of New Jersey Athletic Control Board."

However, the fact that the event was not subject to the regulatory purview of the NJSACB had no bearing on the existence of the documents.

2) "Your request is overly broad and improper."

I did not believe that to be the case. However, in response, I told the Custodian of Records that, for the time being, I would be satisfied with receiving "any script for the main event" pursuant to my request.

3) "To the extent that any such script may exist, it would be the
confidential and proprietary property of Celebrity Boxing."

To support this claim, the Custodian of Records stated, "Celebrity
Boxing Entertainment LLC (CBE), the organizer of the June 11, 2021,
boxing exhibition, repeatedly marked information, documents, and correspondence to the SACB as confidential and proprietary business information [and] stated that the release of the requested information would
cause irreparable harm to CBE, its shareholders, investors and participants."

However, just because someone writes "confidential" and "proprietary"
on a document and claims that the document is exempt from production doesn't make it so. Also, since the scripted June 11 event had already
occurred, there was no longer anything confidential about the script.

Following proper procedure, I asked the Custodian of Records to
reconsider my request. Again, the request was denied. This time, the
Custodian of Records abandoned her first two objections to production,
restated her position that the documents were exempt from production
because they contain confidential and proprietary information, and added
a new excuse—that the documents "were obtained as part of SACB's
review of the event" and thus are exempt from release because they are
"records concerning background investigations or evaluations for public
employment, appointment to public office, or licensing, whether open,
closed, or inactive."

That was blatant nonsense. The "investigation" exemption under
New Jersey law applies to instances where an individual has submitted
an application for public employment, appointment to public office, or
licensing by the State of New Jersey and an investigation of the applicant
followed. There was no such application in this matter.

On July 21, I took things to the next level and filed a complaint
with the New Jersey Government Records Council. In response, the
Custodian of Records conceded that the script at issue exists and had
been transmitted by email to Deputy Attorney General Nick Lembo on
May 23, 2021. But the Custodian continues to claim that the script is
exempt from production for the reasons stated above.

The Custodian has also refused to identify or produce relevant documents other than the script, claiming, "as Mr. Hauser failed to identify
with specificity the records he sought, aside from requesting a copy of

the script, it was not possible to determine the full universe of records that could be responsive."

This is a ridiculous assertion. It's impossible for me to "identify with specificity" the records sought because I don't know with specificity what these records are. I do know that the universe of documents responsive to my request is small and easily reviewable. Indeed, in one of its responses, the Custodian states, "the organizer of the June 11, 2021, boxing exhibition repeatedly marked information, documents, and correspondence to the SACB as confidential and proprietary business information." So obviously, the Custodian has already reviewed the documents.

That's where things stand at the moment. My request for documents is still before the Government Records Council.

There are serious issues involved here. If Odom–Carter was in fact "scripted" (which now appears to be conceded, given the acknowledgment that there was a script), then the NJSACB was correct in not exercising jurisdiction over it. However, if Odom–Carter was scripted, it was marketed in misleading fashion to the public. Pursuant to this marketing, at least some consumers were deluded into paying money for onsite tickets and pay-per-view buys. And more troubling, legal gaming companies posted odds and took bets on a "fixed" match.

On the other hand, if the event was not "scripted," then the New Jersey State Athletic Control Board should have exercised jurisdiction over it.

The New Jersey Open Public Records Act was enacted to protect the public through the free flow of information. Hiding the truth of this matter through a disingenuous response to a valid Open Public Records Act request is a disservice to the public and also a violation of the act.

One has to wonder how many of the other fights that boxing fans have seen in New Jersey in recent months have been scripted.

Some things are far more important than boxing.

Dmitry Bivol Should Not Be Allowed to Fight Canelo Álvarez

"The ambition is global domination. It is like a snowball that keeps on growing. We never stop trying to do more or be bigger or go to new territories."

No, that wasn't Vladimir Putin. It was boxing promoter Eddie Hearn. Hearn, of course, didn't say it in the context of geopolitics. He was talking about Matchroom Boxing and DAZN.

Matchroom and DAZN are now planning to promote and stream a championship fight between Canelo Álvarez and Dmitry Bivol at T-Mobile Arena in Las Vegas on May 7, 2022. Because Bivol is a Russian citizen who lives in Russia, there have been calls to replace him as Canelo's opponent.

On March 8, former heavyweight champion Wladimir Klitschko (who has returned to Kyiv to help defend his Ukrainian homeland against Russian aggression) was interviewed by BBC 5 Live Radio and urged the broadest possible economic sanctions against Russia, including a global boycott of Russian athletes. When asked if Canelo–Bivol should proceed, Klitschko answered, "Absolutely not. Every sanction—and it's nothing against the personalities or athletes, it's about the politics of Russia—every Russian representative in this case needs to be sanctioned because this way we show to Russia that the world is against his [Putin's] senseless war and there is no good in this war.

"To isolate Russia from all sporting competition is not an act of aggression," Klitschko continued. "We do this to stop the war, in the name of peace. I have nothing personal against the athletes, but I have a lot against the aggression of Russian leader Putin. We believe sanctions on different levels, including sport, are crucially important. If you take away sporting competition, the athletes will ask their leader, 'Why will nobody compete against us?' I repeat, this is not against the athletes. It's in the name of peace in Ukraine."

Bivol was born in Kyrgyzstan but has lived in Russia for most of his life and is a Russian citizen. Those who support his right to fight Canelo on May 7 say there's nothing to indicate that he favors Putin's war of aggression and that sports should be kept separate from politics. But the arguments against allowing Canelo–Bivol to proceed are overwhelming.

At the March 2 kickoff press conference for Canelo–Bivol, Dmitry told reporters, "None of us are enjoying what is happening. I have a lot of friends in Ukraine. I have a lot of friends in Russia and my family is in Russia. I wish everyone peace and only the best."

That's an empty statement. I have no idea what Bivol's political views are. He seems to be stuck between a rock and a hard place. One empathizes with the fact that his family in Russia would be at risk if he spoke out against the invasion of Ukraine. The war isn't his fault. But I have more sympathy for the people who are being killed as a consequence of Russia's brutal aggression.

Sports are important to geopolitics. Indeed, it's widely believed that the Chinese government asked Putin to not invade Ukraine until after the 2022 Winter Olympics in Beijing came to a close. Far from being a bastion of goodwill, sports are a moneymaking machine and, to borrow a phrase from Karl Marx, the opiate of the masses.

Despite calls for the United States to boycott the 1936 Berlin Olympics, the games went ahead with American participation. Some people look back fondly on those games because of the gold-medal performances by Jesse Owens. But Germany led the medal count at the 1936 Olympics by a wide margin. The games strengthened Adolf Hitler's standing with the German people and were the subject of Leni Riefenstahl's influential propaganda film, *Olympia*.

Vitali Klitschko's own political career speaks to the power of sports as a platform for political action (he is now mayor of Kyiv), as do the lives of Muhammad Ali and Manny Pacquiao.

Canelo–Bivol isn't just any fight. Because of Canelo's stature, a victory for Bivol would make Dmitry a symbol of Russian might and be heralded as a great victory for Russia. Some people point to the 1938 rematch between Joe Louis and Max Schmeling and ask, "If Schmeling fought then, why can't Bivol fight now?" The answer is that (1) those were different times; (2) even then, there were calls to boycott

Louis–Schmeling II; and (3) it was personally important to Louis that he fight Schmeling to avenge a previous loss, whereas Bivol is a fungible opponent for Canelo. And think of the boost it would have given Hitler's vile regime if Schmeling had won.

Is it fair to deprive Bivol of a large payday, thereby imposing a financial sanction on one man who is not responsible for the carnage in Ukraine?

That's the way economic sanctions work. Is it fair to deprive oil workers in Russia or Russians who work at McDonald's and Starbucks of their jobs? Financial sanctions are designed to burden an aggressor nation's people. It's better than killing them. If Bivol loses the opportunity to fight Canelo, I'll have a degree of sympathy for him. But not as much sympathy as I feel for the people in Ukraine who are being brutalized by the Russian invasion.

Neutrality isn't an acceptable option in the present crisis. In Dante's *Inferno*, it's written of those who refuse to take a stand on moral issues, "Let us not talk of them, but look and pass." Later, those words were interpreted and quoted by John F. Kennedy as, "The hottest places in Hell are reserved for those who in time of moral crisis maintain their neutrality."

As the Irish-born British statesman Edmund Burke wrote more than two centuries ago, "The only thing necessary for the triumph of evil is for good men to do nothing."

Randy Roberts is uniquely qualified to comment on the present situation. Roberts holds the title of Distinguished Professor of History at Purdue University where he teaches a course on World War II. He has also been a visiting professor at the United States Military Academy at West Point, where he taught courses on military history and the history of sport. And he has been honored with the A.J. Liebling Award by the Boxing Writers Association of America for biographies of Joe Louis, Muhammad Ali, Jack Dempsey, and Jack Johnson.

Roberts says unequivocally, "Bivol should not be allowed to fight Canelo. The world community has to put as much pressure as possible on Russia. Sports are a national unifying factor. Sports are a way to measure international greatness. That's why they count Olympic medals. It shouldn't be that way but it is. To deny a world stage in sports to Russia is important. The Russian people aren't responsible for what's happening today in Ukraine. But it's impossible to separate Russia from the Russian people. Denying Bivol the opportunity to fight would be an appropriate extension of economic sanctions.

"This is a scary time," Roberts continues. "Never in my life since the Cuban Missile Crisis have I thought there was a real possibility of nuclear war. I always felt that sane people were ultimately in charge. But Putin doesn't fit that mold because, like Hitler, he shows a willingness to take unthinkable steps. I don't think he has wide support for this war in the military or among the Russian people. There have to be generals in Russia who, right now, are thinking that what's happening in Ukraine is wrong. But can they halt the use of nuclear weapons if Putin orders it?"

Where do we go from here?

First, let's acknowledge the heroic role being played by Vitali Klitschko as mayor of Kyiv. Vitali and Wladimir are inspirational figures.

Yet as of this writing, Matchroom and DAZN are moving ahead with Canelo–Bivol. Let's not forget, this is the same team that staged the 2019 rematch between Anthony Joshua and Andy Ruiz in Saudi Arabia despite compelling evidence that the Saudi government was responsible for the murder of *Washington Post* journalist Jamal Khashoggi in Saudi Arabia's consulate in Istanbul on October 2, 2018.

DAZN founder Len Blavatnik is Ukrainian born and a citizen of both the United States and United Kingdom. His personal fortune has been estimated by *Bloomberg* and other sources as being well in excess of $20 billion. A substantial portion of his wealth came from buying formerly state-owned oil and aluminum assets in Russia as they were privatized by the Russian government.

Blavatnik could unilaterally pull the plug on Canelo–Bivol in an instant. And if he's concerned about the financial impact that would have on Bivol, he could reach into his pocket to make Dmitry whole.

Or maybe, at the opposite end of the spectrum, someone will cynically decide that the controversy over whether Bivol should be in the ring on May 7 is good marketing for Canelo–Bivol and that it will engender more subscriptions and pay-per-view buys.

Meanwhile, DAZN subscribers can cancel their subscriptions in protest. At the very least, if the fight goes ahead, boxing fans should donate $79.99 (the price of the pay-per-view) to a Ukrainian relief fund rather than buy the fight.

Which is more important: being entertained by two men in a fistfight or making an effort to halt a senseless slaughter?

Trash boxing is how boxing is now being portrayed to large segments of the American public.

Triller, Holyfield, and Trump: Did Evander Get Hustled?

PART ONE

On September 11, 2021, Evander Holyfield was knocked out by Vitor Belfort in the first round of a boxing event at the Seminole Hard Rock Hotel and Casino in Hollywood, Florida. There was widespread criticism of the event before it took place and more criticism when it was over. Holyfield is fifty-eight years old and shouldn't be getting punched in the head by men trained in the art of hurting.

Worse, interviews with multiple people involved with the promotion suggest that Holyfield was hustled. That he went into the ring thinking he was about to participate in an exhibition in which neither man would use best efforts to hurt the other, only to find himself double-crossed in a scenario akin to an old-time boxing movie.

How did boxing get into this mess? Read on.

In 2015, two musicians in search of an inexpensive way to edit their work launched a video app called Triller that enabled them and other users to avoid the cost of renting studio space. A year later, Triller was transitioning to becoming a social video app but had still not entered the mainstream consciousness.

Enter Ryan Kavanaugh.

Kavanaugh is a forty-six-year-old businessman, a big concept guy who's adept at raising money. Over the years, he has been enmeshed in a wave of litigation touching upon his professional and personal life

In 2004, Kavanaugh founded an entertainment company called Relativity Media that purported to use sophisticated algorithms to eliminate the risk from film financing. *Variety* named him "Showman of the Year" and he made his way onto the *Forbes* list of billionaires. Then Relativity Media filed for bankruptcy. Twice. Kavanaugh told the *Wall Street Journal* that he took Relativity into Chapter 11 bankruptcy in 2015 "to fend off vulture investors who were trying to steal the company" and that he wasn't involved in the second bankruptcy. In 2018, as reported by the *Los Angeles Times*, Relativity Media sold substantially all of its remaining assets to a holding company called UltraV.

Meanwhile, in 2017, Kavanaugh founded a company called Proxima Media. In 2019, Proxima Media acquired a majority stake in Triller. Kavanaugh sought to position Triller as an American version of TikTok (the Chinese-owned social networking service that was under attack by then-president Donald Trump). To date, Triller has fallen far short of TikTok's success.

In describing Triller, a company press release states, "The Triller Network is a consolidation of companies, apps and technologies. Triller Network pairs the culture of music with sports, fashion, entertainment and influencers through a 360-degree tech and content-based vertical."

Triller became a significant player in boxing when it put together a November 28, 2020, exhibition between Mike Tyson and Roy Jones that engendered an estimated 1.6 million pay-per-view buys. DAZN and Matchroom had jump-started the move of "trash boxing" into the mainstream of the sport when they partnered to stream social media personalities Logan Paul and KSI in a fight on November 9, 2019. Tyson–Jones brought this phenomenon to a new level.

Triller got what it wanted most out of Tyson–Jones—massive publicity and clicks. And the event fit perfectly into what Kavanaugh calls Triller Fight Club's "four-quadrant model" consisting of "influencers, legends, music artists, and contemporary fighters."

More Triller events followed. Most notably, on April 17, 2021, Jake Paul knocked out former MMA fighter Ben Askren in one round. One month later, it was announced that Paul was leaving Triller pursuant to a multi-bout deal with Showtime. The April 17 card also saw a more traditional boxing match between Regis Prograis and Ivan Redkach. The event and others that followed were mired in red ink. But they were aimed at building Triller's base and were showpieces for potential investors.

Meanwhile, on April 14, 2021, Triller announced that it had acquired FITE, a small but successful technology company that has become a leader in the distribution of pay-per-view combat sports events. After numerous snags in ironing out the contracts, the acquisition was finalized in late July.

As all of this was unfolding, Triller was looking for another legendary fighter to showcase. Mike Tyson was unhappy with the money he'd received in the aftermath of his encounter with Roy Jones and, on March 21, issued a statement that read, "Just to be clear, there is no Tyson with Triller fight. I don't know any Triller executives personally. I don't have a deal with Triller or any head executive representing them for the next event. I will never do another event or any business with Triller, so anyone misrepresenting that they own the rights to my name or my next event isn't true. I am not with or ever will be with Triller's Fight Club."

With Tyson unavailable, Triller turned to Oscar De La Hoya.

For more than a decade, De La Hoya was one of boxing's brightest stars. But he's now forty-eight years old and last fought in 2008 when he was brutalized by Manny Pacquiao.

Oscar has been wounded many times, physically and psychologically. The psychological wounds seemed to have caused more suffering than the physical. He has acknowledged having problems with alcohol and cocaine and has been in rehab on multiple occasions. The ravages of his lifestyle and years as a fighter have taken a toll.

Appearing at a March 26, 2021, press conference in Las Vegas to promote the Jake Paul vs. Ben Askren Triller card, De La Hoya took the microphone, announced "July 3, I'm making my comeback," dropped the microphone, and walked off the stage.

The Paul–Askren event, when it came to pass, featured performances by Justin Bieber, the Black Keys, Doja Cat, Saweetie, Diplo, Major Lazer, and what was advertised as "the exclusive world premiere of the hip hop supergroup Mt. Westmore (Snoop Dogg, Ice Cube, Too $hort and E-40)." There were pole dancers with big butts and lots of cleavage. Taylor Hill, Charli D'Amelio, and other social media personalities made appearances.

There was also a lot of weed (much of which was openly smoked on camera) and alcohol. The commentating team of Ray Flores, Mario Lopez, and Al Bernstein was joined from time to time by Snoop Dog, Pete Davidson, and De La Hoya.

Oscar looked bloated, sounded as though he'd participated liberally in hospitality room offerings, and said that he wanted to fight Mike Tyson. Rey Flores observed on air, "Oscar is definitely high."

One might ask why the people around De La Hoya who care about him allowed that scenario to unfold. Four days later, Oscar appeared on "The DAZN Boxing Show" and was asked about his commentating that night.

"I've been in beast mode for about six weeks," De La Hoya answered. "And I got a little into it; you know. I started having a couple drinks. And then they told me, 'Why don't you go and commentate?' And I was like, 'Oh, man! Okay. Okay.' I got a little over carried away. And I apologize. But it's all good. I'm back in beast mode."

Thereafter, Ryan Kavanaugh told *The Sun*, "It was a fun event. You had two people up on stage smoking joints, so Oscar had a couple of drinks. He wasn't falling over. He wasn't so awful that he did something terrible. People love to talk shit. I don't think Oscar was that bad. He was just having fun with it. We told him to have fun with it. We said go and enjoy it. Anybody that has enough time to go onto the internet and start commenting negatively in big ways and making a point of it, they obviously have other issues."

Then, on June 17, 2021, it was announced that De La Hoya would box against former MMA fighter Vitor Belfort in a Triller Fight Club pay-per-view event to be held in Las Vegas on September 11. Belfort, age forty-four, had retired in 2018 after compiling a 26–14 career record and losing four of his last six fights. He'd boxed only once as a pro and that was fifteen years earlier.

"This isn't that WWE theatrics we've been seeing in boxing lately," De La Hoya declared. "This is the real deal, a real fight with real knockouts for a real win. I'm in better shape than I was fifteen years ago. I want to make the biggest comeback in boxing history."

On July 21, Triller announced that De La Hoya vs. Belfort was moving to the Staples Center in Los Angeles. The contract weight was 180 pounds and the bout would be contested over eight two-minute rounds. That brought the California State Athletic Commission into the act.

"We were told that Tyson and Jones would be an exhibition and we regulated it as such," CSAS executive director Andy Foster said. "An exhibition in the State of California is when you don't use your best efforts to win. Here, the fighters want to use their best efforts, so by definition it can't be an exhibition. They want a fight and we'll regulate it as such. They're gonna box and we're gonna score it."

Asked about drug testing, Foster told this writer, "Both fighters will have to pass their medicals. We're still working out the details on drug testing. Most likely, it will be conducted by California, not VADA. I think we'll be focusing on PEDs, not recreational drugs."

As for possible drug use by the TV commentators, Foster pledged, "The commission will control the environment in the technical zone at ringside."

The formal kickoff press conference for De La Hoya vs. Belfort took place on July 27.

"I'm doing it for myself," Oscar told a group of reporters before the formalities began. "I've had a fucking crazy life, you know. I've had a crazy life. And sorry if I get all emotional and shit. I've done this for thirty-five years. I've always done it for my family and fans all over the world. I've gone into the ring and just let it all out because I love what I do. I love what I represent for people. But I'm finally fighting for myself. I can't fucking wait. It's going to be hell, but I've been through hell and back. There is nothing that can break me down, all the shit, all the bull-shit, whatever. I'm strong as a rock. I'm at peace. I finally got here. I'm getting fucking crazy emotional. It's been a fucking struggle. People can talk all the shit they want to but I will never give up. I feel that age is just a number, and I have to literally thank yoga. It's not a fucking joke. Yoga, like really, literally almost saved my life."

That was followed by pronouncements like, "This is not a game. I said, 'Look, if we're gonna do this, let's do it for real. Let's not do this song and dance. Let's not do these exhibitions, you know, that we're tired of.' This is the real thing. And the fact that we both agree that it's gonna be a real fight, it's gonna be a lot of fun. We're gonna kick the shit out of each other. That's one thing for sure. Call me crazy, but I'm looking forward to it. It's gonna be a lot of fun."

Asked about the possibility of fighting Canelo Álvarez, De La Hoya responded, "Why not? It's only power. That's all it is. Power, I can with-stand. Speed, like Pacquiao, is a whole different story. I have a good chin, you know."

Of course, in 2019, Oscar was talking about running for president of the United States.

At times, promoting the Belfort fight seemed like a therapy session for Oscar.

"I was raped at thirteen, from a woman, an older woman," he told Dylan Hernandez of the *Los Angeles Times*. "Thirteen, lost my virginity over being, you know, being raped, basically. I was in Hawaii, I think, at some tournament. She was over thirty-five. You suppress everything. You're living this life, the Golden Boy. But, oh shit, wait, that's still there. Like I never, like, thought about it. I never processed it. I never really thought how my feelings are until one day it just comes out and you don't know how to deal with it."

Over the years, Oscar traded blows with fighters like Manny Pacquiao, Félix Trinidad, Bernard Hopkins, Shane Mosley, Ike Quartey, Julio César Chávez, Pernell Whitaker, and Floyd Mayweather Jr. Later, he offered a stark assessment of the risks inherent in the trade he'd chosen. "I hate getting hit," De La Hoya said. "Getting hit hurts. It damages you. When a fighter trains his body and mind to fight, there's no room for fear. But I'm realistic enough to understand that there's no way to know what the effect of getting hit will be ten or fifteen years from now."

However, at an August 25, 2021, media workout, Oscar declared, "Call me crazy but I just miss it. I missed getting hit and doing the hitting. I wasn't ready to retire after I lost to Manny Pacquiao. I never felt like I was in wars. In boxing you're just as old as how you feel. I went through hell and back treating my body wrong, but these last six months I feel amazing. I refocused myself and rededicated myself and I'm actually doing this for me. I can't wait. I'm going to give the fans a war. I have a good chin and I can take the punch. My inspiration for this fight is Arturo Gatti. I want one of those types of fights."

No one asked about a September 27, 2010, interview with *Broadcasting & Cable*. In that interview, De La Hoya had acknowledged, "I did have tests done after every single fight. My last fight, they found something that they couldn't really understand in my head. It didn't help me to make my decision to retire, but it was obviously a concern. I had second and third opinions. It was something in my head that they thought could maybe have an effect thirty years down the road, but they just weren't sure. Maybe they were being extra-careful."

Then, on September 3, De La Hoya vs. Belfort ground to a halt. Oscar announced that he had tested positive for COVID and that the fight was off. One day later, fifty-eight-year-old Evander Holyfield was substituted as Belfort's opponent.

PART TWO

The last thing a fighter loses isn't his legs, speed, or power. It's his ego.

Evander Holyfield was a great fighter. His victories over Mike Tyson, Riddick Bowe, Buster Douglas, George Foreman, Larry Holmes, and Dwight Muhammad Qawi are the stuff of legend. But Holyfield is fifty-eight years old. Prior to fighting Vitor Belfort on September 11, 2021, he hadn't fought in more than ten years. He had nothing left as a fighter except his ego.

Evander needed money. After the exhibition between Mike Tyson and Roy Jones engendered a reported 1.6 million pay-per-view buys, he thought he knew where to find it. Tyson was a goose that could lay a golden egg. But where fighting Holyfield again was concerned, Iron Mike could have been forgiven for thinking, "Been there, done that. It didn't work out well the first two times, so why do it again?"

On March 22, 2021, Kris Lawrence (Holyfield's manager) issued a media release stating that Tyson's representatives had turned down a $25 million guarantee to fight Evander at Hard Rock Stadium in Miami on May 29. "We thought this was a done deal," Lawrence said. "But it fell apart when Tyson's people declined all offers. We were negotiating in good faith all along and it appears we just ended up wasting our time."

Then Triller came calling.

On April 16, 2021 (one day before Jake Paul vs. Ben Askren), Holyfield and Kevin McBride attended a press conference in Atlanta where it was announced that they would face each other on the undercard of Teófimo López vs. George Kambosos (then scheduled for June 5 at LoanDepot Park in Miami).

McBride—best known as "the conqueror of Mike Tyson"—had last fought in 2011 when he was knocked out by Mariusz Wach at Mohegan Sun in Connecticut. He'd lost six of his final seven fights and was just shy of forty-eight years old.

After losing to Wach, McBride was placed on an indefinite medical suspension by the Mohegan Tribe Department of Athletic Regulation with the notation "needs neuro and MRI." There had been no administrative change in his status since then.

Multiple sources say that Holyfield–McBride was to have been an exhibition with neither man using best efforts to hurt the other. Informed sources say that Evander was to receive slightly more than $7 million and McBride $500,000.

Soon after Holyfield–McBride was announced, Triller moved López-Kambosos to June 19. But when the new date was set, Holyfield–McBride was taken off the card. On May 13, Triller announced that Holyfield–McBride would be rescheduled for an unspecified date in August. At the end of May, as mandated by contract, Triller sent Holyfield a substantial check as an advance. But the fight wasn't rescheduled.

On September 1, Holyfield filed a demand for arbitration against Triller, alleging breach of contract and demanding the unpaid portion (approximately $5 million) of what was to have been his purse for the exhibition against McBride. Then De La Hoya contracted COVID and Triller concluded that it could salvage its September 11 card and settle its dispute with Holyfield at the same time by making Holyfield vs. Belfort. McBride was paid $250,000 in step-aside money, and Holyfield–Belfort was on.

Or was it?

On August 11, 2021, Triller had announced a pay-per-view undercard for De La Hoya vs. Belfort consisting of Anderson Silva vs. Tito Ortiz, Andy Vences vs. Jono Carroll, and David Haye vs. Joe Fournier. Then, California State Athletic Commission executive director Andy Foster refused to sanction Haye–Fournier as an official fight. Fournier is a London-born entrepreneur (inaccurately described as a "billionaire") who'd compiled a 9–0 ring record but whose previous five fights had been against opponents with a composite ring record of 2 wins, 40 losses, and 37 KOs by. Also, Fournier and Haye were friends. At that point, there was talk of a split-site event with Haye–Fournier moving to Miami or, alternatively, being clearly labeled an "exhibition."

Holyfield–Belfort was more troubling to Foster. As a person ages, his or her brain begins to shrink. This means that the veins connecting the brain to its coverings are at increased risk of a brain bleed when the head is struck.

Holyfield is fifty-eight years old and has been hit in the head thousands of times by men who hit much harder than Belfort. But no matter how limited in power Vitor's punches might be—and no matter what the pre-fight understanding between the fighters might have been—any blows to the head that landed on Evander had the potential to cause serious damage.

The California State Athletic Commission refused to approve Holyfield–Belfort.

"I was not agreeable with the match based on a variety of regulatory factors," Foster said later. "There were issues as to whether it was going to be an exhibition or a fight, and we did not have adequate time for Evander to go through an appropriate licensing process."

Then the Florida Athletic Commission allowed what California wouldn't.

"They tried California," Association of Boxing Commissions president Mike Mazzulli told this writer. "Andy turned it down, and I commend him for that. I reached out to the Florida commission on several occasions and did not get a call back. I hope they understand the consequences of something like this. It was dangerous and a disgrace to boxing. It was a fiasco, and I think it was horrible."

But was Holyfield–Belfort to be an exhibition or a fight? Evander and Vitor signed separate contracts. It's unclear what Vitor's contract said. However, multiple sources say that Holyfield's contract made it clear that the fighters would not use best efforts to win the fight.

"I knew from the beginning that it wasn't supposed to be a legitimate boxing match," Mike Mazzulli says. "You can quote me on that. I'm one hundred percent sure the contract was written as an exhibition."

"There were meticulous negotiations as to how things would be conducted," another person familiar with the situation says. "Evander went into the fight thinking that it was an exhibition with each man making an effort to put on a good show for the fans. That was the contractual understanding he had for Kevin McBride and that's what he had here. Evander's mindset was 'we'll go out, put on a show, and get a good payday.'

I don't know what Belfort signed. I only know what Evander signed. Evander had no intention of hurting the other guy."

Multiple sources also say that the contract Holyfield signed contained a confidentiality clause and prohibited him from publicly calling the event an exhibition.

Meanwhile, Triller was promoting the event as a fight. And a compliant Florida Athletic Commission went along with that notion. On September 8 (three days before the event), FAC executive director Patrick Cunningham issued a statement that read, "The Florida Athletic Commission has approved the Evander Holyfield vs. Vitor Belfort bout as a fully regulated professional boxing match. It will be conducted under the Unified Rules of Boxing and scored by three judges on the 10-point must system. All boxers on this card have successfully met all requirements to be licensed by the Florida Athletic Commission."

Similarly, Triller's promotional material for Holyfield–Belfort was marketing the event as a "fight," not an exhibition. And Triller arranged for it to be entered on BoxRec.com (the official registry for the Association of Boxing Commissions) as an official fight. Then Mike Mazzulli stepped in.

"We were not going to allow it to be placed on BoxRec," Mazzulli says. "We contacted them, explained the situation, and BoxRec removed it from its listing of official fights."

At the final pre-fight press conference on September 9, both Holyfield and Belfort presented their encounter as a real fight. When asked specifically if it would be an exhibition, Evander responded, "All I know is, it's a fight and they got the rules. If I can get him in one second, I'll get him in one second. I do what I have to do."

During fight week for Tyson–Jones, Donald Trump Jr. (who has seven million Twitter followers) had sent out five tweets supporting the event and sharing links to promotional videos and pay-per-view ordering information. For Holyfield–Belfort, Triller went one giant step further, offering viewers what it called a "Donald Trump alternative commentary" stream with the former president and his son live onsite giving "unfiltered boxing commentary" at no extra charge on top of the $49.99 pay-per-view buy.

At the September 9 press conference, Donald Trump Jr. talked for thirteen minutes, noting his father's "total recall" of fights from decades ago and voicing the view that it was "really cool" that he and his father would be commentating on the fights. He also opined, "Americans are learning the hard way that they've been lied to and manipulated by the media. You're seeing the results of that every day."

Later in the proceedings, Donald Trump Sr. came on an audio feed and answered pre-screened questions for seven minutes, ending with the thought that, if he had to fight somebody or box somebody, "I think probably my easiest fight would be Joe Biden. I think he would go down very very quickly."

Thereafter, Jerry Izenberg (the dean of American sportswriters who, unlike either Trump, actually served in the Armed Forces), noted that Joe Biden, Barack Obama, and George W. Bush would all commemorate the twentieth anniversary of 9/11 (the day Holyfield–Belfort was contested) by visiting attack sites. Izenberg then closed his column with a thought regarding Holyfield–Belfort: "The bad news: It will cost you $50 to see this farce. The good news: You can save every penny of it by simply not watching."

When fight night came, Rey Flores and Shawn Porter carried the regular (sans Trump) blow-by-blow commentary. Mario Lopez was the emcee. References to a "sold-out arena" were somewhat disingenuous. The Seminole Hard Rock Hotel and Casino theater has three levels. Two of them were curtained off.

Todd Grisham and a series of rotating mixed martial artists were on the alternative commentary desk with Donald Trump Sr. and Jr. Trump Sr.'s comments often centered on himself. Trump Jr.'s comments often centered on himself or his father.

Trump Sr. began his commentary by attacking "some very bad decisions" made by Joe Biden with regard to Afghanistan. Later, in a tribute to America, scantily clad women carried American flags around the ring prior to the singing of the National Anthem, after which the crowd chanted "We want Trump" and "Knock out Biden."

Trump Sr. also expressed delight at being in Florida: "We had a tremendous result in Florida. We love Florida. And they ran the election clean. That's very important. . . . You have a lovely crowd here. You've got so many [pro-Trump] signs. I love the signs. . . . If you do a lot of talking, you have to back it up. I do a lot of talking and I won."

After one fight, Trump Sr. cautioned, "Let's see what happens with the scoring. It's like elections. It could be rigged."

Trump Jr. once again praised his father's recall of fights. But that recall failed Trump Sr. when he started talking about George Foreman vs. Michael Moorer and couldn't remember Moorer's name. Then, while going off on a tangent to show off his great knowledge of boxing, Trump Sr. and Grisham confused Gennady Golovkin with Sergey Kovalev.

The first "fight" of the evening matched David Haye against Joe Fournier in an encounter that had all the credibility of a WWE confrontation but wasn't choreographed nearly as well. Haye fought like a boxing instructor who was sparring with a pupil of limited ability and had promised ahead of time that he wouldn't hurt him. Fournier boxed with the confidence of a man who had an understanding with his opponent that all would be well. This lasted for eight long two-minute rounds, after which the judges rendered an 80–71, 79–72, 79–72 verdict in Haye's favor.

Next up, Jono Carroll won a 97–93, 97–93, 95–95 majority decision over Andy Vences in a tedious affair that saw thirty seconds of action spread over ten rounds. After that, in a matchup of previously retired forty-six-year-old MMA fighters, Anderson Silva knocked out Tito Ortiz in 81 seconds.

Then it was time for Holyfield–Belfort. The contest was scheduled for eight two-minute rounds. Holyfield had weighed in at 225 pounds, Belfort at 206.

Watching Evander in the ring was sad. His balance was poor. His reflexes were shot. He pawed with his jab and seemed to have no defense against punches. Fifty-five seconds into the contest, Belfort landed a straight left to the body that knocked Holyfield off balance and pushed him back into the ropes. Then Vitor attacked. Evander covered up and, seeming to understand at this point that he was in a real fight, threw a wild left hook that looked like it was designed to hurt. But it missed by a wide margin and his momentum caused him to plummet into the bottom ring strand and then to the canvas.

Holyfield rose. Belfort attacked again and, at the 1:22 mark, dropped Evander with a left uppercut to the jaw. Evander beat the count but was in trouble. Showing no mercy, Belfort threw eighteen unanswered punches. One minute, 49 seconds into the round, referee Sammy Burgos stopped the encounter.

When it was over, Holyfield complained to Todd Grisham about the stoppage and said he'd still like to fight Mike Tyson. Belfort said he'd like to fight Jake Paul next and called him "a little bitch."

Several days after Holyfield–Belfort, a source with knowledge of what transpired told this writer, "Evander was fighting Belfort like David Haye fought Fournier. Then Belfort started unloading on him, and Evander realized it was for real and threw a left hook to put him in his place. But he missed, fell into the ropes, and went down.

"I was with Evander in his suite after the fight," this source continued. "One of the first things he said was, 'I couldn't believe how hard the guy was throwing. When I realized he was trying to hurt me, I threw back. But before I could change my mindset and put things together, I got knocked down. I got up and was covering up the way you're supposed to and the referee stopped the fight.'"

So . . . where does all of this leave boxing?

First, Holyfield got a lot of money for being in the ring with Belfort, and that's good. I hope it's invested wisely so he can live off the income and be financially secure for the rest of his life.

Second, to quote Mark Kriegel, "Boxing can't survive, much less grow, if it keeps pushing out its past at the expense of its present and its future."

And as Matt Christie wrote, "I don't care how many new eyes they bring to the sport; creating this new precedent, which essentially says it's okay for boxers who long ago realized they shouldn't be boxing anymore to come back and take more punches is not just irresponsible. It's deadly."

Holyfield–Belfort seems to have performed poorly in the market-place. A well-placed source says that FITE (which had exclusive streaming rights) chalked up approximately 50,000 buys. Add on cable and, most likely, the total number of buys will be in the neighborhood of 125,000.

That's bad news for Triller. Counting fighter purses, music acts, Donald Trump Sr. and Jr. and other talent costs, production, publicity, travel, and the like, the promotion is estimated to have cost between $15 million and $20 million to mount. And unlike some past events that Triller might have classified as loss leaders, this one brought far more bad publicity than good. And no! Not all publicity is good publicity. Triller got dragged over the coals on this one.

Sports have always been about entertainment. And sports are monetized as entertainment. But trash boxing won't save the sweet science. Sports don't thrive on sideshow events. The NBA slam-dunk contest and three-point competition enliven All-Star Weekend, but the league is built around regular-season games and the playoffs. Football fans might be intrigued by the idea of a punt-pass-kick competition between Peyton Manning and Brett Favre, but that competition would never outdraw an NFL playoff game. Boxing can't be healthy if sideshows are the main event.

Keep in mind, though: the proliferation of trash boxing is a symptom of boxing's problems, not the cause. Trash boxing in and of itself isn't bad for boxing. In recent years, boxing has been bad for boxing.

Teófimo López vs. George Kambosos wasn't a six-million-dollar fight.
But it was a good one.

The Strange Odyssey of
López–Kambosos and Triller

PART ONE

On November 27, 2021, Teófimo López fought to defend his multiple 135-pound titles against George Kambosos at the Hulu Theater at Madison Square Garden. The primary storyline coming into the bout wasn't the fight. López was a 9-to-1 betting favorite, and very few people expected López–Kambosos to be competitive. The fight generated publicity in the nine months that preceded it because of its business backstory. But López–Kambosos evolved into a tense, hard-fought, bloody spectacle with Kambosos emerging victorious on a 115–111, 115–112, 113–114 split decision.

López, now twenty-four, turned pro after the 2016 Olympics. Top Rank (his promoter) put him on a fast track, and Teófimo delivered. He won the IBF lightweight title with an impressive second-round knockout of Richard Commey in 2019 and added the WBA and WBO belts to his inventory with a unanimous decision over Vasiliy Lomachenko in October 2020. That brought his record to 16–0 with 12 knockouts.

Kambosos had pieced together a 19–0 (10 KOs) record against pedestrian opposition and became the IBF's mandatory challenger by virtue of a split-decision victory over Lee Selby last year. In theory, boxing's mandatory-challenger rule is designed to ensure that champions go in tough against the best available challenger at least once a year. But it has been subverted to the point where, too often, the mandatory challenger is an easy mark.

When boxing fans talked about dream fights at 135 pounds involving López, Lomachenko, Gervonta Davis, Ryan Garcia, and Devin Haney, Kambosos wasn't even in the conversation. But López was obligated to fight him if he wanted to keep his IBF belt.

Top Rank, which had several years left on its promotional agreement with López, offered Teófimo his contractual minimum of $1.25 million for the bout. David McWater (who manages López) countered with a demand for $5.5 million. With a divide that wide, Kambosos's demands were irrelevant. Under IBF rules, the matter went to a purse bid with the proceeds to be split 65–35 in favor of Team López.

Enter Triller.

Triller is largely under the control of Ryan Kavanaugh, a forty-six-year-old businessman with a checkered past. Triller's foray into boxing started with a commercial success—the November 28, 2020, exhibition between Mike Tyson and Roy Jones. Tyson–Jones was a way to drum up interest in, and exposure for, Triller. But the extraordinarily popular reception that it received encouraged Kavanaugh to delve further into the boxing business. Things have gone downhill from there.

Triller holds itself out as "a vehicle for fighters to grow their brand, connect with fans, and build their social media following as they progress in their careers." Boxing on Triller is largely a social media event, which is not necessarily a bad thing for the sport. These days, presidential elections are won and lost on social media.

But we're living in an age when some businesses are operated as financial instruments to be built up and sold for a profit rather than being run as self-sustaining businesses that are profitable in and of themselves. Triller might fit that mold.

The purse bid for López–Kambosos was held on February 25, 2021. Considerable behind-the-scenes maneuvering preceded the opening of the envelopes.

On February 11, according to a report in *The Athletic,* Top Rank president Todd duBoef sent an email to Kevin A. Mayer (who was about to become the CEO of DAZN). That email read in part, "This is a follow-up to our conversation. Attached is an article which quotes Matchroom's Eddie Hearn's desire to make a bid on DAZN's behalf for Teofimo Lopez v George Kambosos. Top Rank signed Lopez out of the Olympics and is in the middle of a long term Promotional Agreement. Lopez has been a mainstay and anchor on ESPN and ESPN+. If the article is true, I was shocked to see this brazen act by DAZN, particularly after I cleared ESPN programming off of May 8 for DAZN's Canelo v Saunders big event, moving our scheduled event (Ramirez v Taylor) to later in the month. I appreciate your attention to this and look forward to starting our conversations in the coming weeks."

Mayer, according to *The Athletic*, responded, "Thanks for sending this, Todd." He then forwarded his response to DAZN Group COO Ed McCarthy with the notation, "Ed, let's discuss, but I think Todd is making a fair point. He's doing us a big favor on the Canelo fight. Let's think hard about this please?"

"After the email exchange," *The Athletic* reported, "McCarthy and duBoef spoke by telephone. Following that call, duBoef believed that Hearn wouldn't bid on López–Kambosos and that Top Rank could enter a bid that would win the rights to the fight without going far above its original offer that called for a purse of $1.25 million to López."

DuBoef later told *The Athletic*, "Eddie can bid all he wants. But if you're asking me to do things for you and we're talking about business together and things that [DAZN] wants to do internationally, if you're asking more to expand our relationship and 'can you help me here?' I find it to be a brazen act if you're enabling Eddie. Is that collusion? No."

But there was a school of thought that, if nothing more, it was an attempt at collusion.

Meanwhile, Peter Kahn (who managed Kambosos) had his own take on things. Kahn told *The Athletic*, "Top Rank in essence was attempting to bully DAZN into not bidding, which means Top Rank would have been able to come in and possibly steal that bid for a low number. And I really wasn't gonna let that happen. So I basically threw a Hail Mary and I flew out to California. I met with Ryan Kavanaugh. I explained to him the situation. I said, 'Ryan, if you want to show people that you're serious about being in the boxing space, not just about influencers, not just about crossover fights and legends, but if you really want to make a splash, this is your opportunity."

And make a splash, Kavanaugh did. Top Rank bid $2,315,000 at the February 25 purse bid ($1,504,750 of which would have gone to López had the bid been successful). Matchroom, despite duBoef's lobbying with DAZN, bid $3,506,000. Triller bid the outlandish sum of $6,018,000.

"He knows it was a premium," Kahn said later of Kavanaugh's bid. But Kavanaugh bought into Kahn's logic; to wit, "In order to really secure that opportunity and show people that you want to make a statement, that you want to be disruptive, you're going to have to bid this type of number."

Pursuant to IBF rules, $3,911,700 (65 percent) of the winning purse bid was allocated to the López side of the equation. Under the terms of Teófimo's promotional contract with Top Rank, 20 percent of that ($782,340) would go to the promoter. Thus, López and his management team were in line to receive $3,129,360 (far more than the $1.25 million they'd been offered by Top Rank to fight Kambosos).

Arum looked at the bright side of things, saying, "We made a lot of money in five minutes. Almost $800,000 is pretty good money. Shit, that's really great because López vs. Kambosos is not a premier attraction." But he was less philosophical when talking about DAZN and Eddie Hearn.

"He lost and pissed us off at the same time," Arum said of Hearn." It sent a message to us. But he better watch out the next time he goes to a purse bid when the fighters have no connection to ESPN or Top Rank. Maybe we'll jam a bid up Hearn's ass. We'll get back at them. I'm angry at them, yeah."

Meanwhile, Triller issued a press release referencing itself as a "disruptive property" that was "reimagining the sport of boxing for a new, engaged generation." And Kavanaugh proclaimed, "We are working to reshape the vision of excitement and storytelling in a sport we love. We're here as a friend to the boxing world. We're here not to attack it, but to bring entertainment to what has traditionally been a purist sport. Our view is that we want to make it look and feel different. We're going to deliver a different experience that has something for everyone. We want to show we're taking the sport of boxing seriously and respecting boxing. We're not trying to make a mockery of it. That's what this fight does for us."

Triller's purse bid for López–Kambosos made it a player in legitimate boxing. It also meant that Triller was supplanting DAZN as the primary force in inflating license fees in the sport. And—temporarily, at least—it led to artificially high expectations from fighters as to what they might receive for future fights.

Predictably, Hearn used the occasion to take a swipe at Arum.

"Teófimo López took the chance for small money to fight Lomachenko because he believed he would win and he believed he would get the financial rewards he deserved," Hearn said. "But guess what? When he won, they wouldn't give it to him. This whole problem has been caused by Top Rank. Bob's been out there, 'Oh, Eddie Hearn, I'm fucking pissed off that he's bid and he's gotta watch himself now.' Fuck off! It's an open market. If you can't do a deal with your fighter and that comes into the open market, you pay the consequences. And the consequences is some-one else has popped up from nowhere and taken one of your biggest assets on your platform, for ESPN, and put it on another platform. It's a disaster for Top Rank. I told him I'd bid. You want no one to bid so you can get your guy cheap? It doesn't work like that. Don't tell us what we can and can't do. It was arrogance, quite frankly. You think that I would phone a competitor and say, 'Don't bid on this fight'? They created this mess. And it went horribly wrong because we don't get told what to do. The fight come up on the open market. Our broadcaster told us, 'We'd like that fight.' And we bid."

Kavanaugh took a conciliatory tone toward Top Rank after the purse bid, stating, "We are in no way competing with Bob Arum. Eddie Hearn is Arum's true competition. We're just doing it to build a brand. We don't compete with Arum or ESPN because we are a different model. We hope they see us as a way to create more marketing for their fighters. Teófimo will come in with a certain amount of followers and leave with, hopefully, three-to-four times that amount. That will be good for Bob too. We think we're great for everyone in the sport."

Still, the relationship between Top Rank and López had been fractured. And there were people whispering in Teófimo's ear—shouting is more like it—that Arum's public statements and duBoef's email exchanges with DAZN had given López grounds to break his contract with Top Rank.

After the purse bid, Teófimo declared, "I love ESPN and the platform and everything they have done for Team López. However, I am very thankful that my team and I stuck to our guns. We knew what we were being offered was disrespectful, and we expected the open market would value us differently. And it showed today. The six million dollars from Triller says that Top Rank doesn't value the best fighter on their roster."

In response, Arum noted that Top Rank had several years left on its contract with López and said, "Teofimo has a contract with us. There will be regular negotiations on his fights. If he wins [against Kambosos] and comes back to us and wants the same money that he got before, the answer is 'no.' So he sits out for a while. You can't pay what you don't have. He either fights or he doesn't fight. Maybe Triller is so happy with López they will give us a big number and buy out our contract with Lopez, which is fine also."

That earned a rejoinder from López, who proclaimed, "If they can't treat their fighters, or at least me, in a way of respect, then I'll find it somewhere else because I know what I'm worth. Obviously, Triller knows my worth. It sucks, it really does, to have it go this way. So congratulations, Todd duBoef. You lost your best fighter from your stable."

Then Teófimo López Sr. (who trains his son) got into the act, saying, "We already took a low rate for the Lomachenko fight. When we took less money to get those belts, I told my son, 'Once you have those belts, you can do whatever you want.' And that's what we're doing right now. This is big. This is like the Muhammad Ali era when Muhammad stood for his rights."

That was an ill-considered remark. Ali gave up the heavyweight championship of the world and risked going to prison for five years to stand up for his religious beliefs. All Team López did was maneuver to get more money. It had every right to do so. But Teófimo was sacrificing nothing. Indeed, Richard Schaefer (who has never been thought of as a fan of Bob Arum) told this writer, "Let's be fair about it. Top Rank did a fantastic job of building up López. And the fight against Lomachenko— which did the most to make López what he is now—was promoted during a pandemic."

Thereafter, an accord was reached. On June 12, it was announced that Top Rank and López had extended their contract and that the new deal provided for an increase in López's minimum purses moving forward.

Meanwhile, Triller was forging ahead. On March 22, 2021, it announced that Peter Kahn would become Triller Fight Club's chief boxing officer (a position he would hold until stepping down six months later). Jim Lampley was hired to handle blow-by-blow chores for at least four future Triller events (he has yet to call one). And the expectation in some circles was that, going forward, Triller would cherry-pick among high-profile boxing cards that were up for purse bid. But Arum sounded a cautionary note, saying, "They don't know what the hell they're doing. I'll let them do their thing. I'm not going to get involved in the sideshow business."

In other words, it was possible that Ryan Kavanaugh had figured out something that Arum, Hearn, Al Haymon, Frank Warren, and other top promoters hadn't. But it was unlikely. And now that Triller was moving to a new level, it was worth asking, "Could Triller actually promote a major world championship fight? Or would the result be like hanging a painting by a kindergarten student in the Metropolitan Museum of Art?"

PART TWO

Initially, Triller scheduled the lightweight title-unification bout between Teófimo López and George Kambosos for June 5, 2021. But on April 27, it was announced that Floyd Mayweather vs. Logan Paul would be contested on June 6. Wary of the competition for pay-per-view buys, Kavanaugh changed the date for López–Kambosos to June 19. Performances by Meek Mill, Myke Towers, and Lunay were to be included in the show. A reliable source says that Triller's projected budget for the event was $18 million.

Then, on June 15, 2021, it was announced that López had tested positive for COVID-19 and the event would be rescheduled for August 14. On June 23, the fight was postponed yet again, this time to September 11.

There were more changes to come. On July 9, it was reported that Triller planned to move López–Kambosos to a fifth date (October 17) and that the fight would be held in Australia. In response, David McWater (Teófimo's manager) stated that López didn't want to fight in Australia (Kambosos's homeland) for logistical reasons relating to the need for him to quarantine for fourteen days once he arrived there and that he also objected to the new date.

"If they want to move it that far back," McWater said, "the IBF will rule. If we have to, we'll give up the title and [Kambosos] can fight Isaac Cruz somewhere [for the vacant title] for $70,000."

An August 9 IBF ruling split the baby. López–Kambosos, the sanctioning body decreed, could be held as late as October 17. But López could not be required to travel abroad to a location that subjected him to a fourteen-day quarantine period.

Thereafter, the projected date changed again. And again.

On August 23, Triller announced that López–Kambosos would take place on October 5 at the Hulu Theater at Madison Square Garden. It then shifted the date to October 4. López and Kambosos signed contracts for October 4. But on September 20, Kavanaugh told journalist Ariel Helwani that he planned to switch the fight to October 16 at Barclays Center because he didn't want to compete for viewers against the October 4 *Monday Night Football* game between the Las Vegas Raiders and Los Angeles Chargers. Team López objected, citing their already-signed contract and the fact that changing the date a mere two weeks before the fight could wreak havoc with Teófimo's plans for making weight, sparring, and the like. Kambosos also demurred. Then, on September 23, Teófimo López Sr. said that his son had agreed in writing to allow Triller to move the date to October 16, bypassing manager David McWater and attorney Pat English in the process.

On September 27, Triller reached a six-figure settlement with Madison Square Garden, and the issuing of refunds to fans who had purchased tickets for October 4 at MSG began. But Kambosos still hadn't agreed to the October 16 date and was demanding that Triller place his share of the purse in escrow before he flew to the United States for the fight.

There was a school of thought that Kambosos didn't want to come to New York because of the birth of his child and death of his grandfather (both of which occurred on September 24). More likely, he was worried about getting paid the full amount that he would be owed for the fight.

On September 28, Greg Smith (an attorney representing Kambosos) sent a letter to the IBF asking that Triller be declared in default of its purse bid and "barred from future purse bids for its egregious behavior." More specifically, Smith alleged that Triller had violated IBF Rule 10.F.2 ("Failure of Promoter to Comply with Obligation").

Triller suggested in its response that the problems it had endured with regard to López–Kambosos were the result of a cabal among the powers that be in boxing to crush a new entity that was threatening the status quo.

On October 6, the IBF ruled that Triller was in default of its purse-bid obligations and that Matchroom Boxing was entitled to promotional rights to López–Kambosos by virtue of its (second place) $3,506,000 purse bid. It further ruled that Triller, by its conduct, had forfeited its $1,203,600 deposit (20 percent of the winning purse bid), and that this amount would be added onto the purses that the fighters received from Matchroom.

On October 20, 2021, Matchroom announced that López–Kambosos would take place on November 27 at the Hulu Theater at Madison Square Garden and be streamed on DAZN.

During the build-up to the fight, Kambosos said the things that one often hears from a prohibitive underdog:

* ★ "No one has ever turned round to Teófimo and said, 'I'm coming straight at ya. I don't care what you've done.' They've all been scared of him. I don't know why. He's a young little kid. I'm not scared of any man. I'm bigger, stronger, faster, and more explosive and more violent."
* ★ "I know this kid's got a suspect chin. If I can crack him with one shot, the speed and power that I possess and the explosive shots that I pop off, don't be surprised if he goes down in three."
* ★ "I've got a big motor. Every round, I keep getting better and better and keep throwing more punches. My speed and the way I move and explosive power and shots that I land and throw and the punches in bunches and the combination punches that I have in my artillery and my stamina and my fitness is just too much for this kid."

López predicted a first-round knockout and got into the holiday spirit of things with the declaration, "I feel like, if I break his fucking eye socket, I'm sorry but I'm not sorry. I feel like, if I snap his vertebrae, I'm not sorry. I really want to show everybody what my power is capable of and what my mind is capable of. If I really want to hurt someone to that extreme, I will."

There was a stupid cursing and shoving confrontation between Teófimo López Sr. and George Kambosos Sr. during a fight-week media workout, the verbal highlights of which were:

López Sr: "Kambosos, you're gonna get your ass kicked. First round, baby. Fuckin' chicken. Fuck you, motherfucker."

Kambosos Sr: "Fuck off, motherfucker. Come on, you big mouth. Come over here. You wanna walk across this fuckin' line? I'm gonna fuck you up first."

The final pre-fight press conference featured more inane trash-talking with the fighters taking the lead.

"After this fight, I don't want to have no handshake, none of that," Teófimo Jr. told George Jr. "We're gonna put your ass on a fucking stretcher."

Beyond that, López spoke for many when he said, "I'm ready to get this over with. It's been nine months. Get this over with and focus on the bigger fights coming up."

The promotion didn't generate much interest beyond hardcore box-ing fans. College football was entering crunch time. The NFL season was approaching its stretch run. DAZN has limited penetration of commercial markets in the United States. And the fight itself was perceived as being of limited merit.

But López–Kambosos turned out to be a scintillating fight.

López came out hard, almost contemptuously, at the opening bell, gunning for a quick knockout. Kambosos made him miss but wasn't mak-ing him pay. Then Teófimo got careless and George dumped him on the seat of his pants with a sharp right hand as López was loading up for an overhand right of his own. Teófimo was sufficiently dominant for the rest of the stanza that two of the three judges (and this writer) scored round one 10–9 for Kambosos instead of the traditional 10–8 that normally accompanies a knockdown.

Thereafter, López was more controlled in his aggression. He kept pressing the action, stalking, throwing punches with bad intentions. But Kambosos is slick and quick with a good chin and sneaky right hand. He set traps again and again and wasn't afraid to trade with Teófimo when the situation called for it. Also, too often, López stood directly in front of Kambosos without moving his head and paid a price when George got off first.

By round eight, the area around both of López's eyes was bruised and swelling. Kambosos was cut above his own left eye and appeared to be tiring. In round nine, Teófimo landed his best punches to that point in the fight. In round ten, he dropped Kambosos with a chopping right hand behind the ear.

Now Kambosos was fighting to survive. And he did.

In round eleven, with López bleeding badly from a gash on his own left eyelid, referee Harvey Dock called a temporary halt to the action while a ringside physician examined the cut. The fighting resumed. López couldn't close the show. It was high drama.

This writer scored the bout 114–113 for Kambosos. The judges favored the challenger by a 115–111, 115–112, 113–114 margin.

López went into denial mode after the decision was announced, complaining in an in-the-ring interview, "I won tonight. I don't care what anybody says. I don't believe it was a close fight at all. At the end of it all, I scored it 10–2."

The heavily pro-López crowd (which knew what it had just seen) booed Teófimo for that proclamation.

López lost because he was certain that there was no way he could lose. And from the day the fight was signed, he conducted himself accordingly.

So . . . where does the odyssey of López–Kambosos and Triller fit into the overall business of boxing? Let's start with some basics.

Once upon a time, the money that flowed into boxing was generated directly by individual fights. In days of old, the primarily source of income was the live gate. Then revenue from television based on advertising sales and pay-per-view buys became the dominant factor. Smaller revenue streams such as income from sponsorships were also involved. But as of late, television networks and other entities have been putting up money that isn't being recouped from income generated directly by fights.

HBO invested heavily in boxing to build its subscriber base and got good value in return. Boxing fans saw the fights they wanted to see. During the glory years of HBO Sports, being an A-side fighter on HBO didn't just pay well. It gave a fighter credibility. Boxing fans trusted HBO to deliver good fighters in entertaining fights with honest well-informed commentary. The network flourished, in part because of its boxing program.

Premier Boxing Champions was built in large measure on a financial model that relied on a huge influx of cash from investors (who were hoping for a profit but appear to have lost hundreds of millions of dollars).

Then a group of businessmen from the United Kingdom backed by a Ukrainian-born billionaire announced their intention to take over and revitalize boxing in the United States as part of a plan to generate subscription buys for a streaming network called DAZN. To date, DAZN has further marginalized boxing in America and lightened Len Blavatnik's wallet.

In sum, money alone doesn't lead to success. The people charged with spending that money have to spend it wisely.

One year has passed since Triller's November 28, 2020, Mike Tyson vs. Roy Jones offering. As of this writing, Ryan Kavanaugh hasn't come close to duplicating the success that he enjoyed with his initial foray into the sweet science. In early 2021, everyone's eyes were focused on Triller. What would Triller do next? Now Triller is almost an afterthought in conversations about the business of boxing. Most people in boxing no longer consider Triller to be a serious long-term player in the sport. It's good when people put money into boxing. But their business plan has to be sustainable.

Subsequent to this article being written, steps taken by the United States Department of the Treasury (as discussed at pages 81–82 above) diminished MTK's influence in boxing. The extent of Daniel Kinahan's current involvement with the sport is unclear.

Clash of the Clans

MTK Global is a fighter management company headquartered in Dubai. It offers managerial services to more than two hundred boxers (foremost among them, Tyson Fury) and is affiliated with gyms around the world. Its website states, "We have firmly established our presence in over 25 locations worldwide" and lists sites in the United Kingdom, Spain, the United States, Canada, France, South Africa, Brazil, Australia, Kazakhstan, Japan, Denmark, Latvia, and the United Arab Emirates.

Nicola Tallant is the investigations editor for the *Sunday World* in Ireland and has written extensively about organized crime. Now Tallant has authored *Clash of the Clans* (Mirror Books), a work that focuses on Daniel Kinahan, who helped build MTK Global and is identified by Tallant as "boss of the largest organised drug gang to ever come out of Ireland"—an enterprise that, Tallant estimates, has enabled the Kinahan family to amass a "£1 billion drug fortune."

Kinahan, age forty-four, has never been convicted of a crime. But in Tallant's words, "He has been identified in the High Court in Dublin as a senior figure in organised crime on a global scale. And the Criminal Assets Bureau, one of the most respected forces in crime fighting across the world, has said that he control[s] and manage[s] the operations of the Kinahan Organised Crime Group, who have in turn been described as a murderous group who have smuggled guns and drugs into Ireland, the UK, and mainland Europe on a massive scale."

This characterization was echoed by Kieran Cunningham (chief sports writer for the *Irish Daily Star*), who said of Kinahan in a May 31, 2020, podcast, "He was identified by the Criminal Assets Bureau as controlling and managing the Kinahan organized crime group. This is an organization that smuggles drugs and guns into and out of the UK [and] mainland Europe. It has been involved in money laundering. It is a major

275

drugs cartel. It's involved in a feud in Ireland that has killed eighteen people, and sixteen of the murders have been by the Kinahan cartel."

Compared to the crimes that Kinahan is alleged to have committed, Don King was a choirboy in his earlier incarnation as a numbers tsar in Cleveland.

Tallant traces Kinahan's entry into boxing to 2012 when Matthew Macklin (a widely respected middleweight contender) founded Macklin's Gym Mirabella (MGM) in Spain in association with Kinahan. Macklin later sold his interest in the gym, which evolved into the company now known as MTK Global.

In a column for the *Sunday World*, Tallant wrote, "Daniel and Matthew decided they should open a gym to give something back to the community. They found a premises near Puerto Banus where they like to hang out and set themselves up as a not-for-profit organisation. They decided to choose a local charity for sick children to give any money they made to. MGM hosts youth boxers from clubs in Ireland as part of their community service. It gives free training for under-16s. No doubt the kids are impressed with the flash cars that Daniel and his pals drive. I'm sure they couldn't help but notice the massive watch on his wrist. I suppose you could say that, when he wasn't organising drug shipments and murder, he was a pretty good guy.

"MGM is to Daniel Kinahan what Atletico Nacional was to Pablo Escobar," Tallant continued. "Have you heard of Escobar? He is the guy with all the money, the one who ran the Medellin Cartel, the one who remorselessly killed any man, woman, or child that stood in his way. Pablo was a psychopath, but he also loved football and he bought the best players with his blood money so he could control Colombia's finest sport. Daniel likes boxing. I think we can safely say that, just like Pablo Escobar, he orders death in the same way the rest of us might ring for a pizza."

In 2015, an underworld feud burst into the open when Gary Hutch (nephew of mob figure Gerry "The Monk" Hutch) was assassinated in Spain. It was widely believed that Kinahan ordered the execution. At least eighteen people were killed in the internecine warfare that followed. The most notable of these killings occurred on February 5, 2016, at the Regency Hotel in Dublin at the weigh-in for a fight card that was to be headlined by Irish lightweight Jamie Kavanagh. Armed men disguised as

Gardai (Irish police) and carrying AK-47s entered the hotel and opened fire. Kinahan (believed to have been the object of the attack) escaped unharmed. Three people were shot. David Byrne (a friend of Kinahan's) was killed.

Later that year, Kinahan moved to Dubai, which Tallant describes as "a safe place for the likes of the Kinahans," before adding, "It had become a hub for money laundering and a hideout for criminals from all over the world. Amongst the glittering extravagance of Dubai, all money was welcome, no matter how it was earned—and with no extradition treaties with most modern countries, it kept crooks at arm's length from the law."

Reading *Clash of the Clans*, one gets the impression that Kinahan might have relocated to Dubai not just because there's no extradition treaty between the United Arab Emirates and the United Kingdom or Ireland but also because his personal security is better safeguarded there.

Officially, Kinahan has severed his ties to MTK Global. On May 14, 2020, Sandra Vaughan (then the company's chief executive officer of record) told IFL TV, "Everyone knows, legally and legitimately, I purchased the business from Matthew Macklin in 2017. There are no ties to Daniel Kinahan. He hasn't got anything to do with MTK Global. We manage fighters; that's our role. A fighter has a team, not just a manager, a team. And ninety-nine percent of the time, they will have an advisor. That can be Daniel. That can be a family member. It could be a cousin or a father. There is always somebody around them that is giving them advice. We don't employ any of these people. They have got no official connection to MTK Global. They are part of that fighter's team just like we're a member of that team. These are independent professional athletes and will decide themselves who they want to speak to, who they want to train with, and who they want to have with them supporting the team."

That said, it's hard to escape the conclusion that Kinahan is intricately involved in the operation of MTK Global. Indeed, Bob Yalen (identified by the MTK Global website as president and CEO of the company) has relocated from the United States to Dubai.

Meanwhile, shortly after Vaughan's statement to IFL TV, there was a hitch. Tyson Fury, in Tallant's words, is "the Golden Goose" for MTK. The Gypsy King, his former trainer Ben Davison notes, "was struggling in many ways when he was introduced to Daniel Kinahan in early 2017."

Now Fury is The Man in boxing's heavyweight division.

On June 10, 2020, four months after Fury knocked out Deontay Wilder in their second encounter, the Fury and Anthony Joshua camps reached an agreement in principle for a two-fight deal between the fighters. Later that day, Fury posted a video on Twitter in which he thanked Kinahan for his role in arranging the fights with Joshua and proclaimed, "Just got off the phone with Daniel Kinahan. He has just informed me that the biggest fight in British boxing history has just been agreed. Big shoutout, Dan. He got this done, literally over the line."

That earned a sharp rebuke from Leo Varadkar (Ireland's minister for enterprise, trade, and employment) who asked Sky Sports and BT Sport to boycott the fight should it happen. "The Kinahan gang no longer operates from Ireland but from the United Arab Emirates," Varadkar added.

Former Dublin lord mayor Nial Ring supported Varadkar and said, "I have seen what a criminal gang named in open court as the Kinahan organization has done to the north inner city of Dublin. And what they have done should never be forgotten. People in professional boxing should take a look at themselves and who they are dealing with. I would not only invite Fury and the people involved in this over to Dublin to see the devastation that has been caused here; I would also invite them to give some of their massive profits to anti-drug schemes around the world."

After Fury's shoutout to Kinahan, Tris Dixon wrote, "Boxing finds itself at a crossroads. The sport has a divisive powerbroker calling shots at the very highest level. Boxing has needed someone calling the shots for years, but is this the right guy? Kinahan's role in the sport is dominating the front and back pages in Ireland. But boxing, the UK, and the rest of the world doesn't see the story."

In a similar vein, Wallace Matthews took aim at Kinahan and ESPN (which has a multi-bout contract to televise Fury's fights in the United States).

"Right now," Matthews wrote, "an unholy alliance of wiseguys, boxers, and Disney princesses is being formed and presented for your viewing pleasure on the Magic Kingdom-owned ESPN, the self-styled Worldwide Leader in Sports. In fact, the only ones who don't seem to know—wink, wink—about Kinahan's shady past and his involvement with one of their showcase sports is ESPN."

Matthews then proceeded to recount, "An email sent to an ESPN flack seeking comment from its president, Jimmy Pitaro, drew the following reply: 'My pals in programming say we have no relationship with [Daniel Kinahan] and that he's really not involved with our boxing. I don't know him at all. Not much for us to discuss.'"

Pressed for more, the ESPN spokesperson responded, "Not sure what you want me to do here. I'm told we don't deal with the guy. No relationship with him whatsoever. Our agreement is with Top Rank, full stop."

Some blowback against Kinahan did follow—ironically, from the Middle East. In mid-May 2020, Kinahan had been named as a "special advisor" to KHK Sports, an organization set up by Khalid bin Hamad Al Khalifa (a member of Bahrain's royal family and president of that nation's Olympic committee) to bring combat sports to Bahrain. On June 16 (six days after Fury's Instagram post), it was announced that Kinahan would no longer advise KHK Sports.

But Bob Arum (who co-promotes Fury in the United States) took a different tack. Apparently unaware of the party line that Kinahan was no longer involved with MTK, Arum held forth on the subject with various news outlets:

* "Kinahan is one of my favorite guys because I like to deal with guys, no-nonsense people, whose word is their bond, and that's what it's been with Daniel. I think Dan's influence is tremendous because people trust him."

* "Those are allegations, and I don't know anything about that. And they don't really speak to how he [Kinahan] has acted when he has been involved in boxing, which is forthright, honest, reliable. This is not unusual where somebody has some questionable background in the past, then goes into boxing. He's judged for how he acts in the sport, whether as a performer or a businessman. I'm not naive. What did or didn't happen prior to his involvement in boxing is not of a major concern to me. If anybody asked me, I would say without any question that I find him to be an honorable man. Whatever the other allegations are, whether they're true or not, I'm not going to get into it because it's not my business."

★ "Our relationship with MTK has been tremendous and particularly
with Dan, who was the original founder of MTK and now is still
an advisor to them and is in effect our advisor regarding the Mid
East. He's living in the Mid East and he has very good connections.
So we early on ceded to Dan the authority to explore opportunities
in the Mid East on behalf of Top Rank. Because of our connection
with MTK, we've been able to get a whole host of events from
MTK and televise them in the United States on ESPN."

★ We told Frank [Warren] what our preference was, and Frank agreed
to go along. His company is the co-promoter of Tyson Fury. We've
even been talking to Eddie [Joshua's promoter Eddie Hearn]. Let's
not go crazy with everybody talking to different people in the
Mid East. Let Dan field all those proposals and report back to us.
And so that's what we've been doing. That's what Dan is looking
into because everybody trusts Kinahan with handling that situation,
whether it's Eddie or Frank or myself. So Dan is like the captain
when it comes to the practicalities of doing a fight in the Mid East."

But Sky Sports and BT Sport (who would have shared pay-per-view
rights to the Fury–Joshua fights in the United Kingdom had they taken
place) issued public statements distancing themselves from Kinahan. And
Arum then told Gareth Davies of *The Daily Telegraph*, "Over the weekend, I've had a lot of conversations with Tyson Fury. And what we both
decided is that myself, Top Rank and Fury will do all negotiations for
fights in the future. This will eliminate a lot of confusion. We've talked
with Dan—who Tyson and I both love and admire and respect—and he
understands that it's best the negotiations on Tyson's side be handled that
way. He is amenable and satisfied and wished us luck."

That said, it's widely believed within the boxing industry that Kinahan
still has the final say on all matters of substance involving MTK Global
fighters. And MTK has continued to grow. Virtually every major promoter in boxing now does business with it.

On February 1, 2021, *Panorama* (the BBC version of *60 Minutes*) ran a
lengthy investigative piece on the ties between MTK Global and Kinahan.
In response, Robert Smith (general secretary of the British Boxing Board

of Control) noted that Kinahan had never held a license of any kind with the BBBC and added, "We can't stop people taking advice from whomever they want to."

Kinahan was sufficiently stung by the *Panorama* telecast that he issued a written statement to TalkSport.com denying the allegations against him and declaring, "I'm Irish. I was born and raised in Dublin in a deprived area with serious levels of poverty, of crime, of under-investment. People like me, from there, aren't expected to do anything with their lives other than serve the middle and upper classes. Boxing is a working class sport for which I've had a lifelong love and passion. I love the sport of boxing but didn't love how business was done. I got into boxing to make sure that boxers get fairly rewarded and not taken advantage of. The boxers put their lives on the line. It's my mission to ensure that the boxers are financially secure when they finish boxing and healthy too. I have dedicated myself to my work in boxing for over fifteen years. I have started from the bottom and worked my way up. I'm doing all I can to give fight fans around the world the fights they want. My professional commitment is always to the boxers, those who take the ultimate risk. I firmly believe that my success has led to an increase in the campaign against me. Pretty much anything can be said about me or inferred about me, and it goes unchallenged and is sadly believed."

The *Sunday World* (for which Tallant writes) is a tabloid, and she writes with a tabloid flourish. Boxing and MTK Global are only part of her narrative in *Clash of the Clans,* but they constitute the chapters that will interest fight fans the most. There's a lot of material in the book about organized crime in Ireland and the role that Tallant says the Kinahan family has played in it. Readers who are already familiar with the ins and outs of that subject will find it easier to navigate the book than other readers. The uninitiated might have to make a genealogical and organizational chart to fully understand it all.

I don't have the background to evaluate the accuracy of Tallant's writing on matters relating to organized crime. I do know that she's not a boxing writer or an expert on the sweet science. The core of her writing about the business of boxing rings true. But there are times when she gives in to hyperbole. For example, writing about the appointment of Bob Yalen as president and CEO of MTK Global, she refers to Yalen as a "boxing megastar." Yalen is many things. A "boxing megastar" is not one of them.

So where does all of this leave boxing?

Tallant makes the point that, when organized crime moves into a legitimate business, it doesn't necessarily play by the same rules as everybody else. There's an undercurrent of intimidation when dealing with someone who comes from a world in which—to use her words—"a bullet in the head is just another way of doing business." And while Kinahan, as noted above, has never been convicted of a crime, Ron Lewis wrote earlier this year, "There seems to be no rush to return to his homeland in order to clear his name."

At some juncture, the networks that fund boxing in the United States and United Kingdom will have to confront this issue. As a start, they might read Tallant's book, make appropriate inquiries after reading it, and act based on what they determine to be the truth.

Meanwhile, three days after Tyson Fury's June 10, 2020, shoutout to Daniel Kinahan, Tris Dixon summed up the ambiguities involved when he wrote, "Kinahan is two different things to two groups of people. If you read the Irish media, he is the devil incarnate, a mafia kingpin responsible for wreaking havoc in Dublin and further afield. A Google search doesn't do him any favours. Ask those in boxing about him and you would think he's a cross between the Pied Piper and Robin Hood. Boxers are old fashioned. Many of them have come from tough backgrounds, dabbled in crime, been associated with it. And to a man, they say Kinahan has treated them wonderfully."

"It's difficult to prepare for life after boxing." As Sugar Ray Leonard said, "You'll never accomplish anything like you did when you were fighting. But you have to accept that, have to stop chasing that spotlight."

When Is Enough?

On February 12, 2022, Danny Jacobs lost a controversial 115–113, 115–113, 113–115 decision to John Ryder in London. One week later in Manchester, Kell Brook stopped a badly faded Amir Khan in six rounds.

Jacobs, Brook, and Khan are each thirty-five years old. They've made big money in boxing and are "name" fighters who are still marketable. They can pass any physical examination that might be given to them as a prerequisite to being licensed to fight. And each of them is in decline as a fighter.

Weighing the money that these men have made in the past and the physical risks inherent in their continuing to fight, when is enough?

Let's start with Jacobs.

I watched Jacobs–Ryder casually. I didn't score it. My impression (and that of most impartial observers) was that Jacobs deserved the decision. Keith Connolly (Jacobs's manager) spoke to that point, advocating, "Danny can go straight into another big fight. He doesn't need a comeback fight because he doesn't feel like it was a real loss and we don't think that bad judging should be rewarded."

But that doesn't address the larger issue.

Jacobs was once an elite fighter. He rebounded nicely from a loss to Dmitriy Pirog early in his career and was 32–1 (29 KOs) when he fought Gennady Golovkin at Madison Square Garden five years ago. I thought Jacobs beat Golovkin by one point that night. The judges ruled narrowly in Gennady's favor.

Now look at the big picture. Jacobs had knocked out twelve men in a row leading up to the Golovkin bout. In seven fights since then, the only person who failed to go the distance against him was Julio Cesár Chávez Jr. (who quit after five embarrassing rounds). Jacobs was taken the distance by Luis Arias (who has won one of five fights since mid-2017) and Gabriel Rosado (who many people think beat Danny).

Jacobs plans to keep fighting. He knows how to protect himself in the ring. He's a safety-first fighter, even if that means not going all out for the win (as appeared to be the case when he lost to Canelo Álvarez three years ago). Indeed, it's hard to know how much of Jacobs's diminished showing in recent fights has been the result of physical decline and how much has been the consequence of a diminishing willingness to take risks. But the bottom line is that Jacobs no longer fights like an elite fighter. The Danny Jacobs who fought Gennady Golovkin would have beaten today's version of Jacobs convincingly.

Jacobs confronted the harsh reality of his own mortality when he battled cancer a decade ago. His purse for fighting Álvarez was in excess of $10 million and he has been extremely well compensated for other fights. When is enough?

Amir Khan made his mark as a seventeen-year-old silver medalist at the 2004 Olympics and last held a major sanctioning body world title in 2011. Prior to fighting Kell Brook, Khan was knocked unconscious by Canelo Álvarez and took a hellacious beating at the hands of Terence Crawford in a bout that was cut short when Amir claimed he could no longer continue after an unintentional low blow. Earlier in his ring career, Khan was knocked out by Breidis Prescott and Danny Garcia.

Prior to fighting Khan, Brook had been knocked out in three of his most recent six fights (by Golovkin, Crawford, and Errol Spence) dating back to 2016. His most impressive win was a majority-decision triumph over Shawn Porter eight years ago. Kell's recent showing against Khan is tempered by the fact that Amir looked dreadful on fight night. Conor Benn and Chris Eubank Jr. are already calling out Brook in the hope of capitalizing on his name to land a big-money fight.

Jacobs is managed by Keith Connolly, who was honored by the Boxing Writers Association of America as its 2019 Manager of the Year. Connolly's roster of fighters includes young prospects like Edgar Berlanga. It also includes two fighters who, like Jacobs, have made large amounts of money, have marketable names, and are on the downward slide.

Sergiy Derevyanchenko is thirty-six years old. He has reached for the brass ring three times—against Jacobs, Golovkin, and Jermall Charlo. Jacobs and Golovkin beat Sergiy by decision in fights that could have gone either way on the judges' scorecards. More recently, Charlo decisioned him decisively.

Derevyanchenko has lost four of five fights during the past four years. He has taken considerable punishment during his ring career. His purses for fighting Golovkin, Jacobs, and Charlo totaled just under $10 million. He still wants to win a world title. But at what cost?

Adam Kownacki has also been adeptly managed by Connolly. Kownacki is a likable man and entertaining brawler whose approach to boxing seems to be, "I'll hit you and you hit me and we'll do it as long as both of us are standing." Adam is now thirty-two years old with a 20–2 record and was knocked out in his last two fights by a shopworn Robert Helenius. Kownacki is showing troubling signs of the ring wars that he has been in.

Jacobs and Derevyanchenko might still be maneuvered to "world championship" fights against beatable opponents. That will be harder to accomplish for Kownacki. But Adam is a marketable commodity. A good estimate is that he has made close to $8 million in gross purses during his ring career.

There are myriad other fighters who can be similarly defined by large past purses, a still-marketable name, and declining ring skills. The "crazy money" being paid to some boxers today as a consequence of extraordinary spending by DAZN and other entities has created an unusual situation.

Sergey Kovalev was a fixture on HBO for years. The purse for his most recent fight—on DAZN against Canelo Álvarez—has been estimated at $12 million, although $2 million of that is believed to have gone to Main Events (Kovalev's promoter) and another $2 million to Top Rank (for relinquishing certain promotional rights). Sergey is now thirty-nine years old and has lost four of eight fights (three by knockout) since mid-2016.

Chris Arreola is forty and has been fighting professionally for eighteen years. He's one of the most engaging personalities in boxing, exciting in the ring, marketable (although less so now than before), and a poster boy for what a fighter looks like when he's dangerously past his prime.

Other fighters are similarly situated.

So, to repeat the question: When is enough?

Sooner or later, old age catches up with every fighter. He gets hit more than before. Often, he loses fights that he previously would have won.

Getting hit in the head isn't good for a fighter's health. And it's not just getting hit in fights. Sparring in the gym leads to damage, too. The symptoms caused by repeated blows to the head progress steadily long after a fighter has retired from boxing. Also, as neurologist Margaret Goodman points out, "The most difficult aspect of chronic brain injuries lies in the fact that by the time a fighter is showing symptoms, it's too late."

And the condition is largely irreversible.

Counting someone else's money is a questionable endeavor. But if a fighter has made life-changing money, it's sad to think that there will prematurely come a time when he is unable to enjoy it. Former heavyweight Jack Bodell put the matter in perspective years ago when he said, "I had offers to make a comeback but I wasn't going to get any better. I wanted to take care of myself. It's no use being the richest corpse in the graveyard."

Unfortunately, most fighters rebel at the notion that they should stop fighting when there's good money to be made.

In 1955, Jimmy Cannon wrote of Sugar Ray Robinson, "There is no language spoken on the face of the earth in which you can be kind when you tell a man he is old and should stop pretending he is young. He was marvelous, but he isn't anymore."

Robinson fought for another ten years after Cannon penned those words.

"You always think of yourself as the best you ever were," Sugar Ray Leonard has said.

"Fighters," Barry McGuigan noted, "are the first people to know when they should retire and the last to admit it."

If a fighter's skills are fading and he has made enough money that he's financially secure, it's time to stop fighting. Look at Muhammad Ali.

Fighters have to take responsibility for their own well-being. Some do.

Vitali Klitschko had won thirteen fights in a row and was the WBC heavyweight champion when he retired in 2012.

Carl Froch never fought again after scoring one of the most satisfying victories of his career by knocking out George Groves to claim the WBA and IBF crowns in 2014.

Lennox Lewis was widely recognized as THE heavyweight champion of the world when he announced his retirement in 2004. "Deciding to end my career as a professional boxer was not an easy decision to make," Lennox acknowledged. "I've been offered millions of dollars to fight again, which is all the more tempting because I believe that there are more championship-quality fights in me. That said, I am mindful of what happens to fighters in and out of the ring as they age."

More recently, Andre Ward retired in 2017 after unifying the 168-pound belts and moving up in weight to beat Sergey Kovalev twice in fights for the WBA, IBF, and WBO 175-pound titles.

Last year, it was suggested to Ward that he come out of retirement to fight Canelo Álvarez for an eight-figure payday because he still has "one more great fight left in him."

Ward's response was short and smart: "Why can't I just have one more left in me?"

Throwing the book at one fighter won't solve the problem that performance-enhancing drugs pose for boxing.

Óscar Valdez, Phentermine, and the Larger Issue

On September 10, 2021, Óscar Valdez successfully defended his WBC super-featherweight title with a twelve-round decision over Robson Conceição in a bout contested under the auspices of the Pascua Yaqui Tribe in Tucson, Arizona.

That's the short version of what happened. The long version is more complicated.

After their fight was signed, Valdez and Conceição enrolled in the Voluntary Anti-Doping Association (VADA) drug-testing program. Top Rank, which promotes both fighters, forwarded their paperwork to VADA and contracted to pay for the VADA testing. This was in addition to the fighters' mandatory participation in the World Boxing Council Clean Boxing Program (CBP).

In late August, a urine sample taken by VADA from Valdez tested positive for phentermine, a prescription medication used as a stimulant and appetite suppressant. The use of phentermine is classified by VADA as prohibited at all times.

VADA does not adjudicate performance-enhancing drug (PED) matters. It tests fighters and reports its findings to contractually mandated parties. In this instance, after receiving the test result, VADA notified Top Rank, the World Boxing Council, and the Pascua Yaqui Tribe commission of the adverse finding.

Athletes rarely say, "I was using a PED and you caught me." Valdez didn't either. "What I can say," he told Mark Kriegel of ESPN, "is that I'm a hundred-percent clean fighter. I don't know how that got into my body."

Patrick English (the attorney who represents Valdez) voiced the view that herbal tea, innocently ingested, was the most likely source of the phentermine and that various supplements Valdez took during training are being tested for any hint of contamination. He further noted that only a trace amount of phentermine was found in Valdez's system and that all other blood and urine samples taken from Valdez by VADA tested negative.

Those arguments aren't persuasive. Victor Conte (the nutrition and conditioning guru whose involvement with PEDs in conjunction with the BALCO scandal decades ago is a matter of record) states, "There is no connection between any herbal tea and phentermine in terms of molecular structure. No tea has ever been reported as being contaminated with phentermine. Ever in history. If you google 'herbal tea phentermine,' a company called their product by this name as a marketing ploy. But there's not a shred of credible evidence I'm aware of to support the notion that phentermine is present in herbal tea. There has never been a positive test associated with any herbal tea. There is zero connection between herbal tea and phentermine."

Conte also makes the point that, in today's world of micro-dosing, drugs quickly leave a fighter's system. All a negative test result means is that a fighter was clean on a particular day.

But Valdez had an ace in the hole. For purposes of drug testing, athletes are considered either "in competition" or "out of competition." In competition begins at 11:59 p.m. on the night before an event.

When fighters enroll in VADA, they're told that VADA has one prohibited list and that it doesn't distinguish between in-competition and out-of-competition drug use. Thus, VADA classifies phentermine as a prohibited substance at all times.

But—and this is a big "but"—while phentermine is banned in competition under the World Anti-Doping Agency code, its use out of competition is not prohibited by WADA.

Adjudication of Valdez's case was left to the Pascua Yaqui Tribe Athletic Commission (which had jurisdiction over the fight) and the World Boxing Council (whose title belt was at stake). There was one hearing overseen jointly by both organizations. The tribal commission opted to follow the WADA standard and allowed the fight to proceed without punishment of any kind. The WBC's position was a bit more complicated because the WBC Clean Boxing Program is, in theory, guided by VADA standards, and the use of phentermine—even out of competition—is a violation of that program.

However, WBC president Mauricio Sulaimán found a way around this inconvenience, declaring, "This substance [phentermine] does not give you any competitive advantage. It is the equivalent of having three energy drinks." Sulaimán also noted that only a trace amount of phentermine was found in Valdez's system.

The WBC then ruled that it would officially sanction Valdez–Conceição as a title fight. But at the same time, it placed Valdez on probation for twelve months. In addition, Valdez was ordered to take part in and pay for several unspecified educational programs, undergo an unspecified number of random drug tests, and make a minimum of six personal appearances as a WBC Ambassador to promote and educate others with regard to principles consistent with clean boxing.

The WBC ruling ruffled a lot of feathers. Victor Conte is among its foremost critics.

"I've given phentermine to athletes in the past," Conte says. "I know what it does. It's a powerful central nervous system stimulant and one of the most effective PEDs a boxer can use. It increases heart rate and enables the heart to pump more oxygen to muscle tissue which delays the onset of fatigue and helps increase speed, strength, and stamina. It also suppresses appetite and burns calories to help with weight loss. And its use can lead to serious heart problems. Athletes in other sports are suspended for using phentermine. A player in the NBA [Lindsey Hunter] was suspended after he tested positive for phentermine. Jockeys in horse racing are suspended if they use phentermine to cut weight."

Why does WADA allow for the use of phentermine out of competition if it has the performance-enhancing and dangerous qualities that Conte says it does?

"Let's get real about this," Conte answers. "First, WADA's protocols were put in place with an eye toward protecting sponsorship dollars. Too many adverse test results are bad for business. And second, WADA's protocols aren't designed for boxers. If a stimulant is on the banned list on fight night and you acknowledge that it enhances performance, why would it be legal in training camp? Does this mean that someone can use all the phentermine they want up until the day of a fight? That would be dangerous and allowing it to happen would be negligent.

"When Óscar Valdez signed up for VADA testing," Conte contin-ues, "he agreed to follow VADA's protocols, which include not using phentermine in or out of competition. The WBC didn't want to lose its sanctioning fee. The tribal commission didn't want to lose the money that would come in from Valdez–Conceição and future fights. It's as simple as that."

In 2018, Billy Joe Saunders tested positive for the stimulant oxilof-rine, which (like phentermine) is allowed by WADA "out of competi-tion" but is on VADA's prohibited list at all times. Saunders claimed that the oxilofrine came from a nasal spray. The Massachusetts State Athletic Commission denied him a license to box and his planned WBO title defense against Demetrius Andrade was cancelled.

"It is the classic case of rules in one place count for nothing in another," *Boxing News* editor Matt Christie writes. "The problem lies with a com-plete lack of uniformity across the governing and sanctioning bodies. Even more problematic is that the sanctioning bodies appear to pick and choose what rules suit them on a particular day."

Christie is right. There are too many variables. Is there PED testing for a given fight? Which tests? Which commission has jurisdiction over the fight? Who's administering the tests? Is a sanctioning body involved? To cite one example of an absurd situation, human growth hormone and erythropoietin (EPO) are still not on the New York State Athletic Commission's list of banned substances.

Insofar as phentermine is concerned, California State Athletic Commission executive director Andy Foster says, "The California State Athletic Commission views the use of phentermine out of competition in the same way as the World Anti-Doping Agency. Phentermine is not a banned substance out of competition by WADA, so it is not banned by the CSAC either."

Nevada State Athletic Commission executive director Bob Bennett says that Nevada also adheres to the WADA list.

Does this mean that Tyson Fury, Deontay Wilder, Canelo Álvarez, and Caleb Plant can use all the phentermine they want prior to their upcoming fights in Las Vegas as long as it isn't in their system on the day of the fight?

"Not exactly," Bennett answers. "Phentermine is a prescription drug so, if a fighter uses phentermine, he must declare its use on a pre-fight form and answer questions as to where he got the prescription and why he's taking it."

I don't know what Óscar Valdez did and didn't do. I do know that most of the moneyed interests in boxing couldn't care less about protecting the health and safety of fighters except to the extent that they're protecting their own financial interests. Clean fighters have to stand up and take control on this issue. As part of their effort, they should demand one national standard.

As Andre Ward stated during ESPN's coverage of Valdez–Conceição, "We can't keep moving the goal posts."

Investigative reporting can take many forms.

An Open Letter to Gov. Kathy Hochul Regarding the New York State Athletic Commission

Dear Governor Hochul,

I received several text messages earlier this month from someone I don't know who wrote to me about a problem at the New York State Athletic Commission. Two days later, I got a telephone call about the same issue from someone I respect and know reasonably well.

These people reached out to me because, over the years, I've written a series of investigative reports about the New York State Athletic Commission. Sometimes the problems I write about are self-evident. Other times, people contact me regarding issues I'm unaware of in the hope that something I write will lead to positive change. On eight occasions, articles I've written have been honored by the Boxing Writers Association of America as the "best investigative reporting" of the year. In other words, there's some substance to what I write.

I hope this article lands on your desk. The New York State Athletic Commission is a small state agency whose mandate pales in comparison to the job of overseeing public health, public education, mass transit, and a host of other needs. But because it's a small agency, it can be understood and the problems within it can be fixed.

What's happening now at the NYSAC is happening on your watch. Andrew Cuomo is gone. How you deal with this situation will be regarded by people familiar with the issues involved as a litmus test for how you govern as opposed to how you talk about governing.

First, a word about the New York State Athletic Commission, since you're probably only vaguely familiar with it. The NYSAC is charged with regulating combat sports in the State of New York. This means boxing, mixed martial arts, and professional wrestling. You might ask why the State of New York regulates professional wrestling (which is scripted entertainment). The answer is that some NYSAC employees like to be

293

paid a per diem salary in addition to being reimbursed by taxpayers for the cost of meals and transportation to watch Roman Reigns and Brock Lesnar cavort around a wrestling ring. You could save New York taxpayers some money by ending this silly regulatory practice.

The New York State Athletic Commission falls within the jurisdiction of the New York State Department of State. This places it directly under your control.

Some capable, conscientious public servants work at the NYSAC. But too often, political connections take priority over performance. This applies to some—not all—fulltime jobs at the commission as well as the selection of fight-night officials such as inspectors, referees, and judges.

On November 2, 2013, a Russian heavyweight named Magomed Abdusalamov suffered life-changing injuries in a boxing match at Madison Square Garden. Ultimately, the State of New York paid $22 million to Abdusalamov and his family to settle claims alleging substandard medical protocols and improper conduct by New York State Athletic Commission personnel on fight night.

The Abdusalamov case led to an investigation of the NYSAC by the Inspector General of the State of New York that began as a review of the commission's medical practices and expanded into a broader study of its overall operation during the tenure of chairperson Melvina Lathan. The subsequent report of the Inspector General (which was released in 2016 and covered a wide range of issues, many of which were unrelated to Abdusalamov) documented numerous instances of incompetence and corruption at the NYSAC.

There have been periods of good oversight at the NYSAC, most notably during the tenure of David Berlin. In May 2014, in the wake of the Abdusalamov tragedy, Berlin was brought in to serve as executive director of the commission. He was respected throughout the boxing industry as a competent, honest, knowledgeable administrator who refused to put a political agenda ahead of properly doing his job. Most notably, Berlin sought to implement standards and accountability and curb the use of the NYSAC as a favor bank for powerful economic interests and a source of employment for unqualified job seekers with politically well-connected friends. Berlin's approach to his job offended your predecessor. In May 2016, he was fired. Since July 2017, Kim Sumbler (who lives in Canada) has been the NYSAC executive director. Sumbler is more compliant in dealing with the powers that be than Berlin was.

There are two fulltime positions on the NYSAC organizational chart directly below Sumbler—director of boxing and director of mixed martial arts. In recent years, Matt Delaglio and Ed Kunkle have done a credible job of filling these roles. But on September 3, 2021, Kunkle resigned. That set up the search for a new director of mixed martial arts and brings us to the text messages and telephone call that I received earlier this month.

The first text message read, "Are you aware that the NYSAC hired Todd Anderson as the new MMA coordinator after the Commission manipulated job requirements? He would not have qualified under previous posting."

This text was accompanied by a screen shot of a statement posted on social media by a minor MMA sanctioning body official that read in part, "To hire a person with Zero experience as a regulator to oversee and regulate combat sports in NYS is laughable and makes this state what it was prior to 2016. I have no faith in this state, its Department of State, or Athletic Commission."

Then I received additional texts from the original correspondent with messages like, "I do not work for the commission nor have I been in a professional setting with Sumbler. But I have witnessed her nepotism in action with her sister Jackie, and I certainly am aware she's a long term personal friend of Todd Anderson's . . . I do not know Todd. I'm sure he's a nice guy. But I find it odd that she would recruit a personal friend who resides in Canada . . . It's all deeply disappointing and disconcerting. Hiring Todd, who does not have the regulatory experience, is questionable for the integrity of the sport in NYS . . . I reached out to you because something about this scenario doesn't appear ethical or lawful. As a journalist, you have a voice which can be amplified."

Then I received the telephone call that I mentioned above from someone I know and respect who also complained to me about Anderson's appointment. At that point, I decided to do some research.

First, let me address the claim of "nepotism" relating to Sumbler and her sister. Prior to joining the New York State Athletic Commission, Sumbler oversaw combat sports for the Seneca Nation of Indians Athletic Commission. Her sister (Jackie Grant) now has that job. I assume that

Sumbler had some input in her sister's selection. But that doesn't mean it was inappropriate.

Then I turned my attention to Todd Anderson—a retired police officer who lived in Canada through the end of 2021. According to opengovca.com, Anderson was a sergeant with the Niagara Regional Police Service in Ontario. He's also an MMA referee who has been widely criticized for his performance.

Go to Google. Type "Todd Anderson" after "exact word or phrase." Then, after "any of these words," type in "MMA." Now hit Google Search. Some of the headlines that appear are, "Dana White is critical of UFC 208, main event referee Todd Anderson" and "UFC 208: Dana White blasts main event referee Todd Anderson." Scroll down and you'll come to an article entitled "The Top 10 Worst Referees in MMA of All Time." Anderson is #2 on the list. These lists are subjective. You could probably find an article posted somewhere that lists me as one of the ten worst boxing writers of all time. But one UFC insider recently told me, "Todd Anderson is a lousy referee."

Of course, just because someone might be lacking as a referee doesn't mean that he, or she, isn't a fine administrator. So next, I looked at the qualifications required by the New York State Athletic Commission to be its director of mixed martial arts.

Three years ago, when the job opening was posted by the Department of State prior to Ed Kunkle's appointment, the listing read, "MINIMUM QUALIFICATIONS: Five (5) years of supervisory regulatory experience overseeing Mixed Martial Arts (MMA). Three (3) years of this experience must have been in a role exercising management responsibilities over staff."

However, when the same opening was posted by the Department of State on September 20, 2021, it read, "MINIMUM QUALIFICATIONS: Five (5) years of governmental regulatory experience in a supervisory or management role. Three (3) years of this experience must have been in a role exercising management responsibilities over staff."

In other words, it was no longer required that the five years of regulatory experience in a supervisory or management role involve "overseeing Mixed Martial Arts." Instead, the applicant was required to demonstrate "skills with regard to composition of reports and memoranda" and "in-depth knowledge of professional and amateur Mixed Martial Arts (MMA)."

So let's look at Todd Anderson's "five years of governmental regulatory experience in a supervisory or management role," three years of which are required to have been "in a role exercising management responsibilities over staff" and also his "demonstration of skills with regard to composition of reports and memoranda."

A well-placed source at the New York State Athletic Commission says the party line on this is, "Well, Todd was a police officer." A police officer in Canada who doesn't appear to have been in a supervisory or management role exercising management responsibilities over staff.

The same source says that Sumbler led the interview process that resulted in Anderson's appointment.

In an effort to confirm that Anderson had been appointed as the NYSAC's new director of mixed martial arts, I sent two emails to the Department of State public information officer assigned to the commission. Neither email elicited the courtesy of a response. I then sent a third email requesting interviews with Sumbler and Anderson. I hoped to speak with Sumbler, not only about Anderson but also about some of the larger issues that the NYSAC faces today. Again, there was no response.

That's from the Andrew Cuomo school of transparency and open government.

Finally, on January 15, 2022, *Newsday* reported Anderson's appointment.

I don't know Todd Anderson. I don't know anything about his administrative ability. I do know that two people—one of whom I respect a great deal—have concerns about his appointment.

Maybe Anderson will do a good job as director of MMA. But the process doesn't feel right. As the source who telephoned me about his appointment said, "Todd comes from Ontario. He's friendly with Kim Sumbler. It was clear that Kim wanted this from the start, and she chose Todd over at least one applicant who was clearly more qualified than he is. Coming to New York and fighting at Madison Square Garden or Barclays Center is the highest level of MMA in the world. And you're putting someone with no real regulatory experience in charge."

Governor Hochul, when you took the oath of office last August, you pledged to implement "a dramatic change in culture with accountability and no tolerance for individuals who cross the line." That's a direct quote.

Reporting on your January 5, 2022, State of the State address, the *New York Times* recounted, "Governor Hochul vowed to open a new chapter of ethical, more transparent government. The package of ethics and government reforms were meant to hold accountable elected officials in a State Capitol with a long history of graft and corruption."

One component of good government is ensuring that taxpayers get fair value from employees who are on the public payroll. I question whether that's happening now at the New York State Athletic Commission.

As noted above, Kim Sumbler is the NYSAC executive director. According to SeeThroughNY, her salary in 2020 was $133,896. The previous (pre-pandemic) year, it was $132,964.

The New York State Athletic Commission is located at 123 William Street in Manhattan (which, as you know from your travels throughout the state, is one of New York City's five boroughs). Sumbler lives in Ontario. Multiple sources say that, prior to the pandemic, she was seldom in the William Street office and that, after the office reopened last year, she was largely a no-show.

One of the points that the Inspector General's 2016 report made in criticizing Melvina Lathan was that she was only in the William Street office four days a week. For Sumbler, that number might be closer to four days a month. Sumbler has said that she works at home and out of a Department of State office in Buffalo. But to be effective, an executive director should be where the action is.

.Or phrased differently, how many agency heads in your administration lead from their home in Canada? And what exactly does Kim Sumbler do five days a week?

There are also instances where hourly payments to NYSAC employees should be reviewed.

Angela Gagliardi is the assistant chief medical officer for the New York State Athletic Commission. Sources say that, prior to the pandemic, Dr. Gagliardi (listed by SeeThroughNY as an hourly employee) worked from home and came into the office one day a week. Her responsibilities included coordinating medical matters for the commission in addition to attending weigh-ins and fights. In 2019, her salary, as listed by SeeThroughNY, was $185,875.

In 2020 (the first year of the pandemic, when there were virtually no fights in New York), the state paid Dr. Gagliardi $168,980. She was listed by SeeThroughNY as an hourly employee at a pay rate of $78 per hour. This means that, in theory, Dr. Gagliardi worked 2,166 hours in 2020 (42 hours per week).

What did Dr. Gagliardi do to occupy her time for 2,166 hours?

In February 2020, she communicated with close to one hundred NYSAC personnel regarding the manner in which they should rent vehicles while traveling on official NYSAC business. You might ask why New York taxpayers were paying a doctor an hourly rate to do this and whether it could have been done by Kim Sumbler or an office adminis-trator as part of their duties.

Dr. Gagliardi also contacted commission employees (including non-medical and per diem personnel) on a monthly basis in 2020 about the administrative requirement that all NYSAC business be transacted on Department of State servers rather than private email accounts and instructed them to send at least one email each month on their Department of State email account to keep their account active.

In addition, on November 2, 2020, and again on November 6, 2020, Dr. Gagliardi sent emails to the "NYSAC team" stating that she was "assisting with Veterans Day activity" and encouraging veterans and their families to "share a bio, pictures and/or personal stories related to their vast experiences."

Was Kim Sumbler so busy that New York taxpayers had to pay Dr. Gagliardi to do this?

We're living in an era of fiscal challenges. The NYSAC should be run accordingly.

To give you another example of a practice that troubles me: it's an open secret that fighters' purses are sometimes underreported to the New York State Athletic Commission, which enables these fighters and others (who receive a percentage of the fighter's purse) to escape the full state and city taxes that should be paid. One former NYSAC employee told me, "I recall discussing it with Kim and it being on her radar. I don't think there was much interest in pursuing it above her." The rationale for allowing this practice is that, if big-name fighters have to pay all legally mandated taxes, they won't fight in New York.

That's an interesting approach to government. We're going to let a group of people who make millions of dollars for a night's work under-report their income so they (along with some other vested economic interests) can make more money. Try putting that idea in your next State of the State message and see how it's received by healthcare workers and others who pay taxes on their full salary and are having trouble making ends meet.

Administratively, the New York State Athletic Commission is in chaos. As one insider said bluntly, "It's a horribly run administrative nightmare with zero accountability."

Some administrative errors at the commission are embarrassing but not harmful. For example, on January 13, 2022, Kim Sumbler sent a notice to all NYSAC per diem employees regarding a mandatory training session. Several dead people were on the recipient list, one of whom (Dr. Sheryl Wulkan) had died five months earlier.

Other administrative errors are more dangerous.

One of the last UFC events in New York before the pandemic began was held in Rochester. Three fighters on that card (Austin Hubbard, Charles Olivera, and Antonio Carlos Jr.) were allowed to compete even though they weren't licensed to fight in New York. Three weeks later, a boxer with a bullet in his head (Marcus McDaniel) fought at Madison Square Garden without a New York license.

Fighters who have been suspended slip through the cracks and compete in New York while still on suspension. Edgar Soghomonyan was placed on indefinite medical suspension pending neuro-clearance after a second-round defeat in a "Rage in the Cage" MMA bout on October 9, 2021. Twenty-nine days later, he fought in New York in a "Holiday Havoc" MMA contest without his suspension having been lifted.

On January 3 of this year, the NYSAC issued an MMA ID for a mixed martial arts combatant who was sixteen years old. That's two years beneath the legal age for professional combat in New York. Since you're a compassionate woman, I'm sure you'd be concerned if that young man were badly hurt in a fight. And being a practical woman, you'd note the prospect of a litigation settlement rivaling the $22 million that was paid to Magomed Abdusalamov and his family.

You might ask the powers that be at the NYSAC how these things happen. You're more likely to get a call back from them than I am.

The home page on the New York State Athletic Commission website proclaims, "The Commission is committed to health, safety, and integrity with standardized protocols at ringside, enhanced medical screening procedures and strong, effective leadership."

That's a bad joke.

The commission has a medical advisory board. But the board has met only three times since June 2017. In each instance, its business consisted largely of approving the minutes of the board's previous meeting and the appointment and reappointment of NYSAC physicians. Policy wasn't discussed in any meaningful way.

Nitin Sethi (a neurologist whose primary practice is affiliated with Weill Cornell Medicine) is the NYSAC's chief medical officer. Dr. Sethi devotes an enormous amount of time and energy to his part-time position with the commission. He's a valuable asset to the NYSAC and has been steadfast in his commitment to protecting the health and safety of fighters (which, for too many in combat sports, is little more than a rhetorical device). But Dr. Sethi has been limited in what he can accomplish at the NYSAC because of the attitude that the commission overlords have toward medical issues.

The most glaring medical deficiency at the New York State Athletic Commission is the lack of understanding and resolve with regard to the use of illegal performance-enhancing drugs. Illegal PED use is not a victimless crime. It results in fighters being hit in the head harder than would otherwise be the case and thus sustaining more short-term and long-term brain damage. It's one of the reasons that fighters die.

The NYSAC's drug-testing program is fundamentally flawed. The commission takes a pre-fight urine sample from each fighter on fight night. For championship bouts, a post-fight urine sample is also taken. In today's world of micro-dosing, having fighters urinate into a cup on fight night does not constitute a serious PED-testing program. Also, Quest Diagnostics (where the NYSAC sends urine samples) is not accredited by the World Anti-Doping Agency.

The New York State Athletic Commission has an outdated prohibited-drug list and refuses to incorporate the World Anti-Doping Agency's prohibited list by reference or separately list the substances banned by

WADA. Thus, erythropoietin (EPO), blood-doping, and meldonium—
each of which is banned by every credible jurisdiction outside of New
York—are not banned by the NYSAC.

Victor Conte is one of the most knowledgeable people in the world
with regard to illegal performance-enhancing drugs. Google him if you
don't know who he is. He spent four months in prison in 2005 as an
outgrowth of his work with various high-profile athletes. He's now a
forceful advocate for clean sport.

"I find it to be absolutely crazy," Conte says, "that the NYSAC does
not test for EPO. In my opinion, EPO is the most powerful drug that
boxers can use to enhance their performance and the most dangerous and
damaging to the health of both the opponent and the fighters themselves."

If there's a reason other than stupidity that EPO isn't on the list of
banned substances for combat sports in New York, I don't know what it is.

Let me quote something I wrote in 2019 about medical practices at
the NYSAC.

"What precisely should a commission inspector do if a fighter col-
lapses in the dressing room after a fight? Calling a doctor would be a good
start. Okay. How should the inspector call a doctor? Does the inspector
leave the fighter unattended while he (or she) runs to ringside to look
for a commission doctor? That could take a long time. Does the inspector telephone 911? Probably not since, pursuant to NYSAC regulations,
there should already be paramedics and an ambulance on site. Does the
inspector telephone someone at a designated number? I've spoken with
numerous inspectors and other 'back of the house' NYSAC personnel. If
there's a protocol in place, they don't know about it."

In response to this criticism, on February 18, 2020, the NYSAC
approved a thirty-two-page "Medical Emergency Action Plan" that was
sent to all commission employees. The plan, one lawyer said at the time,
is "a plaintiffs' lawyer's dream." It has two flow charts that look like they
were pieced together by a preschool toddler sticking colored rectangles
on a magnetic board and is deficient in myriad ways.

Among other things, the plan contains the statement, "Staff Contact
List/Emergency Contacts. For each event, a list of NYSAC staff working
the event with cell phone numbers will be distributed. Emergency contact information for venue management, EMS and the promoters will
also be included."

Two years later, this emergency contact information is still not being distributed to inspectors on fight night.

Sloppy administration.

I might add here that, on fight nights, the NYSAC also endangers its own personnel by not following its mandated COVID protocols. At a recent fight card at Madison Square Garden, dozens of commission personnel were crammed into a small room at the start of the evening. Social distancing was impossible. Numerous commission personnel, including Sumbler, were unmasked for extended periods of time. One person who was there complained afterward that James Vosswinkel (a NYSAC commissioner and a physician) "was walking around with his mouth and nose uncovered and his mask dangling from one ear."

Many of the commission's per diem employees are poorly trained. It doesn't help for an inspector (some of whom are excellent public servants) to watch a fighter's hands being wrapped in the dressing room before a fight if the inspector doesn't know what to look for (which most NYSAC inspectors don't).

Inspectors whose performance is clearly substandard have been allowed to stay on the job too long. Sometimes this is because they're well connected politically. Other times, it's because those in an oversight role haven't noticed, simply don't care, or are afraid of unwarranted litigation if the employee is terminated.

There are some good referees and judges at the New York State Athletic Commission and also some bad ones.

No referee gets everything right. But when a referee makes a mistake, there should be constructive follow-up by the commission, both with the referee and in the form of an acknowledgment to the aggrieved fighter and the public. This doesn't happen.

As for the judging, I've been at fights in New York when the crowd favorite has been awarded a decision that was so unfair that the crowd actually booed. Fight fans want their fighter to win, but they also have a sense of fairness.

In one instance, a judge's scorecard was so off the mark that, after the fourth round, a deputy commissioner was dispatched to ask him if he was confused as to which fighter was which. That was hard to confuse, since the cards filled out by judges after each round clearly designate a "red" and "blue" corner. The judge denied that he had confused the fighters.

Asked for comment on the judge's scorecard after the fight, a spokesperson for the NYSAC responded, "We have no comment."

A fighter spends years toiling in pursuit of a dream. And it can be taken away in seconds by an incompetent or corrupt judge.

Major sports leagues such as the NFL and NBA acknowledge it when an official makes a mistake. These acknowledgments don't undermine the officiating. They reaffirm the integrity of the officiating process and the commitment of the supervising authority to getting things right.

Kim Sumbler was named acting executive director of the New York State Athletic Commission in July 2017. Soon after that, her appointment became permanent. She has had almost five years to put her imprint on the commission and, for almost five years, I've tried to give her the benefit of the doubt.

Sumbler has proven to be an adept political player. That's a good skill to have. The question is whether she has utilized this skill to make the commission better. Let's look at another case study.

On November 1, 2019, Kelvin Gastelum weighed in for a UFC-244 match to be contested at Madison Square Garden against Darren Till. The contract weight was 186 pounds. It was widely known in the MMA community that Gastelum had been having trouble making weight. Before stepping on the scale, he stripped down completely naked and a towel was lifted in front of him to shield his genitals from public view. Then, to everyone's surprise, his weight was announced as 184 pounds. That was a full two pounds under the contract weight. But—and this is an elephant-sized "but"—video of the weigh-in shows Gastelum resting his elbow on his coach, Rafael Cordeiro, as he stood on the scale. And the NYSAC officials conducting the weigh-in missed it.

You might ask, "How did NYSAC allow this to happen?"

In answering that question, I'll start by noting that weigh-ins for major fights in New York City are usually overseen by deputy commissioners Robert Orlando and George Ward. Orlando and Ward are retired New York City corrections officers. Each man has been with the commission for decades and knows all the tricks. But while on site and readying for the Gastelum–Till weigh-in, Orlando and Ward were advised by Sumbler that they were being replaced at the scales by two less experienced commission employees who had been brought to New York City from upstate. When one of the deputy commissioners asked why they were being replaced, Sumbler told him, "Because I said so."

You're a smart woman, Governor Hochul. Put the pieces together on that one.

There's also a leadership void at the NYSAC at the commissioner level.

The New York State Athletic Commission has five commissioners who, in theory, are charged with making policy for the commission. But the commissioners rarely, if ever, discuss issues of importance. In some instances, they aren't even aware of them.

Lino Garcia is the most recently appointed commissioner. On June 7, 2021, the New York State Senate approved more than fifty last-minute nominations by Governor Cuomo to various state agency boards and commissions without serious discussion or debate. Garcia was among them. He's president of a company called Unanimo Sports Media and has extensive experience in sports marketing. Nothing on his résumé indicates expertise with regard to the issues facing the combat sports industry today. And one might ask whether his day job poses a conflict of interest.

My understanding (which the Department of State won't confirm or deny) is that the other four commissioners are serving on a holdover basis. In other words, their terms have expired and, unless reappointed, they'll stay on until replaced. One of these commissioners (a man of considerable past accomplishment) has significant cognitive deficits due to the ravages of old age. Another has little interest in boxing or mixed martial arts but accepted the position at the urging of a colleague. By and large, they don't understand combat sports from a business or competitive point of view.

Let me ask you a question, Governor Hochul. Before I started writing, I went to law school at Columbia, clerked for a federal judge, and spent five years as a litigator on Wall Street with a law firm called Cravath, Swaine & Moore. I'm politically aware and largely in agreement with you on the issues that the State of New York faces today. I'm pretty smart. Would you hire me to run your gubernatorial campaign? Of course not. Why not? Because I don't have any experience running political campaigns.

So why do you have five commissioners at the NYSAC who, as a group, are largely uninformed about the inner workings of combat sports?

They might be fans. They might be honest, intelligent, hard-working individuals (although one of them, as noted, has serious cognitive issues). But how can they possibly make and evaluate the implementation of NYSAC policy when they don't have expertise in the industry they're charged with regulating?

The people you appoint as commissioners will say a lot about your commitment to good government.

Governor Hochul, in your August 24 speech, you promised "a dramatic change in culture, with accountability and no tolerance for individuals who cross the line." You also declared, "You'll find me to be direct, straight-talking, and decisive."

The New York State Athletic Commission represents an opportunity for you to prove the truth of those words. We're not talking about radical political change or big spending. In fact, the reforms I'm talking about will save the state money. We're talking about competent administration, the implementation of standards and accountability, addressing legitimate health and safety concerns, upholding existing laws, and applying common sense. These are not big lifts.

In 2016, I wrote, "The NYSAC is broken. It can be fixed if Governor Cuomo is more interested in getting it to function properly than in using it as a vehicle for granting political favors and repaying political debts. It's not hard to do the job right if conscientious, hard-working men and women who understand the sport and business of boxing are pressed into service at every level. Political observers should watch the New York State Athletic Commission closely. Not because they care about combat sports; most of them don't. But because it offers an easily understood case study on how Andrew Cuomo governs. Either Andrew Cuomo is serious about good government or he isn't."

Now it's your turn. You might say, "Well, I need to make certain accommodations and put certain people in important positions at the NYSAC and allow certain dicey things to happen to get the campaign contributions and power I need to do good works on a broader scale. That's the way politics works."

Or you might take a different view.

So . . . Governor Hochul . . . will it be business as usual at the New York State Athletic Commission, or do you plan to fix this?

Because of my friendship with Muhammad Ali and other fighters, this book struck a particularly responsive chord with me.

Damage: The Untold Story of Brain Damage in Boxing

Damage: The Untold Story of Brain Damage in Boxing by Tris Dixon (Hamilcar Publications) is an important book.

In 1928, a doctor named Harrison Martland wrote an essay titled "Punch Drunk" that was published in the *Journal of the American Medical Association*. People knew that fighters could be severely injured in fights or even die in the ring. But there were also fighters walking around who were derided as "cuckoo," "goofy," "cutting paper dolls," or "slug nutty." Martland called these fighters "punch drunk" and believed that roughly half of all boxers would fall victim to this condition if they fought long enough. He studied what was happening to men who were being hit in the head again and again in fights and in sparring. And he concluded, "I am of the opinion that in punch drunk there is a very definite brain injury due to single or repeated blows on the head or jaw which cause multiple concussion hemorrhages in the deeper portions of the cerebrum."

As Dixon notes, "Not only did 'punch-drunk' sound like a term of mockery, but the medical professionals who used it said that it happened to sparring partners, to journeymen, to fighters who were not that good. They said it did not happen to the better boxers. But they were wrong." As Sammy Lewis, who owned a nightclub with former light-heavyweight champion Maxie Rosenbloom, said as Rosenbloom's cognitive abilities deteriorated, "If you take those punches, something's got to give."

Over time, the term "punch-drunk" was replaced by "dementia pugilistica" and eventually "chronic traumatic encephalopathy (CTE)." Its symptoms, depending on the sufferer, include slurred or garbled speech, unsteady gait, tremors, loss of analytical ability, memory loss, mood swings, irritability, confusion, depression, and erratic violent behavior.

By and large, the boxing establishment has ignored this issue. When a fighter dies or suffers a life-changing traumatic brain injury in the ring, it's talked about for a while. But the story soon fades away. And little is written, said, or done to address the issue of long-term chronic brain damage.

As Showtime Boxing commentator Steve Farhood told Dixon, "The fighters suffering the effects that they have to live with for maybe thirty or forty years just don't seem to generate the same amount of attention. Boxing does nothing to help them. I also think that the fact that we don't discuss this issue more is emblematic of the fact that a lot of people in boxing, and perhaps boxing as a sport, tends to treat its fighters as disposable commodities. They are warriors as long as they can fight. And when they can no longer fight at that level, they're useless to a lot of people."

Many athletic commissions have failed to implement even the most basic standards with regard to protecting fighters against brain damage. Dr. Margaret Goodman has been in the forefront of those seeking to improve fighter safety in the United States. "Unfortunately for boxing's sake," Dixon writes, "her beliefs and values do not align with the sport's power brokers or their economic goals."

Goodman, for her part, states, "No one wants to give up their piece of the pie, irrespective of what the repercussions are to the fighters. The politics involved in the sport is probably just as important as the actual head trauma the fighters are taking because people don't want to step on other people's toes. In most states, the person running the commission office has no real knowledge of boxing or MMA. They wouldn't know if someone was hurt if you punched them in the head to show them what it was like."

CTE progresses steadily long after a fighter has retired from the ring. It's largely irreversible. Also, as Goodman points out, "The most difficult aspect of chronic brain injuries lies in the fact that by the time a fighter is showing symptoms, it's too late."

"Some fighters feel they have dodged the bullets and retired unscathed," Dixon writes. "But only time will truly tell." In that vein, he recounts attending an International Boxing Hall of Fame Induction Weekend in Canastota, New York.

"It was like a scrapyard of high-price vintage cars that had decayed over time," Dixon recalls. "It was heartbreaking. And the Hall of Fame treats the fighters wonderfully well. It gives them more days in the sun when otherwise they would be forgotten. But it's a fan's guilty pleasure—posing for a picture with someone who is looking emptily into a camera, habitually holding up a shaking fist in a fighter's pose, or watching them sign a scarcely legible scrawl. I've seen the decline of fighters I looked up to, some I idolized and some I've known. And I will keep seeing it. The next wave will be fighters I've watched and become friendly with. Then it will be fighters who I have covered from their debut. Then it will be fighters who weren't born when I started writing about the sport. The brutal wheel will keep turning and fighters will keep getting spat out, broken and damaged. They will be asked to pose, staring vacantly into cameras, to sign autographs with pens they cannot control, using letters they can scarcely remember. This is not all, but it will be some, and more than a boxing man like me should care to admit."

Former *Ring Magazine* editor Nigel Collins echoes that theme, saying, "I went up to Canastota one year with somebody who'd never been before but was a boxing fan. And he was mortified when he saw all of these broken-down people, that some of them could hardly speak. That was a real shock to him. People have asked me about becoming boxers and I say, 'You're going to get brain damage. It's cut and dried.'"

The boxing media rarely acknowledged the problem of chronic brain damage in fighters until Muhammad Ali's struggle became public. And as Dixon notes, "The old punch-drunk terminology was rarely used with Ali. Perhaps they thought it was too cruel a label for a man who had given so much and who had awed the world with his brutal elegance."

But the same media has largely ignored the problem of CTE apart from Ali. And there are times when the cause of Ali's condition isn't honestly addressed.

Three decades ago, I was Ali's authorized biographer. With his consent, I reviewed hundreds of pages of medical records and talked at length with his doctors. There was no doubt in my mind, or that of his primary physicians, that boxing was the main cause of his physical decline at that time.

Ali preferred to think that boxing was not the cause. I believe this was in part because of his vanity as a great boxer. Also, he didn't want to think that boxing—which he loved—would cause a condition like his. Anytime someone talks about studies that show an outsized proportion of football players in the United States suffering from CTE, what they're really saying is that football causes brain damage. What was Ali going to do? Get up and say, "I'm talking the way I am because I boxed too long. Boxing did this to me." The next logical thing to say would then be, "Don't box." And Muhammad wasn't prepared to say that.

Aaron Pryor, one of the greatest fighters ever, suffered from chronic brain damage after retiring from boxing. He died in 2016 at age sixty. Having talked at length with Frankie Pryor (Aaron's widow), Dixon writes, "Frankie wished Lonnie Ali, Muhammad's wife, had publicly acknowledged the reason behind the icon's demise. Frankie felt that their involvement would have shone a light on CTE far faster and would have helped countless more fighters understand and admit to what had happened to them. If boxing could shut down the best—The Greatest—where is the shame in that?"

Frankie Pryor emphasized that point to Dixon, saying, "The one fighter who had the notoriety and could have brought a lot of attention to this was Ali. And then they went off on the Parkinson's thing. That pissed off a lot of people in boxing, that Ali's family chose to say, 'Oh, he has Parkinson's, it has nothing to do with boxing.' It has everything to do with boxing. I don't think it was done maliciously. Maybe Lonnie didn't fully understand the impact. But just to say, 'It wasn't boxing; it was Parkinson's.' No, it wasn't."

Further to that point, historian Mike Silver declares, "The false narrative with Ali has mostly been foisted [by] people who are ignorant of the problem and don't understand it or they're Ali lovers that don't want to believe it. His own family, who are really trying to preserve his legacy in the most positive light, says that he suffered from Parkinson's disease and would have got that if he was a bricklayer. That's ridiculous. Now, would he have developed Parkinson's on his own? Possibly. But you cannot tell me, no logical person would say that someone who has taken whatever it was he took—and he took some horrific beatings, especially to the head—that his brain is not going to be affected by that. He's boxing's poster-person for brain damage."

Fighters like George Foreman, Bernard Hopkins, and Archie Moore—each of whom fought to an old age without apparent ill effects—are the exception to the rule. Looking at some of Ali's better-known opponents from what is often called "the golden age of heavyweight boxing," Dixon cites the early deaths and cognitive/neurological problems suffered by Joe Frazier (dead at age 67), Floyd Patterson (71), Jimmy Ellis (74), Ernie Terrell (75), Jimmy Young (56), and Jerry Quarry (53). Quarry's neuropsychologist said that his brain "looked like the inside of a grapefruit that has been dropped dozens of times."

Dixon also recounts interviews he conducted with a wide range of fighters now suffering from CTE.

"I told my neurologist that sometimes I think about killing myself," Freddie Roach confessed. "He asked me why, and I said, 'It's just fucking difficult sometimes dealing with this shit.'"

"Everybody's concussions are different," Micky Ward explained to Dixon. "Some people suffer from headaches. Some people suffer from depression. Some people get tired. Some people get angry. Some people want to hurt you. Some people want to hurt themselves."

What are Ward's symptoms?

"There are some things like my memory. Long term, I could tell you first-grade things I remember. I couldn't tell you yesterday. If I don't take my medicine, I get snappy, I get edgy. And I didn't have that years ago. I don't have the [slurred] speech, but I have the headaches, the aggravation, and all the crap. It is what it is. Boxing has been this way since day one and it's going to stay that way. Watch. It's sad."

Dixon's re-creation of time spent with Leon Spinks is particularly poignant. Some of what Spinks said was coherent; some wasn't. But one thing Leon said came through loud and clear: "All of the motherfuckers were hard punchers."

Dixon writes well, which is a good start for any book. He's a meticulous researcher, which further elevates his work. There are places where *Damage* is a bit too technical and dry. And there are too many case studies, some of which are close to a century old. But Dixon approaches his subject with sensitivity and he understands its gravitas. He explains medical concepts in a way that the average reader can understand.

And the technical parts in *Damage* are important to informing ring
doctors and other medical personnel associated with boxing about the
issues involved.

Dixon also writes in self-revelatory fashion about his years as an
amateur boxer.

"I wonder if I am damaged," he acknowledges. "I'm forty. I can be
moody. I can be emotional. I can get cranky. My temper can be short. I
was an amateur for ten years. I only had a handful of fights. I was stopped,
but never knocked down—not that that matters. There are four or five guys
I could tell you I boxed more than a hundred rounds with. My defense
was abysmal. I took some blows to the head that really hurt, and some of
them I didn't shake for several weeks. My memory catches me out at times.
There could, of course, be many reasons behind it. But I remember once,
after driving back from a fight in the West of England (stopped in the
second or third round) that I drove clean over a roundabout and did not
think anything of it. In fact, I thought I was being clever. That Saturday
night, I had taken a left hand to the crown of my head when coming in
underneath my taller opponent. I saw some patchy bright colors, felt my
knees buckle, and the pain did not subside for a few days. It certainly was
not helped when I was back in the gym sparring on Monday."

And Dixon recounts a particularly harrowing sequence of events
that occurred when he journeyed from England to the United States to
hone his craft.

"One time when I was sparring with some of the pros in Kevin
Rooney's Catskill Boxing Club in upstate New York, I was clobbered
harder than I can ever recall being hit. My legs bolted firmly to the mat
like I was some kind of robot screwed in the floor. I was stricken, frozen
solid like a block of ice, looking at the light hanging above the ring. A
volley of punches came my way. I clumsily swiped back and the round
passed. The next day, the other fighters and I did our roadwork. I had
a splitting headache from the sparring. It was not the sort of migraine
pain you get around your temples but toward the top and back of my
head. It was like my brain was loose within my skull and, as we ran up
the mountains and along the sweeping roads, it felt as though there was
a rattle in my head. The next day we sparred again, and it was hard. With
hindsight, I believe I was concussed. But when Rooney called me into

the ring, what could I say? I could not take a battering in sparring one day and opt not to box the next. I would look like a wimp. What are you going to say? 'My head hurts from boxing yesterday?' Of course it hurts. It's boxing. You get hit on the head. It's the fight game. Heroic boxers have fought through infinitely worse. I said nothing and boxed, but my timing was off. I felt lethargic and flat. My head felt a great deal worse after the four rounds, too. That rattle did not completely leave through most of the summer. I continued to train in New York, Atlantic City, and other places. I was still getting hit all the time.

"How many times does an ordinary person recall being banged on the head?" Dixon asks. "Maybe once when they stood up quickly somewhere there was a low ceiling, or when they fell off their bike while learning to ride, or perhaps even in a drunken punch-up. But fighters take blows to the head repeatedly, often several days a week. That is where the real danger lies."

Can boxing be made safer?

Let's start with the premise that we're talking about a sport in which the objective is to cause brain damage (a concussion) to an opponent. There are no easy answers. Athletic commissions should be more vigilant in determining who is licensed to box. Ring doctors, referees, and cornermen should be better informed with regard to when to stop a fight. Uniform national medical standards, a worldwide database, and better education for all parties would help.

More importantly, gyms should be better regulated and, in Dixon's view, fighters should spar less.

"It's not the fights," Kelly Pavlik told Dixon. "Fights are the glamorous part that people see. The damage comes in three, four days a week sparring. Some of these guys are doing like three hundred rounds in camp. I can't remember what I did, but it was minimum a hundred rounds in camp and sparring was full go. That's where the damage comes."

Micky Ward concurs, saying, "There's no way they can stop concussions in boxing. The only thing you can do is probably minimize the sparring. What I believe—and I don't know this for sure—is three minors [head injuries] is a major. Just getting stunned in the gym with a right hand or whatever, not hurt, just stunned, that's a minor. I used to get those constantly. I don't know how many of those I had. Full-blown,

I had a whole bunch. But the minors are the ones that you don't think hurt but they still do damage. Then you're going back and sparring again and again."

Wearing headgear while sparring might guard against cuts. But it doesn't protect a fighter's brain against concussions. To the contrary, it makes it easier to shake a fighter's brain because headgear increases the hitting area. Anyone who doubts that assertion should ask themselves whether wearing helmets protects football players from CTE.

But when asked about fighters cutting down on sparring, Paulie Malignaggi answers, "That's not going to happen. If you're going to prepare yourself for a fight, you're going to have to spar a lot of rounds. Otherwise you're not going to be sharp. Fighters have to be fighters."

Tris Dixon has made a major contribution to the health and safety of fighters. Now let's see who's paying attention. *Damage* should be required reading for ring doctors and high-ranking state athletic commission officials. If one of these people doesn't read *Damage*, that person is doing less than should be done in the performance of his or her job. Fighters, managers, and trainers should read it, too.

Sugar Ray Robinson, Joe Louis, and Muhammad Ali—the three greatest fighters of all time—all fought too long. And they all wound up in poor health with significant cognitive issues. There's a message in that for anyone who's paying attention.

Meanwhile, as Dixon states, " It's time to be open about it. It's time to talk about it. It's time boxing confronts its own worst problem, stops ignoring it, and steps up to address it at all levels. Boxers should be told what might be happening to their brains."

I correspond regularly by email with a man named John who loves boxing, understands boxing, and speaks his mind when talking about it. Some thoughts that John has shared with me follow.

Thoughts from a Reader Named John

* "No one tells boxing what to do. That is a fact."
* "No real fighter takes pride in losing with everyone watching. When did that become an act of courage, to make money on losing? That is not a fighter's mentality. Never has been. That is an entertainer's mentality, an actor's job."
* "Boxing fans are the most abused fans in all of sports. Things used to start with the idea of building something up in the boxing ring based on certain principles. I give you an honest display of good boxing, and you pull your money out and say you appreciate it. Now everyone is so wrapped up in getting money. Every step of the way, every person has got to stick their hand in the pocket of the fight fan like you're an idiot to be played. It sickens me."
* "Damn cold out there today. Not everyone knows what it's like to be cold. No one takes the time to write or talk about those things. All we get as fans is 'he grew up in poverty.' You see a fire in a rowhouse. Somebody got cold and did what he could to escape it. Dollar a night floor space. Either you pay it or you walk the streets. One dollar to lay on a floor and defend your space, an imaginary line you make in your mind that will not be crossed. It is your space, your spot, and you hate it. But it's yours and you will protect it. No different in the ring. Someone wants to take your space, so you draw lines that will not be crossed. Do not let him take what is yours. Make him pay if he crosses the line. That's what you have to do to win a fight."
* "Too much money, too much greed, and a long list of other 'too muches' have turned the fight game into what we have today. Years

ago was not my imagination. It was not because I was young or knew nothing about fights. There was a raw power to it all. I've lowered my expectations now. I'm just looking for a good fight. I try and catch a few guys who are not the best, don't have the skills that the big names have, but they have heart."

★ "Let me clear something up. I worked most of my life in heavy construction. I saw men die on the job site. I saw men lose their legs, arms, and eyesight. I know a police officer who walked into a housing project and was hit with several bullets. So I pause when I hear that no one takes the risks that a boxer takes and no one sacrifices as much as a fighter does. There are lots of risk-takers out there doing it to make a decent living and get a better life for their families and themselves. That's not meant to demean the risks in boxing, just to put them in perspective a bit."

★ "Seems like no one fights much anymore, but they do talk a lot."

★ "Boxing is about having to look at stuff that sometimes only a beating can make you look at. Sounds crazy to most folks, but to me it makes a lot of sense."

★ "I don't like celebrity boxing. There's a fake feel to it. And there's another reason I don't like it. If you've been in the ring all your life, it's dangerous enough. But when you've been outside the ring and walk in, it can be bad, very bad. You always think it won't be me. But numbers don't lie."

★ "If you love the fights, logic and common sense have to leave you from time to time. It takes a certain character to follow boxing and not kick it or hate it or even wonder at times why you watch."

★ "Being wrong is just another way to learn. Drop your hands and get caught with a punch and you learn a lot faster than someone telling you where to put your hands."

★ "Anyone who has been around boxing knows about bad influences in life."

★ "I never hit a person with a concern for their health unless it was to damage it. It's the way of a fighter. Nothing personal, but I'm going to hurt you within the rules of the game."

★ "I watched Katie Taylor and Amanda Serrano the other night. A couple of little girls got their asses in the ring and embarrassed men's boxing."

★ "I've been reading about all these big purses for fighters. Money is not about how high you can count. For some of us, it's about survival. Some people don't know what it's like to have a car repair bill that causes you to lose twelve pounds in ten days and have to work overtime in a place you don't want to be at. I get real life in my life every day."

★ "Boxing talk is becoming all about outside the ring, not what's happening in it. It's ninety-nine percent, not about skill, not about development, just speculation about boxers and who they should fight and what should have happened but didn't. All this talking means nothing. All the noise drowns out the quiet truth of a fighter, men who walk into the ring and do what few men are gifted to do."

★ "I do not expect everyone to know from experience what it is like to suffer from hunger. It is not a pleasant thing. Most people think being hungry is having lunch a few hours late. There are people who have grown up and gone to bed hungry many a night. And either you are one of them or you are not."

★ "If you lose the passion for the fight game, it's over. I see it all the time. Fighters just going through the motions. When it becomes a check list, it's time to check out. Don't try to figure it out. Just move on. It's over."

★ "Everyone should get excited about boxing at least once in their life."

Fistic Notes

The first thing that many fighters do after winning a fight is give praise to Jesus.

There's a great deal of combat in the Bible, particularly in the Old Testament. But Jesus was a man of peace. He preached, "Blessed are the meek: for they shall inherit the earth" (Matthew 5:5), and taught, "Ye have heard that it hath been said, 'An eye for eye, and a tooth for tooth.' But I say unto you that ye resist not evil but whosoever shall smite thee on thy right cheek, turn to him the other also" (Matthew 5:38–40).

This leads to a question I've been contemplating lately: "What would Jesus think about boxing?" There are more than a few people on the business end of the sport who one might analogize to the money changers and merchants who Jesus cast out of the temple (John 2:13–16, Matthew 21:12–13). But I'm asking about the actual fight.

What would Jesus think about people participating in and paying to watch combat as a sport? Would he liken it to the horror of gladiators doing battle in the Roman Colosseum? Or would the fact that today's fighters participate of their own free will and rarely fight to the death lead to his being comfortable with boxing?

George Foreman and Evander Holyfield are born-again Christians whose devotion to their faith is well known. I asked each of them, "What would Jesus think about boxing?"

"I have been a Sunday school teacher now for about forty-two years," George told me." It's an ever-learning process. The stories told throughout the Old Testament included great wars and great battles where many lives were lost. 'Violence' appeared in these stories. But from the first story when Adam said, 'This is now bone of my bones, flesh of my flesh,' to Jesus saying, 'Father, forgive them for they know not what they do,' The Bible has been a book of great stories of Love and forgiveness. In the true scheme of things, boxing is no more than a game of 'marbles' that kids play till their knees give out on them."

Evander took a different approach, saying, "Our sport is competitive, not fight to the death. To compete in boxing takes focus and discipline, something Jesus would be proud of. A big difference."

Entire armies have gone to war in Jesus's name. But unlike war, boxing involves the imposition of physical damage and pain for the purpose of entertainment. Jesus lived in a different time with different standards for behavior than our own. But it's hard for me to imagine Jesus sitting at ringside, urging one fighter to inflict physical damage on another.

What would Jesus think about boxing? I'm not a Biblical scholar. I don't have an answer to the question. I'm just asking it.

★★★

Sometimes it doesn't take much for a journalist to get a story.

July 19, 2021, marked the twenty-fifth anniversary of Muhammad Ali lighting the Olympic Flame at the 1996 Atlanta Olympics. Several days before those games began, I was on the telephone with Muhammad.

"Will you be going to the Olympics?" I asked.

"I can't tell anyone," Ali told me. "It's a big secret."

From this, I deduced that Muhammad was in fact going to Atlanta and that he would be lighting the Olympic cauldron. But staying true to the spirit of the occasion, I told no one about our conversation until the opening ceremonies were over.

★★★

Boxing has always been a male-dominated sport.

When we think of great fighters, we think of men like Sugar Ray Robinson, Joe Louis, and Muhammad Ali. Great promoters? Tex Rickard, Don King, and Bob Arum. Trainers? Ray Arcel, Eddie Futch, and Emanuel Steward. Michael Buffer is the greatest ring announcer ever. And so it goes.

The first woman enshrined in the International Boxing Hall of Fame was Aileen Eaton (2002). She got into boxing promotion with her husband. Like Eaton, promoters Lorraine Chargin (2018) and Kathy Duva (2020) had accomplishments in their own right. But the foundation stone for their respective careers was set with their husband.

This year's selection of Laila Ali and Ann Wolfe brings the number of women in the IBHOF "women's modern" category to four. There are also three "women's trailblazers" in Canastota.

That's it. Ten women out of 485 inductees.

No! Make that eleven.

This year's induction class includes Dr. Margaret Goodman.

Goodman, a neurologist by trade, was a ringside physician for the Nevada State Athletic Commission for two decades and chair of the NSAC Medical Advisory Committee for six. In late 2011, she founded the Voluntary Anti-Doping Association (VADA), which has become boxing's gold standard in testing for illegal performance-enhancing drugs.

"I had an epiphany," Dr. Goodman says. "I realized that the horses in show competitions and racing were tested for illegal performance-enhancing drugs more often and more thoroughly than boxers. No one was doing the job properly. I said to myself, 'This is nuts.'"

In 2017, the Boxing Writers Association of America honored Goodman with the Barney Nagler Award for Long and Meritorious Service to Boxing. Previously, she and Flip Homansky (who worked with Margaret professionally at the NSAC and has been her life partner for twenty years) were honored by the BWAA with the James A. Farley Award for Honesty and Integrity.

"Margaret comes from a place of admiration for and caring about the fighters," Homansky says. "Most people in boxing have an ulterior motive. Usually it's financial. And no matter what they say, they come from that place first. Margaret is different. She really is. That admiration and caring are what set her apart. And that's the truth."

The most influential ring doctor ever and the first physician selected for induction into the International Boxing Hall of Fame is a woman.

***

Marv Albert, who turned eighty this year, called what he says was the final game of his illustrious announcing career when the Milwaukee Bucks beat the Atlanta Hawks on June 27, 2021, to claim the NBA Eastern Conference title.

Albert is sportscasting royalty. He began his career in the 1960s as the radio voice of the New York Knicks and New York Rangers and is most identified in the public mind with NBA basketball. But in a journey spanning fifty-eight years, he has called eight Super Bowls, seven Stanley Cup finals, two World Series, and Wimbledon. He's a craftsman who voluminously researched assignments and never just mailed it in.

He also had a droll sense of humor. In 1986, while interviewing St. Louis Cardinals manager Whitey Herzog (who was in competition with Yale president Bartlett Giamatti to become president of the National League) Marv suggested, "Whitey, look at it this way. If A. Bartlett Giamatti takes the job, there would be an opening for you at Yale University."

Herzog was not amused.

Steve Albert (the youngest of three Albert brothers) spent two decades as the blow-by-blow commentator for boxing on Showtime. Brother Al was behind the microphone for *USA Tuesday Night Fights* for sixteen years. Marv has left his own imprint on the sweet science.

"When I was young," Marv recalls, "my dad took me to fights at a rickety arena in Coney Island. They weren't big fights but they were exciting to me. And I remember going with him a couple of times to fights at St. Nicholas Arena. Then I started doing radio for the Knicks and Rangers and going to fights at The Garden."

The most unique setting for a fight that Marv called as a blow-by-blow commentator was Rahway State Prison for the December 1, 1979, contest between James Scott and Yaqui Lopez. The bout was broadcast live on NBC. Scott was serving a prison term for armed robbery. Thus the venue. Ken Norton was paired with Marv as the expert commentator.

More often, NBC paired Albert with Ferdie Pacheco. Two fights from that collaboration stand out in Marv's mind. The first was John Tate's October 10, 1979, victory over Gerrie Coetzee in front of 86,000 spectators in South Africa to claim the WBA heavyweight title. The second was Larry Holmes's first-round obliteration of Marvis Frazier in 1983.

Marvis wouldn't have been in the ring that night but for his father's name. "I always liked Larry Holmes," Marv says. "I thought he was an underappreciated fighter and a good guy. And I liked Marvis. It was a sad situation."

Pacheco later said of his broadcasting partner, "Marv Albert was a pure star. He was motivated and driven by a desire to be perfect. Once he undertook a job, his employer could be sure Albert would devote 110 percent of his waking hours to be the best he could be, which was usually the best in the business."

Marv also called the May 20, 1985, heavyweight championship fight between Holmes and Carl Williams, which was the last heavyweight title fight broadcast live on network television in the United States until Deontay Wilder fought Johann Duhaupas for the WBC belt in 2015. And to bring matters full circle, Marv was behind the microphone for Wilder–Duhaupas, which was contested during a brief flirtation between NBC and Deontay's promoter, Premier Boxing Champions.

Marv also covered boxing for NBC at three Olympic Games: 1988 in Seoul, 1996 in Atlanta, and 2000 in Sydney.

"The Roy Jones robbery was the big story in 1988," Marv recalls. "And another thing I remember about those games was that they had two rings right next to each other with two fights going on at the same time. The bell rang in one ring, and a fighter in the other ring heard it and stopped fighting and got knocked out."

Teddy Atlas, who was paired with Marv at the 2000 Olympics, has his own remembrance of the man.

"Marv is an icon but he's more than that," Atlas says. "He's a consummate professional, and to work with him was a real pleasure. I have my own standards and my own work ethic. And to see the work ethic he had after so many years was very impressive to me. I'll give you an example," Atlas continues. "We had trouble with the names of some of the fighters. Anyone would. We did the best we could. We had the names broken down for us phonetically before each fight. But one time during the action, I referred to one of the fighters as 'the Hungarian fighter in blue.' And the next break, Marv said to me, 'Teddy, you cannot do that.' And he was right. I was taking a shortcut. And if you're a pro, you don't take shortcuts."

"I enjoyed calling fights," Marv says looking back on it all. "The scene, the stories, the characters in boxing, were always intriguing to me."

So . . . is this a firm retirement? Or might sports fans see and hear Marv Albert behind a microphone again?

"It's firm," Marv answers. "I made up my mind. Fifty-five years of the NBA and all the other things I've done is enough. In a way, the pandemic was a rehearsal for retirement. I found myself reading more, working out more, and doing other things to fill up my time. Unlike some boxers, I won't be coming back."

★★★

The award for "double standard of the year" was locked in early by Kate Abdo when Ryan Garcia knocked out Luke Campbell on January 2, 2021. Sean Garcia (Ryan's brother) decisioned Rene Marquez on the undercard. Between those bouts, Abdo (an on-camera interviewer for DAZN) told the boxers' father, Henry Garcia, "You make them pretty. You make them athletic. That's some good sperm you got there, sir."

Now suppose a white male commentator had said that to Richard Williams, the father of Serena and Venus Williams.

★★★

Most boxing fans don't know who Henry Hascup is. But the seventy-three-year-old New Jersey resident has served the sweet science in numerous ways. He has been president of the New Jersey Boxing Hall of Fame since 1986, a contributing editor for BoxRec.com, a charter member of the International Boxing Research Organization, and president of several amateur boxing organizations, He has also been the ring announcer for more than a thousand mostly amateur fights and has eulogized fighters at countless funerals. But it might be that Hascup's most notable contribution is embodied in the emails he sends to members of the boxing community when one of our own dies.

"It started in the 1980s," Hascup recalls. "As president of the New Jersey Boxing Hall of Fame, whenever someone in boxing died, I'd call around to let people know. Then the internet and email came in and I started notifying people that way. I have close to a thousand people on my email list. And the people on my email list have their own email lists. So when someone dies, it snowballs.

"Sometimes I'll read about a death on the internet," Hascup continues. "Usually I find out because someone calls and tells me. Before I send out a notification, I double-check to make sure the person has really died. I've never counted but I'd guess that, over the years, I've sent out notifications for close to a thousand deaths. The hardest thing is when someone calls and tells me that their husband or father has died. In that moment, a four-round fighter is as important as a great world champion."

"I can't say I enjoy doing it," Hascup says. "But it's a service, and I guess I'm the one who's doing it."

★★★

The annual ESPY Awards are a celebration of sports and the role that they play in American society. Jim Valvano, who was dying of cancer, energized the first ESPYs telecast in 1993 with his powerful message, "Don't give up. Don't ever give up." The ESPYs have gotten bigger since then. They're now a mainstream cultural happening. But for knowledgeable boxing fans, their credibility just took a hit.

The ESPYs are (in ESPN's words) about "celebrating major sports achievements, remembering unforgettable moments, and honoring the leading performers and performances" of the preceding twelve months. On June 28, ESPN announced the nominees for the 2022 ESPY awards. The winners will be revealed during a July 20 telecast. Most of the nominees were well chosen. But the nominees for "best boxer" appear to have been chosen with an eye toward promoting fighters aligned with ESPN rather than "celebrating major sports achievements, remembering unforgettable moments, and honoring the leading performers and performances" of the past twelve months.

The ESPY nominees for "best boxer" are Tyson Fury, Katie Taylor, Shakur Stevenson, and Makaela Mayer. In other sports (such as soccer, basketball, golf, and tennis), the ESPYs have separate categories for male and female athletes. Rafael Nadal doesn't compete against Emma Raducanu at Wimbledon or in the ESPY balloting. So it's unclear why Tyson Fury should compete against Katie Taylor.

The ESPYs tilt toward boxers who are aligned with ESPN is more troubling. Fury and Taylor belong on the ballot. During the preceding year, Fury knocked out Deontay Wilder and Dillian Whyte, while Taylor decisioned Jennifer Han, Firuza Sharipova, and Amanda Serrano. The historic nature of Taylor–Serrano validates Katie's inclusion.

But Stevenson and Mayer are a stretch. Both of them have promotional contracts with Top Rank, which has an exclusive licensing agreement with ESPN. During the preceding year, Stevenson beat Jamel Hering and Óscar Valdez. Those were nice wins but hardly remarkable. Mayer's ESPY credentials are limited to decisions over Maiva Hamadouche and Jennifer Han.

Why isn't Oleksandr Usyk (who dethroned Anthony Joshua) on the ballot? What about Terence Crawford (KO 10 over Shawn Porter) and Dmitry Bivol (whose victories included a unanimous-decision triumph over Canelo Álvarez)?

Hint: Usyk and Bivol are currently aligned with DAZN. And Crawford has signaled his intention to leave Top Rank/ESPN to pursue a unification bout against Errol Spence on Showtime-PPV or FOX-PPV.

If Netflix hosted the Oscars and stacked the ballot with Netflix programming, it would be comparable to the ESPYs' handling of this year's "best boxer" award.

When the ESPY nominations were announced, I reached out to ESPN for comment. Initially, I asked, "What is the process by which the four nominees for 'best boxer' were chosen?"

Speaking on background, an ESPN publicist responded, "Nominees are chosen by a mix of ESPN editors, executives and show producers."

"On background" means that a reporter may quote the source directly and may describe the source by his or her position but may not attribute the statements to the source by name.

I followed up by asking, "How many people choose the nominees and what are the criteria for choosing them?"

There was no response.

I'm also curious to know the identity of the "editors, executives and show producers" who selected the ESPY nominees. Did knowledgeable ESPN boxing people like Tim Bradley and Mark Kriegel have a significant voice? I think not. Here, I should note that ESPN analyst Andre Ward is also knowledgeable about boxing. I omitted his name from this paragraph because, given Ward's ties to Shakur Stevenson, he probably shouldn't participate in the nominating process.

In recent years, boxing fans have grown accustomed to boxing tele-casts on all networks being as much about hype as honest commentary. The 2022 ESPY nominations for "best boxer" are about ESPN hyping its own fighters and advancing its own economic interests.

★★★

From time to time, I come across something that someone in boxing has said and make a note to share it with readers at a future date. Herewith some thoughts on boxing:

* Charles Farrell: "If you're in the boxing business, depending on where you're in the boxing business, you're going to have some involvement, if only indirectly, with guns. Your fighter is going to shoot someone or get shot or have a family member shoot some-one or get shot by someone. Your fighter is going to walk into a convenience store in a bad part of town just before it gets held up. There will be territorial gang disputes, confrontations with some-one's husband over a woman you're fucking, conflicts with shady promoters or road agents over skimpy fight payoffs. You will be in the wrong place at the wrong time."
* Tony Ayala Jr.: "I think very little of boxing, To me boxing is just my job. I don't see it as a grand sport. I don't think that winning or losing a fight is the beginning or end of life. I'm asked, 'Aren't you excited that you'll be getting a shot at a world title?' I don't really care whether or not I ever win a world title. What I'm concerned about is the security of my life financially, the paying off of this house I just bought."
* Rocky Marciano: "As people get more civilized, they're going to ban boxing. A hundred years from now, we'll be like the gladiators, something out of history."
* Jimmy Tobin: "No distraction quite compares with watching your guy knock another man senseless. No need to apologize for that or even try to justify it."

★ Archie Moore: "I would rather see Ray Robinson punch a speed bag than watch the average guy go out and fight. There was nobody more beautiful than he was."

★ Larry Merchant: "There are too many governing bodies. They're all corrupt. I think they've replaced the old mobsters with a kind of corporate rule of boxing."

★ Diego Corrales: "I don't bring my children to my fights. I don't want them to be afraid for me. And I don't want them to see that very aggressive hurting side of me either."

★ Tom Gerbasi: "A fighter with nothing left but heart is a tragedy waiting to happen."

★ Carlos Acevedo: "Not many trades are more arduous than boxing where past, present, and future all promise hardship of one kind or another."

★ Goody Petronelli: "We all know what a great chin Marvin [Hagler] had. But even if you have a great chin, the punches hurt."

★ Mark Kriegel: "Fighters tend not to be happy people. Forgive the generalization, but I'm not wrong here. They're mined from dismal circumstances, and the business of boxing does little to leaven their distemper."

★ Floyd Patterson: "We are not afraid of getting hurt but we are afraid of losing. Losing in the ring is like losing nowhere else. A prize-fighter who gets knocked out or is badly outclassed suffers in a way he will never forget. He is beaten under the bright lights in front of thousands of witnesses. He is being watched by many thousands more on television. The losing fighter loses more than just his pride and the fight. He loses part of his future and is one step closer to the slum he came from."

★ Paul Magno: "There are no holy men in boxing at any level."

★ Ferdie Pacheco: "Boxing writers are a rare breed. It's hard to conceive how a body of men can be so filled with their own importance in spite of the number of times they are wrong. They are called experts which does not carry with it the burden of being

THOMAS HAUSER

right most of the time but apparently only means you have a job
writing about boxing."

★★★

One of many divisive issues facing society today is the question of whether
transgender athletes should be allowed to compete in a gender category
other than that assigned to them at birth. Recently, Dr. Nitin Sethi (chief
medical officer for the New York State Athletic Commission) offered
some thoughts on the matter as it relates to combat sports.

Sethi supports transgender rights. He has pledged to protect transgender individuals against discrimination in employment, education, access
to healthcare, and other areas of everyday life. But he is also, in his words,
"committed to the value of fair competition."

"A combat-sport bout," Sethi states, "should occur between two
equally matched competitors. At present, there is no consensus whether
a bout between a transgender woman against a cisgender (biological)
woman is a fair bout between two equally matched competitors."

Metrics such as testosterone levels, Sethi notes, are inadequate to
ensure fairness at the time of the bout. "It can be argued," he posits, "that
by the time a transgender woman combatant launches her professional
career, she has already gone through male puberty, thus conferring her
with the musculature and bony structure of a male. So a transgender
woman combatant may have an unfair advantage over her cisgender
woman opponent."

The converse would be true in the case of a fight between a transgender man and a cisgender man.

"Combat sports such as boxing," Sethi continues, "are unique since
every punch thrown at the head is thrown with the intention of winning
by causing a knockout, which is a concussive head injury. These sports
carry an exceedingly high risk for both acute and chronic neurological
injuries."

Thus, Sethi advocates for "two equally skilled and matched athletes
competing on a level playing field and to keep matches fair, competitive,
entertaining, and, most importantly, safe for all combatants." At the present
level of scientific knowledge, he concludes, allowing transgender athletes

to compete in combat sports raises serious health and safety concerns that he finds unacceptable.

★★★

Boxing fans are familiar with Michael Arkush from *The Big Fight* (the autobiography that he fashioned with Sugar Ray Leonard). Now Arkush has joined forces with NBA great Scottie Pippen on the autobiographical *Unguarded* (Atria Books).

Pippen was on the original "Dream Team" at the 1992 Barcelona Olympics. Four years later, he reprised that role in Atlanta, where Muhammad Ali lit the Olympic cauldron. Ali also attended the United States vs. Yugoslavia gold-medal basketball game in Atlanta and, at half-time, was presented with a new gold medal to replace the one from the 1960 Olympics that had been lost or stolen.

After Ali died, Pippen posted several photos on social media of him-self with Muhammad accompanied by the messages: "Goodbye to the champion of champions. Rest in peace, Muhammad Ali . . . We may never again see an American hero quite like Muhammad Ali. RIP to the greatest champion of all . . . A legend like no other, Muhammad Ali taught us all to dream."

After reading Pippen's autobiography, I was curious to know more about his feelings toward boxing. In a way, it seemed to me that, even though Pippen and Michael Jordan were teammates, Scottie was cast into the role of Frazier to Jordan's Ali. Frazier was Ali's equal in the three fights that they fought against one another. Ali rose to the heights that he did in the mythology of boxing in part because of Joe. But Frazier could never escape Muhammad's shadow.

So I spoke with Scottie.

Pippen doesn't go to fights. But as an elite athlete, he understands the extraordinary things that boxers do in the ring. And he's a fan.

"I was born in 1965," Scottie told me. "So I grew up in the Muhammad Ali era. Boxing was at its pinnacle then because of Ali, Frazier, and George Foreman. Those guys were true champions and they gave us some of the greatest entertainment ever seen."

Did Pippen ever box?

"When I was young, a lot of my friends joined a club and boxed on Saturday nights. But I was never into boxing myself. I appreciate what it takes to be a great fighter. Like all sports, it takes hard work and dedication. You have to outwork your opponent. But boxers have something different inside of them."

Which NBA players does Pippen think would have made the best fighters?

"I think Charles Oakley would have been a good heavyweight," Scottie answered. "But you don't know until you find out about the chin."

Which fighters has Pippen followed in recent years?

"Like everyone, I watched Mike Tyson. And there's my guy from Arkansas, Jermain Taylor. He was a good fighter."

But Ali is number one in Pippen's heart.

"Meeting him at the Olympics was a once in a lifetime experience for me," Scottie reminisced. "I grew up loving Ali. It was amazing, meeting one of my first heroes. He wasn't just a great fighter. He was an advocate and so much more. All people, not just athletes, owe Ali."

★★★

One of many problems that plague boxing today with regard to fighter safety is that medical standards differ widely—and wildly—from state to state. Some jurisdictions require state-of-the-art neuroimaging. Others require none at all. Some states require sophisticated eye examinations. In others, a fighter who's virtually blind in one eye can slide by. Medical records might be retained by commissions for future use, but they're rarely shared with other commissions.

Federal law now mandates the maintenance of electronic medical records for all healthcare providers. This brings the creation of a national medical database for fighters within easy reach.

The Association of Boxing Commissions should create a national medical database for fighters. State athletic commissions that take their responsibilities seriously could keep tabs on fighters through this data base. States that do minimal testing (either because of a lack of expertise or lack of funding) could benefit through the efforts of their more thorough counterparts.

Dr. Nitin Sethi states, "A national medical data base would streamline the process of reviewing medical records prior to a fight and go a long way toward protecting the health and safety of boxers. A boxer's medical history would be readily available at the click of a mouse, making it easier to identify high-risk fighters who need additional testing or closer medical supervision."

A national medical database would also reduce redundancy such as repetitive and costly medical tests (for example, CT scans) and could be expanded to include all post-fight medical care. Securing the database by limiting access to regulators with a legitimate need to know would ensure the confidentiality of the data provided.

The time is now.

★★★

Chris Traietti is a thirty-five-year-old club fighter who has compiled a 30–4 (24 KOs) ring record over the past fifteen years. The most recognizable name on his ring ledger is Mike Lee (who defeated Traietti 99–90, 99–90, 98–91 in 2016). Traietti has entered the ring as a professional fighter 34 times. He deserves credit for that.

Traietti is also a licensed promoter doing business as Granite Chin Promotions. And he's a matchmaker. On April 17, 2021, Granite Chin promoted a twenty-four-bout card in Derry, New Hampshire. The A-side fighter won twenty-three of these fights. But the story goes deeper than that.

The Association of Boxing Commissions maintains a "watch list" overseen by Pennsylvania State Athletic Commission executive director Greg Sirb. The watch list was created to track fighters who have long losing streaks and multiple defeats by knockout and presumably shouldn't be fighting anymore. The list is sent to all ABC member commissions. The assumption is that any reasonable commissioner would look at the list and say, "I'm not going to let these guys fight." But nothing in federal law precludes mismatches and poorly equipped fighters from entering the ring. Each state athletic commission has its own standards and procedures to evaluate and license fighters. So the mantra for many promoters is, "If the commission lets me do it, I'll do it."

The New Hampshire State Athletic Commission lets promoters do it. The April 17 fight card in Derry had TEN fighters who are currently on the ABC watch list.

Roberto Valenzuela, age forty-seven, has 80 losses including defeats in his last 14 fights. He was knocked out in Derry by an opponent with a 21–1–1 (20 KOs) ring record.

DeWayne Wisdom has 56 defeats and has been victorious in 1 of his last 35 outings. He lost to a fighter with a 10–1 record.

Rynell Griffen (2 wins in his last 47 fights) was knocked out in the first round by an 11–1 fighter.

Clifford McPherson (43 losses in a row) was knocked out in the first round by a 16–5–2 opponent.

Theo Desjardin (0–13), Bruno Dias (0–10), and Paulo DeSouza (0–19) were all knocked out, as were Larry Smith (46 defeats), Steve Walker (37 defeats), and Francisco Neto (who now has 9 consecutive first-round knockout losses).

This writer reached out to Traietti for comment. He declined to be interviewed by telephone but responded with an email that read in part, "I am aware of Greg Sirb's email and 'must watch list' that he created and uses to smear promoters and more specifically the NH commission. I appreciate you reaching out for my side of things, sincerely I do, but I feel like it's not productive for me to go on record and state my feelings about certain 'powers that be' in the boxing world."

This situation is not good.

***

Boxing suffered a loss on April 19, 2021, when Bart Barry announced that he was moving with his wife from San Antonio to a small town in Mexico and would no longer write his weekly column for 15rounds.com.

I met Bart at the 2009 Boxing Writers Association of America dinner in New York. Norm Frauenheim (Bart's mentor and friend in addition to being lead boxing writer for the *Arizona Republic*) introduced us. Bart and I chatted again the following night at Miguel Cotto vs. Joshua Clottey at Madison Square Garden. Over time, reading his Monday morning column became a welcome start to my weekly routine.

Bart didn't tweet "scoops" and pretend it was journalism. He didn't report every rumor and every threat by Fighter A to kick Fighter B's ass. Once a week for sixteen years, he wrote a column that captured the essence of boxing and the contemporary boxing scene.

Despite having a remunerative career in banking data analytics, Bart marched to his own drummer. "My wife is Mexican," he explained this week. "Helping her build a house in the mountains of Mexico was the last goal I had. The house has now been built. I have enough money to leave the bank. By this time next week, we'll be fully relocated to a very small, mostly indigenous town in the mountains of Mexico with no reliable electricity, no internet, and no way to watch fights."

Will there be regrets?

"I don't think so," Bart told me. "Seeing the current boxing calendar makes leaving the sport easy."

Each year, the University of Arkansas Press publishes a book with all of the articles about boxing that I wrote the previous year. In assembling the manuscript, I invariably find that I've quoted Bart in it. I also maintain a file with thoughts, quotes, and nuggets of information set aside for future use. Bart is well represented there too.

Herewith, a sampler of thoughts from Bart Barry:

* "When I began covering matches from ringside, I foolishly interpreted my press-row position as a commentary on my merits as a writer. I thought credentialing reflected something different from click-counts and a seat in auxiliary meant you were inadequate as a craftsman."
* "There's the pain of torn flesh or cramped muscles or wheezing breathlessness. And then there's injury. Injury is a non-negotiable signal sent to the central nervous system. One doesn't make his living in athletics without knowing the difference."
* A thought experiment: Imagine Wladimir Klitschko reduced by a foot and 100 pounds and set across from a prime Juan Manuel Marquez or Manny Pacquiao. For a snicker, imagine Deontay Wilder, six inches and 60 pounds smaller and set across from Andre Ward. Then keep the mirth rolling by imagining a 112-pound man with Tyson Fury's toolkit pitted against Roman Gonzalez. Let us

have no more loose talk about today's heavyweight prizefighters belonging on pound-for-pound lists whatever gaudy win streaks they enjoy. They are genetic lottery winners. We don't have to call them great at boxing too."

★ "This year's leading slugger belted forty-three home runs. In 2001, Barry Bonds hit seventy-three. That's the difference between the natural substances and sophisticated training methods now used and steroids. And before anyone offers up a loony rebuttal that boxing trainers have discovered some secret the rest of the sports world knows nothing about, he should visit a boxing gym. Eating ice chips, rubbing one's body with Albolene, and training in a garbage bag is the way most boxers still make weight. From such a laboratory, next year's Nobel Laureate in chemistry is not likely to emerge."

★ "Andre Ward has approximately twice Sergey Kovalev's craft and can fight effectively while moving in three times as many directions as Kovalev, who does incredibly well while moving forward and moving forward."

★ "[Terence] Crawford enjoyed [Jeff] Horn's diminishment. He felt Horn relenting and smiled. This is what makes men like Crawford exceptional. Where something like empathy for a man being stripped publicly of his dignity begins to drain others, such a stripping makes the purest fighters euphoric. It transcends professionalism: I'm not doing this because it's my job. No, I'm doing this because I like hurting you."

★ "Deontay Wilder is a professional athlete who fights like he's insane. Tyson Fury is an insane man who boxes conventionally."

★ "The PBC telecasts have had every ingredient imaginable. Special ring walk music, rotating cameras, monster display boards. It's like they're making a cake. Flour, sugar, butter, chocolate. Wait! Here's a chili pepper. Let's throw that in too. The only ingredient they haven't thrown in is good fights."

★ "Hospitalized twice for COVID since he coldcocked Whyte in their first match, Povetkin looked like he might struggle with a breathalyzer during his ringwalk and couldn't possibly walk a straight line after a couple minutes of moving around with Whyte. Not enough is known yet about the lingering effects of COVID. But we have witnessed steep declines in prizefighters known to have contracted the virus. Boxing with perfect lungs is daunting enough. Boxing with compromised lungs? Heavens. Povetkin looked worse than nonchalant before the match. Then he went through round one with the footwork of a first-hour foal. Alexander Povetkin did not belong in a prizefighting ring."

★ "Ruiz-Joshua II was fat guy versus a nervous one and it failed all expectations. Trust yourself, dear aficionado. Trust your gut on this one. A pundit writing or saying that it was anything better than woeful does so with the same integrity as a waiter embellishing the daily specials or a flight attendant thanking you for loyalty to her airline. Saturday was just awful."

★ "Mexican prizefighters do not wish to get struck in the face any more than any other type of prizefighter does."

★ "Moments are not memorable because someone tells you they'll be memorable. It's not like anyone with access to YouTube could mistake this era for a great one."

★ "Julio César Chávez Jr. built his following the old-fashioned way. He inherited it."

★ "When it gets it right, there's nothing like boxing. And when it gets it wrong, there's nothing like boxing either."

Norm Frauenheim speaks for many in the boxing community when he says, "Bart's a good writer and he always found a different way to look at a particular fighter or fight. It was never boilerplate, always honest. He'll be missed. I know I'll miss him."

★★★

Muhammad Ali gave new meaning to the term WORLD champion. During the course of his extraordinary ring career, he fought in twelve different countries and twelve states within the United States. He also had one fight in Puerto Rico, which is a US commonwealth.

The geographic breakdown for Ali's 61 professional fights is:

Countries—United States (45), England (3), Canada (2), Germany (2), and Switzerland, Japan, Ireland, Indonesia, Zaire, Malaysia, Philippines, and the Bahamas (1 each)

Commonwealths—Puerto Rico (1 fight)

States—New York (10), Nevada (8), Florida (6), Kentucky (5), California (5), Texas (4), Maryland (2), and Pennsylvania, Maine, Georgia, Ohio, and Louisiana (1 each)

That's quite an itinerary.

★★★

Anyone can suggest that a name be placed on the ballot for induction into the International Boxing Hall of Fame. The nominations are then weighed by a review committee that makes recommendations to a screening committee. The screening committee selects the names that appear on the final ballot.

I'd like to suggest a name for inclusion on this year's final ballot that has never been on the ballot before.

Gerry Cooney won his first 23 fights before losing to Larry Holmes on a night when Holmes was as good as he'd ever been or would be ever again. Plagued by substance abuse problems that he conquered after leaving boxing, Cooney retired after losses to Michael Spinks and George Foreman. The only three men to beat him in a boxing ring were first-ballot Hall of Famers.

Cooney electrified the boxing world with his devastating knockout power. In his two bouts just prior to fighting Holmes, he scored first-round knockouts over Ron Lyle and Ken Norton (the latter in 54 seconds). "If Gerry Cooney was fighting today" Holmes told me recently, "he'd be champion. No doubt about it." Hall of Fame matchmaker Bruce Trampler puts Gerry in the top twenty on his list of all-time heavyweight greats.

Cooney never won a world championship. But neither did Jimmy Bivins, Charley Burley, Billy Graham, Cocoa Kid, Lloyd Marshall, Holman Williams, and others who are enshrined in Canastota. Knowledgeable observers can argue over whether or not Gerry deserves to be in the Hall of Fame. But he certainly deserves to be on the ballot ahead of Jorge

Arce, Vuyani Bungu, Yuri Arbachakov, Leo Gamez, Miguel Lora, Orzubek Navarov, and some of the other nominees.

★★★

Floyd Mayweather ventured into the vaccination culture war on October 25, 2021, when he tweeted his support for Kyrie Irving, who has been temporarily barred from playing for the Brooklyn Nets as a consequence of his refusal to be vaccinated.

Speaking directly to Irving, Floyd said, "America gave us the choice to take the vaccine or not take the vaccine. As time moves on, that choice is gradually being stripped from us. It's crazy how people hate you for being a leader. I hope your actions encourage many others to stand up and say enough is enough. Respect to you Kyrie, and power to the people."

But let's not forget: Irving is the same "leader" who, in 2017, proclaimed that the Earth is flat and declared, "When I started actually doing research on my own and figuring out that there is no real picture of Earth, not one real picture of Earth—and we haven't been back to the moon since 1961 or 1969—it becomes like conspiracy, too. The Earth is flat. I'm telling you, it's right in front of our faces. They lie to us."

That bit of genius prompted NBA commissioner Adam Silver to observe, "Kyrie and I went to the same college [Duke]. He may have taken some different courses."

★★★

More on Kyrie Irving, who was subjected to an eight-game suspension in November 2022 after voicing support on social media for a blatantly antisemitic documentary that, among other lies, claims the Holocaust never occurred and that its history has been fabricated pursuant to a conspiracy by Jews to conceal and protect their status and power.

Irving's defenders maintain that he should be free to speak his mind with regard to social issues without fear of reprisal. This raises the question of how they would feel if Tom Brady (or another superstar) tweeted support for a film that claims slavery never existed and that the history of slavery has been fabricated pursuant to a conspiracy by Black Americans to advance their own interests. My guess is that they would call for a severe sanction—and appropriately so.

★★★

Red Smith, one of the greatest sportswriters of the twentieth century, wrote, "Sports is not really a play world. I think it's the real world. The people we're writing about in professional sports; they're suffering and living and dying and loving and trying to make their way through life just as the bricklayers and politicians are."

That's true. But there's also a "real world" for athletes beyond the playing field. And sometimes that world is ugly.

One of the first fight cards I went to when I started writing about boxing was at the Felt Forum at Madison Square Garden on October 4, 1984. A hot prospect named Troy Darrell knocked out an opponent named Pedro Estrada in the seventh round. It was a great fight with rousing back-and-forth action.

Estrada never fought again. Nor was he ever ranked in the top ten by any of boxing's world sanctioning bodies. Instead, he found himself on the FBI's list of "Ten Most Wanted Suspects" and was imprisoned for participating in a drug-related triple homicide.

I remember being shaken when news of Estrada's circumstances broke. Fighters often come from places that are hard and violent. But the thought that, as a member of the media, I'd interacted with a man who was later actively involved in the shooting deaths of three people unsettled me.

I had that feeling again on May 6, 2021, when former Olympian Felix Verdejo was indicted in Puerto Rico on charges that he had kidnapped and murdered his mistress when she refused to have an abortion after becoming pregnant by him. More specifically, it's alleged that Verdejo punched Keishla Rodriguez in the face, injected her with a substance from a syringe, tied her arms and feet with wire, tied a heavy block to her body, threw her off a bridge into a lagoon, and then shot at the body.

Verdejo, like all criminal defendants, is entitled to his day in court. But the evidence against him appears to be overwhelming.

Welcome to the real "real world."

★★★

WORDS OF WISDOM FROM GREAT TRAINERS

Jack "Chappie" Blackburn: "You gotta throw away your heart when you put on those boxing gloves or the other fella will knock it out of you."

Charley Goldman: "The part I like best is starting from the beginning with a green kid and watching him develop. It's like putting a quarter in one pocket and taking a dollar out of the other."

Emanuel Steward: "I make my living by producing winners. That's what I do, so I know what I'm talking about. But the key in boxing isn't the sculptor. It's the marble."

Eddie Futch (when asked how far he could take Duane Bobick): "I'm a trainer, not a magician."

★★★

Ring judge Gloria Martinez Rizzo has turned in some horrible scorecards, most notably her 117–110 tally in favor of Gabriel Maestre in a WBA title fight against Mykal Fox in 2021. But her conduct away from the ring has been worse.

Martinez has a history of making racist comments on social media. By way of example, in a July 11, 2020, post on Twitter mocking Black Lives Matter, she wrote, "Black Goya beans matter." Then, in an August 18, 2020, Twitter post, she referred to Michele Obama as "monkey face."

On June 11, 2022, Daniel Dubois knocked out Trevor Bryan in the fourth round of a WBA heavyweight "world" title fight at Casino Miami Jai Alai in Florida. One of the judges assigned to the bout was Gloria Martinez Rizzo.

Florida governor Ron DeSantis oversees the Florida State Athletic Commission. Perhaps he finds Rizzo's conduct and remarks acceptable. They aren't.

★★★

On July 23, 2022, Indianapolis Colts owner Jim Irsay paid $6.18 million for a piece of leather and base metal listed by Heritage Auctions as "1970's Muhammad Ali WBC Heavyweight Championship Belt Earned in Victory over George Foreman in the 'Rumble in the Jungle.'"

The item description that accompanied this listing read in part, "Here we present the foremost symbol of that glorious achievement, the WBC Heavyweight Championship belt earned for Muhammad Ali's victory over George Foreman in the fabled 'Rumble in the Jungle.' Two Muhammad Ali WBC belts are known to exist, one in a private museum collection unlikely to ever see the hobby's auction block. The only other known surviving Muhammad Ali Heavyweight Championship belt on Earth is presented here. Like many of the greatest relics of Muhammad Ali's career that circulate the hobby today, this belt derives from the famous Drew 'Bundini' Brown storage lockers, their contents entering the collecting community in 1988 after Brown's passing caused the bills to go unpaid."

Now let's probe a bit.

Ali defeated Foreman in 1974. The Heritage description concedes, "The WBC first awarded belts in 1976, the midpoint of Ali's Heavyweight reign." But Heritage goes on to state, "It is important to stress that Ali's WBC reign began in Zaire, the belt a retroactive symbol of that achievement, as well as of the entirety of the subsequent rule."

In other words, the $6.18 million belt wasn't presented to Ali when he beat George Foreman. More likely, according to boxing memorabilia dealer Craig Hamilton, it was presented to Ali around the time he beat Richard Dunn.

The second WBC belt known to be given to Ali wound up with his father (Cassius Clay Sr.), who sold it to a collector named Joel Platt. Platt has established an entity called the Sports Immortals Collection, a Sports Immortals Museum, and a related foundation. But he has kept an eye on the bottom line.

More specifically, Platt has sold shares in his most valuable sports memorabilia through a company called Collectable. Shareholders can resell their shares on the secondary market. If Platt decides to sell an item outright (as he could with the Ali belt), each shareholder will receive a pro rata share of the proceeds.

Contrary to the suggestion in the Heritage listing, Platt divided the Ali belt into 42,800 shares, kept 30,000 shares for himself, and sold the other 12,800 shares for $128,000. The total valuation of the belt at the time of this division and sale ($428,000) might seem low in light of the recent Heritage auction. But consider this history.

The belt that came from Bundini's locker and was auctioned by Heritage on July 23, 2022, for $6.18 million was purchased two decades ago by a collector named Troy Kinunen. Kinunen sold it for $358,500 in a September 10, 2016, Heritage auction. It was then re-offered by Lelands in a September 27, 2017, auction and is listed as having sold for a mere $120,000.

This is the belt that Jim Irsay bought from Heritage on July 23, 2022, for $6.18 million.

And you thought that the price of digital currency was unstable.

Reading Old Books

Old books can be enlightening and a pleasure to read. I'm not talking now about classics. Just good old books that have been largely forgotten.

A well-written old book offers a window onto the distant past. The facts and scenes might be replicated in works written today. But there's a different feel to the way that authors of old books presented and interpreted their subject matter within the context of their time.

This article is about nonfiction books written about boxing in the 1920s and earlier. Some notable writers authored novels about the sweet science during that time. Jack London wrote *The Game* in 1905 and *The Abysmal Brute* in 1913. George Bernard Shaw penned *Cashel Byron's Profession* in 1882. Historian Randy Roberts reminds us that "a novel can sometimes get at deeper truths in a way that a legitimate historian can't."

Be that as it may, this inquiry is limited to nonfiction. In that regard, Roberts cautions, "These old books are historical sources. And you have to weigh them like any other historical source in terms of accuracy. What can you confirm? What biases did the writer have? How much attention did the writer pay to detail? If the writer saw a fight himself, it might add credibility to his narrative. But I rarely use these books as the gospel truth."

Adam Pollack has written a series of exhaustively researched biographies about boxing's early gloved champions.

"I like accuracy, detail, and truth," Pollack says. "And the books you're talking about have very little verification of facts and almost no citation of sources. The authors might have done the best job they could, given the limited resources they had to tap into. But these old books are filled with errors. Writing today, I have the advantage of modern research tools and can access primary sources like old newspaper accounts online."

And what about the autobiographies by John L. Sullivan, James J. Corbett, Jack Johnson, and their brethren?

"For the fighters' own personal feelings and certain insights into how they thought about things, those books are okay," Pollack answers. "But if you're looking for accuracy, forget it. Most of the old autobiographies are self-serving and wildly inaccurate. And most of the time, these guys were talking years later off the top of their head. And they were hit in the head a lot."

Historian Clay Moyle echoes Pollack's thoughts, saying, "People who were writing a hundred years ago couldn't go to BoxRec.com to check on the details of a fight. Writing today, I can go into newspaper archives online, read twenty different articles written about the same fight, and piece the jigsaw puzzle together. Today's research tools are simply better than what writers had to work with a century ago."

With these caveats in mind, I decided to read an old boxing book. I chose *Ten and Out: The Complete Story of the Prize Ring in America* by Alexander Johnston.

"Complete" is a relative term. The book was published in 1927 shortly after Gene Tunney defeated Jack Dempsey in their "long count" rematch to solidify his claim to the heavyweight championship of the world. Joe Louis had yet to reign. Rocky Marciano was four years old. Muhammad Ali and Mike Tyson were unimaginable.

Johnston did his best to be an accurate historian. Indeed, he referenced some of the same issues that Roberts, Pollack, and Moyle flagged a century later, acknowledging, "In digging back into the pugilistic records of this country, the chronicler is confronted by many difficulties. In the early days, records were carelessly kept or altogether neglected. For many of the records, we have to depend on the shifting minds of managers or even the fighters themselves, obviously not the most unbiased testimony that could be obtained. We must rely on the stories of eye-witnesses. And spectators at prize fights are not the most reliable recorders."

Ten and Out begins with a look at prizefighting in England and then, as its title suggests, moves to America. Johnston called boxing "the most exciting form of sport in which man has ever engaged," and added, "Fighting with the fists is not a gentle sport. Blood will be shed, eyes will be blackened, and there may be accidents of a more serious nature." He chronicled what he called boxing's "thuggish past" and its evolution to "a more respectable present," writing, "The bare knuckle days of the prize ring in America were distinctly a bad time. Anyone who talks of 'the good old days of real fighting' is absolutely wrong. They were the bad old days, and the great sport of boxing lived through them because it had inherent rough virtues of its own."

Johnston's work focused in large measure on heavyweights. In his hands, major championship fights were well told, particularly those that involved the violent transfer of power from one champion to another.

Writing about James Corbett's 1892 conquest of John L. Sullivan at the Olympic Club in New Orleans, Johnston recounted, "Sullivan's strength, speed, hitting power, fighting instinct, and ring ferocity would have made him a great fighter in any generation. [But] in Corbett, he met the first exponent of a new boxing generation which was to carry ring skill far beyond anything that Sullivan's era had known. The old boxing could not meet the new skill on even terms. Sullivan relied on paralyzing punching but you can't paralyze a man who refuses to be hit. Corbett was the first real student of boxing. He was always trying new blows and perfecting his delivery of the old ones. He studied defense. Even in the ring, he was perpetually studying the man opposite him."

Then, in 1897, Corbett fell prey to Bob Fitzsimmons.

"They had broken from a clinch near the center of the ring," Johnston wrote. "Jim feinted as if to start one of his left hooks for Bob's jaw when suddenly Fitz straightened up a bit, shot out a long left to the champion's chin, and then, shifting his feet, drove home his right with all the force of his gigantic shoulders behind it to a place just to the right of the heart where the diaphragm begins. Corbett started to fall forward, and Fitz cracked the jaw again with his left but the last blow was unnecessary. The 'solar plexus' blow had done the trick. Gentleman Jim lay and listened to the fateful count. He says that he was conscious when the fatal 'ten' was being counted but that he was absolutely paralyzed. So the first champion of the new dispensation in the boxing game had gone and a new king reigned in his stead, even as he had replaced the mighty Sullivan on the throne."

Fitzsimmons was followed by James Jeffries, who was regaled as a "giant" of a man (which he was for his time). The "giant" stood a shade over six feet, one inch tall and weighed 220 pounds. Johnston believed that, at his peak, "Jeffries could have hammered into submission any pugilist that ever took the ring."

Then Jeffries retired and, after Marvin Hart and Tommy Burns, Jack Johnson ascended to the throne.

Johnston called the search for a great white hope to beat Johnson "one of the saddest chapters in the history of the heavyweight prize ring in America," adding, "Whatever may have been Jack Johnson's failings in personal behavior, he was a fighter. Some competent critics consider him the greatest fighter that ever lived. He was a master boxer with an almost perfect defense and also a smashing wallop. Johnson had learned in his hundreds of ring battles the art of using only as much energy as was needed to carry out any given maneuver of offense or defense. He never allowed himself to be hurried. He conserved his resources of strength and stamina. And when the time came, he was ready for the finisher."

Johnson was succeeded by Jess Willard. Then, in 1919, Jack Dempsey became king.

"Dempsey," Johnston wrote, "believed thoroughly that the best defense is a good offense. From the moment the first gong rang, he was at his man. He seemed to burn in the ring with a cold white fighting rage that made it impossible to call on finesse. His one idea was to get at his man and knock him horizontal. He plunged in almost wide open, leaving innumerable chances for a skilled opponent to hurt him. He had, though, excellent recuperative powers and he was a vicious hitter. His most outstanding quality as a fighter was his fighting spirit. He carried more than his share of the 'killer instinct.' Given his terrific lust for battle with a killing punch in either hand and a physique able to stand up under punishment, we have a very formidable fistic gladiator."

Recreating the moment in Willard's corner after the third round of the carnage inflicted on him by Dempsey's fists, Johnston wrote, "The champion's seconds worked over him. Walter Monahan, who had charge of his corner, said, 'Jess, do you think you can go on?'"

"'I guess I'm beaten,' Willard answered. "I can't go on any longer.'"

"Monahan at once threw a towel into the center of the ring."

"Willard did not quit," Johnston wrote. "He was smashed to a bruised and broken object of pity. As they took him from the ring, his jaw drooped foolishly like a gate that had lost one hinge. If he had gone up for another round, there might have been a fatality."

Johnston had a way with words.

Regarding Jack Johnson's demolition of James Jeffries when the latter attempted an ill-advised comeback at age thirty-five (six years after he'd retired from the ring), Johnston turned the race issue upside down, writing of Johnson, "In the middle of the third round, it seems to have dawned on him that he was this man's master."

Later, setting the scene for the 1921 bout between Dempsey and George Carpentier (boxing's first million-dollar gate), Johnston observed, "Following his usual custom, Dempsey went into the ring with several day's growth of beard on his face. As he sat glowering across at the clean-shaven Carpentier, he looked like a ferocious tramp about to assault a Greek god."

There's also an occasional nod to humor.

Prior to challenging Corbett for the heavyweight crown, Fitzsimmons and an acquaintance named Robert H. Davis listened as Mrs. Fitzsimmons prayed to God for her husband's victory and safety. Davis suggested to the fighter that he do the same, and Fitzsimmons shook his head, saying, "If He won't do it for her, He won't do it for me."

There were parts of *Ten and Out* that I skimmed when reading through it. I didn't feel an obligation to Johnston to read his description of every fight and the events surrounding it. But there's something satisfying in good writing about boxing's early heavyweight champions as written in their time. It draws a reader closer to these remarkable men and the era in which they lived.

A book that was good when it was written will always have something to offer despite the passage of time.

Boxing's library continued to expand in 2021 and 2022.

Literary Notes

Russell Peltz has been promoting fights for fifty years and is as much a part of the fabric of Philadelphia boxing as Philly gym wars and Philly fighters. He was inducted into the International Boxing Hall of Fame in 2004 and deservedly so. Now Peltz has written a memoir entitled *Thirty Dollars and a Cut Eye* that chronicles his many years in the sweet science.

Peltz started in boxing before it was, in his words, "bastardized by the alphabet groups" and at a time when "world titles still meant something."

"I fell in love with boxing when I was twelve," he writes, "saw my first live fight at fourteen, decided to make it my life, and never looked back." He promoted his first fight card in 1969 at age twenty-two.

Peltz came of age in boxing at a time when promoters—particularly small promoters—survived or died based on the live gate. Peltz Boxing Promotions had long runs at the Blue Horizon in Philadelphia and both Harrah's Marina and the Sands in Atlantic City. His journey through the sweet science included a seven-year stint as director of boxing for the Spectrum in Philadelphia. At the turn of the century, he was a matchmaker for ESPN.

Along the way, Peltz's office in Philadelphia was firebombed. That was long after he was robbed at gunpoint while selling tickets in his office for a fight card at the Blue Horizon. Over the years, he was threatened in creative ways more times than one might imagine. He once had a fight fall out when one of the fighters was arrested on the day of the weigh-in. No wonder he quotes promoter Marty Kramer, who declared, "The only thing I wish on my worst enemy is that he becomes a small-club boxing promoter."

Now Peltz has put pen to paper—or finger to keyboard. "The internet is often a misinformation highway," he writes. "I want to set the record straight as to what actually went on in boxing in the Philadelphia area since the late-1960s. I'm tired of reading tweets or Facebook posts or Instagram accounts from people who were not around and have no idea what went on but write like they do."

Thirty Dollars and a Cut Eye is filled with characters (inside and outside the ring) who give boxing its texture. As Peltz acknowledges, his own judgment was sometimes faulty. Russell once turned down the opportunity to promote Marvin Hagler on a long-term basis. There are countless anecdotes about shady referees, bad judging, and other injustices. Middleweight Bennie Briscoe figures prominently in the story, as do other Philadelphia fighters like Willie "The Worm" Monroe, Bobby "Boogaloo" Watts, Eugene "Cyclone" Hart, Stanley "Kitten" Hayward, and Matthew Franklin (later Matthew Saad Muhammad). Perhaps the best fight Peltz ever promoted was the 1977 classic when Franklin knocked out Marvin Johnson in the twelfth round.

There's humor. After Larry Holmes pitched a shutout against Randall "Tex" Cobb in 1982, Cobb proclaimed, "Larry never beat me. He just won the first fifteen rounds."

And there are poignant notes. Writing about Tanzanian-born Rogers Mtagwa (who boxed out of Philadelphia), Peltz recalls, "He couldn't pass an eye exam because he didn't understand the alphabet."

Remembering the Blue Horizon, Peltz fondly recounts, "The Blue Horizon was a fight fan's nirvana. The ring was 15-feet-9-inches squared inside the ropes. No fighter came to the Blue Horizon to pad his record. Fans wanted good fights, not slaughters of second-raters."

That ethos was personified by future bantamweight champion Jeff Chandler who, after knocking out an obviously inept opponent, told Peltz, "Don't ever embarrass me like that again in front of my fans."

Thereafter, whenever a manager asked Peltz to put his fighter in soft to "get me six wins in a row," Russell thought of Chandler. "I enjoyed promoting fights more than promoting fighters," he writes. "If I was interested in promoting fighters, I would have been a manager."

That brings us to Peltz the writer.

The first thing to be said here is that this is a book for boxing junkies, not the casual fan. Peltz is detail oriented. But do readers really need to know what ticket prices were for the April 6, 1976, fight between Bennie Briscoe and Eugene Hart? The book tends to get bogged down in details. And after a while, the fights and fighters blur together in the telling.

It brings to mind the relationship between Gene Tunney and George Bernard Shaw. The noted playwright and heavyweight great developed a genuine friendship. But Shaw's fondness for Tunney stopped short of uncritical admiration. In 1932, the former champion authored his auto-biography (*A Man Must Fight*) and proudly presented a copy to his intel-lectual mentor. Shaw read the book and responded with a letter that read in part, "Just as one prayer meeting is very like another, one fight is very like another. At a certain point, I wanted to skip to Dempsey."

Reading *Thirty Dollars and a Cut Eye,* at a certain point I wanted to skip to Hagler.

There's also one jarring note. Peltz recounts how, when Mike Jones fought Randall Bailey for the vacant IBF welterweight title in Las Vegas in 2012, Peltz bet five hundred dollars against Jones (his own fighter) at the MGM Sports Book and collected two thousand dollars when Bailey (trailing badly on the judges' scorecards) knocked Jones out in the eleventh round.

"It was a tradition from my days with Bennie Briscoe," Russell explains. "I'd bet against my fighter, hoping to lose the bet and win the fight."

I think Russell Peltz is honest. I mean that sincerely. And I think he was rooting for Mike Jones to beat Randall Bailey. But I don't think that promoters should bet on fights involving their own fighters. And it's worse if they bet against their own fighters. Regardless of the motivation, it looks bad. Or phrased differently: Suppose Don King had bet on Buster Douglas to beat Mike Tyson in Tokyo?

Philadelphia was once a great fight town. In 1926, the first fight between Jack Dempsey and Gene Tunney drew 120,000 fans to Sesquicentennial Stadium. Twenty-six years later, Rocky Marciano knocked out Jersey Joe Walcott at the same site (renamed Municipal Stadium) to claim the heavyweight throne.

Peltz takes pride in saying, "I was part of Philadelphia's last golden age of boxing."

An important part.

★★★

Five years ago, Arly Allen wrote an entertaining, well-researched biography of Jess Willard. Now he has turned his attention to a much earlier era.

The Beginning of Boxing in Britain, 1300–1700 (McFarland & Company) explores the murky origins of boxing and its evolution from military combat and crude everyday altercations to the germination of what is known today as the sweet science.

Boxing matches were contested in ancient Greece and Rome. But boxing as a sport disappeared from Europe at the close of that long-ago time. Allen writes, "We are unable to trace any reference to boxing in Western Europe from the fall of Rome (AD 410) until at least the beginning of the fourteenth century. We are unable to find any link between ancient and modern boxing. The best we can do is trace activities that might have influenced boxing. It had to be reinvented in a new form in the modern world."

This new form evolved in part from military combat, which was characterized in the Middle Ages by three distinct types of fighting: (1) with weapons on horseback, (2) with weapons on foot, and (3) on foot with hands in the event that a combatant lost his weapon. Wrestling was taught as a military skill to deal with this latter contingency. It then developed into a non-military sport and an antecedent of boxing.

"When boxing-like activities reappeared in England at the beginning of the fourteenth century," Allen writes, "they were primarily the outgrowth of wrestling. While wresting is not the only source that influenced the development of boxing, it was the primary source and had the greatest impact on the creation of the new sport."

Little is known about the "boxing-like activities" in fourteenth-century England that Allen references. Organized fights began to appear circa 1550. They were, in Allen's words, "rag-tag affairs put on to entertain the meanest sort in society. By 1600," he continues, "separate rules existed that not only gave the new sport form but also allowed it to be recognized as different from wrestling and understood so by the public."

This crude boxing was something more than a fistfight. It was a fistfight governed by the concept of fair play and rules.

"Without rules," Allen explains, "sport would not be sport." In that regard, his thoughts on the boxing ring are instructive. "The ring," Allen writes, "was a spontaneous circle made by individual members of the crowd grabbing hands to create an open space in which the men could fight. The ring was a vital and essential feature of boxing [because] the ring creates order."

The first written notice of a boxing match that Allen has found dates to December 31, 1681, and appeared in a publication called *The Protestant Mercury*. It reports that, the previous day, the second Duke of Albemarle had matched his footman against a butcher and that the butcher "won the prize."

The following year, the Duke was reported to have entertained King Charles II with another boxing match.

Technique and rules evolved thereafter.

"By the early 1700s," Allen states, "boxing had been adopted by all levels of English society. Boxing was displacing the rapier and the duel of honor and was becoming the classical British method of settling quarrels. And boxing had also become an established method of British entertainment."

Allen has conducted an exhaustive amount of research. His work is 150 pages long followed by 6 appendices, 39 pages of notes, and a 14-page bibliography. But a word of caution is in order. I don't have the tools to evaluate the accuracy of Allen's scholarship with regard to England during the years 1300 through 1700 or the credibility of his theories. But some of his assertions seem a bit implausible to me.

Allen states, "The rules of boxing were a powerful force for civilizing society." Were they? Or was it the other way around?

He writes, "Gambling made random play into sport. It converted disorganized local games into the organized national sports that we recognize today. Boxing, cricket, and horse-racing all owe their form and popularity to the control gambling imposed on their rules."

I think that's an overstatement. And moving to modern times, Allen states that Pete Rose was "sent to jail and permanently banned from baseball for gambling on games while he was a player and manager."

No! Pete Rose was banned from baseball for betting on games. But that had nothing to do with his imprisonment. He was imprisoned a year later after pleading guilty to two charges of filing false tax returns that failed to report income from the sale of autographs and sports memorabilia. If Allen misstates that easily accessible fact, can readers fully trust him on more complex historical matters?

★★★

"More than anyone else," Kenneth Bridgham writes, "John Morrissey personified the links between sports, gambling, high finance, politics, and crime in nineteenth-century America."

That's the theme of Bridgham's new book—*The Life and Crimes of John Morrissey*—published by Win by KO Publications.

Morrissey was born in Ireland in 1831 and, as a young boy, came to the United States with his parents. He was a thug and a drunk who made his mark as a bareknuckle prizefighter. Then he became a gaming house owner and was involved with Thoroughbred horseracing at the highest levels. He was, Bridgham writes, "the first true Irish mob boss in American history."

In 1866, backed by New York's corrupt and powerful Tammany Hall political machine, Morrissey ran for Congress. His criminal record at the time included four indictments for assault with intent to kill and three for burglary. Despite his past transgressions, he was elected.

Morrissey was an ineffectual congressman, largely disinterested in and incapable of performing the job properly. After serving two terms, he had a falling out with his Tammany Hall backers and left the House of Representatives. He subsequently served for three years in the New York State legislature after being elected as an anti–Tammany Hall candidate.

He died in 1878 and was inducted into the International Boxing Hall of Fame in the "pioneer" category in 1996.

Bridgham recounts Morrissey's transformation from violent thug to mob boss to a millionaire businessman who "doubtless attained a significant portion of his wealth through means that were illegal." The book is thoroughly researched and gives readers a feel for the squalid underside of life in New York as well as bareknuckle prizefighting in the mid-nineteenth century.

But as Bridgham acknowledges, many of the nineteenth-century tales regarding Morrissey's life are allegorical. Thus, it's sometimes difficult to distinguish fact from fiction. And Bridgham's writing style is a bit heavy.

Despite the book's entertaining storyline, *The Life and Crimes of John Morrissey* reads slowly at times and never quite catches fire. Still, it's an interesting window onto a bygone era.

★★★

Ike Ibeabuchi (who styled himself as "The President") came from afar. Born in Nigeria, he moved to the United States to pursue a career in professional boxing and compiled a 20–0 (15 KOs) ring record between 1994 and 1999. His two signature victories were a 1997 decision over David Tua in an enthralling nonstop slugfest and a fifth-round demolition of Chris Byrd in 1999. Tua and Byrd were undefeated when Ibeabuchi fought them. He was the best heavyweight to ever come out of Africa. One can only speculate what might have happened had he fought Lennox Lewis, Mike Tyson, and Evander Holyfield.

Luke G. Williams recounts Ibeabuchi's life to date in *President of Pandemonium: The Mad World of Ike Ibeabuchi.*

Ibeabuchi had demons. He was mentally ill and violent outside the ring as well as in it.

Eric Bottjer, who served as a matchmaker for Cedric Kushner (Ibeabuchi's promoter), told Williams, "I've been around boxing long enough to realize that it's not a normal profession and a lot of boxers are not normal human beings. But Ike is the only fighter I've ever met who I would say was literally insane. I recall having a conversation with Cedric where I said I thought Ike was a dangerous human being who was capable of killing somebody."

Ron Scott Stevens, who also worked for Kushner, looked back on fight week for Ibeabuchi–Byrd and recalled, "The whole week, I was like, 'Please, let me stay away from this guy!' One day they asked me to bring up some lunch for him. I knocked on the door and couldn't wait to get the hell away. He was intimidating and frightening."

After meeting with Ibeabuchi prior to Ibeabuchi–Byrd, HBO blow-by-blow commentator Jim Lampley told his colleagues, "That man's crazy." But as Lampley acknowledged to Williams, "Everybody in the sport—whether you're Cedric Kushner, Lou DiBella, or Curtis Cokes [Ibeabuchi's trainer]—has the dream to get hold of somebody who might have some conceivable shot at becoming the heavyweight champion. If you can get that championship, it takes your life to the next level. Ibeabuchi was a dream commodity for everyone involved with him."

Thus, the enablers. But eventually Ibeabuchi's conduct went beyond anything that could be enabled.

On August 26, 1997 (less than three months after beating Tua), Ibeabuchi was arrested and charged with aggravated kidnapping and attempted murder. As recounted by Williams, "Ibeabuchi drove his car straight into a concrete pillar on the embankment of a bridge on Interstate 35. With him in the vehicle was the fifteen-year-old son of his estranged girlfriend. Ibeabuchi emerged miraculously unhurt, but his teenage passenger had a broken pelvis, ankle, and jaw, as well as a diagnosis that he might never walk properly again. The authorities assumed initially that it was an accident. After interviewing the teenage boy involved, however, prosecutors became convinced that Ibeabuchi caused the crash on purpose. The boy alleged that Ibeabuchi had initially told him they were "going on a journey." But after leaving Dallas County he decided he no longer wanted to be in the car. When he tried to get out, he said, Ibeabuchi struck him in the face. Ike then continued driving before he smashed the car straight into the concrete pillar.

Eventually, the charges were plea-bargained down. Ibeabuchi pled guilty to false imprisonment and was sentenced to 120 days in jail. "The main issue of the case," District Attorney Ken Anderson said, "was whether or not he was trying to injure the young man. Our final conclusion was that he was severely depressed and was trying to commit suicide."

There was more to come. In December 1998, Ibeabuchi was arrested in Las Vegas on a charge of sexual assault involving a prostitute. But the Clark County District Attorney's office felt there was a lack of evidence and chose to not pursue the matter.

That was followed by a more serious incident at the Mirage in Las Vegas in July 1999. Again, Ibeabuchi sought out a prostitute. Then, according to court papers, he "forcibly detained, battered, and digitally penetrated both the vagina and anus" of the victim. When police arrived at his hotel room, Ibeabuchi barricaded himself in the bathroom after which the police shot pepper spray under the door to force him out. Several weeks later, while in custody, he assaulted a corrections officer.

Ibeabuchi was released on $750,000 bail but arrested again—this time in Arizona—when two female escort-service workers alleged that he had sexually assaulted them and held them against their will. After things were sorted out, he was found mentally competent to stand trial in Nevada and entered into a plea deal that led to a sentence of five to thirty years in prison. Ibeabuchi was also convicted of sexual assault and sexual abuse in Arizona. Eventually, he was paroled in Nevada and taken into custody by US Immigration and Customs Enforcement (ICE) because of his status as a Nigerian national. Next, after being released by ICE, he was taken into custody in Arizona for violation of parole. He was released from prison in Arizona on September 23, 2020, but transferred once again to immigration custody. His future status is unclear.

Ibeabuchi is now forty-eight years old and hasn't boxed professionally for more than twenty-two years. But in today's sordid world, despite his demons, it's possible that he will fight again.

Williams is an accomplished writer. Previously, he authored *Richmond Unchained*—a superb book that recounts the life of Bill Richmond, who rose to prominence, first as a fighter in Georgian England and then as the trainer of Tom Molineaux. Given Williams's credentials, *President of Pandemonium* is a bit of a disappointment. It doesn't have the depth or texture of *Richmond Unchained* and reads more like a long magazine article than the type of scholarly work that he's capable of researching and writing. That said, it's the most comprehensive look at Ike Ibeabuchi that boxing fans are likely to find.

★★★

(Low)life by Charles Farrell (Hamilcar Publications) is described by its author as "a memoir of jazz, fight-fixing, and the mob." Among other things, Farrell (who was a fringe player in boxing in various capacities over the years) writes that he's happy to have fixed fights and wishes he'd done more of it.

Reading *(Low)life*, I couldn't escape the feeling that a lot of what I was reading was embellished if not outright fantasy. But one thing rang true to me:

"You can't be a part-time boxer," Farrell states. "And you can't be in the boxing business part-time. If you box and you're not in the gym every day doing the many things necessary to keep yourself sharp, you will lose and you will almost surely get badly hurt. If you are in the boxing business and are not in the gyms and on the phone and, nowadays, online all day, every day, you will get left behind, lose all your money, and almost surely get badly hurt. The commitment to box or to be in the boxing business precludes doing anything else. When I made my living in boxing, I worked fourteen-to-sixteen-hour days. I'd sleep for four hours a night, still ready to take any calls that came in during those hours. When I got out of boxing, I was instantly left behind. I still watch a lot of boxing. But there are people—even people who don't earn their living at it—who are much more up on what goes on in the sport than I'll ever again be."

★★★

Shot at a Brothel: The Spectacular Demise of Oscar "Ringo" Bonavena by Patrick O'Connor is the sixth book to be published as part of the Hamilcar Noir True Crime Library.

Bonavena was a big, strong, crude heavyweight from Argentina who compiled a 58–9–1 (44 KOs) ring record in the 1960s and '70s but lost the fights that mattered most. Those losses included two defeats by decision against Joe Frazier and a fifteenth-round stoppage at the hands of Muhammad Ali (the only time that Bonavena was knocked out). He was shot to death at the Mustang Ranch (a brothel near Reno) in the early morning hours of May 22, 1976.

The primary villain in O'Connor's telling is Joe Conforte. Conforte had ties to organized crime, was deeply involved in prostitution, and benefited from an intricate web of alliances with state and local officials. "I'm not saying that I bribe officials or anything like that," Conforte explained. "I don't bribe officials. But it doesn't hurt to be on good terms with them."

The shotgun blast that killed Bonavena was triggered by Willard Ross Brymer, who pled no contest to a charge of involuntary manslaughter. The prosecution recommended that he be given a ten-year prison sentence. The judge saw things differently and imposed a two-year term. Brymer was paroled after serving less than eighteen months.

Shot at a Brothel is a workmanlike effort that moves along at a linear pace. The players never really come to life, and the story is told without the drama that one might expect from such a lurid set of facts. Also, there are too many factual errors. For example, O'Connor writes that Muhammad Ali was "largely bankrolled by the Nation of Islam." In reality, the converse was true.

Still, *Shot at a Brothel* offers two footnotes tied to the culture of the 1960s that are worthy of mention.

First, Bonavena's nickname was Ringo—traditionally a name of Japanese origin that means "apple." Ringo Starr (aka Richard Starkey) of the Beatles was given the name because of the number of rings he wore. Bonavena was referenced as Ringo because of his shaggy Beatles-like hair.

And second, Bonavena was not shy about voicing his opinion when Greek shipping magnate Aristotle Onassis (one of the richest men in the world) married Jacqueline Kennedy (President Kennedy's widow). Jacqueline Kennedy was seen by many as the ultimate trophy wife. Bonavena saw things differently and declared, "I don't understand Onassis. He got so much money. Why he got old girl?"

★★★

Championship Rounds, Round 2 is the second collection of articles by Bernard Fernandez to be published in book form. Taken as a whole, the pieces form a tapestry of boxing—a metaphor that came to mind when I read Fernandez's observation that "classic slugfests are just prettier swatches in the patchwork quilt that is the entirety of any boxer's career."

One theme that repeats throughout the book is the sad saga of fighters who fight too long. There's a particularly poignant article written after the death of Matthew Saad Muhammad. First, Fernandez pays tribute to Saad as a fighter in terms of his thrilling ring style and ability to absorb blow after blow and come back from the brink of defeat to win.

"There are fighters," Fernandez writes, "whose claim to fame owed more to indomitable will than to extraordinary skill. The blunt-force trauma guys come forward relentlessly, taking punishment to dish out punishment, their most memorable bouts recalled as bloody wars of attrition that bespeak the beauty that can be found even in the fiercest, most primeval of boxing battles. Matthew Saad Muhammad was such an acclaimed warrior, wearing down opponents in two-way action classics that left a deep impression on anyone who saw him dig inside himself to find, time and again, some last ounce of courage which marked the difference between victory and defeat."

Then Fernandez recounts Saad's financial ruin and the gut-wrenching decision the former fighter made in 2010 to walk into a homeless shelter in Philadelphia.

"I was putting my people up in hotels," Saad recalled. "Buying them cars. I would be nice to other people, help other people out, give to other people. Never once did I think, 'Who's going to take care of me when I'm broke?' Stupid me. I was in a state of shock. I thought to myself, 'Am I really going to go into this shelter?' But I had to go somewhere. My money had run out, bills piling up. I went into the shelter because I hoped it could help me make a change."

At times, Fernandez looks to others for insight; for example, when quoting Teddy Atlas on the two vastly different stages of George Foreman's long ring career.

"The old George Foreman," Atlas opined, "the reincarnated George Foreman that came back after a ten-year hiatus, was tougher than the young George Foreman. He was smarter in a lot of ways. He wasn't better physically, having gotten older and fatter. But he was better in the most important areas. He understood the difference between truth and lie. He bought into a lie in Zaire. He was a bigger, stronger guy than Ali, but Ali made him feel that that didn't matter. George couldn't make the decisions he needed to make. He couldn't endure what he needed to endure. He wasn't tough enough to handle the things that Ali represented that night. When his power didn't work, he didn't have anything else to back it up. George had to live with that for ten years. And living with it was a helluva lot harder than the punches he would have had to take for a few more rounds. So when he came back, he came back tougher. I think the older George Foreman would have beat the crap out of the younger George Foreman."

One thing I appreciate about Fernandez's writing is his creative approach to certain subjects. He didn't just write a review of *The Hurricane* (the 1999 feature film about Rubin "Hurricane" Carter starring Denzel Washington). He watched the film with former middleweight champion Joey Giardello, writing afterward, "The silver-haired senior citizen, unnoticed and unrecognized, settled into his seat for yesterday's 12:30 p.m. screening of *The Hurricane* at UA Riverview Plaza 17 on Columbus Boulevard. Giardello, disturbed by reports his December 14, 1964, title bout against Carter had been severely misrepresented in the film, agreed to accompany me and critique Hollywood's version of the bout which is crucial to the storyline. As depicted in the film, Carter's loss to Giardello not only was the biggest robbery since the Brink's job, it was tainted by the same sort of overt racism that kept landing Carter in prison on increasingly trumped-up charges."

But in truth, the decision favoring Giardello in Giardello–Carter was a fair one. After seeing the movie, Giardello told Fernandez, "For people to spread a pack of lies about me thirty-five years later? This is serious business."

Giardello sued the filmmakers and received a substantial sum in settlement. As part of that settlement, DVDs of the film sold later to the public included a voice-over by director Norman Jewison, acknowledging, "Going back over it, there's no doubt that Giardello won."

In another article, Fernandez writes about the deaths of three Nevada State Athletic Commission referees who died twenty-five years apart: Richard Green, forty-six, suicide by handgun on July 1, 1983 . . . Mitch Halpern, thirty-three, suicide by handgun on August 20, 2000 . . . Toby Gibson, sixty-nine, suicide by carbon monoxide poisoning on November 25, 2008.

And Fernandez addresses the folly of National Football League players who try their hand at boxing with the suggestion, "Try to imagine Mike Tyson or Joe Frazier holding end-of-the-bench roster spots with an NFL team."

There are interesting nuggets of information to be mined from *Championship Rounds, Round 2*. For example, I hadn't known that ring announcer Jimmy Lennon Jr. is a cousin of the Lennon Sisters, who became popular with a national television audience in the 1950s and '60s as a singing quartet on *The Lawrence Welk Show* and later starred in a TV variety show of their own, followed by a successful run in Las Vegas.

And Fernandez has a nice ear for quotes.

From Aaron Pryor: "I'm not bragging or anything, but I was a great fighter once. Not just good, great."

From assistant district attorney Carol Crawford, summing up for the jury at the end of the prosecution's case against Mike Tyson, who was convicted and sentenced to prison after a road-rage attack on two motorists in Maryland: "Imagine what you must feel to have an agitated Mike Tyson coming toward you."

And from Michael Jordan (quoted in a short section entitled "Other Sports" at the end of the book) on his decision to retire from basketball: "I have another life, and I know I have to get to it at some point in time." Then, in a classic reminder of the essence of sports, the man who was arguably the greatest basketball player of all time noted, "I've missed more than nine thousand shots in my career. I've lost almost three hundred games. Twenty-six times, I've been trusted to take the game-winning shot and missed. I've failed over and over and over again in my life. And that is why I succeed."

★★★

A Few More Rounds (Win by KO Publications) is a collection of essays separately written by Jerry Fitch and John J. Raspanti that view boxing through the prism of their own personal experiences. Portions of the book are likely to have more meaning to the authors than to readers. But there are some nice personal touches. Raspanti reflects on his father standing up for John's right to admire Muhammad Ali in an Oklahoma environment that ran counter to that sentiment. And Fitch crafts a moving portrait of heavyweight contender Jimmy Bivins with whom he interacted on several occasions.

Bivins, by the way, engaged in 112 professional fights. Fitch notes that only six of his opponents had a losing record at the time he fought them. And three of these bouts against sub-.500 fighters were contested during Bivins's first year as a pro. That's a staggering statistic.

A Few More Rounds contains interesting nuggets of information. Philomena Gianfrancisco (Tony Zale's second wife) played in the All-American Girl's Professional Baseball League with the Grand Rapid Chicks and Racine Belles from 1945 through 1948. Jean Terrell (Ernie Terrell's sister) replaced Diana Ross as lead singer for the Supremes when Ross left the group in 1970 to pursue a career as a solo artist.

There's also a quote from trainer Virgil Hunter that bears repeating: "I've had kids [with a great attitude] and I tell them what I can do for them. I can train them to be very exceptional at taking care of themselves on the street. As far as the ring is concerned, yes, they can compete. But they're not going to be a world champion. I can train them, and around their block they'll be a legend. But in the ring, it's always talent."

The most thought-provoking essay in the book is by Fitch and is entitled "Mixed Emotions." Fitch began watching boxing in the late 1950s and started writing about it in 1969. But he no longer follows the sport because of the brain damage that it inflicts on fighters.

"When I was defending boxing back in the day," Fitch writes, "I would point out the numerous injuries in other sports. Professional football has had so many players hurt via concussions from blows to the head. Soccer also has come under fire. In some cases leagues are now banning younger players from heading the ball. So other sports do cause injuries, but the focus in boxing of course is to hit your opponent as hard as possible in the head.

"When I watched fights as a young boy," Fitch continues, "I had no clue permanent damage was happening before my eyes. I was not aware of the life altering damage that more than likely was happening. Even when I first started covering boxing and sitting ringside, I never thought much about the negative part of the sport. It was exciting and I thoroughly enjoyed it. I don't ever want to appear as a hypocrite. I will not get on a soap box and call for a ban. I have no regrets that I was once very much involved in boxing. I have no regrets for loving boxing as much as I did. But I no longer can defend the sport. So these days I am strictly a boxing historian."

★★★

Joe Louis vs. Billy Conn by Ed Gruver (Lyons Press) is what its title says it is—a book about the June 18, 1941, heavyweight championship fight between Joe Louis and Billy Conn.

Conn was born and raised in Pittsburgh and grew up fighting. He liked to say that he started in alleys and worked his way up to the streets. He had his first pro fight at age sixteen, defeated five former world champions by age twenty, and was light-heavyweight champion of the world at twenty-one. In a twist of fate, when a heavyweight prospect named Joe Louis fought Hans Birkie in Pittsburgh in 1935, Conn (then seventeen years old) handled the spit bucket in Louis's corner.

Conn was twenty-three and Louis twenty-eight when they fought in 1941. The weight differential between them was enormous. The challenger weighed in at 169 pounds (announced as 174). Louis tipped the scales at 204. Many expected the bout to be a replay of the 1921 "million-dollar-gate" encounter between Jack Dempsey and Georges Carpentier in which the hard-punching heavyweight champion obliterated his charismatic but smaller foe.

But Conn matched up well against Louis in two areas. His footwork was superior and his hands were faster.

More significantly, perhaps, The Brown Bomber was slipping a bit. Fighters got old at a young age in those days. And Louis hadn't fought a top-level challenger since Max Schmeling in 1938, feasting instead on thirteen opponents referred to collectively by some sportswriters as the "bum of the month club."

Louis was a 17-to-5 betting favorite over Conn. The Polo Grounds in New York was jammed with 54,487 fans on fight night. They saw a great fight between two great fighters.

Scoring in New York in 1941 was on a round basis. Conn's footwork and handspeed were dazzling. After twelve rounds, he led 7–4–1 and 7–5 on two scorecards and was even on the third. In the twelfth stanza, he staggered Louis. In today's world, he would have been the new heavyweight champion. But championship fights in 1941 were fifteen rounds, not twelve.

Conn's version of what happened next was, "In the twelfth round, I staggered Louis. It made me feel good. I knew I had the title if I wanted to box for it. But I thought how great it would be to beat the unbeatable Louis at his own game. I went into the thirteenth with the idea of knocking Joe cold."

"Casting caution to the wind," Gruver writes, "Conn went all out for glory. Operating on a knife's edge, the Kid was extending a Homeric effort. If he succeeded, sportswriters would speak of his stunning victory in epic prose which would echo in eternity. There would be odes written in the Old World as well as in the new, paeans to Conn fighting with the passionate intensity of his Irish ancestors."

But, Gruver continues, "trading blows with Joe Louis proved to be a bridge too far." Louis froze Conn with a crushing right hand and, soon after, ended matters with thirteen unanswered blows.

Conn, Gruver recounts, "fell limply like a marionette whose strings had been cut" and struggled to regain his feet. But as the count reached ten, his gloves were still touching the canvas. The time of the stoppage was 2:58 of the thirteenth round.

Had Conn beaten the count, rounds fourteen and fifteen (if there was a fifteen) would likely have gone poorly for him. In all probability, Louis would have won by decision or knockout. Also, while much has been written about Conn going for the kill in round thirteen, Gruver acknowledges that, having fought twelve hard rounds, Conn might no longer have been physically able to maneuver out of harm's way.

The Joe Louis lode has been mined by numerous authors (most notably, David Margolick, Don McRae, Randy Roberts, and Chris Mead). Conn was the subject of an excellent biography by Andrew O'Toole. Gruver's work doesn't have the texture or depth of analysis that these books offer. And he glosses over the endless dysfunctional family struggles that plagued Conn throughout his life culminating in the boxer's sad decline into pugilistic dementia (which O'Toole covered particularly well).

There are also times when digressions interrupt Gruver's narrative flow. The end of round six of one of the most exciting fights in boxing history isn't the place to insert a three-page biography of Bill Corum (Don Dunphy's radio commentating partner that night).

That said, *Joe Louis vs. Billy Conn* is an entertaining read. Gruver brings his subject to life. The fight itself is dramatically told over the course of five chapters. And Conn (who clearly has a place in Gruver's heart) gets his due as a great fighter.

★★★

Clay Moyle is sixty-five years old and has written biographies of Sam Langford, Billy Miske, and Tony Zale. He has also collected boxing books for decades.

Moyle's initial goal was to own a biography of every gloved heavyweight champion. "During that initial pursuit," he recalled earlier this year, "I began to come across other boxing books that I thought might be interesting, so I purchased many of those as well. One thing led to another, and it wasn't long before my new objective somehow became to add every boxing book ever written in the English language to my personal collection."

Moyle acquired 4,500 different titles. The ones that tug most at his heartstrings are books with unique inscriptions. For example, his copy of *God, Gloves and Glory* (a 1956 autobiography by Henry Armstrong) has a lengthy inscription in Armstrong's handwriting that begins, "To the Greatest, Ray Robinson."

Brick-and-mortar bookstores, the internet, auction houses, and personal referrals all played a role in Moyle's collecting. He also bought numerous full collections, which led to his having 2,500 duplicates. "When I got serious about collecting boxing books," he says, "I became knowledgeable about their value. Then I realized I could fund my addiction at least in part by selling the duplicates."

Recently, Moyle and his family moved to a new home. In the process, he packed seven thousand books into 350 cartons. But the new home is short on bookshelves and storage space. Thus, with regret, he has decided to sell his collection.

Craig Hamilton (the foremost boxing memorabilia dealer in the United States) has amassed his own library of six thousand boxing books as a historian, dealer, and fan.

"I don't know of many people who have great boxing book collections," Hamilton says. "But Clay certainly has a very good one. It goes deep into the annals of boxing history and includes a lot of rare titles."

But Hamilton cautions, "It's a tough sell. Collectors are less interested in boxing books now than they used to be. You don't need them for reference because you can go online for information. They don't display like a fight poster or photograph. There are a lot of people who would like some of Clay's books but not all of them."

Moyle estimates that, over the years, he put $185,000 into his collection. In recent months, he has reached out to various collectors and auction houses, but they were only interested in buying the high-end items. A tentative deal with a $140,000 price tag that would have allowed him to keep 250 books of particular sentimental value to him was in place earlier this year but fell through.

"The idea of selling the books is gut-wrenching for me," Clay acknowledges. "I've devoted more than thirty years of my life to building this collection. There are titles that took me decades to find at a price I could afford. I've loved sitting in my library surrounded by these books. But it's time."

★★★

A non-boxing literary note. . . .

With fewer good fights to watch these days and no press conferences or other boxing-related events to attend, I've been reading more lately.

I love books. At last count, I had roughly 4,500 on floor-to-ceiling bookshelves in my apartment. It's a nice collection and a passageway to the wisdom of the ages.

Some of my books are valuable. There's a nine-volume set printed in 1802 that has all of William Shakespeare's plays. Each volume is 27 by 13 inches in size and illustrated with extraordinary engravings. The great majority of my books are of little monetary worth. But the collection as a whole has enormous sentimental value to me.

Several shelves in my library are devoted to young adult classics, many in editions published in the early twentieth century by Charles Scribner's Sons with illustrations by N.C. Wyeth. These books have a special feel. Their heavy paper, large type, exquisite art, and yellowing pages draw a reader back in time.

Recently, I took *Treasure Island* by Robert Louis Stevenson off the shelf and began to read.

Stevenson was born in Scotland in 1850. *Treasure Island* is his most famous work. It appeared in installments in a magazine called *Young Folks* in 1881 and 1882 and was published in book form one year later. "It was to be a story for boys," Stevenson later explained. "No need of psychology or fine writing."

Treasure Island shaped the image of pirates for generations of young readers. It's a wonderful page-turner and an easy read. There's a lot of drama with pitched battles, a map telling the location of buried treasure, and sayings that have become part of the vernacular ("Fifteen men on the dead man's chest. Yo-ho-ho and a bottle of rum.").

Jim Hawkins—in his mid-teens at the time the events in question occur—is the story's narrator. He's joined by characters like Dr. Livesey, John Trelawney, Captain Smollett, Ben Gunn, and—most memorably— Long John Silver.

Silver is the tale's primary antagonist and one of the most treacherous, manipulative, greedy, cunning, clever, opportunistic, deceitful, charismatic characters in young adult literature. Sort of like Don King.

Treasure Island carries with it the imprimatur of the ages and is a gateway to earlier times. Stevenson left the date of the adventure open, but indications are that the tale he recounts is set in the late 1700s. The book itself, though written in the early 1880s, was immensely popular with boys through the first half of the twentieth century.

I remember being seven or eight years old and my father reading *Treasure Island* to me—one chapter at a time—when he put me to bed at night. It was a way of linking his childhood to my own.

★★★

And one more non-boxing literary note. . . .

Recently, I was going though a cabinet and came across a letter that was written to me in 1958 when I was twelve years old. The correspondent was Howard Pease.

For the uninitiated (which includes almost everyone reading this column), Pease was born in Stockton, California, in 1894 and lived in San Francisco for most of his life. He served in the United States Army during World War I and shipped out on several occasions afterward as a crew member on freighters to gather material for books that he was writing.

Pease crafted adventure stories aimed primarily at boys age twelve and older. Many of his books were set on tramp steamers. His first published novel, *The Tattooed Man* (1926), introduced the character of Tod Moran, a young merchant mariner who, during the course of thirteen books, works his way up from boiler-room wiper to first mate. Pease also wrote seven non–Tod Moran novels and two children's stories. To make ends meet, he taught high school English and, later, was an elementary school principal. He died in 1974.

Pease wanted to show young readers what the real world was like. His books touched on themes like racism, drug addiction, and struggles between labor and management. In 1939, speaking at a gathering of four hundred librarians, he decried the children's literature then being published and declared, "We attempt to draw over their heads a beautiful curtain of silk. Let's catch up with our children, catch up with this world around us. Let's be leaders, not followers, and let's be leaders with courage."

Writers as diverse as E.L. Doctorow and Philip Roth cited Pease's books as influencing their childhood. Robert Lipsyte (a much-honored sports journalist who has written several award-winning novels for young adults) told me recently, "I loved Howard Pease. His books took you somewhere. You could travel with his characters. They were long books, but I tore through them. Reading them was a formative experience for me. When you write for young adults, you're also functioning as a teacher. And Pease did that. I wish we had more books like that now."

By age twelve, I'd read all of Pease's books with the exception of *Mystery on Telegraph Hill* (which wasn't published until 1961) and *The Gypsy Caravan* (which had been written in the early 1920s, published in 1930, and wasn't available in any of the local libraries where I foraged for books). This was before the internet and sites like AbeBooks.com. So I wrote to Pease in care of his publisher, asking where I could get a copy of *The Gypsy Caravan*. Several weeks later, an envelope addressed to me arrived in the mail with a return address that read, "Howard Pease, 1860 Ora Avenue, Livermore, California."

Inside, a neatly typed letter dated October 12, 1958, began, "Dear Tom Hauser, It was a pleasure indeed to get your letter. *The Gypsy Caravan* was my first book and is now out of print. I'm afraid you will not be able to find a copy anywhere. I've looked for some without any success. However, that book was aimed at younger readers than you."

Pease then recounted that *Thunderbolt House* was his favorite of the books he'd written, followed by *The Dark Adventure, Heart of Danger,* and *The Tattooed Man.* "My most successful book in sales," he added, "has been *The Jinx Ship,* a book I do not care for much." He closed with "Cordially yours," followed by "P.S. In 1946, I spent the summer not too far from your home on Bell Island near Rowayton, Connecticut. Enjoyed it a lot, too."

In today's world, I can go to AbeBooks.com and, with a few clicks, order a copy of *The Gypsy Caravan*.

Pease's books are more expensive now than most young adult literature from his era. He still has a following among older readers who fondly remember his tales from when they were young.

I have two books by Pease in my home library—*The Jinx Ship* (published in 1927) and *Shipwrecked* (1957). Last week, I decided to spend a night reading *The Jinx Ship*. My copy has "Discard Mt. Pleasant Library" stamped on the front and back end pages. My best guess is that I picked it up at a book sale decades ago.

Stylistically, Pease wrote in a way that was fit for grown-ups but also accessible to young adults. *The Jinx Ship* is 313 pages long and gives readers a feel for what it was like to be a crewman on a tramp streamer almost a century ago. The plot holds together reasonably well with twists that include gun-running, murder, and a voodoo ceremony on a Caribbean island. On the downside, there are demeaning racial stereotypes typical of the 1920s and the culture that Pease was writing about. The "N-word" appears frequently in dialogue.

After I finished reading *The Jinx Ship*, I reread Pease's letter. The paper has aged; the letter was written sixty-three years ago. But it's still in good condition.

"My most successful book in sales," Pease wrote, "has been *The Jinx Ship*, a book I do not care for much."

Why didn't he care for his most commercially successful novel? The romantic in me would like to think that, as an author who confronted racism in his later work, Pease came to have misgivings about that component of his earlier writing. I'll never know. I do know that getting his letter meant a lot to me when I was twelve years old. It still does.

In the National Football League, because of the threat of brain damage, a slap
to the face or facemask is punishable by a ten-yard penalty against the offense
or, if the perpetrator is on defense, five yards plus an automatic first down. And
in football, players are wearing helmets to protect themselves. Contrast that with
slap fighting, where the assailant winds up before hitting a stationary target in
the head as hard as he can.

Slap Fighting: A Bad Idea Whose Time Shouldn't Come

On October 18, 2022, the Nevada State Athletic Commission approved a proposal to categorize slap fighting as unarmed combat that will be allowed when conducted pursuant to rules and regulations promulgated by the State of Nevada and overseen by the commission.

UFC president Dana White, Fertitta Capital (an investment firm owned by former UFC owners Lorenzo and Frank Fertitta), Endeavor (which bought UFC in 2016), UFC chief business officer Hunter Campbell, TV producer Craig Piligan (*The Ultimate Fighter*), and Zeke Capital (a hedge fund) are the primary owners of an entity called Power Slap League, which will be the most obvious beneficiary of the ruling.

During the commission meeting, NSAC chairman Stephen Cloobeck said that a video prepared by Power Slap League personnel that he watched was "highly entertaining" and praised the involvement of "professionals who know what they're doing."

Now let's get real.

MMA writer Ben Fowlkes recently called slap fighting "a nascent sport crawling out of the primordial ooze" and "the dumbest sport imaginable."

"The concept of slap fighting," Fowlkes elaborated, "is about as simple as it gets. Two people stand across from each other and take turns hitting each other in the face with an open hand until, one way or another, someone has had enough. It might be the only combat sport where any form of defense is expressly, explicitly banned."

To repeat; there's no defense. Competitors are not allowed to keep their guard up or move their head. They wait for the blow. How hard they can hit and how much punishment they can take determine who wins. Whoever knocks his opponent out emerges victorious. It's brutal and it's dangerous.

Last year, a Polish slap fighter named Artur "Waluś" Walczak died from brain injuries after being knocked out in a slap fight in Wrocław.

So why is the Nevada State Athletic Commission working with the Fertittas, Dana White, and their brethren to enable this venture?

"We already know the answer," Fowlkes writes. "The answer is money. There's simply no way you can get me to believe that White and the Fertittas and the rest of the gang saw a Belarussian slap fighting competition on YouTube and said to each other, 'This is an important movement and, for the sake of our legacies, we need to be a part of it.'"

Appearing before the Nevada State Athletic Commission on October 18, Hunter Campbell testified that slap fighting intends to follow "an identical template for what we have with UFC events," and added, "We've spent the last year sort of beta-testing this in a controlled environment to really test and see sort of the dynamic of how this would function as an actual league and real sport. What we've found is that this is actually a skill sport; that the participants that are at a high level in this are skilled athletes. They train. They're in good shape. They take it seriously."

As reported by CombatSportsLaw.com, when asked about the NSAC's decision to legitimize slap fighting, Nevada deputy attorney general Joel Bekker (who works with the commission) responded, "I can assure you that licensed doctors with knowledge and experience working with unarmed combat athletes were consulted with to assure that Slap Fighting, like all other regulated unarmed combat sports in Nevada, is conducted as safely as possible with the ultimate goal being the health and safety of all participants."

This writer reached out to the Nevada Attorney General's Office and asked which doctors Bekker was referring to in his statement and which doctors, if any, testified before the NSAC regarding slap fighting. *The* Nevada State Attorney General's Office declined to answer the question other than to state that the doctor in question (apparently there was only one) "has been actively licensed in Nevada since the 1990s and worked for the NSAC in the past." That sounds like the résumé of a physician currently employed by UFC. Where are the independent medical observers?

One might also ask about the "beta-testing in a controlled environment" that Campbell says Power Slap League (or its proxies) conducted. How many times were defenseless combatants hit in the head as part of the testing process? How many of these combatants were concussed? What other injuries did they suffer? How much of the testing process was recorded on video? How much of this video was destroyed? Did the commission ask to see the rest of the video or only the carefully edited "entertaining" video that the commission chair referenced?

Bekker further advised, "Slap fighting competitors are mandated to wear protective gear during their bouts including a tooth/gum shield and cotton ear padding . . . The scoring target area deliberately excludes the eyes, nose, chin, neck, and temple areas of the head and face. Strikes outside that area are considered Fouls . . . All competitions will have 'Catchers' or 'Spotters' behind the defensive competitor to ensure that struck competitors do not hit the ground hard, especially their heads."

The cotton ear padding is supposed to help protect slap fighters against ruptured eardrums. Brain bleeds and the spectre of chronic traumatic encephalopathy are of greater concern.

I'm not an expert on slap fighting. But I've looked at the videos and I think it's awful. The cardinal rule in combat sports is to protect yourself at all times. In boxing or MMA, if a fighter can't defend himself or herself, the referee stops the fight. And the whole point of slap fighting is to hit someone in the head as hard as you can while he or she is not allowed to defend himself.

Dr. Nitin Sethi (a neurologist whose primary practice is affiliated with Weill Cornell Medicine) is chief medical officer for the New York State Athletic Commission. Putting slap fighting in perspective, Dr. Sethi states, "Concussions and acute traumatic brain injuries are common in combat sports. In boxing, every punch thrown at the head is thrown with the intention of winning by causing a knockout which is a concussive brain injury.

"Subdural hematoma," Dr. Sethi continues, "remains the most common cause of boxing-related mortality. Boxers, as you are painfully aware, have died in the ring or in the immediate aftermath of a bout. The ones who survive by undergoing a timely decompressive hemicraniectomy are left behind with devastating and lifelong neurological deficits. The far bigger burden and problem is that of chronic neurological injuries such as chronic traumatic encephalopathy. Unfortunately, this burden remains hidden and comes to medical attention long after the fighter has retired."

Turning to slap fighting, Dr. Sethi explains, "Open-handed slaps delivered with such force to the opponent's face frequently cause the person's legs to buckle, at times suffer momentary—sometimes longer—loss of consciousness, and collapse to the floor. These are all concussive injuries of varying duration. The 'athlete' who is on the receiving end of the slap has no option available to him to defend himself. These 'slaps' will add up. In my professional opinion, those who partake in this 'sport' will also suffer the stigmata of chronic neurological injuries."

Finally, Sethi adds, "I disagree with the argument that better medical supervision of this 'sport' shall make it safer. I am not sure what a physician is meant to supervise here other than being the overseer of concussive injuries occurring under his or her watch."

Dr. Michael Schwartz (the driving force behind creating the Association of Ringside Physicians) is equally pointed in his criticism.

"We've spent so many years trying to educate commissions and fighters about brain damage," Dr. Schwartz says. "And now you have this. These guys get hit in the head. You're inflicting a concussion without allowing the combatant to in any way protect himself. And then he gets hit in the head again. Every concussion is brain damage. The first concussion is damaging. And with second impact syndrome, the second concussion can be life-threatening. It's insane."

Nevada State Athletic Commission executive director Jeff Mullen supported the decision to enable slap fighting. To justify this position, Mullen says, "This sport needs to be regulated. And if we don't regulate it, it will be taking place everywhere all over town without any kind of regulations, without any kind of safety standard. By regulating this, we can make sure that there's doctors there, ambulances there, that the fighters have physicals, they have eye exams, they have MRIs and MRAs. And if we don't regulate it, we're going to have people competing right off a bar stool and it's going to be a dangerous situation. I think, for the health and safety of our constituents, we have to do that."

That's nonsense.

Yes, slap fighting is easy to run as an outlaw sport. There's no ring, just two combatants standing or sitting at a table. They don't even need gloves. But if slap fighting goes mainstream, it will encourage more people—particularly young people—to emulate it. That will mean more slap fighting in casual settings such as school playgrounds and bars.

Maybe someone should seat the NSAC commissioners at a table. Let a 300-pound slap fighter whack each of them in the head. Then let's see if the commissioners want to reconsider their vote.

Meanwhile, don't call it "slap fighting." That cosmetizes the brutality. Call it what it is—"whack a defenseless person in the head as hard as you can to cause brain damage."

Ken Burns Explores Muhammad Ali

"I wanted to write about Muhammad Ali," Wilfrid Sheed told me years ago when we were discussing the text that Sheed had written for an elaborate coffee-table book. "He's one of those madonnas you want to paint at least once in your life."

Ali is also a subject that filmmakers want to make documentaries about. More documentaries have been fashioned about Ali than any other athlete ever.

There was a time when Ali was the most famous, most recognizable, most loved person on the planet. He was an important social and political figure in addition to being a great fighter. One day after Cassius Clay (as he was then known) beat Sonny Liston to claim the heavyweight crown, he met with reporters and told them, "I don't have to be what you want me to be. I'm free to be what I want to be and think what I want to think."

At a time when the heavyweight championship of the world was the most coveted title in sports, that lit a spark that grew into a raging fire. Commenting on the impact of Ali's refusal to accept induction into the United States Army at the height of the war in Vietnam, Islamic scholar Sherman Jackson observed, "You can't teach that kind of thing in lectures and books. That kind of thing has to be modeled."

Now Ken Burns—one of America's most honored filmmakers—has thrown his hat into the ring. Burns rose to prominence in 1990 when PBS aired his critically acclaimed eleven-hour documentary on the Civil War. Since then, he has tackled subjects as diverse as baseball, Mark Twain, World War II, the war in Vietnam, the Brooklyn Bridge, and jazz. In 2005, he explored the life and times of Jack Johnson in a three-and-a-half-hour documentary entitled *Unforgivable Blackness*. Now Burns has returned to the sweet science with *Muhammad Ali*—an eight-hour opus co-directed and written with Sarah Burns (his daughter), and David McMahon (her husband).

Muhammad Ali unfolds chronologically and is divided into four parts designated as "rounds"—a questionable designation since Ali was hardly a four-round fighter.

"Round One: The Greatest (1942–1964)" details Cassius Clay's upbringing in Louisville through his first fight against Sonny Liston with considerable exposition of Nation of Islam doctrine and the allure that it had for Clay.

"Round Two: What's My Name (1964–1970)" covers Ali at his peak as a fighter (Liston II through Ali–Folley with Ali–Quarry I tacked on). Also, Ali and the draft.

"Round Three: The Rivalry (1970–1974)" takes viewers from Ali–Bonavena, through Ali–Frazier I and II up to an introduction of Don King and the stirrings of Ali–Foreman.

"Round Four: The Spell Remains (1974–2016)" begins with "The Rumble in the Jungle" and lays out the remaining forty-two years of Ali's life.

In the interest of full disclosure, I should note that I was one of several people asked by the Corporation for Public Broadcasting in 2018 to review Burns's proposal for the documentary and answer a series of questions keyed to whether or not the CPB should fund it. Given the excellence of Burns's work, I began my evaluation with the thought, "It feels presumptuous to be critiquing a proposal by Ken Burns," and added, "I have no doubt that Ken Burns will do a masterful job in the areas that he covers. His track record speaks for itself. Muhammad Ali is important. And Mr. Burns's proposal, coupled with his reputation for excellence as a filmmaker, promise a comprehensive entertaining look at his subject."

The finished documentary bears out that promise. It's thorough and nicely put together. Burns lays out both the positive aspects and also the ugly underside of the Nation of Islam without sugarcoating the principles that Ali espoused at a time in his life when he adhered to the teachings of Elijah Muhammad. The glorious and ultimately tragic arc of Ali's ring career is well told. The cruelties that he visited on Joe Frazier outside the ring and Ali's profligate womanizing are honestly addressed. The archival footage and still photos are excellent.

Some of the talking heads are exceptionally good. Former WBO heavyweight beltholder Michael Bentt is particularly insightful in describing Ali's ring technique. Professor and media commentator Todd Boyd is a welcome voice. Speaking about Ali's taunting of Joe Frazier, Boyd declares, "Ali is making the sort of jokes that racist white people would make. I feel like, in that instance, he used his powers for evil as opposed to using them for good." Khalilah Ali (Muhammad's second wife) and two of his daughters, Rasheda and Hana, provide valuable personal insights. Veronica Porche (Muhammad's third wife) is a particularly welcome inclusion. And Burns gives ample time to three wise men who covered Ali for much of his journey—journalists Robert Lipsyte, Jerry Izenberg, and Dave Kindred.

Kindred is the most lyrical of the three. Recalling Ali–Frazier III, he states, "They turned each other into monsters. That's boxing at its cruelest. That's what the game is. And they were at their best cruelest that night." Later, commenting on Ali's horribly debilitated physical condition, Kindred observes, "The game that we asked him to play to entertain us has left him looking like this."

On the minus side, the documentary is too long. It's eight hours drag in places. Some of the material (e.g., the extensive film footage from Ali's amateur career and some of his professional fights) could have been shortened with no loss in quality.

More significantly, Burns offers no new interpretations of Ali.

In responding to the Corporation for Public Broadcasting questionnaire, I advanced the thought, "There has been an endless stream of Ali documentaries over the past half century. More are currently in production. For maximum impact and to make a maximum contribution to history, it's not enough for Mr. Burns to do what has been done before better than it has been previously done. He has to break new ground."

How could he break new ground?

"I hope," my response continued, "that Mr. Burns devotes some time to the final twenty years of Ali's life in a more than superficial way. These decades cry out for interpretation. What did Ali mean to the world over these years? Was his legacy corrupted by the calculated filing away of rough edges from his persona and the 'sanitization' of his image by CKX, ABG [two companies that owned commercial rights to Ali's name, likeness, and image], and others for economic gain? Is there still an Ali message that resonates? In memory, can Ali be a force for positive change?

Is there a way to harness the extraordinary outpouring of love that was seen around the world when Ali died?"

"Round Four" of the documentary could have addressed these issues. But it didn't. The last thirty-five years of Ali's life (everything after the end of his ring career) are compressed into twenty-five minutes. And much of this time is devoted to Ali lighting the cauldron at the 1996 Atlanta Olympics.

The 1996 Olympics were an important marker in the public's embrace of Ali. But they were also the point at which corporate America rediscovered Muhammad and the sanitization of his image for economic gain began. This was evident in everything from subsequent advertising campaigns to the 2001 feature film starring Will Smith. Burns's documentary doesn't sanitize Ali. But it doesn't talk about the sanitization either. And that sanitization was a corrosive force.

Decades ago, Alex Haley (who fashioned *The Autobiography of Malcolm X* with its subject) told me, "I think it's important for future generations to know who Muhammad Ali was. So if I were to talk to a young boy about Ali today—a young boy who wasn't alive in the 1960s, who didn't live through Vietnam, someone for whom Ali is history—I'd talk to that boy about principles and pride. I'd say, 'If you really want to know about people and history in the times before you were born, you owe it to yourself to go back, not read books so much, but to go to a library where you'll have access to daily papers and read about this man, every single day for years. That might give you some understanding of who Muhammad Ali was and what he meant to his people.'"

Every single day. Day after day. For years.

Muhammad Ali's spirit is inside all of us. At its best, Ken Burns's film reminds us of how charismatic, charming, electrifying, wise, foolish, generous, loving, cruel, kind, complex, simple, and great Ali could be.

Boxing's cinematic tradition rivals its literary one.

Movie Notes

Body and Soul is on the short list of the greatest boxing movies of all time. It's a wonderful film, worthy of the accolades it has received over the years. John Garfield was the driving force behind it.

Jacob Garfinkle was born in 1913 to Russian Jewish immigrants who lived on the Lower East Side of Manhattan. His mother died when he was seven, and he grew up being cared for by a succession of relatives in Brooklyn, Queens, and the Bronx. A poor student and chronic truant, he joined gangs in whatever neighborhood he lived in. A bout with scarlet fever when he was a boy caused permanent damage to his heart.

Garfinkle became interested in acting as an adolescent, began his career as an actor in live theater, and in 1938 signed a film contract with Warner Brothers (which insisted he change his name to the less ethnic-sounding John Garfield). As Bernard Weinraub wrote in the *New York Times*, "He was one of the first dark-haired, working-class, ethnic outsiders to turn into a Hollywood star. His chip-on-the-shoulder style and his rugged looks often cast him as a social outsider on the screen: a boxer, a gangster, a soldier. The persona affected actors from the 1950s onward."

Garfield is often cited as a predecessor of Method actors like Marlon Brando, James Dean, and Robert De Niro. Many of his films, such as *Gentleman's Agreement* and *The Postman Always Rings Twice*, are widely regarded as classics. Subpoenaed in 1951 to testify before the United States House of Representatives Committee on Un-American Activities that was investigating "communism in Hollywood," he refused to "name names." That refusal damaged his film career.

It should also be noted that Garfield turned down the male lead in the 1947 Broadway production of *A Streetcar Named Desire*, after which the role went to Brando. More tragically, the role of Terry Malloy in *On the Waterfront* was earmarked for Garfield but he died before production began. Again, Brando stepped into the void.

Unlike most actors, Garfield could actually fight a bit. Growing up, he was often in street fights, sparred at a gym on Jerome Avenue in the

Bronx, and, according to several biographical profiles, reached the semi-finals of a New York City Golden Gloves tournament. That brings us to *Body and Soul*.

In 1947, Garfield chose not to renew his contract with Warner Brothers and instead founded an independent production company with producer John Roberts. *Body and Soul* was their first film together. Initially, it was planned as a biopic of former world champion Barney Ross. But when Ross's heroin addiction (a consequence of being treated with morphine for wounds suffered in World War II) became public knowledge, a Ross biopic became commercially unviable and a new script was written by Abraham Polonsky.

Body and Soul is a dramatic exploration of the corrupt underside of boxing. Garfield plays middleweight fighter Charley Davis. Lilli Palmer is cast as Peg (Charley's love interest), while Hazel Brooks is Alice (the conniving other woman). Anne Revere is effective as Charley's mother. There are two particularly loathsome characters—Quinn (a small-time promoter played by Robert Conrad) and Roberts (a mob boss played by Lloyd Gough).

Normally, as per the custom of the time, a white actor would have been cast in the role of Ben Chaplin (the champion who Charley dethrones early in the narrative). But Garfield insisted that the role go to Canada Lee (a forty-year-old Black actor who had fought professionally and compiled a 39–35–10 record before retiring in 1933).

Body and Soul piles double-crosses on top of double-crosses. At one point, Charley (who has reluctantly agreed to throw a fight) tells Roberts, "I still think I could knock that Marlowe on his ear in two rounds."

"Maybe you could, Charley," the mob boss answers. "But the smart money is against it. And you're smart. . . . You gotta be businesslike, Charley. And businessmen have to keep their agreements."

Later, when things get more antagonistic between them, Charley asks Roberts rhetorically, "What are you gonna do? Kill me? Everybody dies."

Body and Soul was criticized in some circles as a "socialist morality drama" that branded the pursuit of money by the powers that be as corrupting society to the detriment of working-class men and women. It also led to increased government scrutiny of Garfield.

Garfield and his wife had three children. His daughter Julie is the only one alive today. Julie followed in her father's footsteps as an actor, appearing onstage with luminaries like Zero Mostel and George C. Scott. She also won a *Variety* Drama Critics Award for her performance as Sonya in the 1971 production of Chekhov's *Uncle Vanya* at the Roundabout Theatre in New York.

"*Body and Soul* is my favorite of the movies my father made," Julie says, "because of the character transformation that Charley undergoes and because the message of the film is so much in keeping with my father's real-life beliefs. It's about learning how to live in this world and be successful without selling out."

Julie was six when her father died.

"There's an incident my mother told me about years later," she recalls. "I was too young to understand it at the time. Canada Lee was dying, and my father drove up to Harlem to visit him. They had become friends. And the FBI trailed my father the entire way. When my father got out of his car in Harlem, the FBI agents got out of their car to see where he was going. He confronted them and said something like, 'What's wrong with you? My friend is dying. Can't I visit him one last time without this?'"

Canada Lee died on May 7, 1952.

Two weeks later, at age thirty-nine, Garfield died from a sudden heart attack. "No actor can be really good until he's reached forty," he had once said.

More than ten thousand mourners lined the streets on the day of Garfield's funeral. It was the largest crowd at a celebrity funeral in New York since Rudolph Valentino's death in 1926.

★★★

In 2003, I was at a fundraising dinner for Ring 8 (an organization that provides financial assistance for former boxers). Jake LaMotta was the scheduled guest of honor. He didn't show.

"Jake wanted to be paid five hundred dollars," Tony Mazzarella, (the guiding force behind Ring 8) explained. "I told him that none of the other fighters had asked for money so why should he be paid? Jake's not a nice guy," Mazzarella added.

That night, I was sitting at the same table as Norma Graziano. She was there to accept an honor on behalf of her late husband.

Rocky Graziano (named Thomas Rocco Barbella at birth) was born on January 1, 1919. He grew up on the Lower East Side of Manhattan and was incarcerated several times before being drafted into the United States Army in 1942. While in the service, he punched an officer, went absent without leave, and served ten months in military prison before being dishonorably discharged.

In ten years as a fighter, Graziano compiled a 67–10–6 record with 52 KOs and 3 KOs by. He was a ferocious puncher best known for three bloody wars with Tony Zale that were contested for the middleweight championship of the world. Rocky won the second of those encounters on a sixth-round knockout at Chicago Stadium on July 16, 1946. He died in 1990.

Norma Graziano was getting on in years when we met at the Ring 8 dinner. As the evening passed, she looked from time to time at an over-head television monitor that was showing black-and-white films of old fights, including Rocky in combat against Tony Zale.

"I can't bear to watch this," Norma said. "I hate to see Rocky get hit. In the beginning, I used to sit at ringside but then it got too hard for me to watch. There were times when I felt like jumping into the ring to help him."

Norma was told that LaMotta might be at the dinner.

"I hope not,' she responded. "Rocky and Jake were from the same era. We all came from the Lower East Side. Jake was a great fighter. Rocky and me, we both respected Jake as a fighter. But I don't like the man."

LaMotta became an iconic figure with the release of *Raging Bull*—the 1980 Academy Award–winning film based on his autobiography. But Graziano beat him to the punch. Rocky's autobiography—*Somebody Up There Likes Me*—was published in 1955 (fifteen years earlier than Jake's) and served as the basis for the 1956 feature film starring Paul Newman.

There have been many biopics about boxers. *Gentleman Jim* (1942), starring Errol Flynn as James Corbett, was one of the first. But *Gentleman Jim* was more fantasy than reality. By contrast, *Raging Bull* was a highly charged, dramatic re-creation of LaMotta's life that bore the imprint of truth. *Somebody Up There Likes Me* was a bridge between the two.

James Dean had been slated to play Graziano. But he was killed in a car crash shortly before filming began, so an aspiring young actor named Paul Newman stepped into the role. Robert Wise (who later won Academy Awards for *West Side Story* and *The Sound of Music*) was the director. Norma was played by Pier Angeli, who had previously enjoyed a romantic relationship with Dean and been engaged to Kirk Douglas before marrying singer Vic Damone.

Somebody Up There Likes Me starts off as trite, but the drama builds over time. When Graziano steps into the ring to face Zale in their second encounter (the climactic scene in the movie), it's hard to not root for Rocky.

The young Paul Newman had a physicality about him, much like Marlon Brando as Terry Malloy in *On the Waterfront*. There was nothing suave in his portrayal of Graziano.

The best lines in the film are reserved for Rocky and Norma. In a particularly good scene, Norma asks Rocky, "What do you do to feel important?"

"You wanna know?" Rocky answers. "Come and see me fight sometime. That's what makes me feel important. I mean, you gotta be there. You got to hear them crowds screamin'. They're screamin' my name. And they're screamin' for me to kill off the other guy. They grab at me when I go up the aisle. That's what makes me feel important."

"I never liked the boxing world," Norma told me over dinner. "But to think that Paul Newman played Rocky...."

★★★

On February 25, 1964, Cassius Marcellus Clay Jr. defeated Charles "Sonny" Liston in Miami Beach over the course of six remarkable rounds to claim the heavyweight championship of the world. Late that night, the new champion found himself in a room at Hampton House (a Black hotel in segregated Miami) with Malcolm X, several other followers of Nation of Islam leader Elijah Muhammad, and football great Jim Brown. Soul singer Sam Cooke (a friend of Clay's) had been at the fight, but there's no historical record of his being in the hotel room with the others that night.

One Night in Miami is built around imagining what transpired in that room among Malcolm X, Cassius Clay, Jim Brown, and Sam Cooke.

Directed by Regina King from a screenplay by Kemp Powers, it's available on Amazon Prime.

The film fits into the genre known as historical fiction. Dramatic license was taken. At times, it's allegorical rather than an accurate factual recounting.

The larger issue is whether the film is impressionistically honest. The answer is "yes."

One Night in Miami begins with the 1963 fight between Clay and Henry Cooper in London. It then segues to Cooke being treated rudely by an all-white audience at the Copacabana, followed by Jim Brown (the greatest running back in National Football League history) being reminded by a patronizing Southern gentleman that he's just a "nigger." Next, we see Malcolm as the Nation of Islam's most charismatic spokesman, after which the scene shifts to Liston–Clay I.

Thirty-four minutes into the film, the drama moves to Hampton House.

Malcolm X, Cassius Clay, Jim Brown, and Sam Cooke were prominent in different ways. Each was young, Black, and famous. But Malcolm was a social and religious figure of considerable intellect while the other three were known as entertainers.

The dialogue between the four men is light at first and then turns serious.

Malcolm is played by Kingsley Ben-Adir. On what should have been one of the greatest nights of his life, his world is slipping away. His deadly rupture with Elijah Muhammad is almost complete. Soon, Clay will abandon him. Ben-Adir comes across as a bit weaker and more tentative than one might expect, although Malcolm's intellect is evident in his performance.

It's hard to imagine anyone playing Cassius Clay well except the young Muhammad Ali. But Eli Goree bears a resemblance to Clay and is pretty good in the role.

Jim Brown was an intimidating physical presence. Aldis Hodge lacks this physicality but his performance is solid.

Leslie Odom Jr., who plays Sam Cooke, has star quality. He's the only one of the four major actors who has the charisma and presence of

THOMAS HAUSER

the man he's portraying. But as a result, Cooke has a stronger on-screen persona than Malcolm. That's a problem as tensions between the two men boil over.

Toward the end of the film, Malcolm reveals that he intends to leave the Nation of Islam because of differences with Elijah Muhammad and will found a new organization. ,

"Who's gonna be in this new organization?" Clay asks.

"I think lots of people will follow me over," Malcolm answers. "Especially if you come with me."

Clay, of course, didn't follow Malcolm. He sided with Elijah Muhammad. One year later, he and Jim Brown were the only participants from the hotel room gathering as portrayed in the film who were still alive. Sam Cooke was shot to death in a California motel on December 11, 1964. On February 21, 1965, Malcolm was assassinated at the Audubon Ballroom in Harlem.

One Night in Miami cautions us that our icons are flesh-and-blood human beings with strengths and flaws. In its best moments, the film is a powerful reminder that the issues of self-respect, Black empowerment, and racial equality are timeless.

★★★

Over the years, several feature films about boxing have been entitled *Knockout*. Recently, I watched the 1941 film of that name.

The plot is typical for its era. Middleweight contender Johnny Rocket (played by Arthur Kennedy) decides to quit boxing and begin a new life with his soon-to-be bride, Angela Grinnelli (Olympe Bradna). Johnny's plan is to become an instructor at a gym and eventually open up a health spa of his own. But his unscrupulous manager, Harry Trego (Anthony Quinn), doesn't want to lose the money that Johnny generates. So he arranges to have Johnny fired from his new job and makes it impossible for him to find employment elsewhere. With Angela now pregnant, Johnny is desperate for money and returns to the ring. Back in action, he catches the eye of socialite Gloria Van Ness (Virginia Field), whose father owns a major newspaper and has assigned his daughter to write about boxing as a lark.

"Maybe I'll write a story about you one of these days," Gloria tells Johnny.

"Well, maybe I'll give you an interview one of these days," Johnny counters.

Eventually, a love rectangle develops. The evil Gloria seduces Johnny as her boy toy. Angela, who still loves Johnny, leaves him because of his philandering and is pursued by the gentlemanly Tom Rossi (Cornel Wilde), who has a crush on her.

Meanwhile, Johnny gets greedier and more insufferable with each ring victory. Finally, he decides to manage himself, at which point Trego arranges for a "chemically prepared mouthpiece" to do Johnny in. Incapacitated as a consequence of being drugged, Johnny is knocked out. Worse, because of his poor performance, he's accused of taking a dive and barred from fighting by the state athletic commission. At that point, Gloria Van Ness loses interest in him.

Thereafter, Johnny fights under assumed names in small arenas across the country, getting knocked out for short money. Eventually, he suffers a brain bleed and is told that his fighting career is over.

"I guess I've been a fool," Johnny tells Angela after she pays his hospital bill despite their being separated.

But Tom Rossi (remember him?) isn't about to abandon his pursuit of Angela. He confronts Johnny and tells him, "I've thought about it a lot. And I figured, if you ever came back, we'd better have it out. You had your chance with Angela and you threw it away. You haven't any right to ask for another. All you've ever given her is a lot of grief and tears. She trusted you and believed in you, and you let her down. The one decent thing you can do now is get out of her life completely so she can have a little happiness. The only feeling she has left for you is pity."

Johnny decides that Tom is right and takes one more fight, knowing that doctors have told him that one more punch could kill him. Angela finds out about it, rushes to the arena, and throws a towel into the ring to stop the fight as Johnny is being brutalized. Johnny and Angela are happily reunited, and he takes a job working at a camp for children.

If that all sounds corny, well, it is.

The fight scenes in *Knockout* are cartoonish. The actors who portray the fighters don't look like fighters. And their boxing technique makes

Logan Paul look like Andre Ward. The film is mindless entertainment. But there are times when it's fun.

★★★

Budd Schulberg is well known to boxing fans for his 1954 Academy Award–winning screenplay *On the Waterfront* and the immortal words spoken by Marlon Brando as Terry Malloy: "I coulda been a contender." Two years later, *The Harder They Fall* (Schulberg's novel about corruption in boxing) was released as a feature film.

RKO bought film rights to *The Harder They Fall* before the book was published in 1947. It planned to cast Robert Mitchum and Joseph Cotten in the lead roles but that never came to pass. Columbia Pictures acquired rights to the property in 1955. One year later, it released *The Harder They Fall* with Humphrey Bogart and Rod Steiger in the pivotal roles. Viewed through the prism of time, the film remains one of the best ever about the seamy underside of boxing.

Bogart plays Eddie Willis, an aging sportswriter in need of a job. Steiger is Nick Benko, a mobbed-up promoter who hires Eddie to oversee a publicity campaign to build interest in Toro Moreno—a giant of a man and a thoroughly inept fighter from Argentina who Benko is navigating toward a title shot through a series of fixed fights.

How inept is Moreno? After seeing him spar for the first time, Willis observes, "A powder-puff punch and a glass jaw. That's a great combination." But as Eddie tells his wife (played by Jan Sterling), "A newspaper job only pays a living. I want a bank account."

When Eddie's longtime friend, sportswriter Art Leavitt (Harold J. Stone), questions him about his involvement with Benko, Eddie responds, "You never played ball with promoters who bought advertising in your newspapers? You did it because you were a nobody. You were afraid you'd lose your job. Now you're a big man. You don't have to lie to hold your job. Well, I do. You think I took this job because I like it?"

Two former heavyweight champions have key roles in the film. Jersey Joe Walcott plays the mononymous George, a trainer who works with some of Benko's fighters. Max Baer is cast in the role of heavyweight champion Buddy Brannen, who Moreno fights in the film's climactic battle.

Moreno is played by Mike Lane—a six-foot, eight-inch, 275-pound professional wrestler who was making his film debut and, in later years, carved out a respectable career as an actor in feature films and television. Moreno isn't supposed to be able to fight. So the fact that Lane looks clumsy and amateurish in fight scenes isn't a problem.

At the close of the movie, Moreno goes into the ring to face Brannen and meet his destiny. His self-delusions have been destroyed. For most of the film, Eddie has wrestled with his conscience and won. Now he's redeeming himself and, as part of that process, tells Toro the truth: "You're not even a tenth-rate fighter. You're what they call a bum. Any saloon fighter could wipe the floor with you."

Eddie and George urge Moreno to use his reach to fight Brannen at a distance and stay down when the inevitable happens and he's knocked to the canvas. But Toro doesn't stay down. Despite being brutalized, he gets up again and again and absorbs a horrific beating before being counted out.

"Why did he take that beating?" Eddie asks George afterward. "Why didn't he fight like you told him to?"

"Some guys can sell out," George answers. "And other guys just can't."

After *The Harder They Fall* was released, former heavyweight champion Primo Carnera sued Columbia Pictures for $1.5 million, claiming that the character of Toro Moreno was based on him (which it was). The case was dismissed on grounds that the film didn't violate Carnera's rights. Years later, Schulberg acknowledged in an interview with *Daily Variety* that Eddie Willis was based on journalist and press agent Harold Conrad.

Unlike Carnera, Conrad was pleased with the film.

And a sad note . . . just prior to the start of filming, Bogart was diagnosed with esophageal cancer. He died on January 14, 1957. Eddie Willis was his final film role.

★★★

More on Max Baer, Primo Carnera, and the movies.

On November 10, 1933, Metro-Goldwyn-Mayer released *The Prizefighter and the Lady*. The plot is simple. Belle Mercer (played by Myrna Loy) is mobster Willie Ryan's woman and sings in his nightclub. She meets Steve Morgan (a bartender in a lesser establishment) when he helps her out after she has been involved in an automobile accident. They fall in love and marry after their first date. Steve (played by Baer) then segues seamlessly from fighting in bars to succeeding as a professional boxer. But he's a profligate womanizer and not at all discreet about it.

Belle leaves Steve and goes back to Willie, although she still loves Steve. Steve then dumps his loyal manager (played by Walter Huston) and eventually gets a title shot against heavyweight champion Primo Carnera (played by none other than Primo Carnera). Jack Dempsey does double duty under his own name as both the promoter and referee for the title fight. There's a nice moment when James Jeffries and Jess Willard in cameo roles are introduced in the ring just prior to the championship bout.

Carnera dominates the action in the early going and knocks Steve down seven times. Then Steve's former manager forces his way into the corner to give advice, and Belle (who has never stopped loving Steve) signals her affection from the crowd. This revitalizes Steve, who proceeds to score seven knockdowns of his own. The fight ends in a draw, after which Steve and Belle are reunited.

Steve is so obnoxious at times that viewers could be forgiven for rooting for Carnera.

The Prizefighter and the Lady was marketed as a mix of romance, drama, and comedy. The promotional campaign proclaimed, "He was a champion in the making—and always on the make. Women have a new heart thrill coming to them. Men, a new idol." The plot is superficial. None of the characters has depth with the possible exception of Willie Ryan (played by Otto Kruger). And the film engages in cheap body-shaming for laughs when the blow-by-blow radio commentator tells listeners prior to the climactic fight that, among the celebrities at ringside, singer Kate Smith is "sitting in seats one, two, and three."

The movie marked the film debut for both Baer and Carnera. Carnera was the real heavyweight champion at the time. Initially, he balked at any involvement with the project because the original screenplay called for Steve to win the climactic championship bout. To satisfy Carnera, the script was changed so the fight ended in a draw.

History sometimes imitates art—or comes close to it. In Baer's next real fight—at Yankee Stadium on June 14, 1934—he fought Carnera and knocked him out in the eleventh round to claim the heavyweight crown.

But he lost the title to James Braddock in his first defense and never fought for the heavyweight championship again.

Boxing trivia buffs will be interested to know that Baer wore his robe from *The Prizefighter and the Lady* with the name "Steve Morgan" emblazoned on the back for his two real championship fights against Carnera and Braddock.

★★★

Muhammad Ali and Malcolm X were two of the most charismatic and important people of the twentieth century. Five years ago, Randy Roberts and Johnny Smith co-authored *Blood Brothers: The Fatal Friendship between Muhammad Ali and Malcolm X*. In the authors' words, it was "the story of how Cassius Clay became Muhammad Ali and the central role Malcolm X played in his life. It is a tale of friendship and brotherhood, love and deep affection, deceit, betrayal, and violence during a troubled time."

Blood Brothers is the most thorough and compelling book written to date on the relationship between these two men. Subsequently, the book gave birth to two film deals. A+E Studios purchased an option to develop it into an eight-part scripted dramatic series. That project may or may not come to fruition. Meanwhile, Netflix bought documentary rights to *Blood Brothers* and released its film in 2021.

The Netflix documentary charts the lives of Cassius Clay and Malcolm X as they intersect and then separate amidst bitterness, recrimination, and violence. Other than Clay's 1964 conquest of Sonny Liston, there's virtually no boxing in the narrative. As with the book, Malcolm's 1965 assassination is the dramatic highpoint of the film.

The documentary has several flaws. First, it repeats the long-discredited story that Cassius Clay threw his Olympic gold medal in the Ohio River after being refused service in a local restaurant. That tale was fabricated by ghostwriter Richard Durham (an editor for the Nation of Islam newspaper, *Muhammad Speaks)* and Herbert Muhammad (a son of Nation of Islam leader Elijah Muhammad) for inclusion in Ali's 1976 autobiography. It's not true; the filmmakers were told it's untrue, and its insertion in the documentary is unfortunate.

The much-needed positive message of self-love and Black empowerment that was central to Nation of Islam teachings is also explored in
the documentary. But more information on the underside of the Nation
of Islam would have been welcome. Yes, viewers are told that Elijah
Muhammad was the father of eight children by six different teenage
girls who were his private secretaries. But that was just one example of
hypocrisy within the Nation. There should have been more exposition.

That said, *Blood Brothers* sets a high standard for any documentary
about Muhammad Ali and Malcolm X that might follow. The archival
film footage and still photographs are superb. A succession of well-chosen
talking heads carry the narrative from beginning to end. Cassius Clay (and
then Muhammad Ali) is shown as he was from 1958 through 1965. His
spirit—and that of Malcolm—is faithfully portrayed. And that's important
because, as professor and media commentator Todd Boyd notes toward
the end of the film, "The Ali that has been presented to the public since
1996 [when he lit the cauldron at the Atlanta Olympics] is a false image.
They've managed to edit out those things that made Muhammad Ali
controversial in another era."

So true. Indeed, when Ali's image was sanitized for economic gain
after the Atlanta Olympics, metaphorically it brought him back to 1960
when twelve wealthy white men known as the Louisville Sponsoring
Group helped launch his ring career and groomed him as a commodity
as they might have groomed a race horse.

Years ago, Ali told me, "When Malcolm broke with Elijah, I stayed
with Elijah. I believed that Malcolm was wrong and Elijah was God's
Messenger. I was in Miami, training, when I heard Malcolm had been
shot to death. Some brother came to my apartment and told me what
happened. It was a pity and a disgrace he died like that because what
Malcolm saw was right. And after he left us, we went his way anyway."

That thought is echoed in *Blood Brothers* by Hana Ali, who recounts
a conversation in 2003 when her father told her that, in Hana's words,
"turning his back on Malcolm was one of his greatest regrets. He wished
he could go back and tell Malcolm that he was sorry and that he loved
him and he was his friend and that he was right about so many things."

Believers might choose to think that Ali has now had that conversation with Malcolm in Paradise.

Fred Levin: An Appreciation (1937–2021)

Fred Levin, the Pensacola attorney who, with his brother Stanley, guided Roy Jones through the glory years of Jones's ring career, died on January 12, 2021, of complications from COVID-19. He was eighty-three years old.

Levin, like Jones, was born and raised in Pensacola. After graduating from the University of Florida School of Law in 1961, he began a legal career that saw him become one of the most successful personal injury trial lawyers in the country. His blunt talk and aggressive style of litigating ruffled some feathers. But during his career, he was on the receiving end of thirty jury verdicts in excess of $1 million and six in excess of $10 million.

Levin's most significant courtroom triumph came after he successfully lobbied Florida governor Reuben Askew (a close friend and former law partner) and the Florida Legislature to revise the state's Medicaid Third-Party Recovery Act. The revision allowed the state to sue the tobacco industry to recoup money expended for the cost of treating smoking-related illnesses. The litigation that followed was Dickensian in length as the tobacco industry used every legal tactic at its command.

Many of Levin's law partners had opposed the idea of the firm serving as plaintiffs' counsel in the case because of the huge outlay in staff and out-of-pocket expenses that would be required to properly litigate the matter. To allay these concerns, Levin agreed to significantly diminish his financial draw for the duration of the litigation. But if the plaintiffs prevailed, he would receive the lion's share of any attorneys' fees that were awarded. Ultimately, the tobacco industry settled the case for $13 billion. The court-approved legal fee was $300 million.

At that point, Levin became a philanthropist. He made tens of millions of dollars in charitable contributions to educational and medical causes. The most notable of these came in 1998 when he donated $10 million to the University of Florida School of Law, the second largest cash donation ever received by a public law school as of that time. One year later, the name of the school was officially changed to the University of Florida Fredric G. Levin College of Law.

Levin's entry into boxing came about largely by chance. In the mid-1980s, his brother Stanley (also a partner in the firm) was on the board of directors of the Pensacola Boys Club where Roy Jones Sr. was teaching youngsters to box. Roy Jr. was one of the adolescents in the program. Then the Boys Club decided to eliminate its boxing program for financial reasons.

"It was only a matter of a couple of hundred dollars," Stanley later reminisced. "So I took the money out of my pocket and gave it to them. That's how I met Roy."

Roy Jr. was thirteen years old at the time. Later, during a period when he and his father were estranged, Roy lived in Stanley's house for a year. When he turned pro after the 1988 Seoul Olympics, the Levins agreed to manage him.

Stanley's primary expertise was in tax law. Like Fred, he had no background in the business of boxing. Initially, there was widespread criticism of the brothers in boxing circles. Boxing writer Michael Katz labeled them "Tweedledumb and Tweedledumber."

But the Levins were undeterred. They formed a corporation called Square Ring to manage Jones's affairs and keep him free of long-term contractual entanglements with the sport's more unsavory promoters. They also negotiated what was then the most lucrative non-heavyweight contract in the history of boxing for Jones with HBO.

"Stanley and Fred were quick to learn and understand the arcane business of boxing," former Time Warner Sports president Seth Abraham (the architect of HBO's boxing program) recalls. "I was always impressed by their openness and candor to acknowledge what they did not know or understand. No boxing question embarrassed them. Once learned, they did not forget the lesson. They represented Roy professionally and with great commitment. They were honest, straightforward, and prepared. Not a motto you find for most boxing buccaneers."

In 1995, the Levins were jointly honored by the Boxing Writers Association of America as "Managers of the Year." Sadly, there came a time when Jones (to his financial detriment) chose to disregard their advice and no longer sought their counsel.

Fred was also a forceful advocate for tolerance and understanding among people of difference races, religions, and ethnic backgrounds. I saw that firsthand in 1997 after Muhammad Ali and I co-authored a short book entitled *Healing* that spoke to the need for those qualities.

Muhammad, his wife Lonnie, and I had visited schools throughout the country with the help of HBO, the Boston Globe Foundation, and Turner Broadcasting. At each stop, we addressed students about the need for tolerance and understanding and gave the students copies of *Healing*. Then I got a telephone call from Fred.

"I like what you and Muhammad are trying to do," Fred told me. "I'd love to put together an event for you in Pensacola."

Fred's idea of putting together an event wasn't opening up a high school auditorium. He rented the entire Pensacola Civic Center at his own expense and arranged for buses to transport 7,600 students to the assembly from high schools throughout Escambia County.

There was opposition in some quarters. Several Christian fundamentalists threatened legal action to halt the assembly, claiming that our appearance was a plot between a Muslim and a Jew to teach heresy to their children. To deal with this objection, the school board decided that a parental consent form would be required for students to attend the assembly. Then, inexorably, the community came together in support of our visit. Florida governor Lawton Chiles attended the event and praised its purpose. I later learned that the son of one of the most vocal opponents of the assembly forged a parental signature on his consent form so he could attend.

The last years of Fred's life were difficult, as they are for many people. His wife Marilyn, who he'd met when they were undergraduates at the University of Florida, died of cancer in 2011 after fifty-one years of marriage. In 2016, Fred was operated on for stage 4 lung cancer that had metastasized to his brain. COVID-19 brought an end to his life. But his legacy lives on.

How generous was Fred? His brother Stanley told me a story once that answers that question.

Stanley (who died in 2009) was having health issues that made it increasingly difficult for him to work. Each day was a struggle. One day, Fred asked him, "How much money would you need in the bank to feel that you and your family were financially comfortable for the rest of your life?"

Stanley said he'd think about it. He went home and evaluated his financial situation. Several days later, he gave Fred a number in the high seven figures. Fred took out his checkbook and, with the stroke of a pen, made his brother financially secure for life.

In 2019, speaking of his philanthropy, Fred Levin said, "If you've been fortunate enough to take care of your family and you've got money over and above that, give it now while you're living. Don't hold it. Instead of waiting to die, give it to different charities. Give it while you're living, name it in honor of loved ones, and get the enjoyment of the gift."

He made a difference.

The ritual ten-count was heard again in 2021 and 2022.

In Memoriam

Hank Aaron, one of the greatest players in baseball history, died on January 22, 2021, at age eighty-six.

Aaron is best known for breaking Babe Ruth's mark of 714 career home runs. He finished his sojourn through baseball with 755 homers, a record that stood until 2007 when it was eclipsed by Barry Bonds. He still holds the MLB career records for most RBIs, most total bases, and most extra base hits, while ranking third on the list for most hits and most games played and fourth in runs scored. He was a thoughtful, gracious man who inspired a generation.

Decades ago, I was conducting research for the book that would become *Muhammad Ali: His Life and Times.* As part of this process, I interviewed many great athletes. Some, like Jim Brown, had played an important role in Ali's life. Others had interacted with Muhammad in a less significant manner. The people I spoke with included sports legends like Bill Russell, Kareem Abdul-Jabbar, Wilt Chamberlain, Ted Williams, and Mickey Mantle. On September 5, 1989, I was privileged to talk with Aaron.

Aaron had broken Babe Ruth's record in 1974, the year that Ali dethroned George Foreman to reclaim the heavyweight championship of the world. The thoughts that Aaron shared with me—one great athlete talking about another—follow:

"I was born in Mobile, Alabama, in 1934. I came up with the Braves when I was twenty. And coming from Mobile, I was very shy. I wasn't satisfied with the way things were, but I felt like I had to do something special in baseball in order to get people to listen to me. By the time Ali came along, things were a little different but not that much. My first awareness of him was when he won the gold medal. And I saw greatness stamped all over him. How great, I didn't know. But I was impressed by his ability and his confidence.

"Being a gifted athlete, being one of the best in the world at what you do, is a great feeling. But sometimes it's kind of eerie because you wonder why you're blessed with so much ability. I'd go up to the plate to face a pitcher and I'd know that, before the night was over, I was going to hit one out of the ballpark. I felt that, and I'm sure Ali felt the same way. That no matter who he got in the ring with, he was better and he'd figure them out. He had all kinds of confidence. And I was the same way. The only thing that scared me was, when I was approaching Babe Ruth's record, I got a lot of threatening letters. I'm sure Ali went through the same thing with letters from people who didn't want him to be heavy-weight champion. Most of that stuff is nothing but cranks. But one of them might be for real, and you never know which one.

"I don't think there'll ever be another fighter like Muhammad Ali. I'm not putting anybody else down. Maybe someone could have beaten Ali in his prime, but I'm not concerned about that. There's just no one who could possibly be as beautiful in the ring as he was. For a guy to be that big and move the way he did; it was like music, poetry, no question about it. And for what he did outside the ring, Ali will always be remembered. When you start talking about sports, when you start talking about history; you can't do it unless you mention Ali. Children in this country should be taught forever how he stood by his convictions and lived his life. He's someone that Black people, white people, people all across the country whatever their color, can be proud of. I know, I'm glad I had the opportunity to live in his time and bear witness to what he accomplished. God gave Ali the gift, and Ali used it right."

I remember very clearly reading to Ali what Hank Aaron had said about him. And Muhammad responded, "Hank Aaron said that about me? I'm honored."

★★★

Leon Spinks enjoyed two moments of adulation and glory in his tumultu-ous life. In 1976, he won a gold medal in the light-heavyweight division at the Montreal Olympics. Two years later, he upset a long-past-his-prime Muhammad Ali to claim the heavyweight championship of the world.

Things went south from there. Plagued by lifestyle issues, mocked by the media and fans alike, Spinks was defeated in his rematch against Ali, lost 17 pro fights, and was knocked out 9 times. Some of the knockouts were inflicted by world-class opponents like Larry Holmes and Dwight Muhammad Qawi. Others were suffered at the hands of fighters like Rocky Sekorski and Angelo Musone.

John Schulian put matters in perspective after Leon's 1978 upset of Ali. Addressing the chorus of disapproval regarding Leon's antics, Schulian wrote, "You might as well get used to the fact that Leon Spinks is Leon Spinks."

Or as Larry Holmes famously said, "Outside the ring, Leon don't hurt nobody but himself."

Leon died on February 5, 2021. The immediate cause was complications from prostate cancer that had spread throughout his body. But physically and cognitively, he had been in decline for years. He was sixty-seven years old.

I interviewed Spinks for the first time in 1989 when I was conducting research for *Muhammad Ali: His Life and Times*. Leon was working in a bar, doing odds-and-ends chores, and drinking more than he should.

"Sometimes what I think about is how my life changed, being champion," Leon told me. "It wasn't right, the way people treated me. I was fighting to get ahead. All I wanted was to make a living, and the world wanted me to be like Ali. I couldn't do what I used to do because everything I did got blown out of proportion. I couldn't be like I wanted to be. Not getting respect didn't matter to me. I don't mind people making fun of me. People always make fun of me. If they don't do it to my face, they're gonna do it behind me. But when I was champion, no one would leave me alone. That's what really bothered me. Everyone wanted me to give them something or do something or act a certain way. And I couldn't do it. I'm Leon Spinks; I'm not Ali. And then, when I lost, people still didn't leave me alone. Even now, they don't let me be."

Then I asked Spinks about Ali's physical condition and whether he felt sorry for Ali.

"What for should I feel sorry for Ali?" Leon answered. " Don't you hear what I been saying? The man's still living. The man's still eating. He's making money. There's a roof over his head. And best of all, whatever happens, he'll always be Muhammad Ali."

Baseball players want to win the World Series. Football players want to win the Super Bowl. Leon Spinks beat Muhammad Ali to claim the heavyweight championship of the world. His place in history is secure. He wasn't a great fighter. But at his best, he was a good one.

★★★

Brian London, who plied his trade a generation before Lennox Lewis destroyed the narrative of "horizontal English heavyweights," died on June 23, 2021, at age eighty-seven.

London was born in West Hartlepool. He turned pro in 1955 and won his first 12 fights, 11 of them by knockout. Then he fought a twenty-one-year-old prospect named Henry Cooper and was knocked out in the first round.

London had trouble against world-class opponents throughout his career. He fought Cooper three times and lost each time. He was knocked out by Nino Valdes, Eddie Machen, Ingemar Johansson, and Joe Bugner, and came up short twice against Jerry Quarry. On a more positive note, he held the British and Commonwealth heavyweight titles for seven months by virtue of a 1958 stoppage of Joe Erskine. He ended his career in 1970 with a 37–20–1 (26 KOs, 11 KOs by) ring ledger.

London's place in boxing history is secure as a consequence of two championship fights. On May 12, 1959, he challenged Floyd Patterson for the heavyweight crown and was knocked out in the eleventh round. More memorably, on August 6, 1966, he fought Muhammad Ali at Earls Court Arena in London.

Ali, age twenty-four, was nearing his peak as a fighter and in the midst of an eight-month span that saw him defend his heavyweight title five times, culminating in a November 14, 1966, demolition of Cleveland Williams. London never had a chance. Ali dropped him with twelve unanswered punches fired within three seconds to end matters in the third round.

Years later, in an ITV Sport documentary, London said of that fight, "I was smaller, fatter, and couldn't punch. He stopped me in three rounds and that was it. I don't think I hit him."

London's passing rekindles two personal memories for me. The first dates to 1989. I was taping an interview with an aging Howard Cosell as part of my research for *Muhammad Ali: His Life and Times*. We were in Cosell's apartment on East Sixty-Ninth Street in Manhattan. Howard was tired, asked to take a short break, and lay down on the sofa. Twenty-five minutes later, still lying down, he began to reminisce—or I should say, sing.

I turned my tape recorder back on:
A foggy day in London town,
Had me low, had me down
I viewed the morning with much alarm
The British museum had lost its charm.

Cosell had transported himself back in time to an August 1966 encounter with Brian London. A somewhat disjointed stream of consciousness followed:

> Flying up to Blackpool. London not there at his training camp. Going to London's home. We flew out of Gatwick in the ABC News plane. His wife, a big-titted woman with a great body. "Where's Brian?" "He's playing squash." Off we go to Whitney Air Force Base. This is the base where they shot *Twelve O'Clock High*. Remember that movie? One of the great motion pictures of World War II. Gregory Peck. Gary Merrill. The son of a bitch [London] was playing squash. And he was a better squash player than he was a fighter. I'll tell you that. Believe me. So they bring London over, and I say to him, "Everybody says you don't have a chance, that you're no fighter at all." He says, "I'm gonna kill you." I say, "It's not me saying it. It's the goddamn newspaper people." He says, "I'll kill those sons of bitches."

My second vivid memory involving Brian London dates to 1991. I was at a dinner in Manchester honoring Ali that was attended by a dozen former British champions. Brian and I were seated next to each other at the dais. When it was his turn to speak, he walked to the podium and began reading remarks that someone else had prepared for him. Clearly, the remarks weren't to his liking. Brian got as far as "Muhammad Ali brought us all a lot of pleasure." Then he stopped reading and proclaimed, "What a load of bollocks. I got no pleasure at all from him. He beat the living daylights out of me."

Maybe so. But later that evening, Brian told me, "If you're a fighter, you want to fight for the heavyweight championship of the world. I did it twice. No one can ever take that away from me."

★★★

Steve Lott died on November 6, 2021, at age seventy-one. Most boxing fans didn't know him. But he played a unique role in the history of the sweet science.

For years, Steve worked with Bill Cayton and Jim Jacobs, helping them build Big Fights Inc. He had an encyclopedic knowledge of their massive fight film library and the history that was embodied in it.

Steve was also Bill and Jim's point person in dealing with fighters, most notably Mike Tyson. He shared an apartment with Mike for several years and was in his corner during the years when Tyson was at his best as a boxer. He was devoted to Mike, in and out of the ring, and never stopped caring about him.

There was one quality that was particularly appealing about Steve. He was extraordinarily generous with his time and knowledge. Time and again over the years, I'd call him with questions about a particular fighter or fight. It could be something as simple as whether or not a film of a given fight existed. If it did, Steve would know about it. And as often as not, a VHS tape of the fight arrived unsolicited in the mail several days later.

Steve loved boxing. He was loyal to his friends and a good person.

★★★

I'd be remiss if I didn't acknowledge the passing of Jeff Wald who died on November 12, 2021, at age seventy-seven.

Wald was a show business manager, then a producer, and later in life, a boxing promoter. The Hollywood Reporter described him as "short, barrel-chested with a gravelly Bronx-accented voice, hot-tempered and prone to fisticuffs."

How hot-tempered?

"In 1980," The Hollywood Reporter recounted, "Wald was arrested after brandishing a shotgun in front of picketing hotel employees in Tahoe.

Wald acknowledges that he thrust the gun into a picketer's mouth. He got 18 months probation and paid a $1,000 fine."

Julia Phillips, in her best-selling memoir *You'll Never Eat Lunch in This Town Again,* wrote, "Wald is always ripping someone a new asshole or tearing off someone's head to shit in his neck."

Over the years, Wald attracted numerous high-profile clients. Sylvester Stallone, Roseanne Barr, Elliott Gould, Marvin Gaye, Donna Summer, Miles Davis, and David Crosby were on his list. He also managed Helen Reddy, which is a story unto itself.

Wald married Reddy in 1966. Four years later, he secured a recording contract for her with Capitol Records. That led to fourteen top-ten hits and four #1 singles, foremost among them the iconic song, "I Am Woman."

"I Am Woman," which Reddy wrote with Ray Burton and sang solo, became a worldwide feminist anthem. Her marriage to Wald ended in 1983 when he was in the throes of a serious cocaine addiction.

"There have been many moments of blinding truth in my life," Reddy wrote in a 2006 memoir. "One was during the dying days of my marriage. Despite all the denials, it was obvious to me that my husband still had a cocaine problem. He had been treated before for his addiction, but his behavior indicated that he was still using—as did his pillow which, by morning, had blood spots, bone fragments, and gristle from his nose embedded in it."

After overdosing in 1986, Wald underwent treatment at the Betty Ford Center in California and was clean for the rest of his life.

What does all of this have to do with boxing?

Wald was a huge boxing fan. In 1997, he and Irving Azoff partnered to promote the final two fights of George Foreman's ring career. More significantly, Wald was the driving force behind *The Contender*—the "reality TV" boxing series that he created with Mark Burnett, Jeffrey Katzenberg, and Sylvester Stallone.

That's where my life intersected with Wald's.

In 2004 and 2005, I wrote a series of articles about *The Contender.* The articles began on an optimistic note. But their tone changed as *The Contender* moved away from what makes boxing great and—with the suicide of boxer Najai Turpin—into scandal.

Wald was displeased with the articles. To put it mildly. At one point, he tried to throw me out of a press conference, only to be overruled by Sugar Ray Leonard (who was involved then with *The Contender*). Not long after that, I was chatting with attorney Pat English at a fight in Las Vegas when Wald approached, stood in front of me, and bellowed, "I want to tell you something. Everyone knows that you and Lou DiBella fuck each other up the ass in hotel rooms."

I assume that Wald was also at odds with DiBella at the time.

And that's how things stood between us until, one afternoon, the telephone rang. To my surprise, it was Wald.

I'd written a series of articles about the decline of HBO's boxing franchise, identifying what I understood the problems to be and suggesting how they might be fixed.

"I've been reading your articles about HBO," Wald told me. "You're right about everything you're saying."

We talked for a while about HBO and boxing in general. Then. . . .

"You know," Wald said. "The reason I was so mad at you for what you wrote about *The Contender* is that a lot of what you wrote was true. I didn't like it, but it was true."

In later years, Wald and I talked on the phone from time to time. Most of our conversations centered on boxing. Jeff understood the sport and business well. On occasion, the conversations were personal.

Once, we were talking about Helen Reddy, and I asked Wald if he took pleasure in knowing that he'd played a crucial role in making "I Am Woman" a cultural touchstone in the women's rights movement.

"I suppose so," he answered. "But to tell you the truth, Helen was bat-shit crazy."

"She must have been," I countered. "She married you."

"Fair enough," Wald said.

The boxing community is incredibly diverse with a wide range of people in it. Jeff Wald was part of that community. He loved boxing. He navigated his way through the business end of the sweet science for years. He was a boxing guy and proud of it.

★★★

Unless he was punching you, Earnie Shavers was easy to like. One of the most devastating punchers in boxing history, he was a charming man with a good sense of humor and a kind word for almost everyone he met.

Shavers was born in Alabama on August 31, 1944, and grew up in Ohio. He turned pro on November 6, 1969, and had 89 fights over the course of a twenty-six-year career, compiling a 74–14–1 record with 68 knockouts. He didn't have the greatest stamina or chin in the world, as evidenced by the seven "KOs by" on his ring ledger. But if Earnie caught you with a good shot before you caught him, you were likely to be gone.

Shavers fought five men who held a version of the heavyweight title at one time or another—Muhammad Ali, Larry Holmes (twice), Ken Norton, Jimmy Young (twice), and Jimmy Ellis. His record in those fights was 3–3–1. He's best known for losses in two of those bouts, his only two title challenges (against Ali and his second encounter with Holmes).

Ali–Shavers was contested at Madison Square Garden on September 29, 1977. Shavers was regarded as a particularly dangerous opponent because of his punching power. Fifty-two of his fifty-four wins at that time had come by knockout, twenty in the first round. "Earnie Shavers takes no prisoners" was the tagline attached to his career. And because Ali was at a point in his own career where he was getting hit a lot, the bout was viewed with trepidation by Ali partisans.

Ali–Shavers showcased Muhammad's drawing power. The bout was broadcast live on home television. Madison Square Garden still sold out. The telecast attracted seventy million viewers. NBC enjoyed a 54.4 rating and 77.0 share. That meant more than half of all the television sets in the United States and more than three-quarters of those in use that night were tuned to the fight.

"Ali nicknamed a lot of the fighters he fought," Shavers reminisced years later. "He called me 'The Acorn' because of my shaved head. Well, Ali found out that night that The Acorn is a hard nut to crack."

In round two, Shavers landed a vicious overhand right. Muhammad was hurt. "Next to Joe Frazier," he admitted afterward, "that was the hardest I ever got hit."

But Shavers had a history of tiring late in fights and was pacing himself for fifteen rounds. So rather than go for the kill, he moved methodically forward and Ali survived the stanza.

After twelve rounds, Muhammad was leading 8–4 in rounds on the two of the judges' scorecards and 8–3–1 on the third. But three rounds remained, and Shavers was coming on strong.

"The thirteenth round was Shavers' best to that point," Pat Putnam reported for *Sports Illustrated*. "The fourteenth was even better. Rocked by hard right hands, Ali survived, but the legs that had carried him through fifty-six professional fights were beginning to fail. At the end of the fourteenth round, the champion had to dip into his reserve of strength just to get back to his corner. Wearily he slumped on his stool, his eyes glazed by fatigue. When the bell for the fifteenth round rang, Ali could barely stand."

"People talk about Manila; they talk about Foreman; they talk about Liston," Putnam said years later. "But to me, the fifteenth round against Shavers was as magnificent as any round Ali ever fought. I don't know where he found the strength and stamina to go on. But he came out for the last round and fought three minutes as good as any three minutes I've ever seen. Late in the round, he even had Shavers in trouble. Only the ropes kept Shavers from going down."

"It was a good fight," Earnie told me when we talked about that night. "In the second round, I hit him with a right hand that hurt him. He wobbled, and then he wobbled some more. But Ali was so good at conning, I thought he was playing possum with me. I didn't realize how bad off he was. Later, when I watched the tape, I saw it. But at the time, I was fooled. And he beat me. When the fight was over, I thought I'd won. But looking at the tape over and over, it was close but I can see how the judges voted for him. I don't think there's a fighter in his right mind that wouldn't admire Ali. We all dreamed about being just half the fighter that Ali was."

Holmes–Shavers II is the other fight that Shavers will always be remembered for.

Earnie landed a lot of devastating punches during his ring career. First-round knockouts of Jimmy Ellis and Ken Norton stand testament to that. But on September 28, 1979, with fifty seconds left in round seven, he landed what he later called the hardest punch he ever threw flush on Holmes's jaw.

Holmes went down like he'd been shot. Somehow, he managed to stagger to his feet and survive the final forty seconds of the round. In round eleven, he knocked Shavers out.

"First, you get up," Larry said later. "Then you worry about whether or not you're all right."

Several years ago, I asked Holmes to compare Shavers and Deontay Wilder in terms of punching power.

"I've never been hit by Wilder," Larry responded. "I've only seen him on television. But can't imagine anyone hitting harder than Earnie Shavers."

Shavers had a sharp wit. Describing the experience of sitting next to Don King on a flight from Paris to New York, he noted, "Don is the only man I know who can talk nonstop over an entire ocean."

Recounting the scene in his dressing room after he was knocked out by Jerry Quarry, Earnie recalled, "I was all alone. Even my shadow was hiding."

Speaking of extramarital affairs, he observed, "When you marry your mistress, you create a vacancy."

Through it all, he was a gracious man.

"Fighting Ali was hard for me to do because he was such a good man," Shavers told me. "He was my idol. Before we fought, he'd helped me out several times; letting me use his training camp for free, giving me advice on what to do against other fighters. I loved him personally, and you hate to see a legend defeated. But at the same time, I was fighting for my family and myself.

"I wanted to be champion of the world," Earnie continued. "And I came close twice—against Ali and against Larry Holmes. Winning those fights would have meant financial security for me. And beating Ali would have been extra special because, when you fought Ali, the whole world was watching. But God had different plans for me, and everything worked out just fine."

Earnie Shavers died on September 1, 2022, one day after his seventy-eighth birthday.

"He was a good man," Jerry Izenberg (the dean of American sportswriters) told me that night. "Write something nice about him."

*For Lloyd Price, 1980 marked a disturbing time in a lifelong friendship
with Muhammad Ali. "I was in Las Vegas for Ali–Holmes," Lloyd reminisced.
"And it sickened me. I couldn't handle it."*

Lloyd Price, Music, and Boxing
(1933–2021)

Music was the lifeblood of the youth culture when I was young. I came of age during the "Golden Age of Rock and Roll" and expanded my appreciation to other eras. I've been fortunate in that the profession I've chosen has enabled me to spend time with some of the icons of my youth. Muhammad Ali heads the list. But there have been many others, including some from the world of music.

Over the years, I've been privileged to meet Ella Fitzgerald, Harry Belafonte, Little Richard, Chubby Checker, Glen Campbell, Mary Travers, Ramsey Lewis, and others. I also spent time with Lloyd Price. Lloyd died in a long-term-care facility in suburban New York on May 3, 2021, at age eighty-eight. A word of remembrance is in order.

Price was born in Louisiana in 1933 and grew up in the segregated American South. He was one of the early pioneers of rock and roll at a time when major radio stations in the United States wouldn't play rock and roll by Black recording artists. Nat King Cole and Johnny Mathis were given airtime. But "race music" was forbidden. That gave rise to a phenomenon known as the "white cover" version. A Black artist like Little Richard would write and record a song like "Tutti Frutti" that received limited exposure. Then Pat Boone or another white singer would release a "socially acceptable" version that might sell a million copies.

In the mid-1950s, a white disk jockey in New York named Alan Freed began playing "race music." The time was right. The Civil Rights Movement was gathering steam. In February 1959, for the first time ever, a rock and roll song sung by a Black recording artist became the best-selling "pop 45" in the nation. The singer was Lloyd Price.

In 1952 at age nineteen, Price had written and recorded a song called "Lawdy Miss Clawdy." Elvis Presley sang the white "cover" version. In

1958, Price updated and recorded a song called "Stagger Lee" that dated back to 1911. "Stagger Lee" rocketed to #1 on the *Billboard* charts in the United States. One year later, Price wrote and recorded "Personality," which became an international hit.

What does this have to do with boxing?

Price had appeared in small clubs after the release of "Lawdy Miss Clawdy." As "Stagger Lee" rose to the top of the charts, he was booked into the Top Hat Lounge in Louisville, Kentucky. When he arrived at the club, a tall, good-looking teenager was waiting outside for him.

"I was on tour," Price told me years later. "Ali was sixteen years old, sitting outside because he was underage and they wouldn't let him in. When I got to the lounge, this crazy kid rushed over, saying, 'Mr. Price, I'm Cassius Marcellus Clay; I'm the Golden Gloves Champion of Louisville, Kentucky; someday I'm gonna be heavyweight champion of the world; I love your music; and I'm gonna be famous like you.' I just looked at him, and said, 'Kid, you're dreaming.' But we got along. You couldn't help but like him. The Top Hat Lounge was a popular place, and each time I played there, I saw him. After a while, I started looking for him and bringing him in with me. He had all sorts of questions—about music and traveling, but mostly he wanted to know about girls. There were a lot of things he didn't know, and he asked me how to make out with girls. He was very sincere about it. I told him, 'Just be yourself, and the girls will like you.' Although as part of the lesson, I gave him a couple of dollars and said, 'Always have some money. That's the beginning of hanging out with the foxes.'"

Thus began a lifelong friendship.

"You have to remember what America was like at that time," Price explained later. "In parts of the country, I'm being booked into white clubs. I'm being booked to do white dances. But I can't stay at the white hotel and I have to go around to the back door if I want a sandwich. I went to some [Nation of Islam] meetings with Ali. For the first time in my life—as a grown man who was a star who had sold millions of records—I heard somebody saying, 'You are somebody.' The language gave you such a lift. You left feeling good about yourself. In the end, it wasn't my thing. But I can understand how Ali got hooked.

"That's how our friendship started," Lloyd continued. "Then, after he turned pro, he came to New York and stayed with me at my apartment several times. Right before he fought Doug Jones, I drove him around town to publicize the fight. That was my red Cadillac he was in."

Price was a savvy businessman. He kept the copyright to most of the songs he wrote and founded several record labels. He's also the man who introduced Ali to Don King.

"I used to go to Cleveland because my song-writing partner, Harold Logan, lived there," Lloyd reminisced. "I knew all the people Harold knew and, through him, I got friendly with Don. One day, I was over at Don's place in the kitchen talking about Muhammad. Don's daughter Debbie said, 'I want to meet him.' It was her birthday. She was about five. So I telephoned Muhammad and he sang 'Happy Birthday' to her over the phone. Then Don got on and started talking. He was strictly a Cleveland man at the time. He didn't know anything about New York or Chicago or Los Angeles. And he was into numbers, not boxing. But that was the introduction. He and Ali got together—once I think it was—and then Don went to prison. But when he got out, you could see the wheels turning in his mind."

After King was released from prison, he prevailed upon Price to call Ali and ask if Muhammad would box in a charity exhibition to benefit the Forest City Hospital in Cleveland. Ali did it for free. History suggests that the primary financial beneficiary of the event was King, not the hospital. Later, Price was a key figure in orchestrating the Zaire 74 music festival in Kinshasa held in conjunction with the historic "Rumble in the Jungle" between Ali and George Foreman.

In 1980, Price tried his best to talk Ali out of coming out of retirement to fight Larry Holmes.

"I kept thinking about a day I'd spent in New York with Ali and Joe Louis maybe ten years earlier," Lloyd told me. "Joe had been with me because there was a little bird singing in my band who he liked a lot. We got together and they were talking, mostly about boxing. I was listening. They got along well that day, no tension of any kind between them. Ali asked, 'Joe, tell me something. What happens in the ring when you get old?' He was asking about Joe's fight against Rocky Marciano, when Joe was thirty-seven years old with that bald spot in the middle of his head, when he got knocked through the ropes and was counted out. Joe said,

'Ali, let me tell you something. When I was young and wanted to throw a punch, I could throw it as fast as I wanted. But when I got old, my brain would tell me to do something and my arms just wouldn't do it.'"

Fast-forward to 1980. "Don't fight Holmes," Price told Ali. "It's over. Father Time is calling. You've got to hear the bell."

"You don't know nothing about boxing and getting old," Ali retorted. "You're a singer, not a fighter."

Then Price told Ali a story about going out on a national tour in 1963. As a favor to a friend who was trying to break into the music business, he agreed to let one of the friend's groups open for him. The arrangement lasted until Price realized that the warm-up act was getting more applause than he was. So, being a showman, he sent them packing with the request that his friend send him a different opening group.

"Who did you get rid of?" Ali asked.

"Some guys I'd never heard of before," Price told him. "Smokey Robinson and the Miracles. And the next opening act made me look even worse. The first night they were on, when they finished their set, there was such pandemonium that I told the band to take a ten-minute break before I went out so the audience could calm down and I wouldn't look bad by comparison."

"Who were they?"

"Three Black chicks called the Supremes."

Price then called his friend (who, of course, was Berry Gordy, in the process of launching Motown records) and told him to stuff his groups where the sun didn't shine. "Just send me one guy to open," Lloyd instructed.

Whereupon Berry Gordy sent Marvin Gaye.

"And that was it," Price told Ali. "I said to myself, 'I don't know what these folks have. But whatever it is, I don't have it.' So I took myself off the road, bought a club in New York [that he called Turntable], and signed a fifteen-year contract to promote concerts for Motown in Manhattan. I heard the bell."

Over the years, I saw Lloyd maybe a dozen times. The most memorable of these occasions was a night when he and Ali were guests for dinner at my apartment. After dinner, I put an old LP of Lloyd Price's greatest hits on the turntable and we sang along. There were seven of us. Ali was beginning to have trouble speaking at that time in his life. But that night he sang louder than the rest of us.

The last time I saw Lloyd, he was well into his eighties, thinner than before and walking with a cane. But his voice was clear. There was a gleam in his eye. And his contagious laugh still filled the room. I'm grateful that I had the opportunity to know him.

Bill Russell once said of Bill Walton, "The community he lives in is the planet."
The same was true of Russell.

Remembering Bill Russell
(1934–2022)

Bill Russell, an inspirational figure and one of the most important athletes in the history of sports, died on July 31, 2022, at age eighty-eight.

Russell revolutionized the game of basketball. Standing six feet, nine inches tall and weighing a lithe 220 pounds, he originated a new style of play. Blocking shots and firing pinpoint passes to initiate fast breaks after grabbing rebounds, playing tenacious defense and transforming the center position from a haven for slow, lumbering giants to one of fluidity and motion.

On the court, Russell lived by the mantra, "Professional athletes are not paid to play. They're paid to win." He was a two-time All-American at the University of San Francisco, where he led the Dons to fifty-five consecutive victories and two NCAA championships. Next, he spearheaded the United States basketball team's gold-medal performance at the 1956 Olympics. Then he became the cornerstone of the greatest dynasty in the history of sports.

During a thirteen-year playing career that began in 1956, Russell led the Boston Celtics to eleven NBA championships. A half-century later, Boston's eight consecutive titles from 1959 to 1966 remain unmatched in professional sports, surpassing the uninterrupted reigns of the New York Yankees (1949 to 1953) and Montreal Canadiens (1956 to 1960).

Russell was a five-time league MVP and twelve-time All-Star. He ended his career with 21,620 rebounds (second most in NBA history) and averaged a mind-boggling 22.5 rebounds per game. Once, he pulled down 51 rebounds in a single contest. Statistics for blocked shots weren't kept when he played. But it's likely that Russell blocked more shots than anyone else in NBA history. He also averaged 15.1 points and 4.3 assists per game.

His confrontations with Wilt Chamberlain from 1959 through 1969 constituted one of sports' most storied rivalries.

But as Steve Kerr recently stated, "What Bill Russell did for his country and for society and the African American community dwarfs what he accomplished on the court."

Harry Edwards (who rose to prominence as the architect of the 1968 Olympic protest movement) called Russell "the heir to Jackie Robinson's struggle."

When the Celtics beat the St. Louis Hawks in seven games to win the NBA championship in Russell's first season, he was the only Black player on either team. He was also one of the first athletes to use his celebrity status to confront racism.

Russell was with Martin Luther King Jr. at the historic 1963 March on Washington. That same year, he went to Jackson, Mississippi, in the aftermath of Medgar Evers's assassination to carry on Evers's work. He actively supported the Civil Rights Act of 1964 and the Voting Rights Act of 1965.

Kareem Abdul-Jabbar viewed Russell as one of his most important role models and recalled, "Some of the things that scared me and bothered me about race relations in America were things that he addressed. He gave me a way to speak about it that had all of the elements of trying to make something better rather than just being angry."

Russell was also the first Black man to serve as head coach in a major American professional sports league.

In the early 1920s, running back Fritz Pollard was the head coach of the Akron Pros in the newly formed National Football League. But Pollard and the league's other nine Black players were removed from the NFL at the end of the 1926 season as the league began to gain a following. Four decades later, John McLendon coached briefly in the American Basketball League (which folded after one season) and American Basketball Association (which lasted for nine campaigns). But at the time, these leagues were secondary institutions.

Russell stepped into an entirely different situation. In 1966, Red Auerbach retired as coach of the Celtics after eight straight championships. In his role as general manager, he designated Russell as his successor. Russell then won two NBA championships as a player-coach and two more in the three seasons that followed his retirement as a player.

I was privileged to interact with Russell on several occasions.

The first came when I was fifteen years old and in high school. In those days, NBA teams played doubleheaders at the old Madison Square Garden on Eighth Avenue and Forty-Ninth Street. And security was light. I'd buy a balcony ticket and a program, walk down a stairway to position myself outside the dressing rooms (which were in close proximity to one another), and ask for autographs as the players came in.

On this occasion, the Knicks were playing the Celtics in the second game of a doubleheader. In addition to my program, I'd brought full-page color photos of Russell and Celtics guard Sam Jones that I'd torn from *Sport Magazine* in the hope that I could get them signed.

Russell was adamant about not signing autographs. I didn't know that at the time. Suddenly, he appeared, carrying a large gym bag. The vision of a giant eagle flashed through my mind.

I approached him and held out the photo.

"Mr. Russell. Could you sign this for me?"

"I don't sign autographs."

"Please."

I don't know why what happened next happened.

Wordlessly, Russell took the pen and photo from my hand . . . and signed.

Decades later, I was talking with him at the screening of an HBO documentary entitled *Bill Russell: My Life, My Way*. I'd come to know him better by then as a consequence of having interviewed him while researching *Muhammad Ali: His Life and Times*.

Russell complimented me on the book. Then I told him about the autograph and he cackled his famous cackle.

"So you were the one," he said.

My records show that I interviewed Russell for the Ali biography on November 21, 1989. At the start of the interview, he told me, "I don't like doing interviews. The only reason I'm talking with you is that Muhammad asked me to."

"I never saw him fight," Russell said of Ali. "I would never go to a fight. I just wouldn't. I went to one a long time ago and I told myself I'd never go back. They're much cleaner on television."

We talked about the idea (floated in 1971) that Ali and Wilt Chamberlain engage in a prizefight.

"I can't speak for Wilt," Russell noted. "I just know that I personally would never challenge a champion in his field of expertise. I would never get in a boxing ring with Ali or on the football field with Jim Brown or on a track with Carl Lewis. I would never impose my thoughts or motivations on someone else. But for me personally, that's just not the way I am."

The heart of our interview concerned a meeting that had taken place in Cleveland twenty-two years earlier. On April 28, 1967, Ali had refused induction into the United States Armed Forces. On May 8, he was criminally indicted. In early June (shortly before his trial began), ten of the most prominent black athletes in America met with Muhammad to discuss his options.

Recalling that day, Russell told me, "I got a call from Jim Brown, who said that Ali was out there by himself and that we should support him in whatever he chose to do. So that was it, really. I didn't go to Cleveland to persuade Muhammad to join or not join the Army. We were just there to help, and I was struck by how confident he was, how totally assured he was that what he was doing was right.

"I never thought of myself as a great man," Russell continued. "I never aspired to be anything like that. I was just a guy trying to get through life. But in Cleveland, and many other times with Ali, I saw a man accepting special responsibilities, someone who conducted himself in a way that the people he came in contact with were better for the experience. Philosophically, Ali was a free man. Besides being probably the greatest boxer ever, he was free. And he was free at a time when historically it was very difficult to be free no matter who you were or what you were. Ali was one of the first truly free people in America."

Not long after the Cleveland meeting, Russell spoke publicly about Ali's draft status for the first time.

"I envy Muhammad Ali," Russell said. "He faces a possible five years in jail and he has been stripped of his heavyweight championship, but I still envy him. He has something I have never been able to attain and something very few people I know possess. He has an absolute and sincere faith. I'm not worried about Muhammad Ali. He is better equipped than anyone I know to withstand the trials in store for him. What I'm worried about is the rest of us."

In honoring Bill Russell with the Presidential Medal of Freedom in 2011, Barack Obama proclaimed, "Bill was someone who stood up and insisted on dignity. He stood up for the rights and dignity of all men."

Bill Russell was a great man. And a good one.

People say that boxing has become a niche sport. But it's quite a niche.

An Inductee Experiences the International Boxing Hall of Fame

PART ONE

On Sunday, December 1, 2019, I arrived home in mid-afternoon after visiting my mother and checked my telephone answering machine. There was a message from Ed Brophy asking me to call him at the International Boxing Hall of Fame in Canastota. When I checked my email, there was a similar message asking me to call Ed.

Earlier in the year, my name had been placed on the ballot for induction into the Hall of Fame for the first time. The public had been told that the names of the newest inductees would be announced on December 4. Like every nominee, I hoped I'd be chosen. Given the realities of the induction process, I doubted that I would be. Still. . . .

"Ed's not a sadist," I reasoned. "He wouldn't be calling to tell me that I didn't get in."

I called Brophy back and he congratulated me on being chosen for induction. There would be a news embargo until the inductees were announced as a group on December 4.

"Please, don't tell anyone," Ed urged.

I honored that request with one exception. My mother was ninety-four years old, an age shadowed every day by the spectre of mortality. So I telephoned her and shared the news.

The International Boxing Hall of Fame in Canastota (a village in upstate New York twenty miles east of Syracuse) exists primarily because of the efforts of one man.

Ed Brophy was born in 1956 and grew up in Canastota. He was an avid boxing fan with a particular affinity for local heroes Carmen Basilio and Billy Backus. In 1954, *The Ring* magazine had launched a Hall of Fame located at Madison Square Garden but it was disbanded in 1987. Similar attempts to establish a boxing hall of fame over the years had floundered. But a voice in Brophy's head whispered, "Build it and they will come."

Brophy secured two New York State grants totaling $50,000 for a feasibility study. Local residents pledged another $25,000 for additional preliminary work. The village and township councils approved small contributions.

And it happened. On June 8, 9, and 10, 1990, the International Boxing Hall of Fame hosted its first Induction Weekend. Muhammad Ali was among the forty-six fighters and seven non-combatants honored.

Brophy has been executive director of the IBHOF since its inception. Boxing owes him a debt of gratitude. The hall has three more fulltime staffers—media director Jeff Brophy (Ed's nephew), events coordinator Zack Babcock, and Rachel Shaw (a secretary-receptionist). The rest of the work is performed by part-time employees and, to a great extent, volunteers.

Inductees into the IBHOF fit into one of seven categories:

* men's modern (last fight no earlier than 1989),
* women's modern (last fight no earlier than 1989),
* men's old timer (last fight between 1893 and 1988),
* women's trailblazer (last fight no later than 1988),
* men's pioneer (last fight no later than 1892),
* observer (journalists and other media), and
* non-participant (others who have made a contribution to boxing in a non-combat role).

Anyone can suggest to the IBHOF that a name be placed on the ballot. These nominations are weighed by a review committee that makes recommendations to a screening committee that, in turn, selects the names that appear on the final ballot.

For the most recent election, the review committee consisted of Nigel Collins, Tris Dixon, Steve Farhood, Bob Goodman, Jack Hirsch, Graham Houston, Dan Rafael, Lee Samuels, and Bruce Trampler. For years, the screening committee was composed of two historians (Hank Kaplan and Herb Goldman) and boxing maven Don Majeski. Kaplan died in 2007 and wasn't replaced. At present, the screening committee consists of Bobby Cassidy, Lee Groves, and Marc Ratner. In future years, Brophy will rotate the names on one or both of these committees.

Once the ballot is finalized, it's sent to electors, who vary in number from category to category. There are roughly 200 electors in the men's modern category. The other categories have fewer electors: women's modern (25), men's old timer (75), women's trailblazer (10), men's pioneer (25), observer (100), and non-participant (100).

I don't want to sound ungracious about a system that elected me. I'm deeply grateful for the honor. But there's room for improvement.

First, there should be more transparency in the voting process. Unlike the Baseball Hall of Fame, the International Boxing Hall of Fame doesn't announce vote totals.

"We feel that, when the inductees are announced, a person is in and that's it," Brophy says of the process. "Each inductee is entitled to the same reception by the Hall of Fame. No inductee should be considered or made to feel less equal than another."

That's a reasonable position. A bigger problem is that the identity of the electors isn't made public (although it's known that all full members of the Boxing Writers Association of America are among those who receive ballots in the men's modern category).

"Making the names public could lead to lobbying and other unnecessary pressure on the electors," Brophy explains. But anonymity can lead to a lack of accountability.

A sometimes ill-informed electorate is an even more serious issue. Many of the electors are relative newcomers to the sweet science and have little understanding of anything that happened in boxing more than a decade ago. And while the Hall says that electors are chosen based on their expertise in a given category, the facts don't always bear that out.

Jackie Tonawanda is a case in point. Tonawanda hung around the fight scene in the 1970s and 1980s, loudly proclaiming herself to be "the female Ali." At one point, she sued the New York State Athletic Commission because of its policy against licensing women to box. She also frequently telephoned editors and writers, urging them to report the results of her latest ring conquest.

The problem is that there weren't any ring conquests. As outlined by Randy Gordon earlier this year in a thoroughly researched investigative report, Tonawanda was a fraud. Her entire ring career (amateur and pro) consisted of one fight—a February 16, 1979, loss to a woman named Diane Clark (who lost her only other pro bout).

Tonawanda was chosen for induction into the International Boxing Hall of Fame's Class of 2021 as a "women's trailblazer" by a voting pool of ten electors. Quite possibly, the number of votes she received for induction can be counted on the fingers of one hand with digits to spare. Her apologists say that Tonawanda's induction can be justified by the publicity she brought to women's boxing. That's like saying Rosie Ruiz, who jumped unnoticed onto the course a half-mile from the finish line during the 1980 Boston Marathon and was declared the winner in the women's division (a designation revoked eight days later), belongs in a track and field hall of fame because of the publicity she brought to women's marathon running.

That said, the International Boxing Hall of Fame in Canastota is far and away the most credible boxing hall of fame that has ever existed.

The press release announcing my selection was made public on December 4, 2019, at 1:00 p.m. Other inductees in the Class of 2020 included Bernard Hopkins, Shane Mosley, Juan Manuel Márquez, Lucia Rijker, Christy Martin, Barbara Buttrick, Lou DiBella, Kathy Duva, Dan Goosen, Bernard Fernandez, Frank Erne, and Paddy Ryan.

I received a lot of congratulatory emails and telephone calls, including one from George Foreman that particularly moved me. Larry Merchant offered the thought, "This is the first time you were on the ballot. That means you're a first-ballot Hall of Famer." Jerry Izenberg (to my mind, the greatest sportswriter of the past sixty years) told me, "To be acknowledged by your peers is a great honor unless your peers are in boxing."

The induction ceremony and related events were scheduled for June 11 through June 14, 2020. Then the coronavirus intervened. Restrictions on social gatherings and travel were put in place. The 2020 ceremony was cancelled, as was the ceremony for the next class of inductees slated for June 2021. Finally, a historic "trilogy" came to pass. Three classes were inducted simultaneously into the International Boxing Hall of Fame from June 9 through June 12, 2022.

The 2021 inductees were Wladimir Klitschko, Andre Ward, Floyd Mayweather, Laila Ali, Ann Wolfe, Marian Trimiar, Jackie Tonawanda, Davey Moore, Freddie Brown, Jackie McCoy, Margaret Goodman, Jay Larkin, and George Kimball.

The 2022 inductees included Roy Jones, Miguel Cotto, James Toney, Regina Hamlich, Holly Holm, Bill Caplan, Ron Borges, Bob Yalen, Todd Morgan, and Chuck Hull.

Of the living inductees, only Klitschko, Rijker, and Fernandez were unable to attend. Klitschko is engaged in the ongoing life-and-death struggle in Ukraine. Rijker was a late cancellation because of the sudden death of a close friend. Fernandez was at home, caring for his wife, who was seriously ill.

Induction Weekend was a walk down memory lane for me. I met Roy Jones for the first time when he fought Jorge Vaca at Madison Square Garden in 1992. I was in his dressing room in the hours before and after six of his biggest fights. I've discussed Pythagorean philosophy with Wladimir and Vitali Klitschko over breakfast and known Laila Ali since she was ten years old. Lou DiBella and Margaret Goodman are longtime friends.

Memories of Induction Weekend and some thoughts on writing follow.

PART TWO

My induction into the International Boxing Hall of Fame came about as a consequence of my writing. So allow me to share some thoughts on the written word.

Alan J. Lerner (who created *My Fair Lady*, *Gigi*, and other musical classics in tandem with Frederick Loewe) observed, "I write not because it is what I do but because it is what I am; not because it is how I make my living but how I make my life."

That's how I feel about writing. I write for history and I write for myself. For history in that I'm creating a record that future generations will read to understand the people, places, and events that I wrote about as I experienced them. And for myself, in that, almost always, I write what I want to write. It has been a long time since I wrote something I wasn't interested in simply for the money.

Joe Parkhurst (a character in a short story by Paul Gallico entitled "The Melee of the Mages") summed up sportswriting with the declaration, "All you do is sit down at a typewriter with a lotta paper and just tell what happens to somebody."

But the craft is more demanding than that. Sportswriting is about sports. But good sportswriting is also about writing.

Jerry Izenberg recently noted, "Too many sportswriters today are nothing more than paparazzi of the written word. A story breaks; they swarm all over it with little or no understanding; and then they're gone. And you hear all the time, 'Oh, didn't he write a great line.' Well, I don't write great lines. I'm a writer."

Asked for more, Izenberg declared, "You have to be a reporter to be a good boxing writer. Yes, you have to be an interpreter and put things in perspective. But facts are at the core of whatever you write."

As a writer, I sit on the easy side of the ropes. I take notes, not punches. But a good writer—like a good fighter—takes risks. That means standing up to powerful interests and telling truths that the powers that be don't want spoken. Over the years, I've given out praise and I've held feet to the fire. I take pride in a comment that Jim Lampley made years ago: "There are two kinds of people in boxing—those who say, 'Oh, boy; Thomas Hauser is writing an article about me,' and those who say, 'Oh, shit; Thomas Hauser is writing an article about me.'"

Prior to beginning my career as a writer, I spent five years as a litigator with a Wall Street law firm called Cravath, Swaine & Moore. Since then, I've written novels and nonfiction books about subjects as diverse as United States foreign policy, race relations, Mark Twain, Charles Dickens, and Beethoven. The first boxing writing I ever did was in 1979 for a magazine called *Gallery*. It was an article about WBA light-heavyweight champion Mike Rossman (whose father's last name was DiPiano). Rossman (known as "The Jewish Bomber") used his mother's maiden name when fighting and wore a star of David on his trunks. I wrote about him through the eyes of his mother. *Gallery* liked the piece and commissioned a second article—a formulaic work that quoted four heavyweights on what it felt like to get knocked out.

In 1983, I decided to write a book about sports. I was a casual boxing fan at the time. My favorite sports were baseball, football, and basketball. A writer can't just walk into Yankee Stadium and talk with the Yankees. But a writer can walk into almost any gym in the country and talk with the fighters who are training there.

So I wrote a book about the sport and business of boxing titled *The Black Lights*. Then I put boxing aside to write a murder mystery, a thriller about a plot to manufacture nuclear weapons for sale to Third World countries, and a book about Chernobyl. In 1988, I was approached by Muhammad and Lonnie Ali, who asked if I'd be interested in writing what we hoped would become the definitive Ali biography. *Muhammad Ali: His Life and Times* was published in 1991. After that, I took a hiatus from boxing until 1999 when I began writing for several internet sites.

When I finished writing *The Black Lights*, I thought I was an expert on boxing. I wasn't. I was an informed fan. Writing about the sweet science for various websites taught me how much I didn't know. And the internet has been an ideal forum for me because I can write as many words as I want to write.

My writing about boxing falls into four categories. First, there's *The Black Lights*. Then there's everything Ali, which includes the big biography, numerous articles (published later in book form under the title *Muhammad Ali: A Tribute to the Greatest*), and the text for three Ali coffee-table photo books. I've also written two novels that focus on boxing—*Mark Twain Remembers* and *Waiting for Carver Boyd*. The novels constitute some of the best writing I've done about the sweet science. But to my mind, my most lasting contribution to the sport has been in the fourth category.

For two decades, I've chronicled the contemporary boxing scene in articles for various websites and print publications. These articles have covered every aspect of the sport and business of boxing. Initially, internet writers were treated as unloved stepchildren by the powers that be in boxing. Inexorably, the walls came tumbling down. I'm now the first writer whose articles were featured primarily on the internet to be inducted into the International Boxing Hall of Fame.

From time to time, I'm asked for advice on what it takes to be a good boxing writer. I often answer, "Rule number one is, 'If there's free food, grab it.'"

But let me give a more serious answer. We're living in an age when responsible journalism is under siege. Too often, good writing and journalistic sensibilities take a back seat to lesser agendas. I'd like to offer some thoughts on what it takes to be a responsible journalist and good writer:

1. Challenge every word you put on paper. Lonnie Ali once asked me to review a short piece she'd written about Muhammad. It was well done but one phrase troubled me. Lonnie had written that Muhammad was "one in a million." But if Muhammad was one in a million, there would have been 350 more people just like him in the United States. "He's not one in a million," I told Lonnie. "He's unique."

2. If you want a reader to know something, make sure it's incorporated in what you write. Years ago, I wrote a spy story entitled *Hanneman's War* that was set in the mountains of Nepal. I got fifty-five rejection letters before landing a publisher. Rejection letters are rarely helpful to an author. They're usually limited to, "Thank you for submitting your manuscript. Unfortunately, it's not suited to our needs." Other times, an author might be left shaking his head. One day, I got two rejection letters for *Hanneman's War*. One of the letters said the book needed more background on Nepalese politics. The other rejection letter said the book needed less background on Nepalese politics. But there was a common thread in that several of the rejecting editors thought the book's protagonist was unsympathetic and thoroughly dislikable. How could these editors think that, I wondered. Didn't they understand how much the character I'd created was suffering? No! They couldn't understand because his suffering was largely in my head. I hadn't spelled it out clearly on paper.

3. Be creative. When John Kennedy was assassinated in 1963 and thousands of journalists descended on Washington, DC, for the funeral, Jimmy Breslin found a way to separate himself from the pack. He interviewed the man who dug the fallen president's grave at Arlington Cemetery. As a journalist, I try to come up with ideas and notice things that other people haven't. As an example, on May 5, 2007, Oscar De La Hoya and Floyd Mayweather fought at the MGM Grand in Las Vegas. Almost two-thirds of the seats in the sold-out arena carried a price-tag of $2,000 or more. There were eight hundred requests for media credentials. Five hours before the main event began, two fighters named Ernest Johnson and Hector

Beltran fought in an eight-round lightweight bout. The doors to the arena hadn't opened when they made their way to the ring. I tracked Johnson and Beltran on fight day and chronicled their experiences in an article entitled "First Bout at 3:05 PM."

4. Journalism involves building relationships. Being able to pick up the phone and call someone for information and insights is invaluable to a writer.

5. Set things up in advance. Years ago, I wrote an article entitled "My 81-Year-Old Mother Meets Don King." The meeting occurred at the final pre-fight press conference for Samuel Peter vs. Jameel McCline at Madison Square Garden. I didn't just show up at the press conference with my mother. I cleared her coming in advance with Alan Hopper (director of public relations for Don King Productions). That meant there was no issue as to whether my mother would be allowed into the press conference. And Hopper arranged for her to meet King. Years later, my mother was in a restaurant on the east side of Manhattan when a loud, booming voice proclaimed, "It's Tom Hauser's momma!" There was a time when Don remembered everyone and everything.

6. Just voicing an opinion doesn't make you a journalist. Back up your opinions with thorough research and facts. And check your facts. All of us make mistakes. In the early 1980s, I wrote a love story titled *Ashworth & Palmer* that was set in a large Wall Street law firm. One of the scenes occurred in a fictitious industrial suburb that I called Unger and located twenty miles north of Cleveland. After *Ashworth & Palmer* was published, I got a letter from a reader who told me that he'd enjoyed the book but thought I should know that twenty miles north of Cleveland would place Unger underwater in the middle of Lake Erie.

7. It's permissible to excerpt and combine quotes from a single speaker. But don't change their meaning when you do it.

8. Respect confidences but don't hide behind them. And don't make stuff up. As attorney Judd Burstein once said in excoriating a writer, "Those little voices you hear in your head aren't sources."

9. Be fair. Edwin Pope (whose writing graced the pages of the *Miami Herald* for decades) felt a responsibility when he sat down to write. "I held the gun," Pope noted. "I didn't want to fire it randomly. I always wanted to be fair, even to people who didn't deserve it." When I finish writing an article—particularly an investigative report—I read it through at least once with fairness to the people I've criticized foremost in my mind.

10. Conduct yourself like a professional. I recall sitting in the press section at Barclays Center several years ago. The writer sitting next to me was on his laptop, surfing the internet for porn. There's a time and place for everything. That was the wrong place at the wrong time.

11. Use the same standard of care for everything you write. Each article with your name on it will become part of your creative legacy whether it's written for an obscure website or the *New York Times*. Also, too many writers today care more about breaking a story than writing well and putting that story in context. I don't care about being first. I want to be best. Whenever you write, ask yourself, "How will this article read years from now?"

12. Don't become a writer for the money. For most writers, the business end of things isn't very profitable. Your satisfaction as a creative artist will be in writing well and getting published.

Boxing is the best writer's sport in the world. If you can't write well about boxing, you can't write.

PART THREE

Prior to going to Canastota for Induction Weekend, I asked some past inductees what the experience was like.

"You get a good feeling being there," Teddy Atlas said. "People come from all over the world for a celebration of boxing. And they respect boxing. They care about boxing. They really do."

"Most people you meet will be very nice," Al Bernstein told me. "And the people who run things are incredibly well organized, so you won't have to worry about where to be at what time or how to get there."

"It was overwhelming," Marc Ratner offered. "I got up to make my speech and turned around. And there were Marvin Hagler, Roberto Durán, and Ray Leonard sitting behind me."

"It was one of the great feel-good experiences of my life," Don Elbaum reminisced. "Now, every morning when I get up, I kiss my ring. Don't ask me why because I don't know why. I just know that it felt so good getting into the Hall and it still feels good. Every day there's sunshine in my life because I'm in the one boxing hall of fame that really matters."

I drove from New York City to Canastota on Thursday, June 9, with my niece (Jessica), her husband (Bayo), and their sixteen-month-old son (Simon). The Hall of Fame arranges and pays for air transportation for inductees. But by the time I would have journeyed to the airport, sat in the boarding area, boarded the plane, flown to Syracuse, waited for my luggage, and got to the hotel, it would have taken as long as driving from Manhattan and been less pleasant. The 250-mile drive took four and a half hours. Simon was remarkably well behaved.

Canastota is nestled in an attractive rural setting and is similar in many ways to what it was fifty years ago. In previous years, inductees had stayed at Days Inn, a stone's throw from the Hall of Fame museum. Not everyone was happy with the experience.

"I've made two great mistakes in my life," Jerry Izenberg told me. "One of them was marrying my second wife and the other was staying at Days Inn."

"Days Inn isn't bad if you don't mind listening to the people in the room next door making love," Craig Hamilton added.

Most of the major Induction Weekend activities would be held at Turning Stone Resort Casino in nearby Verona. This year, that's where the inductees, myself included, were lodged.

It was the first time I'd traveled overnight since the pandemic began. We arrived at Turning Stone at 4:15 p.m. and I checked into my room on the fourth floor. Virtually no one in the hotel was masked, a marked departure from the West Side of Manhattan, which had been my world for the preceding twenty-seven months. I'd decided before journeying to Canastota to adhere to a risk-reward formula. Having been double-vaccinated and double-boosted, I put my mask aside for most of the next few days and went with the flow.

Traditionally, the Hall of Fame's induction festivities take place over the second weekend in June. Executive director Ed Brophy is passionate about the Hall, and that passion is reflected in everything he does. More than 150 volunteers support the effort. Seventy-five percent of them live in Canastota. Virtually all of the other volunteers come from within a thirty-minute drive. None of them are paid. They're uniformly well informed, well trained, and exceptionally nice.

There was a buffet dinner for inductees and their guests in the Mohawk Room at Turning Stone on Thursday night. Not all of the inductees were onsite yet. Those who'd arrived were happy to be there.

"This is a party you don't want to miss," Roy Jones told me.

Friday began with a buffet breakfast in Parlour, a lounge set aside each morning for inductees, family members, and friends. Julian Jackson (a 2019 inductee) was there with his high school sweetheart, who has been his wife for decades.

At sixteen months, Simon (my great-nephew) doesn't talk yet except for the occasional "momma." But he was toddling around the room, high-fiving some of the greatest fighters of our time. It brought back memories for me of Jessica (Simon's mother) sitting on Muhammad Ali's lap and singing the Barney song with him when she was six years old.

Shane Mosley, gracious as always, was in a reflective mood.

"This is bittersweet," Shane said. "When I started boxing, I dreamed about being in the Hall of Fame someday. This is the best validation I could have, but it means that a part of my life I loved is over."

Late in the morning, most of the inductees boarded a bus for a short ride to Theodore's (a restaurant in Canastota), and I found myself sitting beside Bernard Hopkins.

Promoters and managers have their money to count when their careers are at an end. Hopkins (unlike many fighters) has his money (a lot of it) and a legacy of historic proportions.

"I felt complete when I retired from boxing," Bernard told me. "But I'm grateful to be here this weekend. You can lose your money, but history never goes broke."

Hopkins burned a lot of bridges over the years. But he has rebuilt many of them.

"Roy Jones in 1993 was the best fighter I ever fought," Bernard said, looking around the bus. "He was the Michael Jordan of boxing back then and I didn't have the boxing IQ at that time to know how to deal with him."

Marvelous Marvin Hagler once said of Induction Weekend in Canastota, "You run into guys you knocked out or you lost to, and you're able to shake hands and catch up. Fighters are able to laugh and be friendly with one another after a guy's beaten the shit out of you."

That sentiment was on display during lunch at Theodore's. Other fighters in addition to the inductees were sprinkled around the room. Terence Crawford, Shawn Porter, Marlon Starling, Antonio Tarver, Iran Barkley, Junior Jones. There was genuine camaraderie and warmth. Old adversaries embraced. No one tried to one-up anyone else.

Some of the inductees in the room had fought each other in the past. Roy Jones fought James Toney and Bernard Hopkins. Christy Martin battled Laila Ali. In some ways, the scene reminded me of a dysfunctional family reunion with everyone on their best behavior.

After lunch, we got back on the bus and rode to the Hall of Fame museum.

Fifteen years ago, Bill Simmons wrote, "American kids don't grow up hoping to become the next Ali or Sugar Ray anymore. They're hoping to be the next LeBron, Griffey, Brady or Tiger. The thought of getting smacked in the head for twenty years, soaked by the Don Kings of the world, and then ending up with slurred speech and a constant tremor doesn't sound too enticing."

But boxing is alive and well in Canastota. The International Boxing Hall of Fame is limited in physical form to a small museum and outdoor event pavilion. But in the imagination, it's as large and grand as the storied history of boxing.

I'd never been to the Hall of Fame before. The first thing I did on entering the museum was look for my plaque. Then I surveyed the robes, trunks, and gloves worn by legendary fighters, fight tickets, fight programs, and other exhibits.

From Ed Brophy's point of view, the most important artifact in the museum is the ring that was used at various incarnations of Madison Square Garden from 1922 to 2007.

"Think of what happened in that ring," Brophy told me with awe in his voice. "That's where Muhammad Ali fought Joe Frazier and Joe

Louis fought Rocky Marciano. Sugar Ray Robinson won his first world championship in that ring. So many great fighters of the past hundred years fought there."

But the real attraction for me at the museum were the fans. Dedicated, well-informed, passionate fans.

Eyes light up when sports fans in a casual setting come upon a great champion. "Omigod! That's Michael Spinks!" was heard decades ago when Spinks was out in public after dethroning Larry Holmes.

The years pass. The fighter grows older. Maybe on occasion he hears, "I think that's Michael Spinks."

At Canastota, I heard, "Omigod! That's Michael Spinks."

And then there were the autograph seekers.

Eight decades ago, Paul Gallico wrote, "The average man is not requested for his autograph, except on a check, more than once or twice in his life. No one who has not been through the mill has even the faintest notion of how wearing on the nerves and exasperating the constant and unremitting request for autographs becomes."

Certainly, that was true for Babe Ruth and Jack Dempsey (two of Gallico's favorite subjects). But for most of us, being asked for an autograph is an ego boost.

Many of the fans who visit Canastota are collectors.

"You'll sign more autographs in four days than you have in your entire life," Al Bernstein had told me. "The Hall will have all sorts of things for you to sign, and you'll meet hundreds of people who will want you to sign everything else. The first time you're asked to sign your name and put 'HOF' with your year under it, you'll get a little thrill."

When I was young, I was an avid collector. I still have my autograph collection and remember how much it meant to me when someone signed something for me. So in Canastota, I signed and signed.

I signed books, induction programs, photos, gloves, index cards, and more. Most people asking for signatures had a Sharpie in hand.

Signing autographs in Canastota reminded me of an experience I had with Muhammad Ali (who probably signed more autographs than anyone else since the beginning of time).

In 1996, Easton Press published 3,500 copies of a leather-bound edition of *Muhammad Ali: His Life and Times*. Pursuant to contract, Ali and I signed 3,500 signature pages for insertion in the book. I was paid three dollars per signature; Muhammad, considerably more.

"This is fantastic," I told myself. "If I do ten signatures a minute, that's 600 signatures an hour. Divide 3,500 by 600. Wow! I'll get $10,500 for six hours work."

Except when I started signing, I couldn't sign more than a hundred or so pages at a time. "Any more than that," I confided to Muhammad, "and I can't connect the letters properly. Something starts misfiring in my brain."

"Now you know," Ali told me, referring to his own physical condition. "It wasn't the punches. It was the autographs."

There was another buffet dinner on Friday night for inductees, family members, and friends. Then I went to the Turning Stone Event Center to check out the ShoBox fights. Olympic super-heavyweight gold medalist Bakhodir Jalolov was scheduled to face Jack Mulowayi in the main event. But the Golden State Warriors were playing the Boston Celtics in Game 4 of the NBA Championship Finals. I was tired and wanted to see the game, so I left the fights early.

As I walked back to my room, it was clear that Induction Weekend was a magnet for the boxing community. I chatted with Paulie Malignaggi (who I've known since he was twenty years old) and Freddie Roach (whose most endearing quality is that, as his fame and fortune grew, he didn't change). Kevin McBride (the only man in the house to have beaten Mike Tyson) was wandering about.

I signed a dozen or so autographs on my way to the elevators; then went upstairs and watched the game. Stephen Curry erupted for 43 points as the Warriors evened the series at two games apiece. Curry, it occurred to me, plays with the kind of magic that Roy Jones once exuded in the ring.

PART FOUR

Saturday, June 11, began with breakfast in Parlour. That was followed by a bus ride to Canastota for another meet-and-greet with fans. There was a hospitality lounge on the fourth floor at Turning Stone that was open to inductees for most of each day and evening. The turkey and veggie wraps were good.

The first major event of Induction Weekend was the banquet on Saturday night.

"The banquet is great," Al Bernstein had told me. "All of the inductees and other honored guests line up backstage and then they go out to the dais one at a time. It's the biggest dais I've ever seen. And it's wonderful. You look at the people sitting beside you. It's a history of boxing. And you say to yourself, 'Wow! I'm one of them.'"

The banquet, at $175 a ticket, had sold out weeks in advance. Fifteen hundred people were there. All of the inductees except one (more on that later) gathered in a room across the corridor from the Event Center. I thought back to the nights when Roy Jones, Bernard Hopkins, Miguel Cotto, and James Toney had invited me to share the hours in their dressing room before and after some of their biggest fights. Now I was being inducted into the Hall of Fame with them.

At 6:45 p.m., the inductees were introduced and walked out to the dais. I was seated between Bernard Hopkins and Margaret Goodman. Margaret is a sartorial wonder and her outfits had been carefully planned. On this occasion, she was wearing a vintage black Gianni Versace suit with a short skirt and black high-heeled Christian Louboutin shoes. Sunday at the parade, she would wear a gray Dolce & Gabbana suit with gray Gucci pumps. Then she'd change into a white Richard Tyler pantsuit with beige Manolo Blahnik sandals for the induction ceremony.

It's a unique experience to sit at a dais under bright lights surrounded by some of the greatest fighters of our time. Referencing the pandemic and trilogy nature of the proceedings, Bernard leaned over and told me, "I don't think we'll see this again in our lifetime. At least, I hope not."

Floyd Mayweather made his entrance at 7:55 p.m., more than an hour after the other inductees were seated.

Throughout the weekend, virtually all of the inductees had mingled freely with each other and the fans. The women inductees were accorded full respect by the men. Fighters with immense pride put their egos aside to blend as one. Only Floyd carried himself separate and apart from the group.

Everyone who understands boxing respects Mayweather for his work ethic and the skills he exhibited throughout his ring career. But the way he handled himself at Canastota, in my eyes, was disrespectful to the other fighters. Time and again, he acted as though he was above them.

Each of the inductees had been asked to speak for a few minutes at the banquet. Our more formal remarks would come on Sunday at the induction ceremony.

After being introduced at the banquet, Mayweather stood at the podium in a show of emotion (feigned or otherwise) for more than two minutes before uttering his first words. He then said, "I'm not here to talk about me," but managed to get in a few words about "me" ("My body of work is amazing. . . . To be able to leave school in twelfth grade and go pursue my dream and make over a billion dollars; that's truly impressive"). His fifteen-minute speech ran far longer that the remarks of any of his peers.

The most inspirational words of the evening came from Ann Wolfe, who spoke movingly about not knowing how to read and write and thanked her two daughters for helping her fulfill her greatest goal in life—"to be a good mom."

On Sunday, the inductees visited the Hall of Fame museum again; this time for group photos. Mayweather arrived separately with an entourage of thirty people. Later, in his induction speech, he would say that he'd brought seventy members of the Money Team to Canastota. That may or may not have been hyperbole.

At 11:30, the inductees assembled prior to the start of the Induction Day parade. Before journeying to Canastota, I'd been asked what I was most looking forward to about the weekend.

"I've seen a lot of parades in my life but I've never been in one," I answered. "I think the parade."

Good choice.

The parade is like something out of a Norman Rockwell painting. Jim Lampley's voice choked up (a not uncommon occurrence) when he told me, "Those of us who love and care about boxing live in a world of the heart. And that heart is on full display in Canastota. The seemingly hokey experience of getting in a car and riding around this small town waving to total strangers who are waving back to you will be thrilling. You'll remember it for the rest of your life."

"A lot of people will be cheering," Don Elbaum advised me. "And nobody will boo."

"I was a twirler in high school," Kathy Duva reminisced. "So I've been in parades before."

The fact that three classes of inductees would be in the parade and the impact of COVID on local car dealerships had made it difficult for event organizers to round up enough vehicles. Earlier, one insider had suggested tongue-in-cheek that Mayweather be sounded out about bringing some of his luxury fleet to Canastota. But in the end, there were enough cars.

The people of Canastota and the surrounding environs were out in full force. The early forecast had been for heavy rain around noon. But now, rain wasn't expected until mid-afternoon.

We got in our cars in a lot outside the Fiore Funeral Home. Each inductee was in his or her own vehicle and could choose who they rode with. I was in an orange Wrangler Rubicon Jeep with Jessica, Bayo, and Simon. Laila Ali, appropriately, was in a tomato-red convertible (Cassius Clay's dream car). There were twenty marching bands.

The car I was in left the funeral home at 12:10 p.m. and arrived at the end of the parade route twenty-five minutes later. Thousands of people lined the streets, waving and cheering. For most of the ride, I stood on the back seat, waving back at them. At one point, I looked over at Simon, who was sitting on his mother's lap. There's no way to know how a sixteen-month-old toddler was experiencing the sights and sounds of that moment. But from time to time as people waved, Simon high-fived in return.

There was another buffet lunch.

At 2:50 p.m., the induction ceremony began in the Turning Stone Event Center. The posthumous inductions came first. At 3:30, the induction of the living began. I was seated onstage between Lou DiBella and Shane Mosley.

Each of the inductees had been asked to limit his or her speech to three or four minutes. Andre Ward caught my attention with remarks that began, "Give God the glory. I wouldn't want to be in this sport without Him."

Ward then told the gathering, "I'd tell people, 'I'm going to win a gold medal and I'm going to be a world champion,' and people would say to me, 'You're crazy.' But it's only crazy until you do it. Some people like you. Some people don't. Some people criticize you. Some people praise you. But when you make it here to this stage in Canastota, the debate is over."

"I'm not the lead singer in the class of 2022," Ron Borges noted. "But I'm proud to be part of the group."

Each inductee was given a gold ring with a diamond chip in it when called to the podium to speak. The rings aren't as fancy as the ones players get for winning the Super Bowl. But when I put mine on, a jolt of electricity went through me.

Once again, Floyd Mayweather separated himself from the pack. During the induction ceremony, he gestured from time to time to an aide who brought him a drink and a towel to wipe his brow. The event center was well air-conditioned and each of the inductees had a bottle of water by his or her chair so that seemed largely for show.

Inductees had been asked to limit the length of their speeches. Floyd talked for almost fifteen minutes. That was longer than James Toney, Shane Mosley, Miguel Cotto, Juan Manuel Márquez, Ann Wolfe, Holly Holm, Christy Martin, and Laila Ali combined.

Mayweather began his remarks by saying, "Today, I want to talk about me. I want to talk about TBE [the best ever]." He then proclaimed, "I look good. I fight good. I'm undefeated."

That was followed by a lot of bragging about money: "Another great thing about my career is the smart investments that I made. It put me in position to make over a billion and then invest my money and triple it. In thirty-two months, I put myself in a position with a smart business team to make three hundred million dollars a month."

I'm sure Floyd is a wealthy man. I'm also sure he doesn't have three billion dollars and that his income is closer to mine than it is to $300 million a month.

More bragging followed before Mayweather closed with the declaration "I'm the best. I will always be the best. There's no fighter in the past that's better than me. There's no fighter that's in the future that's gonna be better than me. And there's no fighter that's better than me right now. I will always be TBE."

The belief among the fighters I talked with in Canastota was that Ray Leonard and Thomas Hearns would have knocked the "0" off Floyd's record and that it wouldn't have been close. Roberto Durán might have done the job too.

The induction ceremony was long, running until 6:20 p.m. Just before speaking, I decided to begin my remarks by acknowledging the heroism shown in recent months by Vitali and Wladimir Klitschko. The rest of my speech was as follows:

> I've often said that some of the best people I've met in my life are in boxing and many of the worst people I've met in my life are in boxing. But it's never boring and it's a great writers' sport.
>
> Let me start with the fighters. This is your sport. The rest of us are just along for the ride. I'm indebted to every fighter who allowed me in his dressing room in the hours before he fought so I could chronicle that night for history. And I'm equally indebted to all the other fighters in boxing for being who you are.
>
> I'd like to acknowledge the promoters, trainers, managers, matchmakers, ring doctors, television executives, announcers, fellow writers, and all the others in the boxing community who have been so generous in sharing their knowledge with me.
>
> I'm very moved by the thought of each and every person who put a check mark next to my name on the Hall of Fame induction ballot. Voting is anonymous so I don't know who you are. But thank you.
>
> A special thank you to Muhammad Ali.
>
> And thank you to the fans; those of you who are gathered here today and those beyond. One of the nicest things about writing for a living is the realization that, on occasion, someone actually reads what I write. A lot of the motivation for what I do comes from you.
>
> Mike Jones, who managed Billy Costello to a world title, was my first guide through boxing. Four decades ago, Mike said something that has always stayed with me. In closing, I'd like to share Mike's thoughts with you now:
>
> "To understand boxing, you have to understand tradition and what it takes to get inside a ring. You have to learn about promoters and television and what goes on inside a fighter's head from the time

his career begins until the day it ends. You have to grasp the reality of smashed faces and pain, and understand how they can be part of something courageous, exciting, and beautiful. I know, I've been there. And after everything I've been through in boxing, I can look you square in the eye and tell you boxing is beautiful—the purest sport in the world. You can knock promoters. You can knock trainers, managers, even fighters. But don't knock boxing. It's the best sport there is. And anyone who has ever been involved will tell you, it's an honor to be associated with boxing."

After the induction ceremony ended, I went to my room and packed my bags. Then I dropped by the hospitality lounge for some final goodbyes.

One of the tables was piled high with boxes of pizza.

Roy Jones was talking with family and friends. Two of his daughters stood off to the side.

"Is either of you Raegan?" I asked the young women.

"I'm Raegan," one of them answered.

On November 8, 2008, I'd been in Roy's dressing room at Madison Square Garden after his loss to Joe Calzaghe. Raegan was four years old at the time. In describing the scene, I wrote, "Jones sat in a far corner of the room on a folding metal chair with his head down. His twin sons (Deshawn and Deandre, age seventeen) were fighting back tears. His youngest son (Roy Jones III, age eight) stood to the side with tears streaming down his face. Raegan Jones, her hair beaded, as cute as a four-year-old can be, moved to her father's side and put her arms around him. 'I'm a big girl, daddy,' Raegan told her father. 'I don't cry.'"

Time goes by. Raegan is now a young woman and had come to Canastota to share a moment of supreme triumph with her father.

Jessica and Bayo had left Canastota for Martha's Vineyard (with Simon in tow) late that afternoon to celebrate their second wedding anniversary. I drove back to New York with Chris Davis, a friend who works at the same law firm that I worked at decades ago.

Before I journeyed to Canastota, quite a few previous inductees told me that Induction Weekend had exceeded their expectations. I'd known it would feel good. But driving back to New York, I understood that it meant more to me than I'd thought it would.